SUSTAINABLE DEVELOPMENT ON THE NORTH ATLANTIC MARGIN

Sustainable Development on the North Atlantic Margin

Selected Contributions to the Thirteenth
International Seminar on Marginal Regions

Edited by

REGINALD BYRON
University of Wales, Swansea

JAMES WALSH
St Patrick's College, Maynooth

PROINNSIAS BREATHNACH
St Patrick's College, Maynooth

Ashgate

Aldershot • Brookfield USA • Singapore • Sydney

Published by
Ashgate Publishing Ltd
Gower House
Croft Road
Aldershot
Hants GU11 3HR
England

Ashgate Publishing Company
Old Post Road
Brookfield
Vermont 05036
USA

British Library Cataloguing in Publication Data

Sustainable development on the North Atlantic margin :
    selected contributions to the Thirteenth International
    Seminar on Marginal Regions
    1.Sustainable development - North Atlantic Region -
    Congresses
    I.Byron, Reginald II.Walsh, James III.Breathnach,
    Proinnsias
    333.7'2'091633

Library of Congress Catalog Card Number: 97-72670

ISBN 1 85972 649 6

Printed and bound by Athenaeum Press, Ltd.,
Gateshead, Tyne & Wear.

Contents

List of contributors   vii

Editors' preface   ix

Introduction   1
James Walsh and Reginald Byron

**Part One: Concepts, processes and strategies in sustainable
development**

1   Development from below: An assessment of recent experience
    in rural Ireland   17
    James Walsh

2   Sustainable rural development: Concepts, practice and policy   34
    Roberto Chiesa and Patrick Commins

3   Planning for rural and local development in Ireland and Norway   53
    Jørgen Amdam

4   Municipal reform: A prerequisite for local development?   76
    Jens Christian Hansen

5   Training for rural development in the west of Ireland   99
    Diarmuid O Cearbhaill

Part Two: Area-based strategies for sustainable development

6   Towards a sustainable approach to the development
    of the west of Ireland   123
    Micheál Ó Cinnéide

v

7 New trends in Norwegian regional policies   135
Paul Olav Berg

8 Norwegian counties in a Europe of Regions   150
Ragnar Nordgreen

9 Sustainable local development in practice:
The case of Sykkylven   173
Roar Amdam

10 The Welsh language, agricultural change and sustainablity   194
Garth Hughes, Peter Midmore and Anne-Marie Sherwood

Part Three: Sustainable approaches to tourism development

11 Environmental interpretation as a disciplinary interface
in sustainable development   217
Richard Prentice

12 Eco-tourism in remote areas of Norway: Just green veneer?   239
Thor Flognfeldt, Jr.

13 Eco-tourism: Rhetoric or a new prospect for the periphery?   249
Peter Sjøholt

14 A sustainable strategy for scenic landscapes   260
Jeanne Meldon

15 Tourism and alternative employment among farm families
in less-favoured agricultural regions of Wales   267
John Hutson and David Keddie

Part Four: Sustainable development of agricultural communities

16 Farm diversification and sustainability: The perceptions
of farmers and institutions in the west of Ireland   285
Mary Cawley, Desmond Gillmor and Perpetua McDonagh

17 Will Wales stay green in the absence of rural policy?   302
Siân Pierce, Gareth Rennie and Eifiona Thomas

18 The impact of Irish dairy industry rationalisation
on the sustainability of small farming communities   323
Proinnsias Breathnach and Michael Kenny

19 Addressing the sustainability of rural populations:
Migration trends in the Republic of Ireland, 1971-1991   339
Mary Cawley

List of contributors

Jørgen Amdam is Professor in the Department of Commune Planning and Administration at Volda College, Norway.

Roar Amdam is Senior Lecturer in the Institute of Municipality Studies, Volda College, Norway.

Paul Olav Berg is Professor in the Graduate School of Business, Bodø University College, Norway.

Proinnsias Breathnach is Senior Lecturer in Geography at St Patrick's College, Maynooth, Co. Kildare, Ireland.

Reginald Byron is Professor of Sociology and Anthropology at the University of Wales, Swansea.

Mary Cawley is College Lecturer in Geography at University College, Galway, Ireland.

Roberto Chiesa, of Udine, Italy, is a visiting research fellow at Teagasc, the Agriculture and Food Development Authority, Dublin, Ireland.

Patrick Commins is Head of Rural Policy Research at Teagasc, the Agriculture and Food Development Authority, Dublin, Ireland.

Thor Flognfeldt, Jr. is Senior Lecturer in the Department of Tourism and Applied Social Studies, Lillehammer College, Norway.

Desmond Gillmor is Associate Professor of Geography at Trinity College, Dublin, Ireland.

Jens Christian Hansen is Professor of Geography at the University of Bergen, Norway.

Garth Hughes is a member of the Rural Economy Research Group at the Welsh Institute of Rural Studies, University of Wales, Aberystwyth.

John Hutson is Lecturer in Social Anthropology at the University of Wales, Swansea.

David Keddie is a member of the Department of Sociology, University of Portsmouth, England.

Michael Kenny is a member of the Centre for Adult and Community Education, St Patrick's College, Maynooth, Co. Kildare, Ireland.

Perpetua McDonagh is Research Officer in the Department of Geography, Trinity College, Dublin, Ireland.

Jeanne Meldon is Project Coordinator at An Taisce and Bord Failte, Dublin, Ireland.

Peter Midmore is a member of the Rural Economy Research Group at the Welsh Institute of Rural Studies, University of Wales, Aberystwyth.

Ragnar Nordgreen is Senior Lecturer in the Department of Tourism and Applied Social Science, Lillehammer College, Norway.

Diarmuid O Cearbhaill is Statutory Lecturer in Economics at the Centre for Development Studies, University College Galway, Ireland.

Micheál Ó Cinnéide is Associate Professor of Geography at the Centre for Development Studies, University College, Galway, Ireland.

Siân Pierce is Lecturer in the School of Community, Regional and Communication Studies at the University of Wales, Bangor.

Richard Prentice is Professor of Tourism at Queen Margaret College, Edinburgh, Scotland.

Gareth Rennie is Lecturer in the School of Community, Regional and Communication Studies at the University of Wales, Bangor.

Anne-Marie Sherwood is a member of the Rural Economy Research Group at the Welsh Institute of Rural Studies, University of Wales, Aberystwyth.

Peter Sjøholt is Professor of Geography at the Norwegian School of Economics and Business Administration, Bergen, Norway.

Eifiona Thomas is Lecturer in the School of Community, Regional and Communication Studies at the University of Wales, Bangor.

James Walsh is Professor of Geography at St. Patrick's College, Maynooth, Co. Kildare, Ireland.

Editors' preface

This volume brings together nineteen of the thirty papers given to the Thirteenth International Seminar on Marginal Regions held in Ireland in the summer of 1995. Two of the editors, James Walsh and Proinnsias Breathnach, were our hosts for the five days of the Seminar in County Kildare and County Kerry. By tradition, the Seminar participants are enabled to observe at first hand the nature of regional development problems and to meet local officials and practitioners and discuss with them the practicalities of development efforts in their areas by holding the Seminar in two main centres (at least one of them rural), and making field trips to nearby places. On this occasion, the members of the Seminar saw for themselves the impressive efforts being made in the west of Ireland to overcome the disadvantages of remoteness, a thin resource base, and adverse demographic characteristics. Throughout, Jim and Fran were entertaining hosts, whose good humour and wide, expert knowledge of the region made the Seminar both very enjoyable and highly instructive.

It has been impossible within the scope of a single volume to do full justice to all the papers which were given to the Seminar, and it has been the unenviable task of the three co-editors to choose among them. Our criteria have been that they are representative of the regions and economic sectors which are the main concerns of the Seminar, and that they address in stimulating and useful ways the theme of the occasion, "Sustainable Regional and Local Development". The blame for any typographical or stylistic errors in the papers included in this volume, however, lies entirely with Reg Byron, who assembled and copy-edited the manuscript.

Introduction

James Walsh and Reginald Byron

Sustainability is about managing development on a global scale. Its fundamental precept is that providing for the needs of the present generation should not impoverish future generations. At a minimum, this means that, over the generations, the consumption of natural resources should remain constant. Thus sustainability is not concerned purely with the imperatives of here-and-now economics, but involves *moral* and *political* questions: Should we ensure that future generations are no worse off than we are? How can this be done? Sustainability is not the choice of the marketplace, which will always tend toward the short term. Yet economists agree that sustainability is possible.

> Hartwick (1977) shows that the achievement of a constant per capita consumption path (which would satisfy our definition of sustainability) results when all scarcity rent is invested in capital. None of it should be consumed by current generations.
>
> Would all scarcity rent be invested? With a positive discount rate, some of the scarcity rent is consumed, violating the Hartwick rule. The point is profound. Restoring efficiency will typically represent a move toward sustainability, but it will not by itself be sufficient. Further policies must be implemented to guarantee sustainable outcomes. (Tietenberg 1996: 543)

A free marketplace and natural-resource sustainability are not always incompatible, as is frequently assumed, especially by the more radical proponents of "green" policies. While the marketplace, if left to itself, will always tend toward short-term considerations, history demonstrates that capital accumulation and technological progress have expanded the ways in which resources can be used and have permitted rising standards of living despite a declining resource base. Technological processes are

1

continuously forced out of the marketplace by innovations which extract higher value from the same resource inputs, or the same value from lower resource inputs, thus rendering older processes inefficient. The economics of freight transport is a good example of this process: since fuel costs are a major factor in tonne-kilometre pricing, there is relentless pressure toward more fuel-efficient ships, aircraft, trains and trucks.

Yet, quite clearly, it will not always be the case that efficiency and sustainability are compatible. In the case of the freight transport industry, as long as the price of fuel remains below the efficient price, which is a price that would exceed the marginal cost of extraction of the most expensive-to-produce barrel of oil that could be brought onto the market, then scarcity rent is being consumed rather than invested in capital and the resource is being depleted at an unsustainable rate. As the world's reserves of oil diminish, and global inequalities in access to natural resources increase, the issue of sustainability becomes ever-more pressing. Political decisions could be taken to raise the price of oil to its efficient price, for example; but this would have the consequence, as we saw in the wake of the OPEC episode in the early 1970s, of causing the greatest amount of economic distress to the poorest countries and widening the gap between the North and South still further.

Sustainability, then, is a profound global problem that must be addressed on an international scale and will require international co-operation. The global distribution of resources is an essential dimension of the problem, and achieving sustainability will require new forms and forums of decision-making. It is naïve to suppose that these global structures and processes will come into being easily, since they will involve compromises to national dignities and sovereignties amongst competing and sometimes ideologically-antagonistic political systems. Yet sustainability as an issue has gathered a great deal of momentum in the 1990s and has gone far beyond academic discussion, as popular concern has intensified about environmental problems such as pollution, ozone depletion, deforestation, declining reserves of fossil fuel, recurrent famines in sub-Saharan Africa, and threats to the global stock of human cultural resources including the survival of indigenous peoples in less-developed countries and minority cultures and languages in our own societies. In the end, the trans-national political mobilisation of popular sentiment may be the only way to force sovereign states to the bargaining table, and thus to bring about the kind of global sustainability that will ensure that our great-grandchildren, and their great-grandchildren, find the planet as our generation found it.

Sustainability is a concept with a history that extends back to the early 1970s. There have been several important milestones, including the UN Stockholm Conference on the Human Environment (1972), the

Introduction

UNEP/WWF/IUCN World Conservation Strategy (1980), the Brundtland report, *Our Common Future* (1987), the EU Declaration on Sustainable Development at Bergen (1990), the UN-sponsored Rio Declaration on Environment and Development and *Agenda 21* (1992) and the EU Fifth Environmental Action Programme, *Towards Sustainability* (1993). Arising out of this intense intellectual and political debate there has, not surprisingly, emerged a variety of definitions of sustainability. Perhaps the most well-known is the one provided by the Brundtland Commission, which defined sustainable development as

> . . . development that meets the needs of the present without compromising the ability of future generations to meet their own needs; . . . a process in which the exploitation of resources, the direction of investments, the orientation of technological development and institutional change are all in harmony, and enhance both current and future potential to meet human needs and aspirations.

More recently, Khan, writing in the journal *Sustainable Development* (1995) has argued that

> . . . the paradigm of sustainability, which seeks to pursue growth and equity within the context of inter-generational resource stability, sees development as achieving the interlinking objectives of social, economic and environmental sustainability both in the short and in the long term.

Clearly, then, the sustainable development paradigm involves replacing an economically-driven model of development that relies entirely on the notion of continuous growth by one which is multidimensional in that it takes account of the economic, environmental, and sociocultural processes aimed at transforming society in a manner that does not deplete the overall stock of natural and human resources. A fundamental concern of the new paradigm is the concept of equity which has to be measured and assured along three interrelated dimensions: social, inter-regional and inter-temporal. In order to achieve the goal of sustainability it is necessary to adopt a systemic perspective which can focus on a limited number of key organisational principles that are essential for the new paradigm to succeed. These include diversity, subsidiarity, partnership and participation. While concerns about maintaining diversity originated in bio-ecology, the concept of sustainable development also emphasises the need to sustain diversity as a means of maintaining vitality and richness in social, cultural and economic systems.

Subsidiarity is concerned with the distribution of decision-making competencies and power across and between different levels of social systems. According to this principle, structures should be put in place to facilitate the devolution of power and decision-making to the lowest possible level in the administrative hierarchy. Otherwise there is likely to be a tendency towards centralisation which is conducive to the promotion of an unsustainable dependency culture and economy. To some extent subsidiarity can be achieved through the establishment of local partnerships and networks that bring together representatives of statutory, private and voluntary community interests. Partnerships provide possibilities for overcoming some of the problems associated with weak horizontal and vertical integration in administrative systems that were designed for the implementation of top-down approaches to development planning. Successful partnership arrangements need to be guided by strategic action plans to which all partners subscribe. The transition to a partnership approach to local planning involves not only an organisational change as a means of facilitating constructive dialogue between the different sets of actors in the local development process, but also some fundamental shifts in attitudes so that new relationships are forged on the basis of trust, negotiation and equality leading to a gradual strengthening of the partnering process.

A key element in the nurturing of partnerships is a willingness to share power. Participation is concerned with the relationships between individuals or groups and the state institutions. It is fundamentally related to questions and methodologies of empowerment so that individual members of society can have an input into the decision-making processes that affect their future and the future of the places they inhabit (Friedmann 1992). Pro-active strategies for animation and capacity-building are required to facilitate the involvement of individuals and communities who have become alienated from the mainstream processes (Stohr 1992). A focus on facilitating participation is essential in order to guard against widening rifts in society and between localities and also to guarantee the democratic legitimacy and accountability of local representative structures (OECD 1996). Sustainable development strategies require the application of each of the principles set out above to integrated development plans that include environmental, economic and sociocultural dimensions.

In parallel with the discussions over the past decade or more on sustainability, there has also been a paradigmatic shift in analyses of territorial development which is of particular relevance to studies of development strategies in marginal regions. Many of the key features of the new paradigm have been identified by Albrechts and Swyngedouw (1989) and Stohr (1992). Emphasis is placed on concepts such as integrated programmes, coordination and integration, innovation, local participation, mobilising endogenous resources, and institutional thickness (Amin and Thrift 1994). While there is much overlap in the range of concepts and principles that underpin the sustainable development and new spatial development paradigms, there has been relatively little progress to date in merging the two into a more holistic framework.

The general principles set out above concerning the application of the sustainable development paradigm in particular local and regional contexts imply the following requirements: an involvement of local actors who accept sustainability as their core aim, strategically-targeted action plans that are guided by sustainability principles, explicit recognition of the benefits that can arise from an integrated approach to local resource utilisation, and institutional arrangements that are conducive to the adoption and implementation of innovative medium- to long-term strategies.

Putting these principles into practice is not without certain problems, however. As a concept, sustainable development is no longer the exclusive property of academic and professional specialists, but has become part of the popular discourse of social movements concerned with environmentalism (see, for e.g. Milton 1993), which may understand the concept in ways that are not always helpful to specialists, and may indeed impede efforts to implement genuinely sustainable policies. A sense of looming and imminent environmental catastrophe animates much "green" rhetoric, and sustainable development has become something of a catchword for green social movements. As with political rhetoric anywhere, complex concepts and questions soon become reduced to their lowest common denominators, and thus become mere slogans. Sustainable development has come to mean, for many people in western Europe, preservationism: *no* development. In England, virtually any proposed new road, wind-farm, or open-cast coal mine attracts protesters objecting to the consumption of "nature", and using the vocabulary of academic and professional discourse on sustainable development to legitimate their opposition to developments which infringe on the aesthetics of the land-scape. Such debased popular interpretations are not helpful to serious efforts, such as those outlined in this book, to develop and apply the principles of sustainable development to the pressing problems of marginal regions.

The human species lives by, and through, consuming nature; we cannot sustain ourselves on any level without doing so. Ever since humanity began to manipulate the environment and experiment with breeding techniques 10,000 years ago, to produce the cultigens and domesticates upon which the world's population of six billion people now rely, the process of environmental and genetic manipulation required to supply ever-greater quantities of fuel and foodstuffs has been continuous, and will continue indefinitely into the future as long as the human population continues to expand. We cannot turn off the switch, preventing all further development and growth, without enormously increasing insecurities and inequalities, thus hastening the global catastrophe that the radical greens are concerned to avert (cf. Lewis 1992); moreover, as the economists tell us, there is no need to turn off the switch, provided that ways are found to ensure that scarcity rent is invested in forms of capital that will provide for the well-being of future generations.

Other common misunderstandings are that all the environments in which the world's people live have equal potential to sustain their populations at comparable standards of welfare, and that reducing the level of consumption or output in one place---where the natural endowment and its relation to the number of consumers is more advantageous---will benefit people elsewhere. Unfortunately, there will always be some places where the carrying capacity is low and the population is high, and there is a desperate short-term need for *any* kind of amelioration that development efforts can offer, whether based on sustainable principles or not, because the carrying capacity has already gone well beyond what is sustainable; and there will always be other places where the application of policies based on the principles of sustainable development will, in the long run, make very little practical difference in terms of life-and-death economics, because the human population is unlikely ever to approach a point where the environment's capacity to sustain it is jeopardised. The Horn of Africa and the ecologically-unstable fringes of the Sahara Desert are examples of the former; Saskatchewan and Sweden are examples of the latter.

While the general problem of sustainability is a global one, the immediacy and extent of its local manifestations are highly variable, and are not always capable of being compensated directly: consuming a little less land upon which to build a new shopping mall in Norway will not add to the stock of well-watered, fertile soil in Somalia. Such inequalities are not necessarily the recent products of capitalism and colonialism, though these historical processes may have exacerbated inequities in the global consumption of natural resources; they are at least as much the consequence of natural environmental variation together with population pressures. Archaeologists tell us that twenty thousand years ago, long before the development of domesticated plants and animals, there were places where life was easy and sweet, where people lived in permanent villages, had small families and lived long lives, where the incidence of disease and infant mortality were extremely low, and famine was unknown; but there were other places where people's lives were a ceaseless struggle to survive from one day to the next.

Sustainable development means that we should be rather better at *managing* development, if increasingly serious pressures on the earth's resources are to be averted in the future. These pressures will not happen suddenly: their effects will be felt first where the resource base is thin, the carrying capacity is low, the human population is high, and the economic and political leverage available locally to offset bouts of scarcity repeated at steadily decreasing intervals is soon exhausted. The world's poorest countries have begun to feel the effects of pressures on the earth's resources decades or generations---perhaps as much as a century or two--- before they will be as sharply felt in the richer countries of the Pacific Rim, north America, and western Europe. It is an urgent priority that the countries of the North, which can afford it, take the lead and show by example how the principles of sustainable development can be put into practice in ways that will be of immediate, practical benefit to the countries of the South.

The contributions in this book describe small-scale experiments in the application of the principles of sustainable development in the laboratory of the north Atlantic margin. Here, the problem is not one of finding ways of averting an impending famine, or even---for the most part---of coping with heavy pressures on limited natural resources which are in the long run unsustainable; it is, rather, how to maintain and enhance the livelihoods, future prospects and cultural well-being of people who live in communities in sparsely-populated areas, which are in many cases in economic and demographic decline: these are pressures of quite a different kind than those of the Horn of Africa, but which nevertheless threaten the very survival of hundreds of communities across the north Atlantic region. If, however, sustainability is about the *management* of development according to the principles outlined above, rather than the substance of the particular developmental problem being addressed, then the lessons to be learnt in this laboratory will be, we hope, of interest and value to development specialists everywhere.

The papers in this book

The International Society for the Study of Marginal Regions is a unique grouping that brings together academics from several disciplines including sociology, anthropology, folklore, economics, geography and planning, and also public officials involved in local and regional development throughout the marginal regions of the north Atlantic periphery, including the rural margins of Ireland, Scotland, Wales, Norway, and the Canadian maritime provinces. For many years the Society has discussed at its biannual seminars a wide range of theoretical and practical issues concerning the problems and appropriate strategies for developing marginal regions (Byron 1995). In many respects the Society anticipated several of the concerns that have in recent years gained prominence under the rubric of sustainability. Through its seminars it has promoted inter-disciplinary perspectives on problems across many sectors, concern for local diversity in marginal areas, the need for inter-regional and inter-temporal analyses, and the necessity for participative planning and development strategies (e.g., Flognfeldt et al. 1993, Byron 1995).

This book, *Sustainable Development on the North Atlantic Margin,* arises out of the thirteenth biannual symposium of the Society, held in Ireland at St. Patrick's College, Maynooth in 1995. The selection of papers contained here from the original thirty contributions are organised for convenience around four themes. While there are some overlaps between papers and across themes, the editors have decided that as symposium proceedings the papers that were most directly relevant to the overall theme should be included without much alteration apart from normal editing and updating to take account of events since the summer of 1995. Some of the key points of the papers in each section are discussed in the remainder of this chapter, with the emphasis on identifying those items that link to the general issues mentioned above.

Sustainable development: concepts, processes and strategies

Section One explores the concepts, processes and strategies of sustainable development within a comparative framework by reference to recent experiments in rural parts of Ireland and Norway. The opening chapter by Walsh explores briefly the range of processes impacting on marginal rural areas. Four categories of inter-related mega-processes are identified: economic processes linked to Europeanisation and globalisation, social processes affecting demography and patterns of social interaction, political processes reflecting changing ideologies on the role of the state, and technological processes affecting the nature, organisation and location of economic activities. Following on from the analysis of adjustment forces, a set of principles for a new rural development paradigm are outlined. These are based on recent experience throughout the OECD countries and reflect the main issues highlighted in theoretical debates about sustainable development as summarised by Chiesa and Commins. While there appears to be broad agreement across countries in regard to the basic principles, there can be substantial differences in the approaches to implementing new strategies. The levels of coordination and devolution in the public administrative systems can be a major influence on the effectiveness of local planning. This is demonstrated most clearly in the chapters based on recent experiences in Norway and Ireland by Jørgen Amdam and Jim Walsh. Both draw attention to inadequacies in institutional support systems and also to deficiencies in the quality of local planning and the understanding of the processes that need to be supported in order to revitalise the communities and economies of marginal regions.

The issue of the appropriate scale for devolution of administration and responsibility has been intensely debated in Norway. Jens Christian Hansen summarises the need for a re-examination of the map of municipal boundaries in order to achieve a better balance between the competing pressures related to fiscal costs on the one hand, and the goals of a socially-responsive and participative system on the other hand. In attempting to address the fundamental issues that have arisen in Norway, but which have much wider application, he draws attention to the resistance that may be anticipated from the in-built inertia that can characterise area-based democratic systems and which may ultimately frustrate any serious reforms that are designed to improve devolution and local empowerment.

The importance of providing opportunities for innovative training and learning by multi-skilled or polyvalent knowledge-workers who are competent in a business, technological, personal and social sense is documented by Diarmuid O'Cearbhaill. Drawing on the experience of the Master's degree programme in Rural Development provided by University College Galway and others, and supported by the EU EUROTECNET programme, he emphasise the importance of careful targeting of participants, ongoing commitment to research and evaluation, and attention to provision of a range of learning methodologies. Finally, he reminds us of the need to look beyond a narrowly instrumental perspective on education and training.

Area-based strategies for sustainable development

The five papers in Section Two focus on regional and local strategies in Ireland, Wales and Norway. The review of strategies to assist the development of the west of Ireland by Micheal O'Cinneide complements the earlier chapters by Walsh, Amdam and O'Cearbhaill. Among the points made by O'Cinneide are the need to avoid spurious analyses that separate rural from urban areas, and the necessity for educational institutions to foster creativity, entrepreneurship, and positive attitudes to innovation and change. The inefficiencies associated with a highly centralised but uncoordinated institutional system are also highlighted.

Recent changes in the orientation of Norwegian regional policies are documented by Paul Olav Berg. He detects a more market led approach to regional development with the emphasis shifting towards the southern regions, where the greatest potential for economically-efficient returns on government investments exist. Furthermore, following the vote to remain outside the European Union, it is contended that the relative position of Norway's peripheral regions could deteriorate further. The social and environmental aspects of regional policies have been downgraded, which may ultimately lead to an unsustainable development path.

The position of Norwegian regions in the larger framework of a "Europe of Regions" is examined by Ragnar Nordgreen. In a situation where transnational regional cooperation will be largely dependent on initiatives from the regions themselves, he anticipates that the relative position of those regions with a weak tradition of international cooperation will decline further, leading to an increase in inter-regional inequity. In order to prevent such an unsustainable outcome, he urges a more supportive relationship between central government and officials at the regional and local levels of public administration.

The importance of different types of learning as a means of changing attitudes is explored by Roar Amdam in his case study of the preparation of a sustainable development plan for the municipality of Sykkylven in northern Norway. Despite intensive efforts to introduce sustainable development principles into the process, Amdam remained doubtful about the extent to which a fundamental shift from previous practice had occurred. A critical weakness that persisted throughout the process was an inability to devise an action programme for which responsibility for implementation could be distributed across all the participants. The failure at a local level in a project of national importance to find a solution to this question---which goes to the heart of the inter-generational equity issue in the sustainability paradigm---does not augur well for more ambitious projects aimed at sustainable development of larger regions.

Finally, the issues related to the maintenance of diversity---in this case in relation to language and culture in rural Wales---as a sustainable development goal are explored by Hughes et al. This chapter identifies several complex relationships between economic development and minority cultural objectives in marginal rural areas threatened by population decline. Echoing earlier chapters, they advocate a holistic approach to rural development with particular attention to the maintenance of cultural diversity and local identities.

Sustainable approaches to tourism development

Sections Three and Four are concerned with issues that arise in two key sectors---tourism and agriculture---where the need for holistic, integrated long-term perspectives are particularly essential. The tourism papers address questions of carrying capacity, management strategies, sensitive marketing and environmental interpretation in Norway,

Scotland, Wales and Ireland.

The chapter by Richard Prentice at the opening of this section focuses on some core issues in environmental interpretation, which is described as the process of communicating to people the significance of a place so that they can enjoy it more, understand its importance, and develop a positive attitude towards conservation. Interpretation can, therefore, be regarded as experiential, symbolic and educational. As such, interpretation must be regarded as critical to the establishment of a sensitive interface between the requirements of local residents and visitors if tourism is to be developed in accordance with sustainability principles. An inter-disciplinary conceptual framework is proposed as a means of achieving sensitive and effective interpretation of often very fragile and unique elements in the natural and built environment.

The need for careful assessment of tourism carrying capacity in ecologically-sensitive areas is taken up in the contributions by Thor Flognfeldt and Peter Sjøholt. Particular importance is attached to incorporating local knowledge into eco-tourism planning via mechanisms for local participation. In a following paper, Jeanne Meldon proposes a strategy for sustainable management of scenic landscapes which takes account of many of the issues raised in the previous chapters on tourism. The idea of a "scenic landscape forum" is suggested as a conciliation and mediation service to resolve local planning conflicts and also as a centre for advice on design guidelines for the diverse range of projects that are likely to be promoted in such areas.

The concluding comment by Meldon, that from a sustainable perspective, community comes first and tourism second provides an appropriate link to Hutson and Keddie's chapter on the alternative employment opportunities provided by tourism for members of farm families. While engagement in tourism-related activities can bring some economic and social rewards and in the longer term a more positive appreciation of the countryside, the authors also point to some of the costs, particularly the loss of privacy, the risk of being identified as "failed farmers", and the unequal burden that tends to fall on farmers' spouses.

Sustainable development of agricultural communities

The final part of the book explores questions related to diversification strategies; interactions between rural demography, culture and economy; and the impacts of globalisation trends in the agri-food sector coupled with reform of the EU Common Agricultural Policy on the viability of small rural communities in locations where the alternatives to traditional livelihoods are very limited.

Introduction

Cawley, Gillmor and McDonagh, reporting on the context of farm diversification in the west of Ireland, noted that it is seen by many as contributing to the long-term maintenance of farm land, farm businesses and farm families rather than as merely a palliative for short-term income problems in agriculture. To further encourage alternative farm enterprises as an approach to the sustainable development of marginal regions, a number of issues need to be addressed including more attention to assessment of market potential, provision of adequate training and advice, and the development of appropriate support structures.

The sustainability of alternative rural land uses such as forestry are discussed by Pierce et al., who conclude that there is a need for greater participation in rural policy formation and also better co-ordination of programmes and strategies. Breathnach and Kenny trace the growth of dairy processing co-operatives in Ireland from small local units to diverse multinational agri-business corporations. They also examine the local consequences of such changes, especially in the aftermath of the imposition of quota restrictions on dairy farms. In their view, current trends are contributing to a further decline in the rural population which can only be ameliorated by structural interventions aimed at improving access to land and milk quotas.

Finally, Mary Cawley analyses the impact of migration trends in Ireland between 1971 and 1991 on the sustainability of the rural population. Districts with populations of less than 10,000 and character-ised by weak urban employment structures and which were beyond the zone of influence of larger centres of population were particularly vulnerable. By the late 1980s increasingly larger districts were experiencing population losses in their working age groups. While some opportunities have been provided by local initiatives, the scale of the population movements warrants the development of a national strategy for regional development, as suggested by Walsh in the opening chapter.

This collection of papers is timely in that it brings together a wide range of experiences from a variety of disciplinary backgrounds to issues concerned with sustainable development in diverse settings throughout the North Atlantic marginal regions. Despite the diversity of the case studies upon which the experiences reported here are based, there is a remarkable degree of consistency across the contributions in regard to the issues that arise in the identification and implementation of key principles. It is hoped that this book will be of interest to academics and students from disciplines such as geography, economics, planning, sociology and anthropology. It will also be a key reference work for officials involved in the design and implementation of innovative programmes for sustainable development throughout and beyond the north Atlantic margin.

References

This reference list contains a number of items not cited in the text. The intention is to provide a basis for a broader discussion of the issues.

Adams, W. M. 1990. *Green Development: Environment and Sustainability in the Third World.* London: Routledge.

Albrechts, L. and E. Swyngedouw (eds.). 1989. *Regional Policy at the Crossroads.* London: Jessica Kingsley.

Alden, J. and P. Boland (eds). 1996. *Regional Development Strategies: A European Perspective.* London: Jessica Kingsley.

Amin, A. and N. Thrift (eds.). 1994. *Globalization, Institutions and Regional Development in Europe.* Oxford: Oxford University Press.

Bennett, R. J. and G. Krebs. 1991. *Local Economic Development: Public Private Partnership Initiatives in Britain and Germany.* London: Belhaven.

Byron, R. 1995. Introduction. In R. Byron (ed.), *Economic Futures on the North Atlantic Margin.* Aldershot: Avebury.

_____ (ed.). 1995. *Economic Futures on the North Atlantic Margin.* Aldershot: Avebury.

Cohen, M. 1977. *The Food Crisis in Prehistory.* New Haven: Yale U. P.

Daly, H. E. and J. B. Cobb. 1989. *For the Common Good: Redirecting the Economy Towards Community, the Environment and a Sustainable Future.* Boston: Beacon Press.

European Commission. 1993. Fifth Environmental Action Programme: *Towards Sustainability.* Brussels.

European Commission. 1996. *Environmental Protection: A Shared Responsibility.* Brussels.

Flognfeldt, T., J. C. Hansen, R. Nordgreen and J. M. Rohr. 1993. *Conditions for Development in Marginal Regions.* Lillehammer: Oppland College.

Friedmann, J. 1992. *Empowerment: The Politics of Alternative Development.* Oxford: Blackwell.

Hartwick, J. M. 1977. Intergenerational equity and the investing of rents from exhaustible resources. *American Economic Review* 67, December: 972-74.

International Union for the Conservation of Nature. 1980. *World Conservation Strategy.* Gland, Switzerland: IUCN

International Union for the Conservation of Nature. 1991. *Caring for the Earth: A Strategy for Sustainable Living.* Gland, Switzerland.: IUCN

Khan, M. A. 1995. Sustainable development: the key concepts, issues and implications. *Sustainable Development* 3, 2: 63-69.

Lewis, M. W. 1992. *Green Delusions: An Environmentalist Critique of Radical Environmentalism.* Durham, N. C.: Duke University Press.

Milton, K. 1993. *Environmentalism: The View from Anthropology.* London: Routledge.

OECD. 1990. *Partnerships for Rural Development.* Paris.

OECD. 1996. *Local Partnerships and Social Innovation in Ireland.* Paris.

O'Riordan, T. 1993. The politics of sustainability. In R. K. Turner (ed.), *Sustainable Environmental Economics and Management: Principles and Practice.* London: Belhaven Press.

Stanners, D. and P. Boureau (eds.). 1995. *Europe's Environment: The Dobris Assessment.* Copenhagen: European Environmental Agency.

Redclift, M. 1987. *Sustainable Development: Exploring the Contradictions.* London: Routledge.

Selman, P. 1996. *Local Sustainability: Managing and Planning Ecologically-sound Places.* London: Paul Chapman.

Stohr, W. (ed.). 1992. *Global Challenge and Local Response: Initiatives for Economic Regeneration in Contemporary Europe.* London: Mansell.

Swyngedouw, E. 1992. The Mammon quest: globalisation, interspatial competition and the monetary order: The construction of new scales. In M. Dunford and G. Kafkalas (eds.), *Cities and Regions in the New Europe.* London: Belhaven Press.

Tietenberg T. 1996. *Environmental and Natural Resource Economics.* Fourth edition. New York: Harper Collins.

Turner, R. K. 1993. Sustainability: Principles and practice. In R. K. Turner (ed.), *Sustainable Environmental Economics and Management: Principles and Practice.* London: Belhaven Press.

World Commission on Environment and Development. 1987. *Our Common Future.* Oxford: Oxford University Press.

Part One
CONCEPTS, PROCESSES
AND STRATEGIES
IN SUSTAINABLE DEVELOPMENT

1 Development from below: An assessment of recent experience in rural Ireland

James Walsh

Introduction

One of the defining characteristics of the late twentieth century phase of economic and social development is the emergence in many countries of a strong interplay between globalisation and localisation forces. The emergence of new information processing and exchange technologies, new corporate organisational models, and a shift towards a less inter-ventionist role for the state has tended to accelerate the transformation of economies and societies in a way that leads to sharp divisions between those who are and those who are not equipped to adapt to the new circumstances. As state-level bureaucracies seek to adapt to the global forces by becoming more centralised in policy formulation and implementation, there are large numbers of people who are unable to participate, and end up becoming socially excluded.

Policy-makers in Ireland in the late 1980s were faced with the problem of seeking to improve economic competitiveness in order to be able to improve the relative position of the state within a more competitive single market European Union while at the same time seeking to combat the effects of economic restructuring which was leading to large-scale unemployment and further disadvantage of certain groups and localities. Furthermore, the challenge of tackling the various facets of disadvantage quickly lead to a realisation that some institutional innovations were required. This chapter reviews the outcomes from a number of experi-ments in local development over recent years. I begin with a brief overview of the processes of adjustment in rural Ireland. This will be followed by an outline of key principles for local development planning which will be used as yardsticks in the remainder of the chapter for evaluating the outcomes from recent initiatives.

17

Processes of adjustment in rural areas

The starting point in any discussion of rural development must involve a clarification of the concepts of rural and development. While in the past there was a tendency to equate in a facile way "rural" with "agricultural", this perspective is now regarded as much too restrictive. It is estimated that only about half of the residents of the open countryside actually live on farms. Increasing numbers of rural dwellers earn their living from non farming sectors. But even restricting "rural" to the open countryside and places with fewer that 1500 inhabitants is too restrictive. In most recent discussion of rural development in Ireland, there is an acceptance that rural Ireland consists of all locations beyond the immediate environs of the five largest urban centres: Dublin, Cork, Limerick, Galway and Waterford (NESC 1994).

The concept of development has also been the subject of intense debate in recent times. There has been a shift from the perspective that development is primarily about the attainment of economic goals to a more comprehensive notion of a multidimensional process concerned with social and environmental as well as economic objectives. Recent discussions have emphasised the need for development to bring about not only an improvement in the physical and social conditions of people but that it must also contribute to an improvement in the capacity of individuals and communities to control and sustain these conditions. In this perspective "people-development" has to be very closely linked to "place-development", which in turn has implications for the targeting of interventions in a manner that does not lead to further widening of rural social divisions.

The patterns of adjustment that are taking place in rural areas are influenced by several factors which can be conveniently grouped into two categories. The first relates to the restructuring of agriculture and food processing while the second includes those factors that are shaping the restructuring of the non-agricultural sectors. In practice, many of the fundamental underlying processes are common to both categories of restructuring. The following mega-processes may be identified:

- economic processes linked to Europeanisation and globalisation

- social processes affecting demography, and patterns of social integration and interaction

- political processes reflecting changing ideologies on the role of the state,

- technological processes affecting the nature and organisation of economic activities.

In this brief overview it is possible to draw attention to only the main trends associated with each category of process and their implications for rural development. It is important at the outset to note that while the influences on rural places and people are increasingly reflecting their global and European contexts, nevertheless the outcomes can be very dissimilar in different rural areas due to the diversity of their economic, demographic, social, cultural and environmental heritages.

Europeanisation and globalisation

The main attributes of the Europeanisation and globalisation processes are:

- increased emphasis on competition

  removal of barriers to market forces and introduction of positive integration measures,

- increased competition for mobile investments

- concentration of food production and processing

- improved physical accessibility and information flows between major centres of population

- primacy of efficiency concerns in design and delivery of public policies

Among the outcomes from these processes are the following:

- re-focusing of EU policies including reform of the Common Agricultural Policy

- economic restructuring influenced by economies of scale and scope, and by innovation

- a shift towards urban areas in location decisions of major investors, and

- more differentiated spatial divisions of labour, and range of opportunities to enter workforce.

Over the past thirty years there has been relentless pressure on farmers to intensify production, and/or enlarge the scale of their operations in order to maintain economic viability. Extensive re-structuring involving specialisation, scale enlargement and concentration of production in most sectors onto fewer farms in regions with significant comparative advantages has impacted most adversely on small farms operated by elderly farmers specialising on cattle and sheep systems especially in the west and northwest. This has led to a situation where many farms, especially in the west, northwest and parts of the midlands are no longer economically viable and farm households are increasingly dependent on state and/or EU direct income support transfers (Walsh 1993). The recent CAP reform measures have reinforced the tendencies towards larger scale units and increased the reliance of the marginalised on direct subsidies. The future viability of many farm households is now very much dependent on household members being able to secure alternative sources of income. However, the likelihood of being able to do so varies between households due to differences in demographic structure, range of skills available, and location.

The economic viability of many farm households is also strongly influenced by the increasingly pervasive role of agri-business and food retailing corporations. The modernisation of farming has been heavily reliant on purchased inputs which has lead to a strengthening of agri-industrial linkages and a decline of the traditional, often local, sources of supplies. In their place, fewer larger corporations have emerged with interests extending along the entire length of the food chain from the supply of inputs to farmers to the eventual marketing of a variety of processed foods via contracts with the large multiple chain stores in the food retailing sector. Such restructuring in the agri-business sector has impacted negatively at farm level in many instances. The domination of the food retailing sector by large multiples has enabled them to exert pressure in regard to quality, delivery, presentation and ultimately the profit margins of food processors. Indirectly, this can lead to a deterioration in profit levels on farms as farmers are obliged to make new investments, change production practices or improve the quality of their products. Those who are incapable or unwilling to respond are at risk of becoming further marginalised from mainstream agricultural activity. Those farmers operating small units at locations that are remote from the centralised processing units may be particularly at risk.

The manufacturing sector has been characterised by a significant dualism for many years. Apart from the food processing sector, the majority of the most competitive sub-sectors are made up of branch plants of overseas-controlled corporations which are increasingly located in or adjacent to the larger urban centres. In the era of strong regional policy in the 1970s, there was a high level of dispersal of new manufacturing plants which, when coupled with a vibrant agricultural sector in the years immediately following accession to the European Community, led to significant levels of new employment opportunities in rural areas (Breathnach and Walsh 1994). Since the early 1980s, the regional dimension in industrial policy has been given less prominence, reflecting in part the re-focusing of strategy towards the achievement of national goals in the European context. The pattern of widespread dispersal of new investments throughout the state has been largely replaced by a more concentrated strategy, as there are fewer locations that can satisfy the soft and hard infrastructural requirements of firms in sectors such as electronics, data processing equipment, pharmaceuticals, and health care products.

The service sector is the most rapidly expanding employment area. While there has been a general expansion across all regions over recent years, the growth in demand for highly-educated graduates is mostly concentrated in the major urban centres, especially Dublin (Walsh 1995). This has been especially the case for the financial services, tele-marketing, and software sub-sectors. Tourism has for long been seen as an activity that can make significant contributions to the rural economy and to the maintenance of rural employment levels. However, the evidence in this regard is not entirely reassuring. Most of the recent growth has occurred in those parts of the country that already had a strong tourism base (the southwest and west) or alternatively in Dublin. There has been little progress in establishing a thriving sector in the weaker regions. Even where tourism has been well established, there are reservations about the quality, duration and level of wages associated with much of the associated employment.

Social change

The most notable and easily measurable aspect of social change is the demographic adjustment that has occurred especially since the early 1980s (Walsh 1991, 1992). A very sharp fall in fertility coupled with a very high level of net migration throughout most of the 1980s have brought Irish demography into the greying phase of the demographic transition. Of course rural areas have had disproportionate numbers of elderly people for many decades due to selective out-migration. Much of the literature on rural poverty draws attention to the plight of the elderly, who frequently end up living alone or in households without any young members, in locations that are distant from most services, and with limited opportunities for interacting with others in the immediate neighbourhood. Increasingly, the rural elderly feel threatened and insecure as the traditional, more intensive local social networks have broken down. This breakdown can probably be partly associated with the emergence of newer types of younger households with smaller families, high levels of mobility and increasingly dual or multiple occupations. The decline in fertility also has obvious implications for the survival of both primary and second-level schools, which are often regarded as important focal points for rural communities.

21

Another feature of social change that has implications for the long-term survival of rural populations is the impact of the trend towards certification for entry into the labour force. For well over a decade there has been increased emphasis on the need for educational or training qualifications to gain entry to a highly competitive labour market. In response to this trend, more and more students are opting to remain in the educational system for longer periods and seeking to acquire third-level qualifications. The relevance of this trend for the rural population is that as education levels increase so also do the levels of inter-regional and international migration with the decision to attend college often being the first link in an emigration chain (Walsh and McHugh 1995).

Changing ideologies on the role of the state

The processes of economic restructuring that have been under way since the early 1970s have been accompanied by a revision of the dominant ideologies concerning the role of the state in western democracies. The transition to post-Fordism in an era of very high levels of unemployment has contributed to the emergence of a neo-liberal perspective on the role of the state in relation to the economy. This has been accompanied by greater emphasis on privatisation and deregulation. More traditional concerns with intra-state regional policies have been largely abandoned as the effects of restructuring and the pressures related to demographic growth became more pronounced in large urban areas. The shift in focus in regard to the role of the state has given greater prominence to efficiency criteria in the allocation of public resources which has resulted in the rationalisation of the delivery of many services, for example in health, education, security, and postal services. These adjustments have impacted adversely on many rural residents, particularly the elderly, persons with disabilities, and those without access to private transport facilities.

At the same time the scope for action by the state is being limited by pressures from both above and below. Much of the policy direction and many of the programmes that are currently being implemented are linked to EU policies and programmes. At the other end of the political-administrative system, there has emerged a strong sense of localism. This has come about partly in response to the mega-tendencies in the economic, social and political spheres which have left many local communities more vulnerable and threatened. In response there have been intensive efforts to establish, or in some cases re-establish, local identities that can provide an effective means of responding to niches in an increasingly differentiated consumer market. The emergence of localism is also driven by a recognition of the need to give greater effect to the principle of subsidiarity by establishing local structures to facilitate participation by a wide range of interests.

Technological change

Technological change underpins many of the adjustments that are occurring in all spheres of activity. All new technologies bring opportunities and threats. Technological innovations applied to farming have contributed to improvements in the productivity of land and labour. But these same improvements have lead to oversupply in food markets and necessitated a revision of public policies towards more market-led strategies. The adoption of new technologies is usually a gradual process that is mediated by factors such as the level of resources available to potential adopters, demographic and educational attributes, as well as access to suppliers. In practice these influences are likely to lead to highly-differentiated spatial and temporal patterns of technological change across rural areas which can lead to further widening of regional disparities in relation to the economic viability of farm households (Walsh 1992b).

The potential impacts on rural society of the most recent technological revolution remain unclear. While undoubtedly many opportunities will arise in the production of hardware and software, and in a diverse range of applications, there are some grounds for concern about the locational implications of the revolution in information and telecommunications technology. Some may argue that geography does not matter any more in the era of Internet. However, it may be more realistic to consider IT as an enabling technology that is more likely to reinforce existing spatial divisions of labour. A key issue that must be considered is the wider economic and social milieu requirements for the most efficient use of the new technologies. One of the challenges is to identify ways in which the greatest number of people can be equipped to benefit from the opportunities that may arise.

Principles for a new rural development paradigm

The dominant theme in much of the literature on rural development since the early 1990s is that rural development must be viewed as a multidimensional process which requires the adoption of a new paradigm guided by principles such as innovation, integration, co-ordination, participation, inclusivity, sustainability, and an area-based approach.

A seminal influence on the new thinking was the OECD report, *Partnerships for Rural Development,* which concluded that "it is constructive to view rural development as a broad notion, encompassing all important issues pertinent to the individual and collective vitality of rural people and places. It encompasses such concerns as education, environment, individual and public health, housing, public services and facilities, capacity for leadership and governance, and cultural heritage as well as sectoral and general economic issues" (OECD 1990: 23).

The model outlined above implies a gradual process. In that context it is essential to recognise that there are differences between groups and areas in their readiness to embark on the type of multidimensional process envisaged, and to move away from the restricted focus on economic expansion without reference to other dimensions. It is widely accepted in the literature that many groups or areas may well be at a predevelopment stage where intensive animation and capacity-building are required before the wider development agenda can be taken fully on board. Even then there may be a long phase during which expertise is built up.

This view of rural development has been accepted by the National Economic and Social Council in their report, *New Approaches to Rural Development* (1994). This report concluded that "rural and local development has three main elements: predevelopment, reduction of social exclusion, and enterprise development. Rural development policy must address all three elements" (NESC 1994:17).

In order to achieve the objectives set by the OECD and the NESC, it is necessary to adopt a new paradigm based on the following principles:

(a) rural development should be guided by locally-prepared integrated strategic plans,

(b) the emphasis in the local strategic plans should be on achieving outcomes which would not otherwise be achieved by the programmes implemented by the mainstream agencies; innovative actions should be given the highest priority,

(c) in order to facilitate inclusion and coordination, and in order to avoid or resolve local conflicts over priorities that may emerge from different interest groups, local initiatives in rural development should be planned and implemented by local partnerships involving representatives of statutory, private and local community interests,

(d) resources should be allocated to improving the capacity of local representatives to participate in the development process and especially to assist the directors of the local partnership boards to develop their skills so that a genuinely cooperative and pro-active partnership can be established,

(e) the local action plan prepared by the partnership should include measures to facilitate animation and capacity-building; the specific animation and capacity-building actions should take account of the stage of development of the group; expenditure on these measures should be front loaded to the initial phase of the plan, and on-going capacity-building should be targeted towards enhancing the competitiveness of local enterprises by assisting in areas such as management training and marketing,

(f) procedures should be established to ensure that the activities of each partnership complement rather than compete with those of other local development initiatives that may be operating in the area,

(g) mechanisms to counteract dead weight and displacement should be established at the outset,

(h) all programmes undertaken by the partnership should comply with the principles of sustainable development,

(i) mechanisms should be established to facilitate and foster shared learning opportunities both among groups in Ireland and between Irish groups and their counterparts elsewhere in the EU, and

(j) there should be provision for and commitment to both internal and external on-going monitoring and periodic review in order to promote a culture of self-learning, and to enable the partnerships and the parent government department to adapt their programmes from an informed position.

Assessment of recent local development initiatives in Ireland

Following a long period of official neglect of community-based approaches to local development in rural Ireland (O'Cearbhaill and Varley 1995), there have been since the late 1980s a number of initiatives to assist local development. The details of some of these are summarised in another paper (Walsh 1996) and by Jørgen Amdam (this volume). The importance of local development strategies was officially recognised in the *National Development Plan, 1994-1999.* This was followed by an *Operational Programme for Local Urban and Rural Development* (1994-99) which is funded under the European Community Support Framework for Ireland. It provides a framework that enables local communities to become involved in the social and economic development of their areas by promoting enterprise and employment, assisting long-term unemployed and other marginalised groups to become re-integrated into the labour market, promoting education and training measures to tackle exclusion and marginalisation, and assisting groups to regenerate towns and villages. The programme is implemented by County Enterprise Boards and Partnerships for Designated Areas of Disadvantage. In addition to the Operational Programme the EU LEADER initiative has been extended to all rural parts of the state following a successful pilot phase of implementation between 1991 and 1994.

Evaluation studies have been undertaken for each of the recent local development initiatives (see for example O'Malley 1992 on the Pilot Area Programme for Integrated Rural Development [1988-90]; Kearney et al. [1995] on the EU LEADER 1 Initiative; Craig and McKeown [1993 and 1994] on the area-based partnership response to long-term unemployment; and Haase et al. [1996] on Local Development Strategies for Disadvantaged Areas). In addition to the local evaluations, the OECD have also undertaken a review of the impact of local partnerships in Ireland (OECD 1996). A notable feature of these reviews is the extent to which they have adopted qualitative methodologies to focus on the processes involved in local development. A number of conclusions can be drawn from the evaluation studies.

There is general agreement that locally-focused, area-based integrated strategies can make a significant positive contribution to the economic and social well-being of many individuals and their communities. Local development is seen to be much more than simply a scaling down of interventions that were previously organised from the top by centralised policy making units and delivered through sectoral agencies with little attention to co-ordination. Taken together, the various local development initiatives constitute a programme that is guided by a multidimensional concept of development. Economic, social and political aspects of development are well catered for. The main weakness is in regard to the environmental dimension, though this is being addressed in a limited way within the second LEADER programme. More emphasis has to be placed on understanding the processes of local development and on education and training of activists in local development. Such training is required for individuals at both the local and central levels so as to facilitate more cooperation and to bring about a change of attitude that will lead to a greater emphasis on soft support measures instead of the more traditional reliance on financial grants and physical infrastructure.

The initiatives are characterised by a strong emphasis on provision of soft supports and the adoption of pro-active out-reach strategies. In these respects they differ from previous sectoral interventions, which were regarded as bureaucratic and overly-reliant on provision of capital supports. The OECD review team were particularly impressed by the extent to which they regarded the new decentralised economy in Ireland to be more pervasive (in terms of the range of activities undertaken) and more accessible to persons from low wage communities than might have been expected. In fact their overall assessment of the partnerships that they visited was that they are "extraordinarily innovative" (OECD 1996:

26

85). However, they warn against complacency, and more critically they point to the need for institutional reform so that the innovativeness of the experiment can be sustained.

The role of partnerships

The implementation of each initiative has been devolved to local groups that are organised on a partnership basis. Typically, each partnership includes representatives of relevant statutory bodies including the local authorities, the local communities and the local business sector. In the case of County Enterprise Boards, the composition of the boards was decided upon by the parent government department. By contrast, LEADER groups were allowed to determine locally the membership of their boards. For the second LEADER programme, this autonomy has been retained but there is now a requirement that the boards should represent a tripartite partnership. In the case of LEADER boards, the average size was fourteen members, though this varied from five to 21. The size of the boards tended to influence the orientation of the programme of actions undertaken by the groups. Small boards tend to pursue a restrictive agenda which was usually strongly oriented towards enterprise support, while larger boards were often dominated by representatives of several community-based groups. These boards were more likely to lack cohesion and were, therefore, less able to follow a strategic approach (Kearney et al. 1995).

The tripartite structure of most partnerships was successful in facilitating a forging of mutually beneficial links between local community representatives and the statutory agencies. Some groups adopted a brokerage role in relation to the existing agencies which led to some innovative initiatives. What was most significant about these was that, in most cases, it was the LEADER group rather than the agencies that provided the catalyst for ensuring that the events actually happened. The inclusion of private business sector representatives on boards has helped to alter some of the bureaucratic procedures associated with public agencies.

While the partnership model has been found to provide opportunities for innovative approaches to local development, there are still some key issues to be resolved. The extent of centralisation in the Irish administrative system is a constraining factor on the development of effective and dynamic partnerships. While several of the local partnerships have demonstrated that they can be very effective in addressing problems that were previously neglected or inadequately addressed by the larger agencies, there is still an element of distrust, and in some cases antagonism, among some personnel in the longer-

27

established agencies towards the recently established partnerships. The reasons for this situation are due in part to a tradition where the bulk of public finances have been controlled by central authorities, and also the threat to existing power structures posed by the partnerships. Indeed in the case of one of the programmes, the evaluators concluded that some of the key statutory agencies had failed to deliver on any aspect of the initiative (Craig and McKeown 1994).

Another weakness in the effective operation of the partnership model can be the demands placed upon the local community representatives. The time commitment required of voluntary representatives can be excessive. Also, the lack of experience of some representatives can at times prevent them from engaging as equal partners. The evaluators have in all cases recommended that special training should be provided for board members and that there should be provision for rotation of membership after a fixed period in order to reduce the burden that is frequently carried by a few, and also safeguard against the emergence of local cliques which could serve to frustrate the ideal of partnership.

The OECD review was forthright in its view that there is a legitimacy question to be addressed in relation to the position of many of the partnerships which have benefited from a provisional dispensation from normal democratic controls. It is alleged that they have "substantial informal power to direct funds from state agencies to the benefit of their own projects" (OECD 1996: 85). This unsubstantiated assertion may be an overstatement, as the situation so described is likely to arise only when a partnership has matured enough to be able to adopt a strong brokerage position vis-a-vis the better-resourced state agencies. Nevertheless, the report is correct in questioning the extent to which partnership board members are capable of representing the diversity of interest groups within the total population of the partnership area. While success and legitimacy may be temporarily derived from the promotion of innovative projects, in the long run this "can never substitute for electoral review" (OECD 1996: 85). This particular issue has become a major concern of the government-appointed Devolution Commission to consider the proposals for a more effective system of local public administration.

The present institutional system is particularly weak in regard to co-ordination mechanisms, which leads to inter-agency conflicts, lack of synergy, frustration for both officials and target groups, and an over-reliance on informal exchanges which in the long run will inhibit systemic innovation. In regard to the partnerships, there is general agreement that the central support units associated with the parent departments are overstretched, while the local groups are so engaged in trying to implement their own plans that there is very little systematic learning taking place.

The problem of weak systemic learning across the partnerships in each programme is compounded by the extent to which different programmes have overlapping objectives thereby encouraging competition rather than complementary actions between partnerships in the same geographical areas. The situation is not helped by the fact that each initiative is under the responsibility of a different government department and that there is no strong mechanism for central level coordination. At county level, County Strategy Teams have been established to coordinate the implementation of local initiatives. To date only limited progress has been made in this respect, as many of the local partnerships do not appear to be interested in local cooperation---in fact in a number of areas there is a high level of mutual distrust between the partnerships.

Strategic planning

In order to be successful in promoting innovative actions that will lead to outcomes that would otherwise not be achieved, it is essential that the partnerships should be guided by strategic action plans (Ó Cinnéide and Keane 1990). While this is a requirement for participation in all of the programmes, the experience to date suggests that the concept and methodology of strategic planning was poorly understood in most cases. This was partly due to inexperience, but the planning process itself was in many cases severely hampered by a lack of baseline data which hindered the undertaking of a comprehensive SWOT analysis. At the beginning of the LEADER programme most groups clearly had little appreciation of the role of animation and capacity-building functions. Consequently, the substance of many of the business plans consisted of little more than lists of potential projects. The concepts of innovation and integration were generally not well understood, and neither was there much awareness of the potential problems associated with dead weight (supporting projects that would have gone ahead anyway) and displacement (providing support for projects that may force others out of business). In effect much of the local planning is funds-driven and led by consultants who may at times be assisting more than one group. The groups did not have sufficient time to participate fully in the preparation of the plans and to give due consideration to prioritisation of actions. The result was that there was very little sense of local ownership of the plans, which frequently tended to be over-ambitious relative to the experience and resources available to the groups, who were also unable to identify the possibilities for integration. There have been very few instances where local groups have prepared medium- to long-term strategies which were flexible enough to be capable of adaptation to the guidelines for various funding initiatives as they became available. This type of planning has been undertaken only by very experienced groups.

Animation and capacity-building

In addition to the assessment of the partnership models and the extent of strategic planning, the evaluation studies have carefully examined the role of animation and capacity-building in the programmes. This was probably the strongest attribute of the LEADER initiative, which resulted in a very positive new type of relationship between the LEADER group officials and the population which they served. A wide range of activities were undertaken under the general heading of capacity-building. These included training courses in business planning, community leadership, niche marketing of local food products, heritage management, women in rural development, horse breeding, and shellfish cultivation. Other types of capacity-building included the formation of producer and marketing groups, the preparation of local resource audits and sectoral-area strategies, and the establishment of local advisory and mentoring panels.

Most groups engaged in some level of animation and capacity-building, though in many cases it was not seen as a specialist task. In the first year of the programme, some groups did not engage professional animators because of difficulties in raising matching funds, though the requirements in this area were later relaxed. In a few instances the LEADER boards failed to appreciate the role of animators. This happened mostly in those groups which had no prior experience in local development. In fact these groups could be described as local top-down agencies. Following the review of the first LEADER initiative, the operating rules for the second phase of the programme require all groups to allocate resources to animation and capacity-building. While the County Enterprise Boards do not engage in animation to the same extent as LEADER groups, they are strongly encouraged to allocate resources to capacity-building such as provision of mentoring services, management improvement courses, a comprehensive information service through a one-stop-shop, and fostering of a greater sense of enterprise awareness.

Conclusions

In this chapter I have shown that rural areas are undergoing adjustments in response to many factors which have international and national dimensions. The tradition of sectoral planning organised from the centre has frequently led to unintended outcomes such as increased marginalisation and exclusion. In response, a number of experiments have been undertaken that have aimed to facilitate more inclusive and sustainable models of development from below. The local development initiatives that have been reviewed in this chapter demonstrate that much can be achieved when appropriate organisational structures are put in place and strategic action plans are prepared when there is a strong commitment to animation and capacity-building. This chapter has set out the basic principles that are essential for sustainable approaches to local development which include economic, social, political and environmental dimensions. However, the experiments in Ireland are still very marginal to mainstream planning. In this situation, it is necessary to maintain a realistic perspective on what can be achieved through poorly-resourced local initiatives, especially in the context of a highly-centralised administrative system. Local development must be embedded in a more elaborate framework for spatial planning that will also include regional planning and mechanisms for horizontal and vertical coordination across and between the different spatial scales. The experience to date also points to the need for a gradual approach to local development with a differentiation of supports according to the level of experience of the participating groups.

References

Boylan, T. 1996. Rural industrialisation and rural poverty. In T. Haase et al. (eds.), *Poverty in Rural Ireland.* Dublin: Oak Tree Press. Pp. 173-210.

Breathnach, P. and J. A. Walsh. 1994. Industrialisation and regional development in Ireland. *Acta Universitatis Carolinae Geographica, Univerzita Karlova Praha* 24, 1: 67-79.

Curtin, C., T. Haase, and H. Tovey. 1996. *Poverty Rural Ireland.* Dublin: Oak Tree Press.

Craig, S. and K. McKeown. 1993. Interim report to the Central Review Committee on the setting up of twelve-area based partnerships in 1991. Dublin: Combat Poverty Agency.

Craig, S. and K. McKeown. 1994. *Progress Through Partnership.* Dublin: Combat Poverty Agency.

European Commission. 1988. *The Future of Rural Society.* Brussels.

European Commission. 1994. *Ireland Community Support Framework 1994-1999.* Brussels.

Government of Ireland. 1993. *National Development Plan, 1994-1999,* Dublin: Government Publications Office.

Government of Ireland. 1995. *Operational Programme for Local, Urban and Rural Development, 1994-1999.* Dublin: Government Publications Office.

Haase, T., K. McKeown and S. Rourke. 1996. Local development strategies for disadvantaged areas; evaluation of the Global Grant 1992-1995. Dublin: Area Development Management Ltd.

Kearney, B., G. Boyle and J. Walsh. 1995. *EU LEADER 1 Initiative in Ireland: Evaluation and Recommendations.* Dublin: Stationery Office.

Morris, J. and J. Copestake. 1993. *Qualitatative Enquiry for Rural Development.* London: Intermediate Technology Publications Ltd for the Overseas Development Institute.

National Economic and Social Council. 1990. *A Strategy for the Nineties: Economic Stability and Structural Change.* Dublin: Government Publications Office.

National Economic and Social Council. 1994. *New Approaches to Rural Development.* Dublin: Government Publications Office.

O Cearbhaill, D. and T. Varley. 1995. Whither community development in Ireland? In R. Byron (ed.), *Economic Futures on the North Atlantic Margin.* Aldershot: Avebury. Pp. 347-364.

Ó Cinnéide, M. and M. J. Keane. 1990. Applying strategic planning to local economic development: the case of Connemara Gaeltacht, Ireland. *Town Planning Review* 61, 4: 475-86.

O'Malley, E. 1992. *The Pilot Programme for Integrated Rural Development 1988-1990.* Dublin: Paper No. 27, Broadsheet Series, Economic and Social Research Institute.

OECD. 1990. *Partnerships for Rural Development.* Paris: OECD.

OECD. 1996. *Local Partnerships and Social Innovation in Ireland.* Paris: OECD.

Walsh, J. A. 1991. The turn-around of the turn-around in the population of the Republic of Ireland. *Irish Geography* 24, 2: 116-124.

Walsh, J. A. 1992a. Economic restructuring and labour migration in the European periphery: the case of the Republic of Ireland. In M. Ó Cinnéide and S. Grimes (eds.), *Planning and Development of Marginal Areas.* Galway: Centre for Development Studies. Pp. 23-36.

Walsh, J. A. 1992b. Adoption and diffusion processes in the mechanisation of Irish agriculture. *Irish Geography* 25, 1: 35-53.

Walsh, J. A. 1993a. Modernisation and marginalisation under the Common Agricultural Policy: Irish agriculture in transition. In T. Flognfeldt, et al. (eds.), *Conditions for Development in Marginal Regions.* Lillehammer: Oppland College. Pp. 185-193.

Walsh, J. A. 1993b. Planning for local and regional development in Ireland. *Irish Banking Review*, Autumn: 36-49.

Walsh, J. A. 1995. *Regions in Ireland: A Statistical Profile.* Dublin: Regional Studies Association (Irish Branch).

Walsh, J. and C. McHugh. 1995. The Irish school-leaver trail: links between education and migration. *Geographical Viewpoint* 23: 88-103.

Walsh, J. A. 1996. Local development theory and practice: recent experience in Ireland. In J. Alden and P. Boland (eds.), *Regional Development Strategies: A European Perspective.* London: Jessica Kingsley Publishers. Pp. 159-177.

2 Sustainable rural development: Concepts, practice and policy

Roberto Chiesa and Patrick Commins

Introduction

The OECD (1994) notes that more than one-third of the combined population of its member countries live in rural communities, dispersed over 95% of their territories. Traditionally, rural areas have been associated with agriculture but their economic functions are now more varied. The processes of rural change have become more complex. Industrial production, infrastructural provision, residential housing, tourism and natural resource conservation are part of the multi-functional use of rural space. These processes of change do not impact evenly on rural territories but do so in different ways for individual areas, depending on the particular internal and external relationships of any area, and with different positive and negative effects at the local level.

Generally, the "rural" is used to define areas with: (i) low population density, (ii) small-scale centres of population, (iii) high presence of natural environmental elements, and (iv) high economic importance of activities linked to the use of the natural environment. Compared to urban areas, rural areas are often perceived as lagging behind in a unilinear path of economic development. In extreme cases, the negative aspects of this situation are highlighted---economic marginalisation, depopulation, social exclusion.

However, we must consider, in a more positive way, the challenges and possibilities for development which are presented by "lagging" rural regions. As suggested by Langer (1989), there is an opportunity for people in lagging rural regions to take account of the negative effects of past development processes and to seek to transform the conditions of these areas on a different model---an alternative development path. From this perspective, rural communities may be seen not simply as being at an early stage towards an urbanised society, nor as a residuum of modern economic development, but as territorial systems that can develop in different and less intensive ways. The concept of "sustainable rural development" (SRD) could be used to identify the possibilities for a positive pattern of change in rural areas. This development path would maintain the natural and man-made capital of rural areas, meet the needs of their populations, and make a genuine contribution to longer-term human welfare.

The objective of this paper is to outline an approach to rural development based on ideas about the sustainability of rural systems. First, we review the recent literature on sustainable development to try to clarify the different understandings of the concept and the application of SRD in rural studies. Second, using the notion of a local territorial unit (LTU) as an appropriate spatial scale at which to apply SRD and develop action strategies, we describe the criteria and methodological tools for identifying such territorial units. Third, we analyse some research priorities and policy implications related to this sustainability approach to rural development.

Sustainable Development (SD)

Although problems of the relationships between human and environmental systems have always been an issue, the concept of sustainable development (SD) has a recent origin. It is based on the observation that the development process, as it has taken place over the past two centuries and especially in recent decades, reduces environmental resources and has also several negative social, cultural and regional economic effects. The intensification of industrial production, concentration of demographic growth, increasing consumption of non-renewable energy, more waste production, and reduction of forest areas have all proceeded in a manner which does not maximise welfare, and is not sustainable in the longer term. From these considerations the need to define the relationships between societal goals, economic activities and environmental resources has come sharply into focus. Against this background, the term "sustainable development" was first publicised in the World Conservation Strategy in 1981 and subsequently adopted by the Brundtland Report, published as *Our Common Future* (World Commission on Environment and Development 1987).

Different meanings of SD

For the Brundtland Report, sustainable development is that which meets the needs of the present generation without compromising the ability of future generations to meet their own needs. It is not a fixed state of harmony, but rather a process of change in which the exploitation of resources, the direction of investments, the orientation of technological development, and institutional change are made consistent with future as well as present needs (World Commission on Environment and Development 1987: 9).

This definition raised some fundamental ideas that were subsequently elaborated in other work. These included the ethical and equity dimensions of meeting human needs, efficiency in the harmonious economic use of the resource base, and SD as a process involving different spheres of human activity and different institutions. Aspects of economic theory, especially those grounded in the market as a basis for allocating the costs and benefits of production, are questioned in the Brundtland formulation.

Pearce et al. (1989) suggest that there are two different understandings of sustainability. A strong approach links sustainability to the conservation of natural capital in quantity and quality; the second and weaker approach offers the possibility of partial substitution of natural capital by man-made capital. Following this distinction, Turner (1993) classifies the contribution to the SD debate into four categories, as a function of the different ways of conceptualising the relationships between natural, man-made, human and cultural capital: (i) "very weak" sustainability allows perfect substitution between these singular types of capital; (ii) a "weak" sustainability view arises from the consideration that perfect substitution between natural and man-made capital is impossible; this imposes restrictions on resource use in that particular non-substitutable ecosystem qualities must be preserved; (iii) "strong sustainability" rejects as undesirable the prospect of declining levels of natural capital, stressing that considerations of vulnerability, irreversibility, and uncertainty should lead to ways of avoiding environmental degradation. Economic development can be promoted by a more efficient use of resources, not by increasing the use of natural capital; and (iv) a "very strong" sustainability approach puts the focus on the need to limit human impacts on environmental systems and suggests a steady-state economic system where development is possible only in the context of a basic change in social values and ethics. In the case of the first two understandings of SD, careful management and some technical change may be sufficient to reach sustainability whereas, for the latter two, a basic shift in economic and social organisation is necessary---underpinned by change in ideological perspectives.

Redclift (1987) sees SD as different from the standard economic paradigm. Not only is SD based on the assumption that nature represents a stock of limited goods but nature could be understood as an independent system with its own rules and mechanisms, not related to

human use. For Redclift, the natural environment is a social construction, assuming a meaning only in relation to the way society
envisages nature and the practical ways to use or manage natural
resources. Different societies have distinctive conceptions of nature.
Clearly, the implications of this approach are that we cannot analyse
environmental issues without understanding the complexities and
relationships among a range of socioeconomic factors. Reaching
sustainable development in this context means finding institutional
frameworks capable of ensuring a minimum of conflictful relationships
and a new equilibrium between social actions and natural resources.
Technology and markets are circumscribed by social rules, and
conceptions of development must start from the links between environmental knowledge, political processes and the practicabilities of
managing nature's resources (Redclift 1991).

In recent years the debate has moved from the conceptual and
theoretical levels to specifically operational problems including, for
example, dealing with global warming or establishing methodologies for
applying SD approaches, as evident in such analyses as environmental
impact assessments, environmental auditing, resource accounting and
decision-support models (Giaoutzi and Nijkamp 1993). Critics of SD
advert to the ambiguity of terminology, the lack of meaning in the
rhetoric, its weakness as a political idea in the face of the dominant forces
of capital internationalisation, and the absence of concrete operational
tools to give it practical effect (Murdoch 1993, Barcellona 1994).

Sustainability of rural regions

The debate about SD has been introduced into the primary sector mainly
because of the incapacity of technological developments to guarantee the
maintenance of environmental quality in the longer run. Historically,
rural communities have developed distinctive management and technical
tools to earn livelihoods in different environmental circumstances. Often,
but not always, these tools and related methods of production have
achieved a desirable balance between maximisation of outputs and the
conservation of natural resources. Even today, conventional farming
methods are considered as contributing to the implementation of SD
strategies in rural areas. Nevertheless, the striving for increased
quantities of agricultural products and raw materials, the introduction of
new technologies, and the integration of production activities with the
agri-industrial complex, have all changed traditional patterns of resource
use and, in particular, have increased the pressure on non-renewable
resources.

Apart from these trends in production activities, the particularity of rural systems is also related to threats to the existence and quality of life in many rural communities. This vulnerability arises from declining economic opportunities for labour, with consequent out-migration and depopulation. To cope with these threats, and before the advent of SD ideas, many countries had explored new approaches to maintaining the socioeconomic viability of rural communities. Concepts such as community development and integrated rural development came into vogue in this context. Relationships between the changing agricultural economy and the rural economic and socio-demographic change have retained their importance in the literature on SD in rural areas. This provides a starting point to define the characteristics of sustainable rural development (SRD). Before taking on this task it will be helpful to examine some particular aspects of rural reality.

SRD and agriculture

Many approaches to SRD focus on the sustainability of agriculture. Douglass (1984) identifies three main ways by which this issue has been considered. The first simply links sustainability to the capacity to produce enough food for a growing world population. The challenge is to expand food supply by technological innovation and efficiency in production. This position comes from within the dominant Western view of agriculture where faith in the progress of scientific knowledge and technological capacities excludes preoccupation with the future quality of the resource base.

The second view of rural sustainability shifts the debate from the economic to the biophysical area. The problem is seen as one of finding an ecological balance in agricultural systems, of respecting longer-term processes of conserving resources, and limiting increases in output produced from non-renewable inputs. A third perspective is that of the proponents of so-called radical or alternative agriculture. This puts the focus on the relationship between agricultural systems and the social organisation and life of rural people. It considers that modernisation has distorted the traditional management of agricultural resources which had combined a great capacity to respond to the needs of rural people with low-level consumption of valuable resources. Rural sustainability, it is argued, must develop an alternative agriculture which would include some technology but would be based on a new sensitivity to the long-term relationships between resource use and social needs.

These different viewpoints come close to Smit and Brklacich's (1989) three possible meanings of sustainability in relation to the agri-food system: sustainability as food sufficiency over the long-term, necessitating the maintenance of quality and quantity in agricultural land; sustainability as stewardship or a concern for rural resources; and community sustainability or the promotion of good social and economic conditions in rural areas to allow farmers maintain food production over the long term.

SRD and the rural community

Because dispersed population is characteristic of the great part of the Canadian and US countryside the viability of rural communities is an important issue. Much of the North American literature is therefore concerned with the sustainability of rural communities. To Gertler (1994: 69), for example, sustainability means more than aligning technology and market forces with ecological limits; it is first and foremost a social issue. He adds: "Communities and culture are the social fabric that can support socially and ecologically appropriate production and consumption practices". Dykeman (1990: 60) defines a "healthy community" as one that is economically viable, socially vital, and environmentally sound. "The healthy community is one that is continually creating and improving those physical and social environ-ments and expanding those community resources that enable people to support each other in performing all the functions of life and in developing themselves to their maximum potential".

Douglas (1990: 66-72) starts from a definition of "vulnerability" as a susceptibility to changes in social, economic, political, ecological and other conditions which undermine or destroy a community's raison d'être, and eventually its actual existence. The practice of sustainable development means coping with vulnerability, maintaining community vitality, and securing long-term viability.

It will be apparent from the above formulations that economic growth (or improving output capacities) is only part of the development process, not in itself capable of generating sustainable development. For a rural community, survival and development are not only linked to its capacity to meet material needs, but also its social, cultural and self-development needs. Furthermore, the possibility of reaching any individual objective is influenced by progress on the others. A multidimensional, holistic and integrated conceptualisation is therefore necessary in defining rural sustainability.

Defining sustainable rural development (SRD)

The main perspectives examined to this point, mainly sustainability in the ecosystem, in the agri-food system and in the rural community, will help us to define an SD approach for rural areas. Adopting a "strong sustainability" standpoint, we consider that SRD can be understood as a

39

process to enable rural people to improve their biophysical, economic, social and cultural environment. It is a process of constructing socio-economic systems to manage relationships with the biophysical resource base in a longer-term development perspective. A broad range of "fields of activity" must be taken into account. How the various activities are articulated is of critical importance because while the linkages between some activities are potentially synergistic, other relationships are inherently conflictful. For present purposes it will be convenient to categorise the main dimensions of SRD under the following headings: (i) ecological, (ii) economic, (iii) social, (iv) demographic, (v) cultural, and (vi) political.

The ecological perspective of SRD is concerned with the relationships between biophysical resources and human activities. The objective is the conservation or improvement of the natural capital (such as biodiversity and environmental quality), and the efficient environmental use of resources (such as the location of new infrastructure with attention to the quality of the landscape, the use of low levels of chemical inputs in agriculture, waste management, management of tourist flows).

The economic perspective considers the utilisation of capital needed to cope with the work and income needs of the population. The objective is to enhance the longer-term capacity for wealth generation, based mainly on local resources. The attention is on increasing the total capital including human capacities, improving cooperation among enterprises, exchanging knowledge, increasing flexibility in using resources, diversifying the economy, and building the capacities to be innovative and enterprising.

The social aspect takes into account relationships among different social groups, and also the quality of life. The objective is to enhance the quality of the social environment by intensifying community cooperation, fostering integration and social inclusion, providing greater access to basic goods and services for all, widening opportunities for public participation in civic affairs, and creating opportunities for leisure.

The demographic aspect of SRD is concerned with the maintenance of a population in which there is balanced distribution by age and gender, and low rates of out-migration. From the cultural standpoint SRD strategies are concerned with increasing local capacity to create and appreciate cultural values by heightening consciousness about local identity and culture, safeguarding the local heritage, encouraging cultural creativity, promoting exchanges with external cultures, and promoting diversity in the institutional framework (private, public and social) concerned with education and cultural production.

The political dimension of SRD involves building or expanding the capacity of people to manage local resources, as well as their ability to manage the internal and external relationships pertaining to the local area. The strategy has to focus on strengthening local institutions, increasing levels of participation by people in decisions affecting their local community, creating sufficient social consensus for communities to function effectively in implementing SRD, and their integration into, and participation in, mainstream national life.

SRD and territorial scale

To implement this multidimensional approach to SRD there is a need for policies but also for operational strategies, including, in particular, an identification of the spatial scale at which policies are best made operational. Determination of the appropriate geographical level (or levels) is in fact one of the most challenging questions facing the researcher in SRD (Flynn 1992).

Environmental processes, economic and other human activities are likely to have different "appropriate geographical scales" in the context of analysing sustainability. Furthermore, there may not be a correspondence between the spatial location of the cause of some problem and the actual manifestation of the same problem at local level. A clear example is the way in which local economic problems are traceable to global economic change or industrial restructuring. In fact, the concern about environmental issues and SRD started from the discovery of the global scale of environmental problems (for example, acid rain, or the greenhouse effect).

In practice, however, the most promising level for conducting SRD analysis and searching for policy prescriptions is at some sub-national geographical level. Norgard (1988) believes that the regional level is the most appropriate scale. For Giaoutzi and Nijkamp (1993) the meso-level offers the most promising prospects. At the regional or meso-level we can better understand the relationships among local forces, the impact of human activities on the environment, the exploitation of local resources, and the dependencies on external inputs. At this level also it seems possible to find the actors interested and able to improve policies favourable to SRD. Of course, the spatial unit has to be considered as an open entity, facing various interactions with bordering regions and with global forces.

What kind of meso- or regional level?

There are obviously different kinds of regions, even ignoring those defined for administrative purposes. Reference to ecology and economics alone will illustrate the variety of designations possible. Ecology defines the basic analytical entity as the ecosystem. At the meso-level an

41

"environmental region" might define a large ecosystem that has an identity as a result of the development of biological features in particular geographical and climatic conditions. Generally, bioregions do not correspond to other spatial units; they are defined by the main natural factors affecting the environment (for example, river basins or mountains), or by human activities that are important enough to characterise the habitat (for example, the predominant form of land use) (Crivelli and Lepori 1992).

Economists pay little attention to problems of space but two categories of studies are relevant here. The first pertains to analyses of the allocation of economic activities. Economic geographers try to define location patterns and the principles determining the structuring of economic regions. The classic examples are Von Thunen's model of land use, Weber's model of industrial allocation, and Christaller's central place theory for settlements and services. The second contribution of economic analyses comes from studies of regional economic development which define regions in order to examine the internal dynamics of development and the relationships with the national or international economy. Both of these economic orientations consider space as a location of relationships, of interdependence between different activities and actors; they also analyse space as the subject of relationships with the external environment.

However, to solve the problem of identifying a suitable regional level for SRD we need to find a framework which will capture the interactions between environmental and socioeconomic systems. Only a few contributions from the literature on SRD seem to be of help. For Zanoli (1994) the appropriate level for organising rural sustainable strategies is the bioregion, constituted by localised communities with sufficient capacity to control their economy and natural resources, but small enough to allow for the participation and cooperation of their members.. Smit and Brklacich (1989), focusing on the sustainability of agri-food systems, note that the community aspects of sustainability are often examined in the context of relatively small geographic units, whereas the food sufficiency approach typically employs a broader scale. Hilhorst (1990), concerned with analysing the optimal population size for integrated rural development, observes that for this purpose there is considerable agreement that areas should have populations of 50,000 to 100,000 persons, with an urban centre of about 10,000 to 15,000 inhabitants. This range would allow a particular level of decision-making, involving agricultural production, trade, transport, credit allocation and labour markets. For Hilhorst, an area of this scale corresponds in most cases to the range of influence of a rural town, to economic and physical structuring, and to sociopolitical structures. In what follows we concentrate on applying a systems approach to examine more closely an appropriate geographical scale for SRD.

The local territorial unit (LTU)

What is required is a territory where it is possible: (i) to identify different processes (ecological, economic, social, political) having a high intensity of relationship and interdependence; (ii) to analyse the elements of every constituent system and the reciprocal impacts among systems; (iii) to understand factors making for the sustainability of the processes; (iv) to analyse this area as a unity in relation to external forces and to define the regional impact of these; and (v) to find subjects who are willing and able to implement SRD strategies.

The concept of a region, defined in systems terms, seems to fit this purpose. Nir (1987) makes a distinction between zones and regions. "Zone" is based on a notion of homogeneity, whereas "region" reflects diversity, processes and interactions. A model region is defined by the relationships between different points (for example, residence and place of work, production and marketing locations). A "functional region" is defined to fulfil a particular aim, while a "total region" is seen as some part of the earth's surface where the population, organised within certain social, political or administrative boundaries, faces common natural, economic, social and political challenges.

Nir adopts a systems approach to express a total region as a unit composed of different elements, with internal relationships and processes. This conceptualises phenomena, not as isolated items that can only be aggregated to some incoherent totality, but as components of a coherent whole where the relationships between the components and the environment are anchored in interdependent processes. For Nir the system concept bridges the physical and sociological components, using methodologies appropriate to both domains, to deal with different spatial scales and to study dynamic, static or declining regions. However, other regional scientists (Hilhorst 1960, Vartiainen 1987) caution that regions can be understood not only as the socio-spatial organisation of objective reality but also in terms of the subjective categorisations made by communities or individuals.

Here, and taking account of systems analysis, we use the term "local territorial unit" (LTU) to characterise a spatial scale in which the relationships and interdependencies among the different processes (ecological, economic, etc.) are such as to fit with the requirements of analysis and policy in striving for sustainability in rural areas. Then, the problem is to establish a methodology to identify and analyse individual territorial units, within the boundaries of which there are strong relationships among the different subsystems and their constituent elements.

Methodological procedures

The aim of any research project in SRD will influence the analytical approach to defining the LTU. At the same time the nature of the LTU will influence the methodological tools useful to analyse and implement SRD. The analyses will require qualitative and quantitative methods to describe the existing situation, with a particular need to identify internal and external systemic relationships, and the factors influencing development processes. The different relevance of the subsystems, together with the existence of internal functional hierarchies, will allow definition of boundary points between subsystems. A methodology to defining an LTU can be developed in the following five steps:

Step 1: Identifying relevant subsystems

The systems approach stresses the importance of internal processes and the relationships between elements that contribute to the identity of the system. A classification of these subsystems is not easy and, in any case, will depend somewhat on the particular focus of the research. However, the main subsystems will likely relate to (i) the environment, (ii) production, (iii) markets, (iv) the public sector, and (v) sociocultural sphere. The relevant subsystem elements will vary from area to area but, to illustrate, the following can be suggested, corresponding to the subsystems just listed: (a) river basins, orographic features, dominant land uses; (b) local labour market areas, enterprise networks, agro-industry basins; (c) commercial or city-market basins, farm input and output markets, housing market areas; (d) areas of coverage by health, education, mail, transport and other public administration services; (e) areas of influence of linguistic groups, community-based associations or other features of common identity.

Step 2: Developing criteria to establish LTU boundaries

Having identified the main forces creating an area the next step is to establish area boundaries. Subsystems have different shapes and area coverages. A preliminary step, therefore, is to define the spatial scope of the relevant subsystems and examine their degree of coincidence. Obviously, no perfect LTU can be drawn on a map, and especially when physical boundaries do not predominate (as in the case of islands) fuzzy boundaries will be the normal outcome.

Subsystems and their elements not only differ in shape but also have

44

different powers to characterise the whole system. Thus, it is helpful to define a hierarchy using a scale of weights. Techniques of so-called paired comparisons (comparisons of all elements in groups of two, using a degree of relative importance) will generate a set of weights for every element and subsystem. The weights assigned will help to produce a scale of intensity of relationships and to define the boundaries of an LTU. The availability of Geographical Information Systems permits the application of quite sophisticated overlay mapping techniques for this exercise.

Step 3: Analysing the threshold and range limitations

The neoclassical approach to regional studies introduced the concepts of "thresholds" and "range". The threshold idea permits the definition of a threshold population as the minimum needed to support a service. This quantity will very according the type of service; it will differ from country to country and over time, in accordance with technological change, income levels and the different considerations underpinning public service and private provision in a society.

In drawing boundaries of LTUs it will be necessary to have a minimum population size to establish a threshold for internal services within the limits imposed by factors of range. In seeking an LTU for SRD policies, services must be analysed in a broad way, considering the need for internal capital and knowledge accumulation, and the quality of life for the local population.

Step 4: Comparing the LTU with administrative and statistical areas

In many countries there are clear and stable administrative boundaries at localised area levels (such as communes). These structures represent an element of structuring and stability in rural communities (for example, in being essential to local identity), but LTUs may have to link the smaller-scale units into a functional framework. In other countries where local administrative units are lacking and only counties or regions constitute the local authorities, administrative boundaries present fewer problems and LTU boundaries can be modified to coincide with administrative boundaries.

Step 5: Developing a participatory process

The results of analytical exercises of the kind just described must be communicated to the public and private actors with a stake in the sustainable development of the LTU. This will be only the first step in a process of institutional collaboration and participatory decision-making.

Procedures for an SRD Strategy at LTU Level

To move towards a strategy for implementing sustainable development, we need to describe further the characteristics of an LTU, taking account of its nature as an open spatial system. In this context four main groups of features are relevant: (i) structure, (ii) internal inputs, (iii) external input, and (iv) output.

The LTU's structure is the result of the human activities (past and present) in an area, in coping with the positive and negative natural elements (for example, accessibility, physical characteristics, natural resources). The structure is the concretely visible manifestation of the processes and interactions operating inside the area. The LTU's structure and its response to internal and external inputs have an important bearing on the development of the LTU.

The internal inputs are the demographic, economic, political and cultural qualities of the population, together with the LTU's environmental qualities. The external inputs are the sum of the influences impacting on the LTU from other regions. The output from the LTU is composed of tangible goods, capital, quality of the environment, cultural values and creations that can be used by the LTU population or by the external population when inside the area (through tourism, for example) or outside the area (through purchasing exports, for example).

In practice, most of these factors can be assessed by quantitative variables and indicators, but the system approach permits the use of qualitative data expressed on an ordinal or nominal scale. The structure can be described, for instance, by the relationships between production structures and population (such as hectares per farm labour unit), or by the presence or absence of some elements. Quantification of internal inputs gives the basic set of information necessary to evaluate the present situation compared to the situation produced by a different development path. Environmental quality, economic and social characteristics, or cultural assets can be described by sets of indicators as appropriate for characterising the development position. External inputs are defined only in part by quantitative indicators (such as import flows, state aid flows or capital flows). A schedule of qualitative indicators of external elements influencing the LTU's structure and internal input will be useful in capturing all external relationships. Similarly, while the LTU's output can be expressed by quantitative variables (such as the value of goods produced), qualitative indicators can be formulated to describe the creation of cultural outputs, political power or social values. Proceeding on this basis, it is possible to define the most important relationships and interdependencies characterising a dynamic LTU system. Models can be designed to describe important subsystems, leading to the construction of an aggregated model for the LTU.

Making inventories of resources (internal inputs, and structures, for example) and of external inputs, and identifying the relationships between them, are common to many types of assessments in area development but they are fundamental to defining an SRD strategy. The next phase is based on the specification of "orientors" (or dimensions of development), on the determination of the empirical referents of each orientor, and on the selection or construction of sets of indicators to reflect these orientors and empirical referents. Bossel (1987) defines basic orientors as a limited set of system (or subsystem) characteristics which ensure the viability of the system and its capacity to function in a way which preserves its integrity and allows it to develop according to its potential. The basic characteristics suggested are: (i) physical existence (essential to the life or continuity of the system); (ii) freedom of action (capacity to exercise autonomy); (iii) security (capacity to cope effectively with threats); (iv) efficiency (economical use of a system's resources); (v) adaptive capacity (capacity to change and control that change); and (vi) responsibility (a characteristic of human systems which recognises their obligations to their own system and to other systems, now and in the future).

To illustrate, and taking the environment as a subsystem at an LTU level, we may set out the following orientors and empirical referents, in the context of formulating an SRD strategy.

Orientor (Dimension of Development)	**Empirical referents**
Existence needs	Maintaining environmental quality
Freedom	Capacity to maintain biodiversity
Security	Avoidance of irreversible risks
Efficiency	Efficiency in resource use for ecological balance
Adaptivity	Resilience, or instigating change which is functional for an ecosystem
Responsibility	Taking measures to conserve natural capital endowment

Every empirical referent can be expressed as a set of objectives, and any objective can be stated in the form of indicators or measurable variables. For instance, environmental quality can be measured in terms of the quality of the air, or water, or the relative absence of environmental degradation.

The next step towards an SRD strategy is to analyse and assess processes of change, comparing actual measures with objective or benchmark indicators. The extent to which the basic orientors are being met, or can be met, will be the main criterion for determining the desirability or otherwise of any pathway of change. Information on this basis is essential for identifying needed policy interventions and for the guidance of decision-makers. However, the important point about SRD is that it involves a multiplicity of objectives, and decision makers have to find ways of structuring a hierarchy of goals, making trade-offs, balancing risks, and reducing the probability of undesirable goals. A number of different ways for dealing with this problem have been proposed (Keeney and Raiffa 1976).

Research implications

For the research community, achieving a common understanding of SRD will not be easy. Economists, sociologists, geographers and ecologists are each concerned with only part of what is a comprehensive field of study. Each discipline has its own conceptual framework, its units of analyses and methodologies, whereas there will be a need for common or complementary research orientations congruent with the multidimensional scope of SRD.

Pathways towards a knowledge base for SRD will have to be found through (i) improving specific disciplinary-based information, (ii) communicating that knowledge to researchers in related fields of study, (iii) developing interdisciplinary research on SRD, and (iv) communicating scientific information to society in general and embracing "non-academic" knowledge.

Each relevant scientific field must first improve its own repertoire of research information, paying particular attention to identifying and filling information gaps pertaining to SRD. There is a need to open research fields in such a way as to increase cross-disciplinary understandings, and to share information as to how research problems are defined and methodologies used in different disciplinary perspectives. There is also need to improve the mechanisms by which multidisciplinary research teams can be set up and made to function effectively in undertaking theoretical and applied research relating to SRD. In this regard a major research aim would be to share knowledge on the functioning of the various LTU subsystems and to design measures for tracing their reciprocal relationships. Clearly, researchers in an SRD context need to pay attention to communications within the scientific community. But they must also communicate their knowledge and its possible applications to the people who live and work in rural areas. There are a number of reasons for this: adherence to the principles of access to information and participation in decision-making, understanding the value criteria by which people make strategic choices in their lives, and allowing the possibility that non-academic knowledge may usefully supplement the scientific analyses of researchers.

Policy implications: from sector to territory

A strategy for sustainable development in rural areas, based on an LTU approach, will have implications for the general structure of public administration and for the implementation of regional and rural policies. In regard to public administration there may be need for a shift in the allocation of functions between national and local or regional institutions, so that functions of overall consideration and control will reside at central level while implementation of actions will be organised at the meso-level. It may be necessary to reorganise local administration, aggregating small units and strengthening the territorial identity of the new groupings. Regionalisation of national agencies may be required but it will be essential to coordinate their activities in multidimensional programmes encompassing the environment, the economy, social practices, and the cultural heritage. In fact, in the European Union Commissioner Fischler (1995) has acknowledged that, in a Union extending from Lapland to Andalucia, many citizens do not understand common policies except with reference to their own concrete regional reality. The risks of such poor understanding will increase with EU enlargement. Arguing that there is a case for a radical simplification of what is done at EU level, Commissioner Fischler added that simplification would probably imply the concession of more latitude to Member State or regional authorities in implementing decisions taken at EU level.

Formulating programmes and strategies for the sustainable development of rural regions will, of course, have implications for research policy. The concerns here are not alone the provision of adequate funding for the studies required but also the nurturing of multidisciplinary and cross-national collaboration, as well as encouraging the favourable disposition of administrative agencies towards providing much of the kinds of data needed.

Territorial policies will have to take priority over centralised and sectoral policies. Guidelines for the implementation of territorially-based policies must be grounded in the acknowledgement of the uniqueness of every region (or LTU), and in a recognition of the strong inter-relationships among economic, social and environmental problems. Policies must also put the emphasis on the development of indigenous resources, on nurturing local expertise, on increasing the capacity to exchange information inside a region and across regional boundaries. For EU policies, in particular, the concept of sustainable development means an acceptance of the possibility that regions may have different paths of development based on their specific characteristics. In this way

EU policy can give expression to a broad concept of development, one that enhances the richness of the Union's diversity.

Conclusions

"Sustainable development", as a multidimensional concept of development, can be addressed through the analysis of the complex relationships among the biophysical, economic, social and cultural dimensions of contemporary life. From this basis the systems approach---as understood in many disciplines---provides a coherent conceptual framework (i) to identify the dynamics and interdependencies between systems of human activity and ecosystems, (ii) to allow collation of analyses and information derived from different research fields, (iii) to make comparisons between different systems, and (iii) to incorporate both explanatory and prescriptive purposes.

A systems analysis offers a way of overcoming operational problems in finding a strategy for SRD. Principally, it can help to delineate an appropriate territorial scale, given that SRD is primarily a spatial concept. The systems approach to regional analysis is congruent with the task of identifying a "local territorial unit" for analysing sustainability issues and prescribing policy interventions.

A sustainability perspective on rural development impels changes in the way in which development problems have been traditionally defined, and in the value criteria by which policy prescriptions can be proposed. Considerations of economic efficiency in resource use have to be balanced by regard for the longer-term maintenance of natural and human systems. Rural policies are emancipated from any ties to the narrow requirements of facilitating agricultural adjustments. Sectoral development agencies must take a more holistic view of the development process. And while researchers in the individual disciplines must consolidate the knowledge base within their own particular fields, they must also be willing to relate their work in rural development to that of scholars in other disciplines.

Acknowledgements

The authors wish to acknowledge the financial support of the European Union, through its Human Capital and Mobility Programme, in preparing this article.

References

Barcellona, O. 1994. La pericolosa favola dello sviluppo sostenibile. *Capitalismo, Natura e Socialismo* 11: 72-82.

Bossel, H. 1987. Viability and sustainability: matching development goals to resource constraints. *Futures* 19, 2: 114-128.

Crivelli, R. and B. Lepori. 1992. Un approccio spazio-instituzionale allo sviluppo sostenibile e al cambiamento strutturale. *XIII Conferenza Italiana di Scienze Regionali,* 1: 191-212.

Douglass, G. K. 1984. The meaning of agricultural sustainability. In G. K. Douglass (ed.), *Agricultural Sustainability in a Changing World Order.* Boulder, Colorado: Westview Press. Pp. 3-29.

Douglas, D. J. A. 1990. Rural community development and sustainability. In M. E. Gertler. and H. R. Baker (eds.), *Sustainable Rural Communities in Canada.* Saskatoon: ARRG. Pp. 66-72.

Dykeman, F. W. 1990. Sustainable community: meaning and approach. In M. E. Gertler and H. R. Baker (eds), *Sustainable Rural Communities in Canada.* Saskatoon: ARRG. Pp. 59-65.

Fischler, F. 1995. *Study on alternative strategies for the development of relations in the field of agriculture between the EU and the associated countries.* Agricultural strategy paper. Brussels.

Flynn, A. (ed.). 1992. *Rural Sustainability.* ESRC Countryside Change Initiative, Working Paper 32. University of Newcastle-upon-Tyne.

Gertler, M. E. 1994. Rural communities and the challenge of sustainability. In J. M. Bryden (ed.), *Towards Sustainable Rural Communities.* University of Guelph. Pp. 69-78

Giaoutzi, M. and P. Nijkamp. 1993. *Decision Support Models for Regional Sustainable Development: an Application of Geographic information Systems and Evaluation Models to Greek Sporades Island.* Aldershot: Avebury.

Hilhorst, J. G. M. 1990. *Regional Studies and Rural Development.* Aldershot: Avebury.

Keeney, R. L. and H. Raiffa, 1976. *Decisions with Multiple Objectives: Preferences and Value Tradeoff.* New York: Wiley.

Langer, A. 1989. *Modernizzazione e vie autonome allo svilluppo.* Udine: C. L. Borgo, Aquileia.

Murdock, J. 1993. Sustainable rural development: towards a research agenda. *Geoforum* 23, 3: 225-241.

Nir, D. 1987. Regional geography considered from the systems approach. *Geoforum* 18, 2: 187-202.

Norgard, R. B. 1988. Sustainable development: a co-evolutionary view. *Futures* 20, 6: 606-620.

OECD. 1994. *Creating Rural Indicators for Shaping Territorial Policy.* Paris: OECD.

Pearce, D., A. Markandya and E. B. Barbier. 1989. *Blueprint for a Green Economy.* London: Earthscan.

Redclift, M. 1987. *Sustainable Development: Exploring the Contradictions.* London: Methuen.

Redclift, M. 1991. The multiple dimensions of sustainable development. *Geography* 76, 1: 36-42.

Smit, B. and M. Brklacich. 1989. Sustainable development and the analysis of rural systems. *Journal of Rural Studies* 5, 4: 405-414.

Turner, R. K. 1993. Sustainability: principles and practice. In R. K. Turner (ed.), *Sustainable Environmental Economics and Management.* London: Belhaven Press. Pp. 3-36.

Vartiainen, P. 1987. The strategy of territorial integration in regional development: defining territory. *Geoforum* 18, 1: 117-126.

World Commission on Environment and Development. 1987. *Our Common Future.* London: Oxford University Press.

Zanoli, R. 1994. Agricoltura, sviluppo rurale e ambiente. Paper presented to XXXI SIDEA Seminar, Compobasso.

3 Planning for rural and local development in Ireland and Norway

Jørgen Amdam

A new interest in planning for rural development

Both in Ireland and in Norway, changes in agricultural policy and new development problems in rural communities dependent on agriculture have led to new national strategies for rural development. These include new funds and initiatives for rural development, and for the diversification of economic activities on farms and in rural communities (Keane 1992; NESC 1994; O Cinneide 1995; St. meld. nr. 33, 1992-93; St. prp. nr. 8, 1992-93). These changes have created a need for the development of strategies on local level, and a need for mobilisation from the bottom. To some extent it can be said that this focus on planning processes is initiated from the top; that is, having an adequate local planning process in place is increasingly necessary in order to obtain programme funding from higher levels of government.

In Ireland the EC/EU LEADER and LEADER II programmes and various national programmes have created new needs for rural planning processes to obtain access to funding for comprehensive local development. New institutional partnerships between private and public organisations are established to do the planning, and to execute the implementation of approved plans and actions (Ó Cinnéide 1995). In Norway there is a long tradition of comprehensive commune and county planning that includes land use planning and the development of local economies as well as the development of welfare-related activities and the preservation of nature. Planning concerns are defined by local governments themselves and can include problems like dealing with the effects of urban growth in rural areas. Our experience is that rural planning processes that cover only economic development and employment, and which do not include the provision of public services like education, kindergartens, homes and services for the elderly and the disabled, as

53

well as preservation of nature and strategic land use, will not be able to deal effectively with issues that are important for rural development or for the development of local communities. Rural development planning processes and rural development policy must be comprehensive and integrated, covering all the issues that are important for the well-being of local inhabitants and communities and for the recruitment of new inhabitants and activities, as well as reduction of out-migration and close-downs of activities.

In this paper I shall attempt to compare development planning processes in rural areas in Ireland and Norway. This study is based on my close acquaintance with Norwegian planning processes in theory and practice and a more superficial knowledge of Irish planning processes based on published materials and discussion with colleagues at the Centre for Development Studies at University College Galway, where I spent a sabbatical year in 1993-94.

Planning initiatives and processes are organised differently on various administrative and functional levels, and are dependent on national traditions in the way that public and private activities are organised, and how they articulate with one another. In this comparison, I ask (a) Who is responsible for planning---who can legally decide a plan and implement it? (b) What is the content of planning and how are planning processes organised? (c) What means are available for the implementation of plans and planned activities and who controls these means? (d) How are private planning and development initiatives organised and treated by public agencies? (e) What is the attitude to planning and the implementation of plans from public organisations? and (f) How is the private-public relationship in planning and implementation managed?

Comparison: perspectives and challenges

Ireland, of all the so-called "European welfare states", when compared with Norway and the other Scandinavian countries, has the most different system of local government and local development. Is there anything the Nordic countries can learn from Ireland? In Norway, the system of local government:

- controls/spends approximately the equivalent of IR£14 billion or 22% of our GDP; IR£8.5 billion is spent by the communes. This compares with approximately IR£1.2 billion spent by local government in Ireland.

- is divided into 19 counties and 439 communes, both systems covering the whole country, compared to 28 counties and approximately 85 county boroughs in Ireland, the last group covering only 15% of the population (Chubb 1992), mostly urban areas.

• involves over 14,700 elected representatives on the county councils (1,099) and commune councils (13,648) (Offerdal 1991) or 0.3% of our population. This compares with 1,700 elected representatives or 0.05% of the population in Ireland (Barrington 1980, 1991).

• controls a local provider system to satisfy local needs in health, education, social care, local development services, and so on, employing over 350,000 public-sector employees (35,000 in administration) or 18% of our work-force.

While, in Norway, most of the production of public goods (except defence, police, universities, etc.) is delegated to communes and county communes under combined national and local democratic control, in Ireland the responsibility for such production is mostly delegated to state-sponsored bodies under central political control. Ireland is a very centralised welfare state, while Norway has a system of welfare communes and counties where the state defines minimum goals through planning, legislation and national production standards of quantity and quality, and by the allocation of funding.

Norway has a two-level system of politics and administration for welfare production: local communes and regional counties, each having directly-elected politicians. This system was established in 1973 when county councils were elected directly for the first time. Except at the commune level, the structure before 1970 was almost like the Irish structure today. There were numerous national agencies with local production systems organised functionally, having different territories for hospitals, education, etc.

Local government in Ireland is organised on a more ad hoc basis; some towns and all cities have their own councils and administration. A county council and its administration are responsible for (mostly rural) areas not covered by these urban districts. Eighty-five percent of electors are governed directly by county councils. Local government in Ireland is responsible for fewer activities than local government in Norway; mostly land use planning, infrastructure and housing. Direct engagement in local economic development is a voluntary activity for local government and depends on co-operation and partnership with state-sponsored bodies and funding from national and EU agencies. The economic power of local government is low compared to Norway: spending is approximately IR£1,200 million or 4% of GDP. Public spending on education, hospitals, etc. is organised by sub-national organisations or regional state-sponsored bodies (there are only eight or nine regions for the whole country), where county councils are represented in governing committees with other stakeholders. Much welfare production, which in Norway is organised by county councils and local communes, is organised by national or regional state-sponsored bodies, which are comparable to state directorates or companies in Norway.

The commune system and local development planning in Norway

In 1965 a system for local and regional integrated territorial planning was introduced, with a structure that—interestingly—was almost the same as that which Ireland is trying to develop today, except for planning on the commune level. Norway was divided into approximately 100 local planning regions, or labour markets, covering from two to twenty communes each, and five sub-national regions (North, Mid, West, South, and East Norway). From 1965 to 1970, much local, regional and sub-national development planning was carried out, which was financed by central government. Partnership committees have a leading role in the planning process on sub-county and sub-national levels, but there was no direct connection with political or administrative structures that could implement the planning initiatives which were initiated at the local level.

What was learned was that the technical production of plans and the implementation of plans functioned as two separate activities. In most situations, local administrative and political organisations as well as state authorities could not or would not carry out local-level planning initiatives. Except for a few regions, the political-administrative apparatus of the local communes and counties tended to ignore these plans if they did not fully agree on the content. State agencies had a different territorial orbits of responsibility than the planning regions. They had no obligation to coordinate their activities with regional and sub-national integrated plans and continued their own totally independent functional-sectorial planning. Commune-level planning, with an appropriate political and administrative system made responsible for the implementation of the proposals, was demonstrably more successful in those cases where it has been tried: at least it was related to land use planning (Næss 1995). This experience, and other analyses, especially research on power structures in Norway initiated by central government (NOU 1982: 3, Hernes 1978, Olsen 1978), led to the complete reform of local administration in Norway starting in approximately 1970 and is still continuing.

The communes, whose territories were changed in 1967 because of changes in communications, were made responsible for all basic public services. Instead of direct sector economic transfers to institutions and activities on local level, an income system has been developed where each commune is granted an appropriate income related to population, age structure, population density, etc. The local planning process has been extended to cover land use planning, economic development and the development of public services. Special funds for economic development are allocated to rural and peripheral communes for the support of small-scale projects. The former state agriculture office, which existed in almost all agriculture communes, was transferred to the communes in 1993.

Political-administrative organisation on the county level was completely restructured in 1973. A new "commune" for the whole county was established with a directly-elected county council and a corresponding administration, and was made responsible for the provision of services difficult to provide on commune level, such as hospitals, secondary education, communications and regional economic development. All state agencies with administrations and institutions on the sub-national level were required to use the county borders as their administrative borders. Almost all such agencies now have their own regional administrations in each county capital (the taxation authorities, the insurance agency, the labour market agency, the agriculture agency and state church hierarchy are typical examples) or is integrated into the county administration (the regional development fund and the road authority are typical examples). Other authorities (the fisheries agency, the state house bank, etc.) have offices that cover from one to five counties.

A county planning system was been introduced under the political authority of the county council. The planning process tries to integrate the activities of the county, the communes and state agencies. The county has no authority over state agencies, but the final decisions on county plans are made by central government, which can instruct state agencies directly. Since 1985 many "bottom up" experiments on commune and county level have been carried out: political-administrative systems were given freedom to organise their own activities. This led to new legislation for communes and county communes in 1993, which gave them almost total freedom to organise their own production---including the right to give economic responsibility to community and partnership committees.

In Norway, a comprehensive strategic planning process is a part of the formal and continuous planning system on commune and county levels as presented schematically in Figure 1. Often the strategic part of this planning process is more rhetorical then real. Trends and tradition are more important then planning activities like producing scenarios of possible alternative futures, the discussion of important goals connected to values and interests, and strategies for reaching aims. The planning process connected with the commune's strategic plan is used to coordinate and control all the activities inside the territory of the commune, and all administrative activities of the commune as an organisation. The system is supposed to be continuous; every commune and county is expected to undertake comprehensive strategic planning (Amdam 1992). The process has the following elements:

1 Strategic planning is carried out in four-year cycles as a part of an overall twelve-year plan.

2 Each four-year programme includes a budget which is an economic plan for the commune's activities but also includes other activities in local economic and welfare development.

3 An annual budget is decided every year.

4 Project planning for land use, new schools, roads, etc., is carried out on a continuing basis.

5 Yearly evaluation reports of ends and means, and progress in planning and development, are produced.

Within this process, it is possible to have special programmes for functions like schools, territorial parts of the commune and for areas of special effort like support for new firms and small businesses. Strategic economic development planning is now seen as an important part of this process, necessary to obtain state economic support for local economic development funds.

The commune structure and the planning system are matters of continuing debate. Examples of questions raised are: should the minimum commune size be 5,000 inhabitants to be really effective? (NOU 1993:15). Is the direct election of a county council necessary? Is the county commune necessary? What should be the responsibilities of the county council? (hospitals take over 50% of county commune spending: should the government itself be responsible for hospitals and the county council more responsible for all kinds of publicly-financed regional economic development activities?). The planning process might function well in some communes and counties, but others are lagging behind:

> To the extent there have been changes in power and influence, there has been a professional take-over; the administration having gained increased control over policy formulation and the day-to-day running of municipal activities. Politicians find it difficult to exercise political management and control by discussing overall strategies and past performance only . . . . At the same time, we can observe---as an apparently contrasting feature---broad normative support for the new

planning models among politicians and administrators alike. (Kleven 1993:7)

Rural planning processes in Ireland

Compared to Norway, Ireland seems to lack an established, coordinated strategy and policy for regional and rural development planning based on local interests and local government. Local planning is ad hoc and project-oriented, perhaps more oriented at trying to obtain funding from the government (and/or from the EU), than developing self-reliant local strategies for local development which can function as guidelines when trying to get access to the means to carry out specific strategies, projects and tasks. Since local government (county councils, etc.) is responsible only for land use planning and urban and village renewal, it is difficult for them to introduce comprehensive and continuous rural and regional planning. Such planning needs authority across sectors and local communities, which the county councils lack.

Related to rural and regional economic development, and under pressure from EU, three levels of territorial, and to some extent comprehensive, planning is being implemented under the *National Development Plan 1994-1999*. Sub-national planning in eight regions is being carried out by a new regional authority. This new planning structure is intended to promote the coordination of the provision of public services at regional level. Partnership regional committees and authorities (but often with different territories) are responsible for much of the service provision on the local level in Ireland like education, hospitals, etc., and most state-sponsored bodies have some form of regional headquarters with territories that correspond approximately to the eight new regions. The new regional authority has representatives from these and other state-sponsored bodies as well as from county councils and other stakeholders.

The task seems to be to identify conflicts, especially between public interests and organisations and if possible to negotiate compromises, which means that the planning process in reality is based on voluntary coordination. Another task is to produce plans and analysis which can be used in the national development planning process and to obtain support from Brussels. This organisational structure and the defined tasks correspond to the less-than-successful sub-national planning process in 1960s Norway. The difference is that this planning process operates in order to get more money for the region, while in the former Norwegian system, the planning process was intended to influence national sectoral planning.

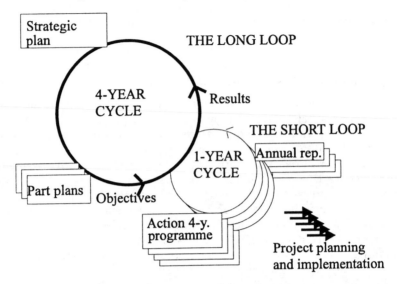

Figure 1   Commune planning structures and processes in Norway

Initiative	Responsible Local Body	Responsible Government Body
Local Enterprise	County Enterprise Boards	Dept. of Enterprise and Employment
Integrated Development of Designated Disadvantaged and Other Areas	Area-Based Partnerships	A.D.M. Ltd.
Urban and Village Renewal	Local Authorities	Dept. of Environment
URBAN	Local Development Companies	Dept. of the Taoiseach
LEADER II	Local Development Companies	Dept. of Agriculture, Food and Forestry

Figure 2   Local development initiatives in Ireland

Source: Ó Cinnéide 1995

New county enterprise boards have been organised, which are responsible for co-ordinated economic development planning on county level, and for support services and funding for small-scale initiatives and local enterprises (currently, the level of support is under IR£5,000). This planning activity can be seen as a parallel to strategic economic development planning on the county level in Norway. The difference is that this planning process is organised by a new set of organisations in Ireland and governed by partnership committees operating within problematic planning horizons with little direct authority if the participants do not support their plans and initiatives. The corresponding strategic economic development planning in Norway is carried out by the county commune, with the active and legally-defined participation of state agencies and other stakeholders. The planning process is directly connected to the county's department for economic development which controls the means for economic development and in most counties has the active support of the state agencies for agriculture, fisheries, employment etc., which have regional offices in each county and have the same administrative territory as the county commune.

In Ireland, there is no local political-administrative structure which can be made responsible for planning and implementation, and which can give the continuity and integration which is needed for the development of a self-governed, comprehensive planning process. On all levels it is expected that this planning process will be led by partnership committees with representation from the county councils, other public agencies, industries and voluntary organisations. It is believed that this co-operation will lead to better---because voluntary---coordination.

These new experiments in territorial planning in Ireland seem to be built on a functional approach (functional regions) instead of a democratic-administrative approach (administrative regions); this is understandable, since Ireland lacks a local government system corresponding to that in most countries in Europe. But this does not mean that Ireland lacks rural development planning. In fact Ireland has a great deal of rural and local planning activity. But this planning is mostly done by voluntary or partnership organisations on a regional and/or local basis, and is mostly related to the need to get access to funds from EU or from the state (cf. Ó Cinnéide and Walsh, this volume).

The development of local capacity to investigate, lead and control development is seen to be of paramount importance according to this new approach. In this respect local area based partnerships of state, statutory, voluntary and community groups are regarded as the core around which national rural development policy in Ireland is built. . . .

it is recommended that these partnerships emphasise: (a) the adoption of a strategic planning approach at the local level; (b) the promotion of innovative projects and processes; (c) capacity building and animation; and (d) community and group projects. (NESC, 1994)

This new national approach has led to the *Operational Programme for Local Urban and Rural Development 1995-1999*. This is composed of three national sub-programmes: (a) local enterprise, (b) the integrated development of designated disadvantaged areas, and (c) urban and village renewal (see Figure 2 (O Cinneide 1995). In addition to the operational programme, there are two further initiatives under the Community Support Framework which form part of Ireland's local development strategy: the EU URBAN and LEADER II initiatives. Local authorities are responsible for urban and village renewal only, and can apply for support from this national initiative. The county enterprise boards are responsible for local enterprise and local economic development planning related to this support scheme, while local or territorial partnerships are responsible for the three other initiatives. To obtain support from EU initiatives such as URBAN and LEADER II, or the national integrated development initiative, formal partnerships or companies related to the specific initiative must be organised, accepted and made formally responsible. The partnership must produce an integrated (comprehensive or sector) strategic development plan with a budget according to rules connected with each specific initiative, and the partnership is responsible for implementation of the approved plan. The normal "negotiation and implementation" planning process is illustrated in Figure 3, where the responsible government body (see Figure 2) plays the role of the EU Commission, and the responsible local body plays the role of Ireland in the planning process connected to each local development initiative. The EU Commission also takes direct part in the planning process connected to URBAN and LEADER II.

Typically for Ireland, a local territory can be covered by various "sector or integrated" partnership groups with support from different national or EU initiatives. Coordination must be done locally, which has led to a growing interest in strategic integrated planning at the local level (O Cinneide 1995) to develop a territorial strategy for self-governed local development which can be adapted to top-down initiatives. This is an adaptive planning approach (Amdam and Veggeland 1991, Friedmann 1973) which is necessary because local initiatives and partnerships usually have no secure existence and little local economic support.

NATIONAL DEVELOPMENT PLAN
THE PLANNING PROCESS, BRÜSSEL - DUBLIN

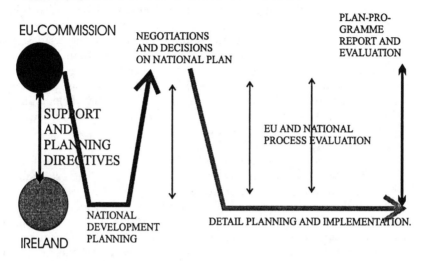

Figure 3   Interaction between Ireland and the EU Commission

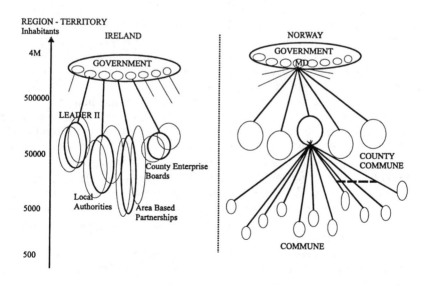

Figure 4   Comprehensive rural planning in Ireland and Norway

Planning structures and activities in Ireland and Norway

Based on the discussion above, I have selected six criteria which I will use to compare rural planning in Ireland and Norway. I have also selected four territorial levels for evaluation. To compare rural and local planning, either a territorial or a functional approach can be used, or both may be used together. Integrated or comprehensive planning is usually territorial, as it is intended to develop a specific region with specific territorial challenges and to co-ordinate activities and development initiatives related to the needs of the specific territory (Friedmann and Weaver 1979, Amdam 1992, 1995b). This is the reason for selecting a territorial- and level-oriented evaluation here.

The legal responsibility for planning and implementation on various levels is related to the democratic-administrative structure. In the Norwegian tradition a democratically-elected council is responsible for comprehensive planning, and for coordinating planning between sectors for the full-scale development of the territory that the democratically-elected council is responsible for and elected from. This means that the most important planning processes are managed by communes and county communes and are politically led by the commune and county commune councils.

Ireland has no corresponding nationwide political-administrative local structure except on county level which in many rural counties, compared to Norway's rural counties' huge areas, is nearer to functional regions based on local labour markets. The planning authority on county level is divided between county councils (land use planning) and county enterprise boards (economic development). Various partnerships related to specific national and EU initiatives and with different territories are important to understand rural planning.

To compare rural planning I will discuss planning activities on four territorial levels. At the local community level, we can imagine a village having approximately 500 inhabitants. A local village in Ireland of this size might have one or two pubs, a few shops, a primary school, a post office (perhaps) and other infrastructure. In Norway, such a village might be called a *bygdelag* or a school district with a primary school, a kindergarten, a local shop, a post office (perhaps) and a community hall. This level is important for cooperation between farmers and other local people in such local initiatives as tourist facilities, cooperative initiatives related to farming, etc.

At the next level up the scale is the commune or parish level: territories having approximately 5,000 inhabitants (between 1,000 and 10,000 in most rural areas). The territory of the rural commune in Norway was traditionally identical with a parish; communes owned church buildings as well as schools, etc. A rural parish in Ireland and a rural commune in Norway are approximately of the same population size and geographical area. Travel time by foot or boat decided the geographical size of a parish in both countries.

A more encompassing territorial level is that of the "region" which is identified for development planning purposes, containing typically between 10,000 and 100,000 inhabitants in rural areas---usually an integrated labour market and an "urban" core with rural surroundings. In Norway this is usually an "urban" commune (town) surrounded by three to ten rural communes (the Ålesund region is a good example, with 60,000 inhabitants in the labour market region; of these 35,000 are in Ålesund town; there are about 150,000 inhabitants in the economic market region as a whole [Amdam 1995a]). In Ireland, the relevant unit is typically a county borough: a town like Galway surrounded by rural areas, usually covered by the territory of a county enterprise board. Functional (integrated) planning in Ireland is organised around partnerships and local development companies with different territories related to the specific initiatives (see Figure 2). Sector planning is organised according to the administrative territories of state-sponsored bodies and these territories differs between sectors.

Finally, there is the county level, in rural areas comprising approximately 100,000 inhabitants in Ireland and 200,000 inhabitants in Norway. This is an administrative region which can cover the same area as functional planning regions, but is usually bigger than functional planning regions in Norway. In Ireland there are 28 counties and 36 county enterprise boards. This means that functional development regions and counties are on approximately the same level as in Ireland. Ireland also has planning activities on a sub-national level in eight planning regions, which are the responsibility of the regional authorities, but this level of is not included in this analysis since Norway has no corresponding planning level except some sector planning related to hospital regions. Planning on this level is usually not directed towards rural problems.

Planning activities vary greatly on different levels between the two countries, especially on the local community and commune level. This is due to differences in administrative-political systems and planning processes. Norway has well-developed systems for continuous integrated planning on commune and county level which also encompass economic development planning for rural areas, while Ireland has developed a system for integrated planning in partnership regions related to specific national and EU initiatives. Most of this planning is carried out on a level corresponding to functional regions and/or counties.

Much public money is today available for rural development in both countries, but its allocation is organised differently. In Ireland most funding is allocated from the national or EU level and is controlled directly by state departments or by state-sponsored bodies. This allocation is governed by the *National Development Plan 1994-1999* and the *Operational Programme for Local Urban and Rural Development 1995-1999* (O Cinneide 1995). This is also the situation for funding related to economic development, welfare production, etc. (see Boyle et al. 1994).

In Norway most public funding for rural development has been de-centralised to county communes, communes or state agency offices on county level. Except direct transfers (subsidy, "positive taxation" and public insurance) between the state and inhabitants/enterprises (Amdam 1995b) which of course are very important in Norway, most public welfare production is carried out by communes and county communes and usually rural communes spend more per inhabitant than urban communes due to the commune income system. Annual quotas for rural development are allocated to each county, controlled by the state agri-culture office in each county and a committee with nine political members and three representatives from farmers' organisations. Annual quotas for regional development are allocated to the county and to the communes. They are controlled by county or commune councils according to national regulations and national and local goals. Regional and local goals related to the use of such funding are developed through the commune and county planning processes. In some counties (especially the free counties, see Amdam 1994, 1994b, 1995) integrated strategies and development plans across state sector boundaries and the county commune, for the use of the total "basket" of funds usable for rural and regional economic development have been developed, while cooperation in other counties is more ad hoc.

The new approach in Ireland is that a local partnership can have funding devolved to it from an initiative if their plan is accepted. An area-based partnership or a local development company can then use the funds according to the goals and regulations in the accepted plan or contract and can distribute these funds to those local enterprises and organisations which apply for loans or grants, or to finance their own tasks. This is also the situation in Norway, except that communes, county communes or state agencies on the county level play the part of partnerships in Ireland. While partnership organisations are usually project organisations with an uncertain future in Ireland, funding is controlled by permanent public organisations in Norway, usually with strong local political influence.

Partnerships in Ireland are usually built on a tripartite representative model of public, private and community interests which include representatives from public agencies and state sponsored bodies, private companies, enterprises and organisations, and community groups (Boyle et al. 1994). This means that community groups can influence economic development planning and the corresponding distribution of funding if they have, or can gain access to the networks of representation involved in these partnerships. But this can sometimes be difficult in large areas; community groups or small enterprises may have to work hard to establish and maintain lines of communication in areas covering 100,000 inhabitants. As shown by Boyle et al. (1994), "formal" representation in partnership committees does not automatically lead to good communication with or representation by important stakeholders. This is also dependent on attitudes and expectations, the communication and planning models used, and the means chosen to mobilise stakeholders (Amdam 1992, 1994b, 1995b, 1995c).

In Norway, these are also important matters. The lines of communication, in terms of geographical distance, are short: the commune level is close to its electorate and enterprises, in some situations too close. Decisions about funding are mostly already planned for; usually communes therefore have limited funds which can be used to give ad hoc loans and grants to enterprises to develop products, study markets, etc. (normally the equivalent of IR£5,000 to 10,000 per enterprise); this is of the same order as the funding available from the county enterprise boards in Ireland. Most such public funding is controlled on county level, usually by committees dominated by county politicians and representatives from stakeholders. Delegation to administrative agencies of decisions concerning small-scale aid is practised in most counties, so that the committees and political organs concentrate only on large-scale issues (Amdam 1994b). A study of political decisions related to the development fund in three counties in Norway showed that in only 1% of cases was the political decision contrary to the proposal from the administration (St. meld. nr. 33 1992-93). But in a political-administrative system where local goals are developed through active strategic and operative planning where major political, administrative, union and business leaders participate and where conflict cases are discussed before decision proposals are written, an increased local "harmony" is to be expected.

Comprehensive strategic planning carried out by a commune or county commune (Norway) or a partnership (Ireland) can be problematic for public sectors if it is in conflict with their own sector-functional planning, regarding goals, initiatives, projects, implementation programmes, etc. Integrated strategic planning is in reality a voluntary process both in Ireland and Norway related to state agencies and state-sponsored bodies. Because of their strong sector (segmented) power-base, my experience both from Ireland and Norway is that territorial planning more often must adapt to sector planning, then sector planning adapts to territorial planning. Coordination is needed to get good development strategies in rural as well as in urban areas (Bennett and McCushan 1993, Stöhr 1990, Friedmann and Weaver 1979), but such coordination is seldom accomplished through formal structures. Joint development efforts will function properly only if leaders of important organisations develop real networks of communication and develop real partnerships related to planning and development (Amdam 1994, 1994b, 1995c). Domain defence and negotiations related to marginal problems are more common among leaders of organisations, if there is no trust and open communication between them.

Trust and open communication are also important regarding private, public and community cooperation. There is a systematic difference between Ireland and Norway. In Ireland, integrated strategic development planning and the implementation of such plans are done by partnerships, while in Norway integrated planning is the responsibility of communes and county communes and with representation from enterprises and communities. Responsibility for implementation of programmes and projects is in Norway usually given to the public organisation which is responsible for this theme or it is "contracted out" to private organisations. Representation from the electorate in political councils and committees differs greatly between the two countries since Ireland lacks commune councils.

Comprehensive and rural planning activities compared

There is no formal (political) organ responsible for integrated planning or development in the two countries on the local level. Some communes in Norway have elected local committees, but these have mostly a reactive responsibility, responding to initiatives from the commune. In both countries, development initiatives on this level must come from local voluntary organisations or individuals who mobilise and organise people. Some communes have introduced strategic and mobilising planning on local level (see Amdam 1992, 1995), but this is not a common activity. More common is open meetings on community level where planners present proposals and invite comments, usually connected to land use planning or the comprehensive planning process, which is a reactive approach.

In Ireland, development initiatives must be channelled through sectors (state-sponsored bodies) or related to national or EU initiatives; the county has few means and responsibilities except land use planning and infrastructure. Local cooperatives and development companies owned by local inhabitants are often important as initiators of development or as helpers for individuals or enterprises, but such organisations have an uncertain economic basis. As I understand the situation, there would be relatively few such development companies covering a given village with only 500 inhabitants. The real difference is that local communities in Norway have the commune organisation as the nearest "rich" partner. Many initiatives are referred to the commune as a "local problem solver" where development officers and public servants are supposed to be helpers for local initiatives. Local development problems are usually an important issue in the comprehensive commune planning process. Keeping these matters on a local level as far as possible is an important political matter.

When it comes to the commune-parish level, we can speak of two different worlds when we compare Ireland and Norway. My own experience from living almost one year in a small Irish community (Moycullen, Co. Galway), is that the local public service level in Norway is extremely high compared to Ireland, especially related to social care like services to old people, kindergartens, libraries, cinemas, etc., and access to local politicians (Amdam 1994a). Moycullen parish, with about 4,000 inhabitants, in Norway would certainly have been a local commune with its own council with about 30 representatives on the commune council and another 100 inhabitants elected by the commune council as members of committees. The commune would have its own administration, including a planner, an economic development officer, and an agriculture office. It would have kindergartens, schools up to the age of 16 years of age, institutions and services for old people, a "culture house" with a cinema, a library, etc., and sport fields and houses owned and serviced by the commune. The only public service I found in Moycullen was schools up to the age of 14. The cost is of course higher local taxation, but the total taxation level in Norway is not much higher than in Ireland. On the other hand public servants are paid relatively less than public servants in Ireland. The truth is that the decentralisation of the responsibility for public services has created many public jobs in remote areas in Norway. In rural communes between 15 and 20% of all inhabitants at work are employed by the commune or county commune (especially women). Our local government structure, and its growing welfare responsibilities, is in fact an important part of our strategy to maintain the population in remote areas.

The commune is responsible for integrated development planning in Norway and for the implementation and/or coordination of public initiatives. If such planning is done at all on the parish level in Ireland, it is initiated by private or partnership development organisations in order to get money from different national or EU initiatives. On the level of functional regions, there is no formal political organ responsible for integrated planning in either of the two countries. In Ireland functional regions are often planning and implementation territories related to EU initiatives like LEADER II and URBAN and national initiatives related to disadvantaged areas (see Figure 2). The formal responsibility for planning and implementation programmes is given by contracts to local development companies or partnerships, which must be organized according to EU or national initiative regulations related to stakeholders. To get access to funding, such regional partnerships must often produce integrated development plans, as O Cinneide (1995) has shown in his example from Inishowen. In Norway we have seen cooperation on this level between counties and communes as well as private organisations which produce integrated strategic plans as part of the county planning process. There are also examples of establishment of regional inter-communal development funds and organisations, etc. (Amdam 1994b).

At county level, planning activities are more equal on this level if the new integrated economic development planning that the Irish regional enterprise boards are responsible for is included. The difference is that a territorially-elected political council is responsible for comprehensive planning in Norway, while a partnership organisation with small political representation and limited political legitimacy is responsible in Ireland. Norway has a twenty-year tradition of comprehensive planning on county level, while this planning activity is new in Ireland. My experience is that the Norwegian county planning is starting to function well in most counties today. More realism and operational organisation of projects and tasks are on the agenda now through active cooperation across sector boundaries connected to development of visions, goals, strategies and tasks. System changes on national level, so that funding for regional development is allocated according to plans and implementation programmes proposed from the county (Amdam and Herse 1995), can increase the importance of planning at this level.

Since comprehensive planning on this level in Ireland is carried out to get funding, the "implementation" process of realistic strategic and integrated planning can take less time than in Norway. But Ireland has a coordination problem related to comprehensive planning on this level since at least four partnership organisations are expected to do comprehensive strategic planning to get access to funds (these are the regional enterprise boards, LEADER II and URBAN local development companies, as well as area-based partnerships for designated disadvantaged areas). Some kind of coordination of integrated planning is needed. Only the future will show whether Ireland is able to develop a coordinated continuous strategic planning system on this level. The close connection to EU planning activity and the national development planning process should mean that comprehensive planning will continue to be done in the future, but will this be built on learning processes in established public organisations like county planning in Norway?

Conclusions

This paper has shown that Ireland and Norway have different paradigms related to local comprehensive planning. In Ireland local planning means "planning on a sub-national level", while in Norway local planning means "planning on a sub-county level". This difference is closely connected to differences in local government in the two countries. Norway has a two-level system comprised of counties and communes, while Ireland has an ad hoc system. While local government is responsible for comprehensive planning and coordination of public and other activities in Norway, local government is responsible only for land use planning in Ireland.

Challenges for Ireland

Provoked by national and EU initiatives, comprehensive planning at the local level is carried out by different partnership organisations connected to different state departments as illustrated on Figure 4. The same territory is covered by different organisations with their own varied planning regions, all producing comprehensive plans to obtain funding for their own activities which "compete" for users. Sector planning is done by state-sponsored bodies which also have different administrative and planning regions. There is, therefore, a tremendous coordination problem on the local level, and this is the biggest challenge to the development of an integrated rural planning system in Ireland. Instead of coordinated and integrated comprehensive planning, what so-called comprehensive planning is done in Ireland is merely project planning to get access to money for a specific partnership organisation; it is not comprehensive planning in the sense used in Scandinavia.

The Irish system leads to problems related to democratic representation and legitimacy: partnerships are easily dominated by a local self-appointed elite who are not directly accountable to the local electorate. Questions can be asked about what influence local communities in reality have upon partnership organisations, their planning and decisions (Walsh 1995). As project organisations with no "continuous life", short-term projects and activities which can provide finance for the organisation will usually be preferred to long-term perspectives, planning and development initiatives for which future funding is uncertain. The experience in Norway is that partnerships are effective organisations when they are related to the planning and implementation of specific projects, but comprehensive local planning must be led by representative political bodies (Amdam and Amdam 1990), and the planning process itself must activate partners. What is or should be more important for a commune or county council than integrated development of the territory they are elected to govern?

In Ireland, fundamental changes in the structure of local government have been discussed for years (Advisory Expert Committee 1991; Barrington 1989, 1991; Chubb 1992; Government of Ireland 1991) but without result. The attitude of influential organisations like NESC (1994) which rejects the idea that local government should have a coordinating role in rural development and comprehensive planning as in Scandinavia, means that a change in the near future is not likely.

Challenges for Norway

After more than twenty years of comprehensive planning in Norway on county commune and commune level, the planning process is starting to function effectively in rural development, but it is mostly related to activities that local government is responsible for. Outside public activities, county and commune planning has mostly been an exercise without means if a partnership with state agencies is not functioning properly on county and commune level. Experience from the "free counties" (Amdam 1994b) has shown that such public partnerships are possible and that coordinated development strategies and programmes can be developed on county level. The challenge now is to develop such partnership between different public organisations, especially on the county level. My hope is that changes to planning and allocation systems for rural and regional development between state and county level will lead to further improvements in network- and partnership-building on county level. Counties like Sogn og Fjordane, Oppland, Aust-Agder, Nordland, Nord-Trøndelag (Amdam 1994, 1994b, 1995, 1995b) have shown that better cooperation on county level can lead to county development programmes that integrate cooperation from private organisations as well as communes.

References

Advisory Expert Committee. 1991. *Local Government Reorganisation and Reform*. Dublin.

Amdam, J. 1992. Local planning and mobilization: experiences from the Norwegian fringe. In M. Tykkyläinen (ed.), *Development Issues and Strategies in the New Europe*. Aldershot: Avebury Press.

_____. 1994. Dei samordnande frifylka. Volda: Møreforsking. Volda.

_____. 1994a. Irland---den motsatte vegen i lokalt utviklingsarbeid. Arbeidsnotat. Volda: Møreforsking.

_____. 1994b. *The Coordinated Free-counties of Aust-Agder and Nordland.* Arb. rap. nr. V9410. Volda: Møreforsking.

_____. 1995. Statleg styring og fylkesvis planlegging: evaluering av politisk og administrativ organisering av bygdeutvikling i Nord-Trøndelag og Oppland. Forskingsrapport nr. 1. Volda: HVO-Møreforsking.

_____. 1995a. The future of the Aalesund region. In R. Byron (ed.), *Economic Futures on the North Atlantic Margin: Selected Contributions to the Twelfth International Seminar on Marginal Regions.* Aldershot: Avebury Press.

_____. 1995b. Challenges in regional development work. Paper presented to the Norwegian Forum for Planning Education, Lillehammer, 20-21 June 1995.

_____. 1995c. Mobilisation, participation and partnership-building in local development planning: experience from local planning on women's conditions in six Norwegian communes. *European Planning Studies* 3 (3).

Amdam, J. and R. Amdam. 1990. Strategisk og mobiliserande planlegging: kommuneplanlegging etter dugnadsmetoden. Oslo: Samlaget.

Amdam, J. and Ø. Herse. 1995. ES-prosjektet som døme på statleg programarbeid. Arbeidsrapport nr. 5/95, Høgskulen i Volda. Volda: Møreforsking.

Amdam, J. and N. Veggeland. 1991. *Teorier for samfunnsplanlegging.* Oslo: Universitertsforlaget.

Barrington, T. J. 1980. *The Irish Administrative System.* Dublin: Institute of Public Administration.

_____. 1991. Symposium on local government reform. *Journal of the Statistical and Social Inquiry Society of Ireland* XXVI.

Bennett, R. J. and A. McCoshan. 1993. *Enterprise and Human Resource Development: Local Capacity-building.* London: Paul Chapman.

Boyle, G., J. Walsh, et al. 1994. *EU LEADER I Initiative in Ireland. Evaluation and Recommendations.* Dublin: Dept. of Agriculture, Food and Forestry.

Chubb, B. 1992. *The Government and Politics of Ireland.* London: Longman.

Friedmann, J. 1973. *Retracking America: A Theory of Transactive Planning.* New York.

_____. 1987. *Planning in the Public Domain.* Princeton. New Jersey: Princeton University Press.

Friedmann, J. and J. Weaver. 1979. *Territory and Function: The Evolution of Regional Planning.* London: Arnold.

Government of Ireland. 1991. *Local Government Reorganisation and Reform.* Dublin.

Hernes, G. 1978. *Forhandlingsøkonomi og blandingsadministrasjon.* Oslo: Universitetsforlaget.

Keane, M. 1992. New directions in the formulation and implementation of rural development policy. In M. Ó Cinnéide and M. P. Cuddy (eds.). *Perspectives on Rural Development in Advanced Economies.* Galway: Centre for Development Studies.

Keane, M. J. and M. S. Ó Cinnéide. 1990. Applying strategic planning to local economic development: the case of the Connemara gaeltach, Ireland. *Town Planning Review* 61 (4): 475-486.

Kleven, T. 1993. Environmental concerns in municipal planning -problems and research challenges. Oslo: NIBR.

National Development Plan 1994-1999. 1994. Dublin.

NESC. 1994. *Rural Development. Executive Summary.* Dublin: National Economic and Social Council.

NOU 1982:3. *Maktutredningen.* Oslo.

NOU 1992:15. *Kommune- og fylkesinndelingen i et Norge i forandring.* Oslo: Kommunaldepartementet.

NOU 1993:15. *Kommune- og fylkesinndelingen i et Norge i forandring.* Oslo: Kommunaldepartementet.

Næss, P. et al. 1995. *Land Use Planning and Cost-effectiveness.* Oslo: NIBR.

Ó Cinnéide, M. 1995. Strategic planning for the integrated development of rural areas in Ireland. Paper presented at the Norwegian Forum for

Planning Education, Lillehammer. 20-21 June 1995.

Offerdal, A. 1991. Kommunepolitikaren---rolleforventning og røyndom. In J. Naustdalslid (ed.), *Kommunal styring.* Oslo: Samlaget.

Olsen, J. P. (red). 1978. *Politisk organisering.* Universitetsforlaget. Oslo.

St. prp. nr. 8. 1992-93. *Landbruk i utvikling.* LD.

St. meld. nr. 33. 1992-93. *By og land hand i hand.* KAD.

Stöhr, W. (ed.). 1990. *Global Challange and Local Response: Initiatives for Economic Regeneration in Contemporary Europe.* London and New York: Mansell.

Walsh, J. 1995. *Local Development Theory and Practice: Recent Experience in Ireland.* Maynooth: Dept. of Geography, St. Patrick's College.

4 Municipal reform: A prerequisite for local development?

Jens Christian Hansen

Introduction: conditions for local development

The aim of this chapter is to trace the history of municipal reform in Norway, with an emphasis on three events. The first was the establishment of municipalities in 1837. The second was the reform initiated in 1946 and brought to an end in the mid-sixties. The third was the appointment of a government commission in 1989, its report from 1992, the government's white paper in 1995, and the public debate resulting from the commission's work. Parliament decided in 1996 that no boundary changes should take place without the consent of the municipalities involved. The commission's report concentrated on the future administrative map of Norway. But form and function are closely related, and the debate has focused on local empowerment versus national control. The paper ends with a discussion of potential effects of municipal reform or status quo for local development in marginal regions.

Local development can take many forms. The two theoretical extremes would be one where local development is totally controlled from above, and one where local development is the aggregate outcome of unrestricted individual activities. The extremes are of interest only in so far that we know that alternative options are found along a continuum between these two ideal types. Local development always depends upon control of resources. The struggle for control of resources may theoretically take place without any kind of public intervention, but usually there is some form of direct or indirect control. If the resources are considered of value to several contenders, public intervention will be necessary to prevent savage over-exploitation or struggles between rival groups of resource users. As already indicated, public intervention may develop into absolute public control.

This chapter deals with resource control in regions which originally were settled by people who produced what they needed for their daily lives, but where changes in the value of resources modified the production system. Two major systems of change should be specified. One is a system of degradation within a traditional economy of self-sufficiency. Over-exploitation of hunting and fishing grounds, soil degradation and vegetation changes turn pioneer fringes into areas of retreat and abandonment. The other system of change is related to increased market value of local resources, leading to conflicts between traditionalists and modernisers, between satisficers and optimisers. The latter were far too often interested in rapid, short-term profits. Local histories abound with examples of such transitions between old and new. They are often abrupt and easy to identify, but sometimes slow and less easy to see, except with hindsight. Local economies become more and more dependent upon changes in technology and markets. These changes have not necessarily been for the worse. New jobs were created, and the economy diversified. Individual profits could be taxed and used for public infrastructural investments and for extensive public services. But periods of crisis also occurred, and often the public sector had to come to the assistance of those who suffered, to mediate in conflicts, and eventually take control of resources. The emergence of services in health care, education and social assistance also gave new roles to the public sector. The more general these services, the stronger is the case for local responsibility.

Both the production and the consumption side of an economic system thus offer opportunities for local empowerment. How should local interests then be defended? In most western countries, political-administrative institutions have been set up on local and regional levels. Historically, their original objective was to serve the interest of central authorities, and they were often moulded upon pre-existing administrative delimitations, of which the ecclesiastical were the most important. But gradually the local political system became more powerful, partly through top-down delegation of power, partly through bottom-up political initiatives. There are, however, great variations between countries in western Europe. Generally speaking, the process of local political empowerment has gone further in Scandinavia than in many countries further south. I shall now turn to the Norwegian experience (Hansen 1970).[1]

Municipal reform in Norway, 1837

The political union between Denmark and Norway was dissolved in 1814: "the end of a four hundred years' night". A new constitution was drafted and passed into law by a constituent assembly, and the new nation began its work by setting up and developing national institutions. In the 1830s, the time had come for local political reform. The towns already had a system of elected councillors, cooperating with local state officials. But most Norwegians---90% of a population of 1.2 million---lived in rural areas, and here the administration was run by government civil servants. In 1837, Parliament voted a law establishing local self-government on two levels: municipal and county. Of these, the municipal level became the most important. The administrative map of Norway in 1838 showed a mosaic of 392 municipalities: 37 existing towns and 355 rural munici-palities, with great variations in population and area. In most cases, the boundaries of the new rural municipalities followed those of the existing *prestegjeld* or ecclesiastical vicarages.[2] In peripheral areas, the result was that many of the new municipalities covered vast expanses of land. People lived in villages or hamlets, divided by water and uninhabited stretches of wilderness. Most municipalities consisted of many small local communities, and it took a long time to develop a community spirit on municipal level. What in fact happened in the period after 1838, was a splitting-up of municipalities. In many cases, the new municipalities adopted the boundaries of church parishes. The number of municipalities almost doubled in one hundred years, and this happened despite a rapid development of sea and land transport. By 1930, the process of sub-division of municipalities had come to an end. The alternative process, that of amalgamation, did not take place in peripheral parts of Norway.

The Schei commission: a long look at the local political system

Norway was shrinking geographically. Human mobility increased, not only during people's lifetimes, but also in daily life. The demand for private and public services increased, and small market towns grew up in peripheral Norway. The Labour Party, in power since 1936, put the development of a welfare state on the agenda, with the emphasis upon health and education. To make these services available to everybody, they had to be decentralized to a local level. But then the municipality needed to have a sufficient population base for these services, and this was clearly not the case in many rural areas. In 1950, almost 40% of the municipalities had less than 2,000 inhabitants. The government set up a commission in 1946, named after its chairman, Nicolai Schei. Its task was two-fold. It was to evaluate the existing municipal system against the new political, economic, and geographical development trends. If it found that a reform was necessary, then, provided that Parliament accepted its analysis, it was charged to come up with concrete proposals.

There was nothing radically new in such an approach. Across the border, in Sweden, a commission had been set up in 1943, and it presented its principles in 1945. The follow-up was rapid. Parliament passed the necessary laws, and the actual reform took place in 1952. The number of municipalities in Sweden was reduced from 2,500 to 1,000.

By then, the Norwegian commission had presented its report on objectives and principles. It took the government and Parliament another five years to follow up with legislation. Then the commission spent another decade in preparing the implementation of the reform, with the result that the number of municipalities was reduced from 750 to 450. By then, the Swedes had already discovered that the 1952 reform did not go far enough, and between 1969 and 1974 the number of munici-palities in Sweden was further reduced, from 1,000 to less than 300. The idea was to establish municipalities which functioned as local labour and service markets, and geographers did much of the preparatory work for the second reform (SOU 1974: 1-4). The Danes were late in presenting their proposals for reform (1966), but by 1970 reform was completed, and the number of municipalities was reduced from 1,400 to 275. The reasons that things went so rapidly in Denmark were partly geographical. Denmark is a much smaller country than Norway and Sweden, so even a radical reform did not have the negative spatial consequences that arose in the more sparsely-populated parts of the Scandinavian peninsula. But the principal cause of the rapid reform in Denmark was the procedure chosen. The political system delegated the whole process to the civil servants of the Ministry of the Interior, who completed their work with minimal political intervention. The Danes used a top-down procedure, while the Norwegians and Swedes used a mixed method, with proposals made by the ministries involved, but with considerable local horse-trading all through the system. The Schei Commission travelled widely, and often listened to local objections to amalgamations. In Finland, a third procedure was chosen: it was left to the municipalities to take initiatives. It should not come as a surprise that this bottom-up model resulted only in a small reduction, from 520 to 460 municipalities.

Table 1 sums up the Nordic experience. By 1990 the average population of the Swedish municipality was 30,000, in Denmark 19,000, in Finland 11,000, in Norway 9,000. In Norway, 20% of the munici-palities had less than 2,000 inhabitants (40% in 1950). It should also be mentioned that only 4% of the total population lived in these communes. The process of amalgamation had been a turbulent one. The Labour Party in the meantime has lost its absolute majority in Parliament. Coalition governments were less eager to press for amalgamations. After 1970 there have been some cases of amalgamation in urban regions. On the other hand, some "forced marriages" in rural areas ended in divorce. At present (1996) there are 435 municipalities in Norway.

Table 1
Municipal reform in the Nordic countries after 1954

	Denmark	Sweden	Finland	Norway
Commission appointed	1958	1943	1967	1946
Proposal presented	1966	1945	1972	1951
Legislation passed	1967	1946	1977/78	1956
Reform	1962-1970	1952	voluntary	1960-1967
No of municipalities before reform	1938	2498	518	744
No of municipalities after reform	275	1037	460	454
Second round of proposals		1959-61		1992
Legislation passed		1962		-
Reform		1967-74		-
No of municipalities after reform		278		-
No of municipalities 1990	275	284	460	448
Average population	19.000	30.000	11.000	9.000
Median population	9.700	15.700	5.000	4.400

Source: NOU 1992, 15: 237

Table 2
Municipal election 1987, 1991 and 1995;
parliamentary elections 1989 and 1994

	Per cent of total vote				
Party	1987	1989	1991	1993	1995
Labour Party	36	34.5	30	37	31
Conservative Party	23	22	21.5	17	20
Centre Party	7	6.5	11.5	17	11.5
Socialist Left Party	5	8.5	11.5	8	6

Table 3
1994 referendum results in Norway by centrality
("Yes" as a percentage of votes)

Centrality	1972	1994
3 (cities)	57.5	56.0
2	45.5	47.5
1	33.0	34.0
0 (periphery)	28.5	28.0
(NORWAY)	46.5	47.8

Source: Statistisk Sentralbyrå 1995

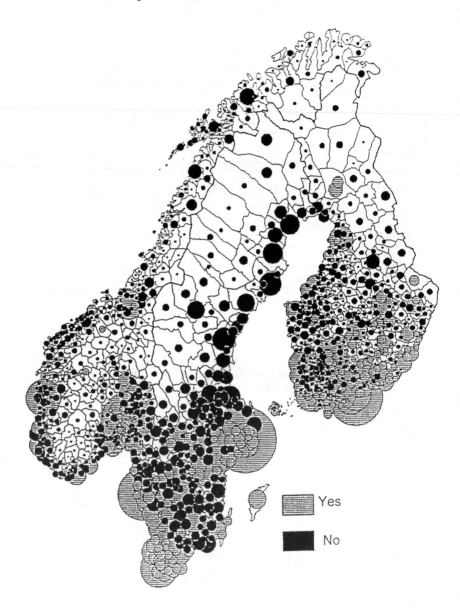

Figure 1 Geographical distribution of the results of the referenda in Finland, Norway and Sweden on EU membership, in proportion to the population of municipalities, autumn 1994

The Christiansen commission

After the Schei Commission had finished its work, the societal processes which had justified the reform accelerated even further. Road transport development increased local and regional accessibility. The urbanisation process persisted, and the fastest growth was found in small- and medium-sized local and regional centres. The main cause of this growth was the growth in service industries, and particularly in public services. In 1990, municipal consumption, county municipalities included, accounted for almost 13% of GNP, double the level of 1960.

Municipal consumption accounted for approximately 60% of total public sector consumption in 1990. The municipal sector's total revenues for 1992 have been estimated at over NOK 150 billion, of which some NOK 56 billion were central government transfers. Municipal employment in 1962 was 98,000 man-years, in 1990, 326,000. Central government employment in the same period increased from 88,000 to 141,000. The slower growth in central government employment is explained by continuous transfer of responsibilities from state to county and municipal level. It is important to remember that the boundary reform carried out in the 1960s took place too early for it to take into account these fundamental changes in the framework conditions of the municipal sector. It has been asserted that an entire welfare state was developed between the previous reform and the municipal sector's present tasks and system of management. A slump in the Norwegian economy in the late eighties made it clear to government that public expenditure could not go on growing. The municipal sector, it was asserted, was costly and there was room for efficiency measures.

In April 1989, a new government commission (the Christiansen Commission, named after its chairman) was appointed. The 13 members were representatives from political parties, government administration, organisations and research institutions. The Commission's mandate was to study the effects of boundaries as a general framework condition, and to propose theoretical guidelines for the future delimitations of such boundaries. The Commission presented its published report in May 1992 (NOU 1992:15).[3] The commission selected fifteen criteria for the evaluation of municipal and county municipal activities:

Criteria for the evaluation of services:
1 Adaptation of services to the needs of the population
2 Degree of self-financing
3 Exploitation of economies of scale
4 Importance of geographically-contingent cost factors
5 Extent of unintended effects of one administrative unit on another

6 Ability to manage own economy and services
7 Equality and accessibility of services
8 Conditions for national economic management
9 Conditions for legal safeguards

Criteria for evaluating community development:
10 Physical planning
11 Local industrial and commercial development
12 Environmental protection

Criteria for evaluating democracy:
13 Participation of the population
14 Local affiliations
15 Local influence

(Ministry of Local Government and Labour 1992:8)[4]

The significance of the current municipal boundaries is then evaluated for each of the fifteen criteria. Some of the implications of interest to marginal regions are summarised below. First, the evaluation of the services criteria:

The populations of small municipalities (defined in the survey as less than 9,000 inhabitants) are more satisfied with the services available, and small municipalities have a greater ability to adapt services to changing needs. On the other hand, large municipalities offer a broader range and extent of services. As a rule, municipal measures implemented in large municipalities are self-financing to a greater extent and are more financially sustainable. Small municipalities are generally more dependent on central government funding and to a lesser degree bear the costs of municipal services themselves.

There are advantages of large-scale operations within municipal administration, primary schools, health institutions and public works. The operating costs of these services are high in small municipalities. The disadvantages of operating on a small scale are considerable for municipalities with less than 5,000 inhabitants. For certain services economies of scale may be achieved even with more than 5,000 inhabitants, and for some services the settlement pattern is a decisive factor. The economies of scale are linked to the extent of the services, and are not always determined by the size of the municipality.

The smallest municipalities find it more difficult to recruit staff possessing the necessary expertise in the field of financial management and services, but they are also easier to administer. Large municipalities necessitate greater coordination and control, and seem to give administrators and special interest groups greater latitude to bring pressure to bear on popularly-elected representatives.

84

For the majority of municipal services, the variation in operating expenses per inhabitant is greatest in the smallest municipalities. This is due primarily to the fact that income disparities are greatest in these municipalities. Thus, the equalization of incomes among the smallest municipalities seems to be advisable from a distributional standpoint. Alternatively, income equalization may be achieved by merging rich and poor municipalities into large municipalities when geographical conditions so permit. The boundaries may also have certain implications for the structure and scope of the overall economic management of the country. Based on the above, certain general conclusions regarding the expediency of the present municipal boundaries may be drawn. There are problems in connection with both the size and the delimitation of municipalities. Firstly, geographical divisions have been frozen by municipal boundaries, while patterns of settlement and communications have changed. This has made it difficult to effectively utilize continuous stretches of built-up areas and improve the accessibility of services, and has created a new dependence between municipalities as regards land use planning and environmental protection.

Secondly, the expansion of municipal services has resulted in growing economies of scale which have in turn resulted in grater cost disadvantages for small municipalities. New demands for services have generated a greater need for specialized expertise that is difficult for small municipalities to meet without incurring disproportionately high costs. Thirdly, the increase in and specialization of municipal services impose new standards of management, coordination and expertise. While the effect of this trend are difficult to ascertain, it seems to constitute a disadvantage for both the smallest and the largest municipalities; the former lack the necessary expertise and the latter encounter problems with regard to coordination and management. Fourthly, the central government has compensated through the system of transfers for the disadvantages experienced by the small municipalities. This has resulted in a low degree of self-financing and an extremely high level of cost per inhabitant. There is a considerable imbalance in the system of financing municipal services according to the size of the municipality.

It is evident from the foregoing discussion that services may be used as an argument on behalf of both small and large municipalities. The strength of small municipalities lies in their ability to adapt their services to the needs of the population and any new needs that may arise, and in their transparency. However, there is no doubt that these advantages have a financial price.

Municipalities with less than 5,000 inhabitants have on the average a considerably higher level of total expenditure per inhabitant than the others, and are heavily dependent on central government transfers. Due to the disadvantages of small-scale operations, these municipalities are considerably more expensive to run, with costly administrative and municipal infrastructural services. Many small municipalities incur extra costs for certain services due to a dispersed pattern of settlement, but this does not explain all the disparities.

There are few significant links between municipal boundaries and national economic management in Norway. The most important connection is the extent to which the boundaries provide good conditions for sound financial management; the larger municipalities can offer a broader range and scope of services and can more easily recruit the necessary expertise for financial management and the development of services (ibid.:15-7).

The Commission then turns to implications of municipal boundaries for community development:

The implications of the current municipal boundaries for community development have been evaluated on the basis of the criteria of physical planning, local industrial and commercial development, and environmental protection. A discussion of the three criteria brings to light a number of common characteristics. Firstly, the role played by the municipalities, both in local industrial and commercial development and in environmental protection, is growing and evolving. At the same time, physical planning is also becoming increasingly important, partly as a result of greater national ambitions to achieve a pattern of development that is more environmentally sound. Secondly, these three tasks require much the same from the municipal institution in terms of capacity and expertise in municipal administration and in terms of the municipalities' ability to solve tasks of a regional character, i.e., tasks that extend beyond the boundaries of the individual municipalities. It is the opinion of the Commission that the present municipal boundaries do not provide a satisfactory basis for the acquisition of expertise and for geographical coordination within the fields of physical planning, local industrial and commercial development and environmental protection. Another disadvantage of the present boundaries is that they maintain units with an economic base that is too dependent on a single industry and thus too vulnerable. This makes it more difficult for municipalities to pursue a local policy aimed at developing industry and commerce.

On the other hand, the present municipal boundaries also entail certain advantages. The proximity of the municipal authorities to the inhabitants can generate the necessary motivation and commitment with regard to both local industrial and commercial development and environmental protection, thereby facilitating the achievement of these tasks (ibid.: 18).

Finally, the Commission turns to the aspects of local democracy:

> The implications of the current municipal boundaries for democracy have been evaluated on the basis of three criteria which cover various aspects of local democracy, i.e. participation, local affiliation and local influence. Political participation exists in many forms, and the Commission has concentrated on the most important types. Studies show that small municipalities probably provide the best opportunities for traditional forms of participation, through political positions and direct contact between the population and politicians. Participation through special campaigns and special interest organizations can best be promoted in larger units (ibid.: 18).

The Commission concludes that there is a need for nationwide municipal boundary reform and then turns to the theoretical guidelines for a boundary revision. It formulates three main principles and three subsidiary principles:

Main principles:

1 Municipalities should be delimited in such a way that they constitute geographically functional units adapted to a common housing and labour market and the location of private and public services.

2 As far as possible, municipalities should have at least 5,000 inhabitants.

3 The total area of a municipality should be such that the inhabitants of the municipality are ensured acceptable access to the municipal centre and the most important public services.

Subsidiary principles:

4 In amalgamating municipalities, the emphasis should be placed on creating units with one municipal centre.

5 In cases of smaller-scale boundary adjustment, great emphasis should be placed on the wishes of the population concerned.

6 The primary consideration in delimiting municipal boundaries should be the activities of the municipalities. At the same time, municipal boundaries should provide a foundation for efficient administrative boundaries for central government administration at local level, when this does not conflict with the other principles of delimitation (ibid.: 41-2).

The hostage to fortune eventually turned out to be the second main principle, where a concrete number was given; that of a lower size limit of

5,000 inhabitants. In the debate which followed the publication of the report (see below), this number got most of the attention. It is therefore necessary to mention that this principle was qualified as follows in the report:

Given Norway's geographical conditions, it is impossible to indicate any absolute figure as a norm for the minimum size of a municipality. The limit of 5,000 inhabitants is therefore intended as a recommended guideline to be used when no other decisive factors necessitate smaller municipalities. The main reason why, in the opinion of the majority, it is advisable that municipalities be of a certain size is to ensure that it will still be possible to maintain generalist municipalities with a uniform distribution of functions and a common national system of management for the municipal sector.

The majority emphasises that municipalities today have developed into vital social institutions charged with carrying out and co-ordinating a broad range of demanding social tasks. A basic principle of earlier reforms in municipal administration has been that municipalities should have equal status in terms of the tasks imposed upon them by law and in terms of central government management. The majority considers that this principle should continue to be applied in revision of administrative boundaries. References is made to the mandate and the Commission's detailed account in Chapter 1 of the municipal system to which boundaries should be adapted. The limit of 5,000 inhabitants is also based on considerations of cost efficiency in municipal administration and in the provision of municipal services. Municipalities of a certain size are also required in order to ensure the necessary expertise to be able to maintain a satisfactory range of municipal services. The majority underscores the fact that benefits of large-scale operations have been demonstrated in municipal admin-istration, primary schools, health institutions and public works. The large number of sparsely populated, small municipalities entails unnecessarily high socioeconomic costs for these services. Emphasis is also placed on the fact that significant economies of scale and a greater need for expertise have been demonstrated in central government administration at municipal level, thereby underscoring the general need for larger units. The majority also stresses the importance of increasing the population in the smallest municipalities so as to create less vulnerable, more viable municipalities, thereby strengthening their role in community development. Emphasis is placed on the fact that all municipalities should be able to provide favourable conditions for the further development of a more genuine local self-government. In the opinion of the majority, boundary revisions designed to create larger units should not result in municipalities with services that are less accessible than the accepted norm in other municipalities in various parts of the country. With this in mind, and on the basis of the majority's own evaluation of what should be considered acceptable in sparsely populated areas, a recommended norm is proposed for acceptable accessibility of no more than 60 minutes' travel one way" (ibid.: 42:3).

The report was endorsed by a majority of eleven members. One member, representing the Centre Party, did not see a need for reform, but held the view that voluntary cooperation between municipalities would be an adequate alternative. She felt that the criteria related to evaluation of services and community development had been given too much attention, and that local values had been neglected.

The debate

When the report of the Christiansen Commission was published on May 20th 1992, the political context was the following. The optimism of the mid-eighties had gradually been replaced by pessimism. Unemployment increased, manufacturing industries shed labour, the fisheries went through an ecological crisis, agriculture became more and more dependent upon government subsidies. The Labour Party had been in power since 1986, although there had been a short interlude from October 1989 to November 1990, with a coalition government headed by a Conservative prime minister. The municipal elections in September 1991 showed a swing in the electorate from Labour to the Centre Party and the Socialist Left Party (table 2).

In the debate which followed the publication of the Christiansen report, the Centre Party gained the initiative and set the agenda. The dissenting view won widespread support. The easiest way to attack the Commission was to focus on the criterion of a lower limit of 5,000 inhabitants. The qualifications and reservations made by the Commission (see the section above) were ignored. Since more than one-half of the municipalities fell below this threshold, and since so many people in the small municipalities were employed in the public sector, any hint of a change provoked them. During my work in the Commission, where we travelled widely all over the country and met many people, and as a participant in many public meetings after the report had been published, I became convinced that scepticism and rejection of the report was related to a general fear of change more than being a result of an evaluation of the criteria. At this point, it should be emphasized that small municipalities in Norway did not have a more difficult economy than larger municipalities, thanks to a system of government transfers which favoured small municipalities. Those with less than 5,000 inhabitants received on an average transfers corresponding to about one-half of the total income budget. The proportion of transfers fell with increasing population size, to around 30% in municipalities with more than 10,000 inhabitants (St. meld. 32, 1994-95, appendix, p. 16). One could say that budget work in the small municipalities began by estimating the expenses, and then asking the state to top up the income budget to ensure budget balance. A recent survey about the quality of municipal services shows that people generally speaking are satisfied: 78% of those living in municipalities with less than 2,500 inhabitants, 82% of those living in municipalities with between 10,000 and 20,000 inhabitants, to mention the extreme values (St. meld. 32, 1994-95, appendix, p. 63). Under such circumstances, the strategy of most municipalities was to defend their position in the welfare state in order to develop the local economy, and not to enter into new alliances. In addition to its status quo policy, the Centre Party also focused on the bottom-up/top-down dichotomy, claiming that a reform along the lines suggested by the Commission would strengthen the power of bureaucrats and weaken the local political system. It is worth noting that the Centre Party, with 12% of the electorate in 1991, had 30% of all mayors in 1992, and that three-fourths of these were mayors of municipalities with less than 5,000 inhabitants. The debate continued during summer and early autumn. But gradually the European question entered the political scene.

Sweden had taken Norway by surprise when it applied for membership in the European Union on July 1st 1991. Finland's application on March 18th 1992 was even more surprising. In the view of the Norwegian government, Norway ought to follow its neighbouring countries, and applied for membership on November 24th 1992. Most of the Labour Party group in Parliament supported the government, but as in the case of the 1972 referendum on membership in the EEC, Labour votes were split in the middle. The publication of the Christiansen Commission report (NOU 1992: 15) therefore came at an inconvenient time for the government. It had to handle two crucial centre-periphery debates at the same time. Since the European question was the most important, and subject to a tight time schedule, the government in August 1992 decided to send the report on a hearing to all municipalities, counties and relevant organizations, and gave them 16 months of reflection time before responding.

Before coming back to the question of municipal reform, it is necessary to present the debate on membership in the European Union. The Swedish and Finnish economies took a turn for the worse in the beginning of the 1990s; the national debt increased and the number of unemployed increased rapidly. A mood of crisis developed. Membership in the EU was considered a necessary condition for economic re-structuring. A comfortable majority voted "yes" in the Finnish referendum in October 1994, and in November a small majority of the Swedes voted for entry in the European Union. In late November, 52.2% of the Norwegians voted "no" (as against 53.5 per cent in 1972).

The political mobilization of those opposing membership was much stronger in Norway than in the neighbouring countries; they had the experience. The Labour minority government led by Mrs Brundtland was in a delicate position. The economic performance of Norway was far better than that of its neighbours, and in fact better than that of most members of the European Union. It was not easy for the government to convince the electorate of the economic urgency of joining Europe. The government hesitated to confront its main adversaries (The Centre Party and the Left Socialist Party) because it knew that this would provoke a substantial minority within the Labour Party. It therefore had to concentrate on obtaining a favourable protocol of terms of entry as a result of the Brussels negotiations. Good terms might convince the Euro-sceptics to vote "yes". The lesson from 1972 was that the "no" majority was formed by numerous minorities, not necessarily in mutual agreement, such as farmers, fishermen, defenders of Christian (Protestant) and cultural values, and people worried about the future of marginal areas (Myklebost and Glässer 1996). Between the 1972 and 1994 referenda, the Norwegian economy had changed radically. Primary and secondary activities employed 46% of the workforce in 1970, 28% in 1990. The decline of the exploitation and industrial transformation of natural resources, traditionally very important for peripheral regions, affected many specialised production regions and communities, resulting in a decreasing and ageing population. The political significance of marginal regions in decline extended beyond the regions directly affected. The Norwegian periphery, covering vast expanses of sparsely and often recently-peopled land, acquired a symbolic value for those who opposed the political integration of Norway into the EU. This explains why questions related to agriculture and regional policy were important in the debate preceding the 1994 referendum. But the government probably underestimated the scepticism of many of those who worked in the tertiary sector. The tertiary sector employed 54% of the working population in 1970, 72% in 1990. The growth of the public services sector has been particularly strong. It employed 13.5% of the working population in 1970, 35.5% in 1994. In 1970, 58% of those working in the public sector were employed by counties or municipalities; the remaining were employed by the state. In 1994, counties and municipalities employed 75% of those working in the public sector.

The importance of counties and municipalities in the production of health and social services and education has already been mentioned in the section above. They receive considerable economic transfers from the state in order to ensure the service level defined by Parliament. In practice this means that "poor" counties and municipalities receive higher transfers than "rich" ones. In some peripheral municipalities up to 75% of the income comes in form of government transfers. National norms guarantee a high level of public services, thereby generating local employment.

Women got the majority of the new jobs in public services. Around 1970, 45% of Norwegian women were in the labour force, 63% in 1990. One-third of the female working population were employed in the public sector in 1970, one-half in 1990. In the 1972 referendum, 76% of the women voted, in 1994, 88%. One reason why the female participation rate increased could well be that women working in local public services were afraid of losing their jobs. An argument often used by those who opposed membership in the EU was that since Norway would have to subsidise poorer regions in southern Europe, the government would have to reduce public spending, and that peripheral regions would suffer most from these cuts. Many women were mobilized because they were convinced that a "no" vote would save their jobs. In polls preceding the referendum, more women that men said they would vote "no".

Table 3 shows clearly that the centre-periphery dimension was important in the EU vote as well as in the debate on the proposals of the Christiansen Commission. As in 1972, the "no" vote in 1994 was very high in small, rural municipalities. In the major cities there was a "yes" majority. In municipalities with centrality 0 (more than 45 minutes' travel to nearest urban settlement with at least 5,000 inhabitants), the "no" vote in 1994 was in fact slightly higher than in 1972. The "yes" vote was slightly higher in 1994 in small- and medium-sized towns and in municipalities within daily commuting distance from them (centralities 1 and 2). Only in the larger city regions (centrality 3) was there a "yes " majority. It was slightly lower in 1994 than in 1972, a reflection of the increasing social cleavages within major cities during the seventies and eighties.

A map of votes (figure 1) by municipality shows a marked north-south divide in all three countries. In Norway, the north is totally dominated by "no" votes. The "yes" municipalities are concentrated around the larger cities and towns in the southeast and along the coast as far as Bergen. Almost all the small municipalities with a large public sector and which were dependent upon substantial economic transfers from central government had "no" majorities.

What happened to municipal reform after the "no" to Europe vote?

By temporarily taking the municipal reform off the agenda in 1993, and by tolerating two views on Europe within the Labour Party, the government had chosen a strategy which paid off in the 1993 parliamentary election (table 3). But Labour's victory was also a result of a deep split between opposition parties on the European issue. The most important "no" party, the Centre Party, continued its rapid ascent, whereas the pro-European Conservative Party suffered heavy losses. The opposition had a majority in Parliament, but the split on the European issue made a new coalition government impossible. After the "no" victory in the 1994 referendum, the Centre Party turned to municipal reform as an issue where it could pursue its political agenda, that of defending the periphery from the centre. Through its dissenting minority position in the Christiansen Commission, it had given itself a watchdog role.

The hearing process after the publication of the Christiansen Commission report, initiated in August 1992, ended in December 1993. The secretariat of the Christiansen Commission then set out to draft a white paper on the basis of the report and the comments received. The plan was to send this white paper to Parliament in January 1995. The documentation process continued. New and updated information about the structural and economic characteristics of the municipalities and county municipalities was collected and analysed. Much work was done on the boundary problems in urban regions. The material from the hearings was systematised. A first draft was ready by the end of November 1994.

The Minister of Local Government and Labour stated in interviews that the white paper would be sent to Parliament at the planned date. But in January 1995 the process suddenly was halted; the chairman of the Labour Party put his foot down. The Commission had expected an immediate follow-up of its work. Its suggested time schedule implied that the reform should have been implemented by January 2000. But this was too risky, seen from a political point of view. When the white paper was finally published on May 12th 1995, it suggested a slower approach (St. meld. 32, 1994-95). A new national commission was to be appointed, to function until the end of 1999. This commission was to coordinate the reform process, and to present drafts of possible changes of the municipal map. The local process was to be coordinated by the county prefects and extensive local participation was envisaged. The white paper explicitly invited municipalities to take an active part in formulating alternatives. Revised legislation was to be presented to Parliament in 1996, and proposals for boundary changes were to be ready by the end of the century, at latest. Elections for new municipalities were envisaged to take place in 1999. But the white paper extended the electoral process to 2003.

It was clear that the government and the Labour Party was trying to avoid a direct confrontation with those who did not want reform. The root of the problem was that most small, peripherally located munici- palities were heavily dependent upon government transfers. The Christiansen Commission had approached this problem by advocating amalgamations as a means to improve economic efficiency. Since this strategy evidently had its weaknesses, the government appointed another commission in February 1995, chaired by Professor Rattsø, one of the members of the Christiansen Commission. The Rattsø Commission was asked to evaluate the existing income system of municipalities and counties, and to come up with proposals for changes in the system in order to ensure a just distribution of state block grants to local authorities. The commission's first report (NOU 1996: 1), published in January 1996, looked at expenditures related to health and social services, as well as other expenditures. It found that the small, peripheral municipalities had received economic compensation for being small (measured in population) and large (measured in distances), and that most of them could offer their inhabitants a satisfactory range of public services. On the other hand, many central, urbanised munici- palities had had an increasing load of problems related to the general problem of social exclusion, and in many cases they were not capable of offering their deprived citizens the services they were entitled to. The Rattsø Commission worked from the assumption that these imbalances should be adjusted within an economic system of redistribution, and in annex to the report in fact calculated the effects of their proposals for each municipality.

This was too much for those who were to be the losers. The govern- ment soon realized that the Centre Party in particular would gain from the heated debate on redistribution which followed immediately after the publication of the report. But it was still within the power of the Government to initiate changes in the transfer system without going to Parliament. The government had chosen a model where the "re" had been taken out of the redistribution. The idea was to increase transfers to the municipalities in need, and freezing transfers to those who are well off. There would be no immediate redistribution within a zero-sum game, but since the increase in block grants would go to municipalities who up to 1996 had been losers, there would be a long-term redistribution effect. A long-term implementation of proposals made by the Rattsø Commission might in theory lead to amalgamations of municipalities, since the preferential treatment given to small municipalities might gradually be reduced. This, at least. is what the opposition feared.

While the Rattsø Commission was working on its report, the political process related to the white paper on the administrative map of Norway continued. One issue discussed in the white paper was use of local referenda. It considered the results of these referenda as advisory, but the outcome of local referenda should be only one of several elements in a decision process, and the final decisions should be made by Parliament. This procedure was quite similar to that used in the 1960s reform. The crucial point was that the drawing of the political-administrative map of Norway should a national responsibility. Only three weeks after the tabling of the white paper, Parliament received a proposal from the Centre Party instructing the government to respect municipal council votes and local referenda. No boundary change should take place without local consent. On June 1st 1995, Parliament gave assent to the proposal by 81 votes to 58. A slightly-stunned Minister told the press: "We will have to consider this decision in connection with the revision of the law on municipal reform. But the law still has precedence over parliamentary decisions". The immediate reaction of the member of Parliament who had tabled the motion was: "This is not exactly a bad case to present when we now are beginning the municipal election campaign" (municipal elections were to be held in September.) An editorial in *Bergens Tidende* (June 6th 1995) summarized the case: "Parliament (through this vote) has made it a rule that it will never pass laws unless those affected by the legislation have accepted the proposals in advance. Such a procedure makes life easy for members of Parliament, but being free from responsibility may easily turn into irresponsibility". The vote was a victory for the Centre Party. The other opposition parties who had not yet taken a firm stand against the white paper were now beginning to question their strategies.

The Committee on Municipal Affairs in Parliament tabled its motion on the white paper on May 30th 1996 (Innst. S. nr. 225, 1995-96), and the debate in Parliament followed immediately after (Forhandlinger i Stortinget, June 7th 1996). The committee had agreed on a compromise which in practice buried the Christiansen Commission report and the government white paper. By 90 votes to 68, Parliament invited the government to appoint a commission to look at the division of responsibilities, tasks and functions between the state, the counties and the municipalities. The government was asked to present the mandate of such a commission to Parliament for approval. In practice, this proposal turned the attention away from the political-administrative map and towards the question: who does what? In reality, form and function are linked, so sooner or later they will have to be analysed in context.

In another vote, Parliament (by 92 votes to 65) asked the government to go through the Municipal Law and other laws and directives on municipal organisation in order to facilitate voluntary inter-municipal cooperation. In a third vote, Parliament (again by 92 votes to 65) stated that it at present does not see a need for a municipal boundary reform, and that it therefore rejects the proposal of the white paper to set up a commission to coordinate the reform process.

Conclusions

The municipality in Norway has two main tasks. One is to ensure that national standards of welfare are maintained. National government gives the municipalities the means through earmarked transfers and block grants. The advantages of decentralization of these functions lie in local insight about problems to be solved, which may give better results than top-down blueprint solutions. Municipal autonomy is, however, dependent upon national resource allocations. As long as these are sufficient, if not abundant, there are no good reasons for municipal boundary reform. And since most municipal activities are related to the local implementation of national welfare goals, other potential forms of local empowerment remain in the shadow.

Norway has upheld a regional policy for more than thirty years where local initiatives in job creation, and in physical and environmental planning are encouraged, and these local initiatives are channelled through the municipal political and administrative system more frequently than in most European countries. The Christiansen Commission emphasised the importance of local empowerment related to these tasks. They do not add up to much in the municipal budget, but they are closely related to quality of life and prospects for future generations. Some may think that these tasks could best be carried out by county or national institutions. The Commission wanted to give the lowest political level a leading role in the shaping the local living environment (positive autonomy), in addition to the distribution of welfare according to national standards (negative autonomy). The Commission argued that this strategy of local empowerment would have better chances of succeeding in larger than in small municipalities. By rejecting the commission's report and the white paper and refusing boundary reform, the political parties which are in favour of local empowerment may have chosen a strategy which eventually will strengthen national empowerment.

Notes

[1] The two introductory chapters in this book deal with the history of municipal reform in Norway between 1837 and 1970. There is an English summary (pp. 139-42).

[2] There are two kinds of parishes in Norway. A parish may be a vicarage (prestegjeld), but it could also be the area served by one church, a church parish (kirkesogn). In sparsely populated regions, one vicar often had to serve more than one church.

[3] The report gives information about previous reforms, and is the base document for this chapter. On pp. 357-8 there are references to commissioned working papers and reports used in NOU 1992:15.

[4] The following references to the Commission's work (NOU 1992: 15) are to a large extent quotations from an unofficial English summary of the report (Ministry of Local Government and Labour 1992). I permit myself to use this document, since I was a member of the Commission. The Commission evaluated municipalities (kommuner) as well as county municipalities (fylkeskommuner). This chapter deals only with the municipalities.

References

Forhandlinger i Stortinget. 1996. No. 262, pp. 3932-75, 3998-4001.

Hansen. J. C. 1970. *Administrative grenser og tettstedsvekst.* Oslo: Universitetsforlaget.

Innst. S. nr. 225. 1995-96. *Innstilling fra kommunalkomiteen om kommune- og fylkesinndelingen.* Oslo.

Ministry of Local Government and Labour. 1992. NOU 1992: 15. English summary: Municipal and county boundaries in a changing Norway.

Myklebost, H. and E. Glässer. 1996. Das norwegische Nein zur EU. Politisch-geographische Analyse der Abstimmungen von 1972 und 1994. *Geographische Rundschau* 48: 285-291.

Nord 1995: 22. *Regional utveckling i Norden: NOGRAN:s årsrapport 1994/95.* Helsingfors.

NOU 1992: 15. *Kommune- og fylkesinndelingen i et Norge i forandring.*

Oslo.

NOU 1996: 1. *Et enklere og mer rettferdig inntektssystem for kommuner og fylkeskommuner.* Oslo.

SOU 1974: 1. *Orter i regional samverkan.* Stockholm: ERU.

SOU 1974: 2. *Ortsbundna levnadsvillkor.* Stockholm: ERU.

SOU 1974: 3. *Produktionskostnader och regionala produktionssystem.* Stockholm: ERU.

SOU 1974: 4. *Regionala prognoser i planeringens tjänst.* Stockholm: ERU.

Statistisk Sentralbyrå. 1995. *Folkeavstemningen 1994 om norsk medlemskap i EU.* Oslo.

St. meld. nr. 32. 1994-95. *Kommune- og fylkesinndelingen.* Oslo: Kommunal- og arbeidsdepartementet.

5   Training for rural development in the west of Ireland

Diarmuid O Cearbhaill

Rural sustainability: From agriculture to community

Most of the earlier debates on sustainability emphasised physical rather than human issues. For example, negative manifestations of degradation of the rural environment, associated with agricultural and other production systems, enlargement of farms, declining farm numbers and the contraction of country towns, were attributed to the single-minded pursuit of productivity and efficiency in agriculture. In the wake of the predominance of monodimensional bio-technical views, the arguments of more people-oriented social scientists have taken a broader view in suggesting that more attention be given to linking sustainable production to sustainable community development, where farm and non-farm groups can both contribute to the strengthening of the social fabric of the countryside (Lawrence and Stehlik 1996).

Lawrence and Stehlik agree with Shaffer's earlier assertion that sustainable communities possess a political economy and other social constructs that permit the orderly and efficient maintenance and use of community resources and facilities and which facilitate community interaction with wider social and economic processes. They cite Shaffer's identification of four micro-level characteristics of those communities which are economically viable and socially sustainable:

> A general concern about (and some dissatisfaction with existing proposals to deal with) issues facing the community; a positive approach to innovation and local achievement; a good deal of community discussion; and past evidence of implementation of community decisions. (Shaffer 1994: 268)

Progress on these fronts is contingent on various external factors and forces, including investment in human capital.

Training: changing imperatives

Investment in education and training, by adding to the stock of expertise accumulated by individuals and groups, can also be for the good of society as a whole. Since the 1960s or so, the endowment of human capital and the dissemination of higher technological skills have been suggested by neoclassical economists, among others, as important factors in promoting economic growth and advancing overall welfare. For example, these factors are seen to help various sectors within society, including rural interests, such as the farmers, cooperatives and local NGOs, which reap the resultant advantages of improved economic performance and efficiency, higher levels of innovation, the adoption of new technology and the diffusion of information (Begg et al. 1991: 204, Ó Gráda and O'Rourke 1995: 202-205, Caldarini and Mantino 1994).

More recently, variants of the arguments in favour of investment in human capital have been posited by social scientists in relation to the benefits that are seen to arise from the "public good" known as "social capital". Social capital, which is analogous to, and enhances the benefits of, physical and human capital, refers to features of social organisation such as networks, norms and trust that facilitate co-ordination and cooperation for mutual benefit. Studies of rural development and path dependency suggest the growing importance of vigorous networking and collective action on the part of indigenous grassroots associations in securing innovative training schemes and establishing extension programmes. Resultant learning and information and the creation and use of local knowledge can be as essential to economic growth and as germane to regional development as traditional physical investment, appropriate technology and market competitiveness (Putnam 1993, Morgan 1995).

At European, national, regional and sectoral levels, the challenges of social, economic and technological change have called for a greater commitment to and cooperation in developing learning and training policies. The European Council in Essen (1994) underlined job-creating economic growth, competitiveness and an active social dimension and their implications for training policy and practice that would respond to the continuing changes in the labour market; the need to improve employability and social cohesion; the need to improve European competitiveness; the impact of industrial and technological change associated with the Information Society where access to and the processing and diffusion of information are transforming work organisation; and the need to develop life-long learning and promote the concepts of personal development, social competence and active citizenship (LEONARDO Vademecum 1995).

Within the broad context of intangible investment highlighted in the white paper *Growth, Competitiveness and Employment* (1993), the European Union (EU) has encouraged the improvement of vocational training policy and practice designed to cope with the accelerating pace of technological change. Emphasising the importance of life-long learning, along with education and research that would inform and guide the national policies of member states, the EUROTECNET Programme (199095) has promoted transnational innovatory and pilot projects in vocational training to take account of ongoing technological change by means of conferences in innovative training needs analysis; transfer of innovative methodologies for planning and management of training; training providers as innovative centres for enterprises; and innovative pedagogical approaches and methodologies (Le Magazine 1994). Among the seventeen Irish EUROTECNET projects was the Master's Programme in Rural Development (MRD) established in 1985 and now conducted at University College Galway (UCG) in collaboration with FAS (the Training and Employment Authority) and classified by EURO-TECNET under the category of the development of cooperatives and rural SMEs. Several of the evaluative criteria adopted by EUROTECNET are relevant to and cited in this paper: context and focus; target groups; learning methodologies; research and evaluation methodology; cooperation; and economic sectors.

In Ireland itself, the previous emphasis on the provision of physical or "hard" infrastructure gradually gave way to a more integrated policy which was directed towards the achievement of greater cohesion within the Single European Market. This more recent policy highlighted the importance of "soft" infrastructure, and in particular, the quality of human resources as a critical variable in promoting national, regional and local development (Davis 1992). The Culliton report, *A Time for Change: Industrial Policy for the 1990s* (1992) emphasised the key roles of education and training in industrial development. A report by Roche and Tansey (1992) on industrial training in Ireland to the Culliton group recommended the option of dividing FAS into an industrial training division and an employment support division in the interest of providing the greatest potential impetus to industrial training in the shortest possible time. An Economic and Social Research Institute study on enterprise-related training and state policy in Ireland argued that the training of employees is lower than the European average and is, therefore, unlikely to be sufficient to bridge deficiencies in qualifications and skills. The same study outlined the research priorities needed to provide basic information essential to policy formulation in the area of training (O'Connell and Lyons 1995). The white paper on education, *Charting our Education Future* (1995) promised the establishment of a further education authority to provide a coherent national development framework, appropriate to the importance of vocational education and training and adult and continuing education.

In *Education and Training Policies for Economic and Social Development,* the National Economic and Social Council (NESC 1993) presented a wide-ranging contribution to the debate initiated by the green paper, *Educating for a Changing World* (1992). NESC's strong view that education and training policies should be considered together reiterated the joint approach initiated in the 1960s by *Investment in Education* (1966). NESC's comparative analysis of the links between the standards of human capital and competitiveness and skill levels was combined with an examination of the educational basis for skill development, mainly for industry. It concluded that

> policy must coherently promote skills and competences which advance economic development; the distribution of these skills must represent an equitable response to the needs of the population as a whole; and the institutional arrangements must be as efficient and effective as possible. (NESC 1993)

In effect, NESC disregarded current functional boundaries in its concern with issues of equity, efficiency and their full policy implications for education and training (NESC 1993: 17). Little or no attention was given in the NESC report to training for the agricultural and rural sectors, but these were the subject of other NESC and Teagasc reports (see below).

Rural training

Alongside educational institutions, such as universities, regional and agricultural colleges in Ireland, the two leading national training agencies---Teagasc and FAS---have been striving to adapt their training programmes, at the risk of competing or overlapping with each other and about 30 other agencies,to the changing needs of a debilitated rural fabric. The terminal decline of small-scale agriculture, the outmigration of youth because of poor employment prospects and the withdrawal from many rural towns and villages of public services and amenities all compound each other, raising doubts about the future viability of many such communities (Barrett 1996).

Teagasc, the Agriculture and Food Development Authority, which provides advisory, research, education and training primarily for the agriculture and food industry, also contains a corps of specialists within its Rural Development Service that increasingly emphasises the development of alternative enterprises, leadership and vocational training and community tourism projects (Whiriskey 1994). The report of Teagasc's review group Strategy for Rural Development Training (1993), pointed to future requirements and new directions in training provision.

The review group identified the need for three new training programmes, with appropriate certification: a certificate in Rural Enterprise involving a multi-skilled programme; a Diploma in Rural Enterprise for persons wishing to develop their own commercial enterprises or to become involved in community-based enterprises or projects; and a Diploma in Rural Development for those promoting rural development in a professional or voluntary capacity, such as project managers or workers, animators or local leaders.

To achieve effective co-ordination of training provision, a Rural Training Advisory Committee (RUTAC) and a special priming fund were recommended, but the financing and implementation of these two proposals were deferred until 1996. In the light of the experience gained from existing area-based integrated initiatives (e.g., LEADER, PESP companies and anti-poverty projects such as FORUM), NESC agreed in *New Approaches to Rural Development* (1994) that animators using a proactive energising approach to area-based integrated development (AID), should be professionally trained in a wide repertoire of managerial, organising and co-ordinating competences for which various training providers already offer programmes (Commins and Keane 1994: 226).

For its part, FAS, which has a national network of 20 training centres, many of which serve rural areas, established in 1994 a new Community Employment Programme which emphasises more substantial training elements over and above those contained in the previous programmes which it replaced. Thus, Community Employment differs from and improves on the work experience element of the former Teamwork and the Social Employment Scheme in providing more funding for structured development and training in personal and technical skills (Barrett 1995a). The West Region alone had as many as 4,000 participants and 160 temporary full-time supervisors employed by sponsors by the end of 1994 on projects funded by FAS at an annual rate of over IR£20 million. FAS's commitment to the long-term unemployed and its contribution to local community development afford remoter areas one of the few opportunities for groups and individuals to show their skills and advance their personal development through non-commercial projects, involving heritage, arts, culture, tourism and environment and education (Barrett 1995b: 17-26). Clearly, the wide range of training provided by FAS in developing community based initiatives to meet these and other community needs through Community Employment, its Community Youth Training Programme, its Community Response Programme (also known as the Local Training Initiative) and its Community Enterprise Programme hinges on the existence of a cadre of "trainers of trainers" having the requisite vocational, integrative and personal skills for rural and community development. Much of that "training of trainers" is provided through the various academic departments, the Centre for Development Studies and the Adult and Continuing Education Programme at University College Galway (UCG) where comprehensive educational, training and research and planning services for local and regional development initiatives, both statutory and voluntary, have been greatly expanded over the past few decades.

Expanding role of rural development

Rural development may be said to refer to the improvement of living conditions in regions where agriculture plays a diminishing but still crucial role, within a context of overall regional development that also embraces industry and services. The notion of integrated development was adopted by the EC (now the EU) and national institutions in the 1980s in their recognition that development is not confined to any one sphere or sector. Thus the EC Commission's approach, as outlined in *The Future of Rural Society* (1988), which anticipated the gradual completion of the large single market by 1992, was guided by the basic considerations of economic and social cohesion; the adjustment of farming and the rural economy to market structures; and the protection of the environment. The Commission also acknowledged the importance of vocational training, innovation and the dissemination of new information and telecommunications technology as prerequisites for the development of rural society. Article 130a of the Maastricht Treaty on European Union (1992) subsequently prescribed in relation to economic and social cohesion that, in particular, the Community should aim at reducing disparities between the levels of development of the various regions and the backwardness of the least favoured regions, including rural areas. As part of its integrated approach, the *National Development Plan 1989-1993* included the promotion of farm viability, the development of non-agricultural activities in rural areas and the expansion of forestry and fishing.

Within the *National Development Plan 1994-99*, Operational Programmes for Rural Development (OPRDs) contain rural development and training dimensions. In the wake of CAP reform and with the advent of the GATT agreement, the OPRDs include sub-programmes on the diversification of the rural economy, small and community enterprises, rural infrastructure, human resources and training for agriculture, forestry and fisheries. Rural development is also being supported through the Objective 1 Community Support Framework 1994-99 which gives a high priority to human resource development by strengthening education and training structures and by improving the quality of continuing education and training through actions most likely to have a long-term impact on both urban and rural development. With a view to integrated local development in rapidly changing circumstances, European Social Fund support in the form of a global grant, administered since 1992 by Area Development Management (ADM), emphasises local capacity-building and community development for which pre-training, training and pre- and post-advisory and counselling services and technical assistance are all envisaged.

The first LEADER initiative (1991-94) provided global support for rural development action groups throughout the Community, including 16 Irish rural groups, and encouraged the use of modern technologies and vocational training in the business plans of partnerships involving community organisations, private organisations and statutory agencies. It is envisaged that training for Rural Development will be strengthened in the second LEADER initiative but also extended further in INTER-REG II which contains a particular focus on cross-border cooperation, involving investment in training and education within the broad area of human resources.

The Government's commitment to intensify the support for rural development initiatives, including alternative farm enterprises, agri-tourism and local community-based initiatives, was reiterated in the Programme for Competitiveness and Work (PCW). On the basis of the hindsight gleaned from area-based pilot partnerships, the PCW suggested that "strengthening the competitiveness of rural economies and providing adequate safeguards for the vulnerable in rural society requires an integrated approach and effective partnership between state organisations, social partners and the voluntary sector" (PCW 1994).

Twelve area-based partnerships had been set up in 1991 on a pilot basis under the Programme for Economic and Social Progress (PESP) to deal with long-term unemployment. Integrated approaches to rural development are used by some such partnership companies (e.g., Meitheal Mhaigheo) which put a strong emphasis on capacity-building and advocating education and training as key elements in the promotion of a greater enterprise culture for local development. Many of these groups, now being extended from the original 12 to 43 groups, will, therefore, require additional and appropriate training in rural development for the remainder of the present decade.

Clearly, then, Rural Development and the associated training needs have now moved up on the development agenda at EU, national and local levels. The Rural Development Programme at UCG, which caters for the participants in many of the above programmes, enterprises, initiatives and partnerships, helps to strengthen their developmental skills and potential by improving their understanding of, and capacity to grapple with, the dynamics of rapid rural change and issues of sustainability.

Origins and objectives of UCG training programme

It was thanks to the vision of Professor Michael Cuddy, head of the Department of Economics at University College Galway and colleagues from the departments of Economics, Geography, and Sociology, that the Master's Programme in Rural Development (MRD) was originally conceived early in the 1980s. However, it took some years to make headway as no government department or state agency was willing to support it. Ultimately, AnCO, the predecessor of FAS, became convinced of the need to help those already engaged in rural development activities to carry out their work more effectively and efficiently. Accordingly, AnCO committed itself to funding and collaborating on a pilot basis in this training project which was to run over a two-year cycle with financial support from the European Social Fund, commencing in 1985. The programme is now in its sixth cycle and it continues to secure vital assistance from FAS. During the three cycles commencing in 1989, its benefits and potential were recognised further afield by the International Fund for Ireland which awarded substantial scholarships to meritorious participants from both sides of the border.

Proceeding from the previously mentioned assumption that investment in human capital is in the last analysis a basic prerequisite for sustaining and revitalising rural life and modes, the main objective of the Programme in Rural Development is to train personnel in general and specific aspects of rural development in order to facilitate the co-ordination of, and participation in, bottom-up initiatives and to strengthen the delivery of top-down policies. The purpose is to ensure that top-down and bottom-up approaches to development are mutually reinforcing, thereby enhancing the economic, social health, recreational, physical and cultural environment of rural communities. This synergetic programme is aimed at persons engaged in development activities in both the public and private sectors (Table 1).

The two-year Master's programme has an enrolment of about 20 to 25 students, and admission is open to persons who hold a primary degree or equivalent and who have a satisfactory level of experience in economic or social development activities. A small number (five to seven persons) of candidates for an associated one-year qualifying Diploma are selected from suitably qualified non-graduates engaged in developmental activities. Enrolments to both programmes are strictly limited in order to maximise staff-student contact. The programme is intended for persons in numerous public development agencies, leaders and animateurs associated with regional, rural and community development groups, such as

Community Councils, Development Associations, Chambers of Commerce and credit unions, and various rural and community development support organisations. Participation by personnel drawn from this wide cross-section of public agencies, including government departments and the voluntary sector, enriches discussions and workshops with a diversity of experience. The trainees are obliged to liaise closely with a community development association, council or such like; this helps to create among local groups a greater awareness of new technological concepts and applications.

Orientation and organisation of the Master's programme

The vocational orientation and integrative approaches to the programme seek to advance the trainees' professional expertise, methodological competence and the socio-personal capabilities. The acquisition of "key qualifications" based on these three areas (Köster 1994) is directed towards enabling graduates to plan strategies and to organise and apply better work processes, innovative techniques and informed decisions appropriate to rural development. In addition, the programme is meant to boost the capacity of local leaders and highly-motivated individuals to communicate, and cooperate with or within rural development agencies and community organisations, such as County Enterprise Boards, LEADER companies, PESP partnerships, integrated resource development companies, anti-poverty projects, Irish Rural Link, NOW- and ADM-supported groups.

Three distinct training methods are used in the Master's programme, namely, coursework (including case studies), workshops, and a research dissertation. The course in the first year includes a number of modules which survey and analyse Irish and European rural development and is taught on an inter-disciplinary basis by staff drawn mainly from the social sciences and business school departments. These modules address the major constraints on development and the principal policies relating to the various sectors. Quantitative, technological and evaluative skills relevant to rural development are the subject matter of another module. The course in the second year deals with selected topics concerning economic, legal, administrative, business, social, political, community, cooperative, planning and environmental aspects of rural development. An important feature of the programme is a workshop series conducted by distinguished personnel drawn from Irish and EU development agencies, including several MRD graduates. These workshops and field trips are designed to complement the coursework. Each participant is obliged to carry out an in-depth project relating to the work of his or her own agency or other development activities, which is presented in fulfilment of the dissertation requirement.

EUROTECNET criteria for evaluation of UCG training programme

EUROTECNET has recognised the need for technological innovation and change at the level of competence development and vocational training. Its purpose is "to identify the kinds of innovations to be promoted in European Vocational Training Systems, and to support a network of projects which are implementing these training innovations." The lessons learned from these projects can help policy-makers and training professionals to bring about or replicate change but also to plan better for the future (*EUROTECNET News,* June 1992). It should be noted that this EC/EU action programme to promote innovation in the field of vocational training resulting from technological change did not begin to take effect until after 1st January 1990, i.e., four to five years after the commencement of the MRD programme. Obviously, the innovative objectives, content, guidelines and community measures of EUROTECNET set out in Articles 1 to 5 of the Council decision (NR89/657/EEC) did not have any bearing on the implementation and development of the training programme at UCG, which is more broadly focused. Nonetheless, the latter has measured up to several EUROTECNET criteria subsequently formulated such as (a) impact on vocational training systems; (b) its transfer potential; (c) use of technology; (d) involvement with national agencies, industry and education; (e) association with transnational projects; and (f) its interaction with other European programmes and initiatives. As already noted, the MRD training programme fits neatly into a recent classification system within the EUROTECNET network which categorises training projects under such headings as: (1) the focus of training innovation, (2) target groups, (3) learning methodologies, (4) technological applications, (5) development of new technologies, (6) research and evaluation, and (7) cooperation with other bodies.

(a) Impact of UCG programme on training in rural development

Viewed at several levels and from various perspectives, this very practical postgraduate training programme can be deemed to have progressed very satisfactorily in terms of transferring innovation, new technologies, and vocational training. More than 90 graduates who have successfully completed the Master's programme over five two-year cycles between 1985 and 1995 have been rigorously trained in general and specific aspects of rural development. Comparatively few participants have failed to last the course of this demanding programme involving considerable commitment to serious study from those who have travelled from as many as 21 counties---mainly in the "disadvantaged" west and northwest (Figure 1).

The majority of the participants in the first four cycles were public sector employees, notably teachers and educationalists, ACOT/Teagasc advisors and development officers, but a different pattern began to emerge in the fifth (1993/95) cycle when most trainees (18 of a total of 24) consisted of community enterprise and voluntary workers within the private sector or were self-employed (Table 1). The exposure of the trainees to a broad range of internationally-recognised expertise, principally in the social sciences exerts, as noted above, a positive effect and appreciable influence on a wide cross-section of public agencies, regional bodies and local communities.

The first-year programme (shared with the Diploma students) covers two broad areas: Rural Development, and Techniques of Analysis. Rural Development provides a background and theoretical basis for the more specialised disciplinary modules of the second year. The Techniques of Analysis are designed to enhance the analytical, descriptive and prescriptive skills of practitioners of rural development. In the teaching of these techniques use is made of state-of-the-art technology in such areas as information and decision support systems (see also [c] below). The eight modules contained in the more detailed programme of the second year continue the upgrading of the developmental skills and innovatory potential of the trainees.

In the module on Enterprise Management and Development, for example, the applied aspects of rural development, including such topics as business innovation, opportunities for new ventures and project feasibility analysis (undertaken in workshops consisting of small groups of trainees) are explored in collaboration with the local Business Innovation Centre (BIC), which is part of a much wider network funded by the EU. The practical nature of group projects completed by participants in this module is illustrated by an investigative report on Recreational Sport Fisheries, published by the Northern Regional Fisheries Board in 1995. Other recent projects included a model for the financial planning of oyster farming operations; biomass; computer tutorials; a rural arts and crafts training centre; and a study of the potential of a community centre.

The action-research orientation of the dissertations undertaken individually by the trainees is normally based on in-depth projects relating to their own agency or other development activities. The pragmatic nature and innovatory features of many of the minor theses successfully completed to date, some of which carry a potential for transfer abroad, are indicated in Table 3. The findings of all of these research projects are available for consultation through the Centre for Development Studies at UCG. An edition of twelve of these, which are contained in the publication *Rural Crisis: Perspectives on Irish Rural Development* (Varley et al. 1991), has been circulated and reviewed internationally. *Gleanings from Leuven* (O Cearbhaill 1992) encapsulated general aspects of rural development within the EC as well as more particular programmes and initiatives within the context of European Integration.

(b) Transfer potential of programme

The innovation that lies in training together agents and other personnel who are actively leading or engaged in rural development but normally working separately and independently of each other creates a synergy which can be translated into multiplier effects in the areas served by them. For example, several of the fourth group of trainees, consisting of public service employees (seventeen), community workers (six) and private individuals (four) have been applying locally the results of their action-oriented research to organic farming, tourism development strategies, information technology needs of agri-tourism community groups, the potential of micro-food industries, the participation of women in rural tourism, fisheries development, and heritage management (Table 2).

(c) Use of technology in training programme

Instruction in techniques of analysis includes, in addition to information and decision support systems, (mentioned at (a) above), new approaches to report writing; information sources and scientific methods; survey methods; computer based data analysis; cost-benefit analysis; accountancy; and group dynamics

(d) Involvement of training programme with national agencies/ industry/education

As already indicated, among national training agencies, the most substantially and directly involved in the programme is FAS, which provides essential funding and collaborates in the planning and monitoring of training. Teagasc, in its role as the national agricultural training authority, provides teaching inputs but also directly supports the cost of attendance at the programme of some of its own staff members specialising in rural development. Similarly, the Industrial Development Authority, County Development/Enterprise Teams, Shannon Development and Udaras na Gaeltachta, all of which are concerned, inter alia, with the development of SMEs, have sent personnel for training on the programme as well as providing frequent contributions to it in the form of teaching, seminars and workshops.

Table 1
Participants in MRD/DRD programme, 1985-95

	1985/ 87	1987/ 89	1989/ 91	1991/ 93	1993/ 95	Total
Public Sector Employees						
Teachers	2	5	3	3	1	14
ACOT/Teagasc	3	3	-	4	-	10
Education Officers	2	1	1	1	1	6
Development Officers	1	1	1	2	1	6
Health/Social Welfare	1	1	-	3	-	5
Gaeltacht/Udaras	1	1	-	1	-	4
Coillte	-	-	2	-	-	2
Other	2	1	3	2	3	11
TOTAL	12	13	10	17	6	58
Community Enterprise/ Voluntary Workers	5	5	4	6	9	29
Private Sector/Self- employed (e.g. Business, Farmers, Accountants, Priests)	2	-	4	4	9	19
TOTAL	**19**	**18**	**18**	**27**	**24**	**106**

111

Table 2
Breakdown of participants in MRD/DRD programme, 1993-94
(n = 21)

Public Sector Employees (6)

Teachers	1
Development Officer	1
Community Employment Supervisor	1
Agricultural Development Advisor	1
Cultural and Language Officer	1
Education Co-ordinator	1

Community Workers (8)

Community/Enterprise Workers	8

Private/Self-employed (7)

Farmers	2
Priest	1
Managers/Proprietors	4

Table 3
Breakdown of rural development projects, 1985-94
(n = 100)

1.   Rural Development

Policy and Planning   7

2.   Environment and Natural Resources

Land Use   3
Roads and Transport   1
Water $\frac{1}{5}$

3.   Human Situation and Resources

Population Migration   3
Communities   3
Grassroots organisations (co-operatives and self-help groups)   19
Women $\frac{2}{27}$

4.   Economic Utilisation of Resources

Employment and Labour   3
Agriculture, Forestry and Fishing   13
Industry   9
Tertiary Sector (Tourism) $\frac{13}{38}$

5.   Public Services

Local Government   1
Extension, Education and Training   15
Health and Welfare $\frac{7}{23}$

Total   **100**

Classification based on *Rural Development Abstracts*

113

Figure 1   Participants in MRD/DRD programme by county, 1985-94

The interdisciplinary teaching and training, provided mainly by staff drawn from UCG, are complemented by regular contributions (sometimes on a reciprocal basis) from several other third-level institutions including The Queen's University of Belfast, Trinity College Dublin and University College Cork. Additional links are now being forged with the Rural College at Draperstown, Co. Derry, where a new Graduate Diploma/ M.Sc. in Rural Development, accredited by Queen's University, replicates many of the features of the MRD model pioneered at UCG. A network was established by graduates of the programme in 1990 to create an active core of expertise in the field of rural development in order to help Irish communities meet the challenge of rural decline. This group maintains liaison with the European Centre for Information and Promotion of Rural Development (Carrefour) which is located at the Centre for Development Studies, UCG. The Carrefour Manager conducts seminars on different aspects of EC policy relating to rural development in Ireland (e.g., technical assistance, information technology, environment) and provides much practical advice to students and graduates in the course of their research.

(e) Association of programme with transnational projects

Students and graduates of the programme are encouraged and helped to get involved in transnational projects for rural development. An intrinsic part of the training is the week-long programme on rural development conducted by the Irish Institute for European Affairs in Leuven, Belgium, in collaboration with FAS, the Department of Architecture and Planning, The Queen's University of Belfast and the Irish Planning Institute. Much informal interaction and many personal contacts have been established and maintained with institutions concerned with the problems and potentials of disadvantaged rural areas (e.g. University of Aberdeen, Arkleton Trust in Scotland and Kommunalentwicklung Rheinland-Pfalz Gmbh in Germany). Through the initiative of some of the programme's earlier students and graduates, a regional twinning project was set up in 1988 between Connemara and Flanders. This continuing link provided by Fionntar Flanders led to the training of Connemara craftsmen in Flanders and the promotion of several cultural exchanges between local groups from both regions.

(f) Interaction of programme with other European programmes and initiatives

MRD graduates have risen to prominence in EU policy-making institutions or agencies. For example, one has until recently served as one of the Irish representatives on the prestigious EU Economic and

Social Committee. Indeed, some of them claim to have been instrumental in planting the seminal ideas that culminated in the EC LEADER rural development concept that eventually emanated from Brussels at the instigation of Commissioner McSharry. The fourth cycle of the programme included students who, in the course of their work, were involved in one or more of the following EC schemes: EUROFORM (training in rural tourism in the Gaeltacht); NOW (training in organic farming for women and the establishment of a training and employment centre for rural women in Connacht); LEADER (multi-annual, multi-sectoral development programmes for rural areas in the Gaeltacht, Arigna Catchment Area and South Mayo); and ORA (use of new information technologies for rural tourism development). The breakdown of projects in Table 3 masks a significant body of research on EU policy concerning rural development, including the Common Fisheries Policy, the Environmentally-Sensitive Areas scheme, Livestock Headage Premia and Telematics for Rural Development.

Conclusion

According to *EUROTECNET News* (June, 1992), innovation in European training systems entails a series of actions in both the public and private sectors which respond to future long-term needs:

> Tomorrow's technology demands that knowledge workers are trained today. These workers must be multiskilled/polyvalent who are competent in a business, technological, personal and social sense. They must be capable of autonomous actions, in relation to changing roles, continuously learning, updating skills, and working on their own initiative within an enterprise. They must also be able to work with people from different technical/professional/cultural backgrounds, customers, managers, etc.

The foregoing discussion suggests that the objectives, impact and transfer potential of UCG's innovative training programme all serve the task of coping with recent and anticipated technological changes within its broader remit of advancing and promoting rural development and serving the particular needs of declining rural areas, mainly in the west of Ireland (Melo 1992). More specifically, the programme can be deemed to match up well with particular EUROTECNET criteria used to track and classify innovative training programmes by reference to their focus, target groups, research and evaluation, and learning methodologies. The focus (context and area) of the training is such as to have considerable potential to exert a positive impact on policy formation and other training systems in terms of developing new curricula in cooperation with other bodies at national and regional levels. The target group consists largely of people at work, trainees and instructors and managers in a disadvantaged region but young people, unemployed adults and women form only minorities within the programme. Research and evaluation are strongly represented by the great majority of projects that can be categorised as action-oriented. Learning methodologies include the use of multiple technologies and combined training approaches to innovation and rural enterprise.

As to improving the quality of training in the existing programme, the possibilities of making greater use of cost-effective front-line technology are reviewed in the planning of each two-year cycle. Attention is currently being given to the feasibility of extending the programme's impact elsewhere (e.g., in collaboration with educational and training institutions in the north of Ireland). Accessibility of other remote and less-developed areas to such training would, however, hinge on the establishment of transnational partnerships with other institutions and the availability of more resources for such purposes as distance education and multi-media technology. In this context COMETT's earlier call for projects within EC and EFTA countries relating to Strategic Planning of Education with Open Learning and Distance Education as Tools for Regional Development (SPOLDERD) might be suggested as a useful model or precedent. Cooperation in the use of such technology in third-world countries could also be envisaged by UCG in collaboration with FAS and appropriate international agencies.

For the more immediate future, the LEONARDO programme, proposed by the European Commission in order to implement a Community vocational training policy, as envisaged under Article 127 of the Maastricht Treaty, opened up the opportunity to rationalise and consolidate the four programmes of PETRA, FORCE, EUROTECNET and COMETT. This common framework embodies adaptation to industrial change, improvement of initial and continuing training, access to vocational training, cooperation between training establishments and firms and exchanges of information and experience. Building on the experience gained from these earlier programmes, priority is to be given to developing transnational cooperation and to boosting the capacity for innovation on the training market by means of pilot projects to design training actions on a transnational basis; exchanges of trainees, specialists and decision-makers; and surveys, analyses and exchanges of data (LEONARDO Vademecum 1995).

Such aspirations should, however, be tempered with a realisation of the necessity to maintain traditional values in education and training as well as creativity, diversity and local cultures. As Professor Mike Cooley, an eminent engineer and systems designer from the West of Ireland, in his classic study of human and technology relationships, *Architect or Bee?: The Human Price of Technology,* has put it: "As we approach the 21st century, we require the perspective of a historian, the imagination of a poet, the analytical capacity of a scientist, and the wisdom of a Chief Seattle" (Cooley 1980).

In trying to make sense of the future, Charles Handy in *The Empty Raincoat* calls for a philosophy that re-grounds life and work in three senses---a sense of continuity, a sense of connection (or community) and a sense of direction (Handy 1995). These three purposeful senses are the touchstones by which future education and training, incorporating rapid changes in information and communication technologies, can be judged and applied in terms of responding to the overall and particular problems associated with sustaining and developing rural society in marginal regions. While certain educational and training methodologies and contents would be common to many rural development programmes, the associated institutional arrangements, including technology, animation and applied research, would have to be adapted to the specific needs and different stages of the development process and conform with the pace imposed by the local situation (Melo 1992: 204-205).

References

Barrett, T. 1995a. Local development: a brief guide to some state organisations and European organisations in local economic development in Counties Galway and Mayo. Mimeo.

_____ 1995b. *Community Employment and Training Schemes: West Region.* Galway: FAS.

_____ 1996. Organisational explosion as a response to the local development problem. Lecture to Rural Development students at University College Galway, 22nd January.

Begg, D., S. Fischer and R. Dornbusch. 1991. *Economics.* 3rd edition. London: McGraw-Hill.

Caldarini, C. and F. Mantino. 1994. Human capital in Italian agriculture and role of education and extension. Paper read at an international symposium on system-oriented research in agriculture and rural development, Montpelier, France, November.

Charting our Education Future. White paper on education, 1995. Dublin: Stationery Office.

Commins, P. and M. Keane. 1994. *Developing the Rural Economy:*

Problems, Programmes and Prospects. NESC Report No. 97. Dublin: NESC.

Commission of the European Communities. 1988. *The Future of Rural Society.* Commission communication to Parliament and the Council. Bulletin of the European Communities, Supplement 4/88.

Commission of the European Communities. 1993. *Growth, Competitiveness and Employment.* White paper. Brussels and Luxembourg: Office for Official Publications of the European Communities.

Cooley, M. 1980. *Architect or Bee? Human-technology Relationship.* London: Langley Technical Services.

Davis, J. P. 1992. Introduction. In J. P. Davis (ed.), *Education, Training and Local Economic Development.* Regional Studies Association (Irish Branch).

Education and Training Policies for Economic and Social Development. 1993. Report No. 95. Dublin: NESC.

Education for a Changing World. 1992. Dublin: Stationery Office.

Eurotecnet. 1994. *Le Magazine.* Luxembourg: Commission of the European Communities Task Force: Human Resources, Education, Training and Youth. Spring Issue 1.

Eurotecnet News. 1992. Commission of the European Communities Task Force: Human Resources, Education, Training, Youth. Brussels: Eurotecnet Technical Assistance Office.

Grimes, S. 1992. Information and communication technologies: the prospects for rural areas. In M. Ó Cinnéide and M. Cuddy (eds.), *Perspectives on Rural Development in Advanced Economies.* Galway: Centre for Development Studies, Social Sciences Research Centre, University College Galway. Pp. 123-135.

Handy, C. 1995. *The Empty Raincoat: Making Sense of the Future.* Arrow Business Books.

Köster, E. 1994. Does agriculture need new training methods? Paper read at 19th International Course on Vocational Education and Training. Centre International d'Etudes Agricoles (CIEA) Seminar, Grangeneuve, Switzerland, August.

Lawrence, G. and D. Stehlik. 1996. A direction towards sustainability? Australian rural communities and care for the aged. *Journal of the Community Development Society* 27, 1: 45-55.

Leonardo da Vinci Programme: Vademecum. 1995. European Commission Directorate General XXII: Education, Training and Youth, unit B: cooperation in the field of vocational training.

Melo, A. 1992. Education for training and development. In M. Ó Cinnéide and M. Cuddy (eds.), *Perspectives on Rural Development in Advanced Economies.* Galway: Centre for Development Studies, Social Sciences Research Centre, University College Galway. Pp. 199-207.

Morgan, K. 1995. Institutions, innovation and regional renewal: the development agency as animateur. Paper prepared for the Regional Studies Association Conference, *Regional Futures: Past and Present, East and West,* Gothenburg, Sweden, May.

National Development Plan 1994-99. 1993. Dublin: Stationery Office.

New approaches to Rural Development. 1994. NESC Report No. 97, Dublin: NESC.

O'Connell, P. J. and M. Lyons. 1995. *Enterprise-related Training and State Policy in Ireland: The Training Support Scheme.* Economic and Social Research Institute Policy Research Series No. 25.

O Grada, C. and K. O'Rourke. 1995. Economic growth: performance and explanations. In J. W. O'Hagan (ed.), *The Economy of Ireland.* Dublin: Gill and Macmillan. Pp. 198-227.

Programme for Competitiveness and Work. 1994. Dublin: Stationery Office.

Putnam, R. D. 1993. The prosperous community: social capital and public life. *The American Prospect,* Spring, 35-42.

Roche, F. and P. Tansey. 1992. *Industrial Training in Ireland.* Dublin: Stationery Office.

Shaffer, R. 1994. Rural communities and sustainable development. In D. McSwan and R. McShane (eds.), *Issues Affecting Rural Communities.* Townsville: Rural Education Research and Development Centre.

Strategy for Rural Development Training. 1993. Report of Review Group. Teagasc.

A Time for Change: Industrial Policy for the 1990s. Report of the Industrial Policy Review Group (the Culliton Report). 1992. Dublin: Stationery Office.

Whiriskey, J. 1994. Teagasc. In *Rural Development in Operation.* Dublin: Teagasc.

Part Two
AREA-BASED STRATEGIES
FOR SUSTAINABLE DEVELOPMENT

6 Towards a sustainable approach to the development of the west of Ireland

Micheál Ó Cinnéide

Introduction

When considering the issues and challenges facing the west of Ireland it is well to remember that regional disparities in levels of development exist in most countries. These disparities are reflected in indices such as income per capita, participation in the labour force, levels of unemployment, migration rates and patterns, demographic trends, social and physical infrastructure, innovation capacity, business start-up and survival rates, and general levels of competitiveness (Walsh 1995).

Peripheral rural regions, such as the west of Ireland, almost invariably rank as particularly deprived regions. This is reflected above all else in the long-term demographic decline which has characterised marginal rural areas in very many developed countries for more than a century. Rural depopulation is likely to continue and may even accelerate, regardless of whether unfettered market forces are allowed to concentrate economic activity on urban core regions or regional policy measures succeed in dispersing growth to regional centres. This is so because the changes wrought to the rural economy through the deployment of new production technologies in the agricultural sector are set to continue. The fundamental restructuring of agriculture proceeds unabated. Farmers have been attracted to an industrial model of production, characterised by increased scale, capital intensity, specialisation, and close links with the agribusiness sector, because of a belief that production efficiencies would lead to financial success. As a result they have greatly increased productivity per farm, per hectare, and per person engaged in agriculture (Troughton 1992). This, however, has not led to prosperity in the countryside. On the contrary, the vast majority of farmers have been marginalised and this process continues with the growing concentration of farm production in agri-industrial regions

123

characterised by good soils, favourable topography, and large farm structures. Most of the rural world is denied its traditional economic role. Faced with natural resource limitations on the range of farming activities and locational limits on the range of non-farming activities, these marginalised rural areas are increasingly associated with forestry, extensification, and environmental conservation. Such roles do not augur well for the future of rural communities and unless new economic activities are introduced into the countryside much of the rural world inevitably will die.

The west of Ireland is no exception to this general characterisation. The combined population of the province of Connacht and the three counties of Ulster declined by 23% between 1926-91 during which time the population of the rest of Ireland has increased by no less than 35%. Between 1926 and 1961 the Dublin Region was the only region to have a population increase and, by 1961, almost one-third of the country's population resided there. Except for a short period during the late 1970s and the early 1980s, the demographic decline of the western counties has continued unabated. While some urban centres within the West Region, such as Galway City, Westport and Letterkenny are growing strongly in recent years, the predominantly rural districts are in steep decline. Population decrease was recorded in all but six of the 48 rural districts in the western counties during the intercensal period 1986-91, with some rural districts such as Enniskillen and Castlereagh declining by 9.3% and 8.3% respectively in five years. Ominously, many medium and small size towns are also in decline, with towns like Tuam declining by as much as 9.2% and Boyle by 8.3% during 1986-91 (Cawley 1995). Rural areas and even towns elsewhere in the country also have experienced decline but nowhere has that decline been as prolonged or as pronounced as in the west of Ireland.

Several other indicators confirm the existence of significant regional disparities within Ireland. Although unemployment is now all too common throughout Ireland, including Dublin, the rate of increase in the number on the live register since 1990 has been much greater in the West Region (40.7%) than elsewhere (26.7% for the country as a whole). The economy of the West Region is much more dependent on agriculture than other regions and since farms are smaller and most are engaged in less profitable enterprises such as cattle and sheep, problems abound. Poverty afflicts people in all parts of Ireland but it is a fact that there are more poor people in rural Ireland than in the major urban centres (Jackson and Haase 1996). We can reasonably conclude that there are large inter-regional disparities in levels of well-being within Ireland. The west, midlands and border regions, in particular, rate badly. The unfavourable relative locations of these areas combined with inferior infrastructural provision in terms of roads, railways, telecommunication nodes, airports, third-level educational institutions and other services have left these areas with very limited employment opportunities and resultant high levels of outmigration and population decline.

Regional intervention

Should governments intervene with the spatial pattern of development? The EU has become increasingly concerned and active in promoting regional development throughout the member states in recent years. Article 130a of the Treaty on European Union states that in particular, the community shall aim at reducing disparities between the levels of development of the various regions and the backwardness of the least favoured regions, including rural areas. Clearly the principle of cohesion looms large in EU policies and Ireland, classified as an Objective 1 region, has been a major beneficiary in this regard. In practice, the EU has strongly supported regional development, particularly since the reform of the structural funds that targeted increased aid on Objective 1 regions and also with the establishment of a cohesion fund.

Ironically, however, concern for regional development within Ireland, a major beneficiary under EU regional policy, has waned in recent years. The Underdeveloped Areas Act of 1952 acknowledged the need for a regional approach to economic development. However, except for a brief period, notably during the 1970s, when, for example, the Industrial Development Authority successfully pursued explicit regional job creation targets, commitment to the notion of regional development policies has been weak. The current national development plan (1994-1999) refers to a determination on behalf of the government to promote balanced regional development but little explicit provision has been made within the operational programmes to ensure its attainment. Nor are the new regional authorities that were established in 1994 making any obvious impression on the over-centralised approach to development that is characteristic of Ireland. The strong arguments that Ireland make in favour of regional intervention at EU level do not appear to carry the same conviction within Ireland. This I believe, is a mistake.

Three arguments are usually advanced in favour of explicit regional development policies. One relates to social justice or fairness: that people in different regions should have comparable access to employment, education and other services. This argument is not particularly strong. It has led mainly to redistributive regional development policies which have not been very effective.

Another argument, derived largely from utilitarian motives, relates to a concern for the rural environment. It is claimed, for example, that the countryside is of economic value (e.g. as a tourism product) and that much of that value derives from the human presence and imprint on the landscape. The Aran Islands, for example, attract very many more tourists than the Blasket Islands, largely because the former have living communities whereas the latter have been depopulated.

Perhaps the most telling argument in favour of rural development policies relates to the evolving sub-optimal geographic pattern of economic activity, due in large measure to firms not having to internalise many social costs (environmental pollution, accidents, traffic jams). Current economic accounting does not reflect these costs so that only partial estimates are available. It is generally recognised, for example, that the external costs of current transportation systems amount to "at least 3 or 4% of GDP" (Commission of the European Communities 1993). These costs are, of necessity, ultimately borne by society at large. The EU white paper, *Growth, Competitiveness and Unemployment* (1993) concludes that market prices will have to internalise systematically all the significant but hidden welfare costs that they generate to society. Undoubtedly, these costs increase with increasing geographic concentration of economic activity. Most small-scale projects in rural areas have minimal costs of this nature. Were firms obliged to bear these external costs, it is likely that many would choose to locate in such a way that these costs and their associated ill-effects on society would be minimised. A more dispersed pattern of economic activity would likely ensue. We can conclude that market forces are generating an economically inefficient geographical pattern of activity and so national welfare is lower than it would be in the presence of policies which influence the location of activity (NESC 1994). It follows that, insofar as regional and rural development policies promote a more even distribution of economic activity, they minimise these costs thereby benefiting the nation as a whole.

Acceptance of the aforementioned arguments leads to the conclusion that rural regions fulfil vital functions that benefit rural and urban dwellers alike. The popular but wholly inaccurate view that rural and urban societies exist simultaneously but separately hinders the formulation of policy measures that would address escalating problems of societal instability (Wilkinson 1992). Claims that funding for rural and regional development policies is misdirected in the light of the very serious problems that characterise many inner cities are both divisive and spurious. Much of the urban malaise is rooted in the forced migration of the rural population to urban centres in search of economic opportunities. Short-term solutions focus on alleviating urban problems in situ. These are both necessary and desirable. However, curtailing the growth of large urban centres, by stemming the rural-urban migration flows, must feature prominently in the broader, longer-term solution. This can only be done through the creation of new employment opportunities in the regions. Rural and regional development, therefore, are everybody's business. In view of the declining political influence of regions beyond the greater Dublin area, associated with the contraction of the rural constituency, it is important that this message gains widespread currency.

Approaches to regional development

Considering the inevitable decline in agriculture and the desirability of creating alternative employment opportunities in rural areas, the question arises as to what measures are likely to be most effective in diversifying the rural economy. In the context of Ireland within the European Union we must ask: What policies are likely to strengthen the competitiveness of rural areas so that they too can benefit from increased opportunities associated with an expanded single market?

The answer to that question appears to have changed radically in recent times. During the 1960s and 1970s, the preferred answer in Ireland and elsewhere focused on attracting inward investment in the form of branch plants of multi-national manufacturing companies by providing financial incentives, a skilled labour force, satisfactory physical and social infrastructure, etc. It must be said that this strategy worked very well in Ireland during the 1970s as evidenced by the migration turnaround and population growth that were widely recorded during that decade (Horner 1986). Since then, however, confidence in this model of regional development has waned. This resulted not just from the frequent closure of branch plants in the face of global recession, but also because of disillusionment with the extent to which they developed local linkages, promoted innovation, and generally led to self-sustaining growth. Although these criticisms are valid, they do not mean that the quest for inward investment should be abandoned. Most regions in Europe still strive to attract inward investment. Even so, the inadequacy of this approach to regional development is widely acknowledged leading to new regional strategies in most developed countries.

Instead of an emphasis on attracting outside investment in manufacturing, the new theory and practice of local economic development concentrates on enhancing local communities' abilities to create and retain employment from within (Teitz 1994). The development of local capacity to instigate, lead and control development is seen to be of paramount importance according to this model. This is clearly a very sophisticated approach which emphasises knowledge, research, innovation, education and training. The education system's capacity to dispel

feelings of apathy and dependency and to foster creativity, entrepreneurship and positive attitudes to innovation and change is of crucial
importance in the local development model (OECD 1993). These requirements represent an enormous challenge to the planners and deliverers of
educational and training services. One goal, as heretofore, must be an
appropriately skilled labour force. Now, however, that labour force must
also be instilled with a spirit of engagement, a self-help attitude, and an
entrepreneurial and innovative leaning.

It is extremely doubtful whether that goal is being targeted sufficiently clearly, let alone being fully realised. Some interesting and encouraging developments are taking place, however; for example, efforts to
promote entrepreneurship in schools. New university courses in areas
germane to local and regional development have been developed by our
universities (for example, the Master's degrees in Rural Development and
Community Development at University College Galway). However, it
appears to me that our education and training system as a whole has not
responded sufficiently to this challenge. The provision of these services is
dominated by the suppliers with the target population having very little
influence on what is taught, where it is taught, when it is taught or how
it is taught. This is scarcely in keeping with the recently published white
paper on education which refers to placing the learner "at the centre of
the education process" (Department of Education 1994).

In my opinion, there is need for a much more custom-tailored approach
to the provision of these services, and unless we get this we run the risk
of squandering resources on education and training interventions that
are not sufficiently targeted on the real needs of our society. No doubt
the question of inadequate resources is a constraint. So too is the fact
that many educators and trainers are ill-prepared for this new challenge.
I do not wish to over-emphasise the economic development role of
education. The more fundamental roles of developing the full potential of
each human being and informing the value system of our society must of
course, be fulfilled. In many respects, however, these roles are mutually
reinforcing. Irish business does not require an education system that is
narrowly focused on training future employees. To quote a spokesman
for the Irish Business and Employers' Confederation: "The need is to
produce well-rounded individuals, confident in their own abilities,
equipped with problem-solving skills, initiative and creativity and committed to the constant development of their skills and knowledge. We
want individuals who are self-reliant, capable of analysis and critical
thinking and willing to change. Everyone would benefit from an education system which delivers on these needs" (Madden 1995).

A related issue is the range and quality of business services and
technical assistance available in rural areas to the promoters of SMEs.

In the course of the past year I attended a number of workshops, in widely separated parts of rural Ireland, to which principals of SMEs and others with business ideas were invited, so as to establish how LEADER II funding could best be used to promote enterprise in these areas. In all cases I was struck by the particular emphasis placed on the need to provide a comprehensive range of "soft supports" both on a systematic basis, for example through organised courses and, especially, on a referral basis in response to the precise needs of individual project promoters. Attention has been drawn already to this need in various reports (e.g. Euradvice 1994) and some praiseworthy attempts (notably through the business innovation centres) have been made to redress this problem. The newly-established county enterprise boards are also charged with the provision of management development support targeted on the particular needs of local small businesses (McCarthy 1994). In addition, several LEADER companies are proposing to make this type of assistance available but, even if they have sufficient funding, it is doubtful whether they will be able to access the necessary quality expertise, particularly in the remoter rural areas.

Another critical issue relating to rural development is the extent to which rural areas can offer a pleasant, functional living environment. This involves not just the quality of the natural and built environment but also the range of public services and amenities which are available locally. A recent major study of the changing geography of employment in Great Britain between 1981 and 1991 reveals that whereas total employment contracted by 612,000 jobs (7%) in London and principal cities, it expanded by 280,000 (17%) in the remoter, mainly rural areas (Keeble and Tyler 1994). The main factor underlying this very significant urban-rural shift of economic activity in Great Britain during the 1980s, according to the authors, is that "rural settlements have been able to attract a relatively high proportion of actual or potential entrepreneurs, largely because of their desirable residential characteristics". Entrepreneurs are migrating from urban centres and are bringing with them ideas and expertise relevant to setting up new enterprises. Moreover, the study concluded, they have been more adept than their urban counterparts at targeting new and emerging markets, particularly for specialised and technologically sophisticated small batch products; they undertake more frequent product and service innovations, and they exploit competitive advantages resulting from the direct benefits of a high amenity environment, high quality labour force, good industrial relations and lower costs, together with indirect advantages associated with the improved accessibility to modern telecommunications, good transport, business and financial services in many rural settlements in Great Britain. The policy implications of these findings are clear. In a nutshell, the quality of the total environment in rural areas must be enhanced to the point where people with business ideas and urban-derived know-how will choose to locate. This is a necessary precondition for business success in the countryside. Ongoing attempts to effect increased efficiencies and economies in the delivery of various public services (for example by closing sub post offices, police stations, schools and by centralising medical care facilities) are likely to militate against the successful promotion of business in the countryside.

Another requirement for effective regional development is the development of institutional capacity at local and regional levels to prepare, implement, monitor and evaluate an integrated development strategy (Ó Cinnéide and Keane 1990). Traditionally, development programmes have been centrally planned and implemented through vertical structures which link action on the ground to various government departments but which have relatively few horizontal links, resulting in lack of co-ordination at the local level (NESC 1994). The regions in Ireland largely have been the object of top-down planning processes with little or no attempt made to take account of differences between localities or indeed to encourage and harness local energies. In general, local communities were given little opportunity to influence the broad thrust of the economic development of their areas. And even though seven sub-regional review committees were invited to make submissions regarding the content and strategy of the current national development plan, it is primarily a plan that has been prepared from the centre with regional considerations having only minor impact.

The superimposition of centrally-devised development plans on the regions has not been very successful. Consequently, an approach that facilitates widespread community participation in all stages of the development process is strongly advocated. This does not exclude a meaningful role for central government. On the contrary, the active cooperation of various stakeholders, ranging through central government departments, regional development agencies, local development bodies, community organisations, professional and commercial associations, as well as private individuals is required. Local partnerships of public, community and private actors are regarded as an ideal vehicle for facilitating such cooperation. Through them, well-defined local development strategies may be prepared and the exact role of each player in implementing the plan may be detailed. In this way it is possible to provide a coordinated custom-tailored response to the precise needs of each locality.

Numerous examples of local area partnerships are currently functioning in the west of Ireland. Several of the existing LEADER companies are so structured, and a specific recommendation arising from an evaluation of LEADER I is that local group structures should be based on

a tripartite partnership involving representatives of community organisations, private sector business interests, and the relevant statutory
agencies including the local authority (Kearney et al. 1994). The PESP
companies are another example of local area partnerships in practice.
Doubtless, more will follow as the government's operational programme
for local development is implemented as part of the national development
plan, 1994-1999 (Government of Ireland 1993).

Although the establishment of these local area partnerships is a step
in the right direction, it is doubtful if they command the necessary
support and commitment from the various stakeholders, the necessary
resources, and the necessary authority and standing to discharge the
onerous task of devising and implementing highly-integrated and
innovatory local development strategies. The LEADER I evaluation, for
example, noted that the LEADER companies were particularly weak at
strategic planning. There is a grave danger that these local partnerships
will expend the bulk of the funds at their disposal in a way that mimics
existing agencies and that the development of bold and imaginative
innovatory collective answers will be neglected. Rather than providing
for the proliferation of such local partnerships, it might be wiser to
concentrate initially on bringing a smaller number to the stage where
they can discharge their assigned roles effectively and efficiently.

It is between the local level and the national level that the biggest gap
exists with regard to institutional mechanisms for elaborating and implementing an integrated development strategy. At the upper level there is
no established way of relating regional roles to state-level objectives. At
the lower end of the scale there is no effective mechanism for linking the
extensive number of private, cooperative and community based agencies
including chambers of commerce, enterprise trusts, representative
associations, area-based partnerships, LEADER groups, etc. Yet, integration and coordination is absolutely necessary to avoid duplication and
to promote synergy. A partial solution may be achieved through the
county strategy teams that the government have proposed in the operational programme for local urban and rural development (Government of
Ireland 1995). At the regional level the new regional authorities have an
opportunity to promote coordination through the regional strategic plans
that they have been requested to produce. Early indications are that
neither of these bodies command sufficient resources and authority to
give meaningful effect to these exercises. This situation must be
redressed. In the case of the west of Ireland, in particular, the establishment of a Minister for Western Development and a Western Development
Commission may represent the best opportunity of achieving a
regionally-specific coordinated development programme.

Conclusion

Except for a brief period during the 1970s, the long term decline of the west of Ireland is continuing unabated. There is a fairly general acceptance that the rural habitat, economy and society are worth saving. Arguments that the crises afflicting many urban centres merit greater attention are spurious insofar as one cannot be divorced from the other. Town and country are closely interconnected. Many would argue that at least part of the long-term solution to urban malaise is to be found in the countryside. Creating the economic opportunities in rural areas that would stem or even reverse rural-urban migration flows is not easy. Current wisdom points towards an endogenous approach to regional development. Central to this is the development of human capacity at the individual level, at the community level, and at the institutional level to chart and implement custom-tailored development strategies. This places local actors centre stage and challenges the education and training systems to ensure that the human resource is equal to this demanding and unfamiliar role. The education system's capacity to foster creativity, entrepreneurship, and positive attitudes to innovation and change is of crucial importance in the local endogenous development model. The provision of an adequate level of physical and social infrastructure so as to ensure a pleasant, functional environment is another precondition for success. Finally, the institutional capacity to elaborate and implement a coordinated regional development strategy is another imperative.

References

Cawley, Mary. 1995. Town population change 1986-1991. Paper presented at Conference of Irish Geographers, St. Patrick's College, Maynooth.

Commission of the European Communities. 1993. *Growth, Competitiveness, Employment: the Challenges and Ways Forward into the 21st Century.* White paper. Luxembourg. 151 pp.

Department of Education. 1994. *Charting our Education Future.* White paper on education. Dublin: Stationery Office.

Euradvice Business Consultants. 1994. *Developing the West Together: A Crusade for Survival.* Galway: Developing the West Together.

Government of Ireland. 1993. *Ireland: National Development Plan 1994-1999.* Dublin: Stationery Office.

Government of Ireland. 1995. *Operational Programme: Local, Urban and Rural Development 1994-1999.* Dublin: Stationery Office.

Horner, Arnold. 1986. Rural population change in Ireland. In P. Breathnach, and M. Cawley (eds.), *Change and Development in Rural Ireland.* Maynooth: Geographical Society of Ireland Special Publications 1: 34-47.

Jackson, John and Trutz Haase. 1996. Demography and the distribution of deprivation in rural Ireland. In C. Curtin, T. Haase and H. Tovey (eds.), *Poverty in Rural Ireland: A Political Economy Perspective.* Dublin: Oak Tress Press in association with Combat Poverty Agency. Pp. 59-85.

Kearney, Brendan, Gerry Boyle and Jim Walsh. 1994. *EU LEADER I Initiative in Ireland: Evaluation and Recommendations.* Dublin: Department of Agriculture, Food and Forestry.

Keeble, David and Peter Tyler. 1994. Enterprising behaviour and the urban-rural shift. Paper presented at the 25th annual conference of the Regional Science Association, Dublin.

Madden, Declan. 1995. Education slow to respond to business. *The Irish Times.* Monday, 5th June.

McCarthy, Denis. 1994. Arrangements under the CSF to support local development. Paper presented at Communicating Europe Conference, Cork.

NESC. 1994. *New Approaches to Rural Development.* Dublin: National Economic and Social Council. Report No. 97.

Ó Cinnéide, Micheál and Michael Keane. 1990. Applying strategic planning to local economic development: The case of the Connemara gaeltacht, Ireland. *Town Planning Review* 61 (4): 475-486.

OECD. 1993. Background document. Paper presented at conference on local development and structural change: A new perspective on adjustment and reform, Paris. 50 pp.

Teitz, Michael. 1994. Changes in economic development theory and practice. *International Regional Science Review* 16 (1&2): 101-106.

Troughton, Michael. 1992. The restructuring of agriculture: The Canadian example. In I. R. Bowler, C. R. Bryant, and M. D. Nellis (eds.), *Contemporary Rural Systems in Transition.* Wallingford: C.A.B. International. Pp. 29-42.

Walsh, James A. 1995. *Regions in Ireland: A Statistical Profile.* Dublin:

Regional Studies Association.

Wilkinson, Kenneth. 1992. Social stabilisation: The role of rural society. In M. S. Ó Cinnéide and M. Cuddy (eds.), *Perspectives on Rural Development in Advanced Economies.* Galway: Centre for Development Studies, University College Galway. Pp. 25-35.

7 New trends in Norwegian regional policies

Paul Olav Berg

Background

Norwegian regional policies are more than the specific measures of regional development policies which were introduced through the North Norway Development Programme in 1951-52. A comprehensive regional policy, which includes the various forms of governmental influence on regional development, can be dated back to the 1920s and 1930s. New economic policy legislation was at that time introduced, with the aim of strengthening the position of agriculture and fisheries on the domestic market. These and other economic policy measures had also an obvious regional policy profile. The same thing can be said about the government transfers which were introduced to relieve crisis-stricken municipalities, resulting in the establishment of a special Tax Equalisation Fund for municipalities in 1936.

Post-war regional policies were carried out on two different levels: at a level of ad hoc, piecemeal development measures; and at a level of comprehensive development planning. On the former level, particular measures and programmes have been applied in order to stimulate economic activity and employment in regions which have fallen behind as industrialisation and urbanisation processes have occurred. The most important measures have been investment grants and business development grants, risk capital, special regional and trade-oriented programmes and a regional differentiation of employers' contributions.

Of far wider scope and importance, however, is the comprehensive regional policy which includes various additional forms of government influence on regional (and local) development. Such influence is applied through government transfers to various industries, mainly agriculture, fisheries and certain manufacturing industries dependent on government support for survival. The geographical distribution pattern of the government framework grants to communes and counties clearly influences the conditions for regional and local development. The same is obviously the case for the geographical pattern of the government's investments and operating expenses. Similarly the extended range of the social security net through National Insurance has had obvious consequences for the welfare of the population in all parts of the country. Through legislation and other administrative regulations, for instance the allocation of fishery quotas, decisions are made which have obvious consequences for regional development.

Questions might be raised as to whether the various policy elements of the comprehensive regional policy have been pursued in accordance with regional policy goals. Since sector-based policies will often dominate regionally-oriented policies, an antagonism will exist, where regional policy will often have to give way (Friedman and Weaver 1979, Berg, 1987). In spite of this, the sector-oriented policies have often had a built-in regional policy profile. The present welfare society is to a large extent the result of a process where the government has drawn up guidelines, defined standard levels and co-financed investments and operating expenses of the various services which make up the welfare society. The majority would argue that the present welfare society, with its merits and disadvantages, is a result of the fact that the decentralisation of services, covering all parts of the country, has been successfully developed through the comprehensive regional policy. Cabinet minister Gunnar Berge, of the Ministry of Municipalities and Labour, recently put this as follows:

> [Comprehensive] regional policy has always been important in Norway. It has contributed to the preservation of a scattered settlement pattern, at the same time as we have succeeded in offering welfare for everybody wherever they live. (Quoted from a statement on regional policy in Stortinget, 16th May 1995)

More market, less political steering

Regional policy is a very important part of the Norwegian scene. It has to be like this in a country characterised by large internal distances and large natural differences between parts of the country and between regions. The task of the regional policy is to make the country function as a unity, so that the people, irrespective of region or part of the country, can benefit from the development of the welfare society. Our main goal is to contribute to the development of viable regions in all parts of the country through a comprehensive regional policy. This goal remains firm.

Regional policy will contribute to the release of the development potential which exists in the various parts of the country. The conditions differ. Therefore the regional policy efforts must be adapted to the situation in the individual region. (*ibid.*)

In his statement to Stortinget, the Minister of Municipalities and Labour emphasized that the main goals of the regional policy remain firm. This emphasis may be seen as a reaction to a situation which has arisen since the autumn of 1994, where there has been some uncertainty regarding the government's intentions of maintaining the regional policy efforts at the present level (Furre 1995). This uncertainty is based on the following two circumstances. First, like other western European countries, Norway is at present recovering from the recent deep depression, while a serious structural unemployment problem remains. The crisis has subdued domestic inter-regional migrations, at the same time as the unemployment problems which previously characterised the peripheral regions are being experienced in the central parts of the country. These circumstances, together with recent changes in the domestic political situation connected to Norway's rejection of EU membership in the referendum in November 1994 (this will be further commented on later), have contributed to a situation where the very basis for a regional policy which has been pursued since the early 1950s has been questioned.

Second, the international trends in the direction of "more market and less political steering", following in the wake of the upheavals of the 1980s in eastern Europe and the Soviet Union, have also reached Norway; these trends appear to have been strengthened as a consequence of Norway's rejection of EU membership. The liberalisation of market regulations, which may be difficult to separate from an ordinary reform activity with the aim of furthering efficiency in public planning and administration, has already resulted in important changes in the use of policy measures and in institutional set-ups.

At the same time this will have great consequences for comprehensive regional policy, inasmuch as the position of the peripheral regions will be weakened. At present governmental committees are working on several issues where the probable outcome also seems to point in this direction. In addition, Norway has undertaken obligations as a consequence of the GATT/WTO agreement and the EES agreement, which may also seem to point in the same direction. This has created some uncertainty regarding the government's intentions for the regional policy in the years to come.

This paper will discuss some changes which have been implemented and some current inquiries which may be expected to have consequences for comprehensive regional policy. These consequences will be commented on later, in relation to the current domestic political situation, which may be expected to last up to the next general election in the autumn of 1997.

Changes in ad hoc regional development measures

During the last four or five years, grants from the government's budget for ad hoc regional development measures have been somewhat reduced, from 1,785 million kroner in 1991 to 1,586 million kroner in 1995, whereas the support through the regional differentiation of the employers' contribution has been increased to some extent. However, of greater importance are several institutional changes which have been proposed and have partly been implemented.

In 1993, the former Regional Development Fund, which dates back to the early 1950s, was merged with three other government financial institutions. The RDF was merged with the former Industribanken, which was established in 1936 in order to give loans to the manufacturing industry, together with two other, minor government financial institutions serving trade and industry. The new institution, named the Norwegian Industrial and Regional Development Fund (SND), has so far continued with the financial measures and grants previously administered by the four former institutions.

As a consequence of this merger, an important symbol of regional policy was to a large extent "neutralised". Another consequence seems to be that the hitherto most forceful measure, the investment grant, will lose some of its importance in the future. The investment grant was introduced in 1969, in order to stimulate investment in buildings and machinery within the development regions. It attempted to achieve this by reducing the capital costs of firms by means of grants. From April 1995 the investment grants may cover up to 35%, 25% or 15% of the investment costs, depending on the geographical location of the firm. Small and medium-sized firms may obtain total grants up to 50%, 30% and 25% of investment costs (Kommunal- og arbeidsdepartementet: Forskrifter og rundskriv S. nr. 94/6629 U, June 1995). In addition, a business development grant was introduced, covering 50% of "soft" investments in market inquiries, training and improvement of skill levels in firms, etc. This form of grant, which existed parallel to the ordinary investment grants directed towards "hard" investments, was given increased importance during the 1980s. As a precondition for obtaining investment grants in recent years, it has been an increasing demand that an investment project should also contribute to development and innovation . This has recently been emphasized by the SND in a circular letter dated February 1995 (SND, 1995):

Creativeness in existing enterprises. Existing enterprises can be given investment grants in order to finance investment projects in connection with substantial expansion of the production of existing products, substantial change-over to new and (for the enterprise) more efficient technology, necessary new equipment for the manufacture of new products, as well as investment in more modern and rational buildings, equipment, etc. Lesser single investment projects and routine investments for maintenance purposes should not be financed by grants.

Whereas the investment grants originally were given as a general reduction of the capital costs of projects which were found supportable, this emphasis on the development and innovative dimension implies that the original subsidising of capital costs which was originally built in to the investment grants will lose some of its effects through time. An additional precondition which is emphasized in SND's circular letter is that a supportable project should "as a minimum be of positive economic value for the community, the grant excluded" (*ibid.*). This last precondition implies a clear intensification of the conditions for obtaining investment grants.

Will the counties be left out of the implementation of regional policy?

Since the early 1950s the counties have been responsible, in the first instance, for dealing with applications from enterprises for grants, loans and guarantees addressed to the former Regional Development Fund and, at present, to the SND. At present, the counties are authorised to make decisions regarding individual projects within a total commitment of six million kroner to a single enterprise, and are responsible for losses exceeding certain limits. This has represented an important development function for the county, which has thus been able to impose its own priorities in the economic development of the county.

In March 1995 a working group appointed by the Ministry (Steineutvalget 1995) presented its report. A majority of the group proposed that the responsibility for dealing with applications for SND's regional development funds should be transferred from the county to SND's own decentralised administration, reporting directly to SND's head office in Oslo. SND's administration would be expanded in order to serve the counties all over the country. A minority of the working group favoured maintaining and to extending the present role of the counties, in collaboration with the SND and within certain limits of authority. The group's report is at present subject to a hearing, with the deadline for comments set at August 20th 1995.

According to the majority proposal, the counties would in future have "responsibility on a strategic level" for planning the implementation of both the enterprise-oriented and the other regional development measures financed from the budget of the Ministry of Municipalities and Labour. However, the SND will have the operational responsibility for the implementation of these measures. The operational responsibility of the counties will occur only in the implementation of the indirect measures, i.e., grants for municipal infrastructure. If these proposals are carried through, an important regional development function will have been transferred from the counties to a centrally-steered administrative agency. A possible consequence of this is that general economic and political considerations could be given priority over regional development considerations. Based on previous experience, for instance from the first regional planning efforts in the early 1950s, it may be expected that strategic planning on county level, which does not have a direct influence on the implementation of the corresponding measures, will, over time, attract less attention.

From differentiated employers' contributions to transport subsidies

The geographical differentiation of the employers' contributions to the National Insurance scheme constitutes the most important measure of ad hoc regional policy. This differentiation was introduced in 1975. For the time being the duty rates in five different regional development zones, delimited mainly from north to south, are respectively 0.0%, 5.1%, 6.4% and 10.6% of the wage costs, whereas the highest rate, which applies to zone number 1, is 14.1%. The loss of revenue to the government, calculated as the difference between the highest and lowest rates, has been calculated to 4 billion kroner for 1995 (Hervik and Johansen 1992). With the exception of the civil service, the reduced rates apply to all employers, including local and county authorities. This differentiation is evidently an important regional development measure, reducing wage costs by 14.1% in the development zone 5 (the county of Finnmark and seven communes in the northern part of the county of Troms) and by 9% in zone 4 (the rest of northern Norway and Namdalen in North Trøndelag).

According to a EU resolution of June 1st 1994, which was accepted by the EES countries on July 20th 1994 (reprinted as Appendix 1 in Mønnesland, 1994), the differentiation of the employers' contribution, with the possible exemption of development zone 5, must be abolished by the end of 1996 for firms in the private sector exposed to international competition. It is supposed to be replaced by a transport subsidy, which can be applied to the same geographical areas covered by the differentiated employers' contribution rate (letter to the Norwegian Ministry of Trade from the EU Commission dated September 2nd 1994).

According to EU's regulations of June 1st 1994, which are expected to apply also in the EES countries, the transport subsidy will be used to compensate for extra transport costs only (Mønnesland, 1994, 1995). Consequently, it may be expected that the new transport subsidy, in contradistinction to the present differentiated employers' contribution, cannot be applied on a general basis, but will be delimited to firms which incur extra transportation costs. Furthermore, it may be expected that the subsidy, one way or the other, will have to correspond to actual transportation costs. A consequence of this will be that many employers who at present benefit from differentiated rates of employers' contributions will be excluded from the new transport subsidy.

As a consequence of these changes, which have partly been decided on administratively (the investment grant) and which may be adopted by the Stortinget (SND/the counties) or as a consequence of international agreements (the employers' contribution), the effects of ad hoc regional policy will most probably be reduced in the future.

Changes in comprehensive regional policy

Comprehensive regional policy has over time constituted a relatively stable structure, which has been of great importance in developing the geographical distribution of the welfare society and the regional balance of employment and settlement patterns. At present, several of the policies constituting the comprehensive regional policy are subject to considerable changes, of which the regional consequences are not always obvious in advance.

Agriculture

Agricultural subsidies from the government's budget amounted to 12,251 million kroner in 1994 (St. meld. nr. 1, 1994-95; Nasjonalbudsjettet 1995, table 5.1). This constitutes 56% of the total transfers to the industrial sector. Agricultural subsidies have been slightly reduced over the last few years. In addition there are indirect subsidies from import restrictions, which bring the total agricultural subsidies close to 20 billion kroner. The importance of agricultural subsidies as part of the comprehensive regional policy is obvious. This means that the changes which the agricultural policy is undergoing, i.e. as a consequence of the GATT/WTO agreement, will also have regional policy consequences.

Over the years, agricultural policy has been criticised for having an insufficient regional policy profile, for instance with reference to the fact that large transfers have been made to grain-producing farms located in the central parts of the country where there are "good alternatives" for employment and incomes within daily commuting distance (NOU 1984: 21A). In recent years the regional policy profile has been strengthened to some extent, as cattle, dairy and sheep farming has been given somewhat better conditions in comparison with grain production. Recent research shows that income per hour and net income per farm has a relatively even geographical distribution (NILF 1995). However, returns are still best from combinations of grain production and pig farming, a typical farming strategy. Agricultural subsidies, which have been characterised by their complexity and complication, are at present being simplified, for instance by linking a larger part of the subsidies to the acreage of the individual farm. The effects of this revision of the regional policy profile of the agricultural subsidies are as yet little known.

Fisheries

Transfers from the government's budget to the fisheries have been drastically reduced over the last few years, from 1,563 million kroner in 1990 to 464 million kroner in 1994 (St. meld. nr. 1, 1994-95; Nasjonal-budsjettet 1995, table 5.1). This implies that quota regulations and the geographical distribution of quotas are more important than before for the regional distribution of economic activity connected with fisheries. For several decades there has been a marked conflict of interest between the ocean-going fishing fleet, which to a large extent uses active fishing gear like trawls, etc., and the coastal fishing fleet, which mainly uses passive fishing gear like nets and long-lines. Since the ocean-going fleet is to a large extent located in western Norway, and the bulk of the coastal fleet is located in northern Norway, this conflict of interests also has a geographical north-south dimension. The fishermen's own organisations, in which western Norway is strongly represented, have traditionally had strong influence on the formulation of the fishery policies. This is also the case when it comes to the distribution of fishing quotas.

Northern Norway's share of the total catch was reduced from 35% in 1981 to 23% in 1989 measured by quantity, whereas the share of cod and cod-like species was reduced from 69% in 1977 to 56% in 1989 (Hershoug and Hoel 1991). In 1989, quota regulations based on individual fishing vessels were introduced. These regulations were based on the vessel's catch in previous years. This contributed in some degree towards an increase in northern Norway's share of the catch. However, western Norway has in the last few years again increased its share of the total catch. This may be related to the allotment of more and increased quotas and better recruitment of fishermen in the western than in the northern parts of the country.

The principle of vessel-based quotas has the unfortunate side-effect that the value of the fishing vessels increases, reflecting the market value of the quotas. This makes it difficult for young people to buy second-hand fishing vessels, thus hampering recruitment to the fisheries. A possible explanation of why western Norway has had stronger recruitment than the northern parts of the country may be that the ocean-going fisheries in western Norway have better conditions for recruitment, since higher earnings are possible than in the coastal fisheries (Lindquist, 1994).

Manufacturing

Government transfers to the manufacturing industry amounted to 5,737 million kroner in 1994, which constituted 26% of the total transfers. These have been stable for several years. To this can be added a loss of revenue from exemption from energy and environment duties, amounting to 2,300 million kroner in 1994. Direct transfers include industrial and regional policy transfers through the SND. Transfers to the shipbuilding industry, which is mainly located in northwest Norway, were reduced from 2,021 million kroner in 1993 to 1,398 million kroner in 1994. This reduction was neutralised in the same year by an extraordinary subsidy of 875 million kroner to the food manufacturing industry. This branch of the manufacturing industry has a more even geographical distribution, with some concentration in the largest towns. The regional impact of transfers to the manufacturing industry is difficult to estimate at present. In the long term programme of 1994-97 (St. meld. nr. 4, 1992-93). the government has warned that during the programme period the government will concentrate on "reducing the transfers to industry, at the same time as important goals for the industrial and regional policy are attended to".

The total transfers to the industrial sector from the government's budget amounted to 22 billion kroner in 1994. This amount is ten to fifteen times higher than the transfers through the ad hoc regional policy. Transfers to industry are gradually being changed at present, partly as an adaptation to international agreements and partly as a result of changed priorities in national policies. A clear picture of the regional policy effects of these changes is not yet possible. However, the general impression is that national, industrial policy considerations have been given increased priority over the last few years.

The municipal sector faces far-reaching changes

In 1992, a committee appointed by the government presented an evaluation of the present geographical division of communes and counties, with proposals for fundamental territorial restructuring (NOU 1992:15). The committee recommended far-reaching reform, through which the future communes and counties are delimited as functional regions with a guiding minimum size of 5,000 inhabitants for communes and 200,000 inhabitants for counties. However, the geographical extent should not exceed an area which would still ensure an acceptable access to the municipal and county centres and to the most important public service supplies. More than half of the country's present 435 communes have less than 5,000 inhabitants.

After the committee's report had been subjected to extensive hearings, the Ministry for Municipalities and Labour presented in May 1995 a white paper on the division of communes and counties (St. meld. nr. 32, 1994-95). The Ministry did not follow up the committee's proposals for the minimum sizes of communes and counties. The white paper sets the stage for a dialogue between government authorities and the regional and local authorities concerned, with the aim of forming a proposal for a new geographical division by the autumn of 1999. On May 16th, Parliament decided by a majority of 72 against 40 votes that future changes in the structure of communes and counties, as a fundamental principle, should not include units where the council, or the inhabitants through a referendum, have decided against amalgamation (proceedings of Stortinget 1994-95, nr. 31, May 24th 1995).

Since the main part of the revenues from taxes and duties falls to the state while a considerable part of public services is supplied by communes and counties, government co-financing of the costs of local and regional service supplies can be seen as a natural part of the division of labour between national and regional and local government. In 1995 the income from local and regional taxes and duties is expected to amount to 93 billion kroner, whereas the additional government transfers will amount to 59 billion kroner. Of this amount, 17 billion kroner are distributed as earmarked transfers, while 42 billion kroner are distributed as block grants according to set criteria. Of this, 22 billion kroner go to the communes and 20 billion kroner to the counties.

Block grants are given partly as co-financing of municipal and county expenses according to set criteria, e.g. demographic, reflecting the costs of service production. Partly, also, they are given as a compensation to communes for extra costs, for instance for schools and care for the elderly. A smaller part of the block grants are given as income compensation to communes with a tax income per inhabitant below the national average. Such income compensation is at present given to 340 of the country's 435 communes. Both the grants for compensation for costs and for tax income imply financial equalisation between strong and weaker communes and counties. This gives the transfer system a regional policy profile. This profile is supposed to ensure an adequate minimum service supply in all parts of the country. Such a profile is not new, but can, as mentioned initially, be traced back to the establishment of the Tax Equalisation Fund in 1936. In the succeeding decades this regional policy profile has been extended as part of the development of the post-war welfare society. When the state government in this way ensures the supply of fundamental welfare to all parts of the country, this may be seen as an important part of the comprehensive regional policy.

The new system for distributing the government block grants which was introduced in 1986 initially carried on this regional profile. However, this profile has to some extent been weakened through changes in the criteria which have been introduced subsequently (Berg 1995). When the last changes in the criteria were brought into effect in 1994, the ministry decided to "make visible" an increased minimum income guarantee for the three northernmost counties and to the communes of northern Norway. This increased minimum guarantee had previously been built into the grants for income compensation which had been applied to this region. This "northern Norway grant", which constitutes a part of the regional policy profile of the transfer system, at present amounts to 942 million kroner to the communes and 635 million kroner to the counties. This constitutes 21.6% of the total block grant to northern Norwegian communes and 16.6% of the block grant to northern Norwegian counties. This "making visible" has contributed to a critical debate, where more centrally-located communes and counties have questioned the regional policy profile of the transfer system. Even though this debate is probably just beginning, it has already reached a level where allegations of "over-fulfilment of regional policy goals" lie just below the surface.

In February 1995 the government appointed a committee with a mandate to evaluate the transfer system and to put forward proposals for changes. A preliminary report is to be presented by January 1996, and the final report will appear one year later. Professor Jørn Rattsø of the University of Trondheim chairs the committee, which in addition to two other economists consists of representatives from relevant ministries and three representatives from local and regional government. The composition of the committee has met with protests from peripherally-located communes and counties due to the fact that all three members representing local and regional government have their geographical background in the Oslo region (i.e., the communes of Øvre Eiker (near Drammen), Oslo and the county of Akershus (near Oslo).

The committee's mandate focuses on the distributive functions of the transfer system, without reference to the system's functions and importance in a regional policy context. The design of the mandate, where the committee is asked to "undertake a broad, professional evaluation of the transfer system", suggests that the ministry is interested in decreasing the significance of the political as well as the regional policy aspects of the matter. There is considerable suspense attached to the question of which regional policy profile will be built into the proposals eventually presented by this committee.

New trends in Norwegian regional policies?

The ongoing changes in governmental influence on regional development, which have been referred to above, should be seen against the background of the current domestic political situation in Norway. In a referendum in

November 1994, Norway said "no" to membership in the European Union. This event has had clear domestic political and parliamentary consequences. Political parties which had earlier formed coalition governments, were situated on opposite sides of the debate on Norwegian membership. Such minority or coalition governments, where both the Centre (Agrarian) Party and the Conservative Party have had important roles, have for the last 30 years constituted the only alternatives to minority governments based on the Labour Party. During the present "post-EU period", up to the next general election in the autumn of 1997, there seems to be no plausible alternative to the present social democratic minority government. The lack of such an alternative gives the present government a stronger position than perhaps any government has had at least since 1965.

As with other western European countries in recent years, Norway has also been influenced by market-liberal ideological currents, pointing in the direction of more market and less political influence. These ideological currents have also to some extent been adopted within the Labour Party, where there seems to be a considerably greater uncertainty than before as to what extent influence should be exercised and what direction this influence should take (Eriksen, 1991). A consequence of reduced ambitions for steering, at the same time as the market is given a wider scope, will inevitably be that the position of "the periphery" will be weakened while market forces favour "the centre", i.e. the more central parts of the country. Exposing the economy to fiercer international competition will be an inevitable consequence of the GATT/WTO agreement and the EES agreement, which Norway has recently signed. In order to avoid situations where Norway is accused of breaking the competition regulations of the EES agreement, the government has emphasised that the new regulations should be adhered to as far as possible. This will in itself accelerate the structural impacts of internationalisation.

In addition, Norway's "no" to the European Union may have consequences for the political counter-measures which will be applied to peripheral regions in the form of regional policy measures to compensate for more open competition, both internationally and nationally. At present several structural programmes[1] are being prepared and will be implemented in the neighbouring countries of Sweden and Finland in collaboration with the EU. In these programmes, the problem regions' strengths, weaknesses, opportunities and threats are analysed, and the EU together with the national governments are co-financing measures with the aim of preventing problems and stimulating development in these regions.

From the Norwegian side, an interest has been expressed in participating in EU's INTERREG programme (Minister Gunnar Berge's statement in Stortinget May 16th), with 100% Norwegian financing, in order to prevent problems which are about to arise in the border regions with Sweden and Finland as a result of the current turn of competition in Norway's disfavour. However, any programme work corresponding to EU's other structural programmes is not being carried out in Norway at present. This implies that Norway's problem regions are not being given the same attention in national planning as is the case in the corresponding regions in Sweden and Finland. At the same time these Norwegian regions are exposed to negative effects as a result of reduced national ambitions for planning and as a result of the transition to an economy more exposed to both national and international competition.

That considerable uncertainty has arisen in Parliament regarding the consequences of the recent regional policy signals from the government can perhaps be read from the following decision, which Parliament decided by 60 votes to 52 after the previously mentioned statement made by Minister Gunnar Berge (proceedings of Stortinget 1994-95, nr. 31, May 24th 1995):

> The Government is asked to decide on routines which ensure that consequences for regional policy are reviewed as part of the basis for decisions when Stortinget decides whether policy is to be changed in important spheres of society.

It remains to be seen what consequences such a fundamental decision will have in practice. If this decision had been reached before the evaluating committee for the system of transfers to local and regional government was appointed, such a passage would have had a natural place as a supplement to the committee's mandate. Ex post facto it may be rather doubtful whether it is possible to have the mandate supplemented on this point.

After Norway's earlier "no" to membership of the then-European Community in 1972, the Norwegian periphery where, as in 1994, the opposition to membership was strongest, emerged from the referendum with a considerably strengthened position in the domestic political arena. As the examples which have been given in this paper suggest, Norwegian peripheral regions are facing the opposite situation after the 1994 referendum. The development of Norwegian peripheral regions in the near-term future is uncertain.

Note

[1] EU's structural programmes for Objective 6 (sparsely populated regions), Objective 5 (agricultural regions), Objective 2a (industrial depressed regions) and the INTERREG programme (development in international border regions).

References

Berg, P. O. 1988. Sector versus region: the stalemate of Norwegian regional development policies in the 1980s. In R. Byron, (ed.), *Public Policy and the Periphery: Problems and Prospects in Marginal Regions.* Halifax: The Queen's Printer, for the International Society for the Study of Marginal Regions.

Berg, P. O. 1995. *Det kommunale inntektssystemet---distriktspolitikk eller storbypolitikk?* Rapport 1. Høgskolen i Bodø: Avdeling for sivil-økonomutdanning.

Eriksen, O. E. 1991. DNAs styringsfilosofi i 1970- og 80-årene. Prøveforelesning til den filosofiske doktorgrad ved Universitetet i Tromsø 27 og 28 september.

Friedman, J, and C. Weaver. 1979. *Territory and Function: The Evolution of Regional Planning.* London: Edward Arnold.

Furre, B. 1995. *Bygde-Norge må igjen slå alarmen på.* Kronikk i *Aftenposten,* 18.2.95.

Hersoug, B. and A. H. Hoel. 1991. *Hvem tok fisken?* Landsdelsutvalget for Nord-Norge og Namdalen.

Hervik, A. and R. Johansen. 1992. *Geografisk differensiert arbeids-giveravgift.* Møreforskning Rapport M9202. Molde.

Kommunal- og arbeidsdepartementet. 1995. *Bedriftsrettede distrikts-politiske virkemidler forvaltet av Statens nærings- og distriktsutviklings-fond (SND) og fylkeskommunene.* Forskrifter og rundskriv. S. nr. 94/6629 U, Juni 1995.

Lindquist, K. B. 1994. *Regionale utviklingstrekk i norsk fiskerinæring.* Bind I og II. Doctoral thesis, Institute of Geography, University of Bergen.

Mønnesland, J. 1994. *Noen regionale virkninger av EU-medlemskap.* Arbeidsrapport, Norsk Institutt for By- og Regionforskning (NIBR). Kap. 9 + Vedlegg 1: EUs regler om regionalstøtte i tynt befolkede områder, vedtatt 1/6 1994, tiltrådt av EØS 20/7.

Mønnesland, J. 1995. *Ressurslikhet eller resultatlikhet. Har vi en luksuspreget kommunesektor i nord?* Paper given to the Kommunenes Sentralforbunds landsdelskonferanse for Nord-Norge, Tromsø, 15-16 May.

NILF (Norsk institutt for landbruksforskning). 1995. *Utsyn over norsk landbruk. Tilstand og utviklingstrekk 1994.* NILF-rapport 1.

NOU 1984: 21A. *Statlig næringsstøtte i distriktene.* Innstilling fra

Bygdeutvalget.

NOU 1992:15 *Kommune- og fylkesinndelingen i et Norge i forandring.*

Statens Nærings- og Distriktsutviklingsfond. 1995. *Prinsipper for bruk av tilskudd i SND.* Produktrundskriv nr. 2/95, datert 16/2/95.

Steine-utvalget. 1995. *SND regionale forvaltningsapparat: Rapport fra arbeidsgruppen.* Rapport avgitt 31.3.95. Statens nærings- og distriktsutviklingsfond.

St. meld. nr. 1, 1994-95. *Nasjonalbudsjettet 1995*, tabell 5.1.

St. meld. nr. 32, 1994-95. *Kommune- og fylkesinndelingen.*

St. prp. nr. 1, 1990-91. Statsbudsjettet medregnet folketrygden ("Gul Bok").

St. prp. nr. 1, 1994-95. Statsbudsjettet medregnet folketrygden ("Gul Bok").

Stortingsforhandlinger. 1994-95. Nr. 31, 22-24 May 1995.

8 Norwegian counties in a Europe of Regions

Ragnar Nordgreen

Introduction

A significant recent development in Europe is, it is said, a strengthening of the regional level and a parallel decline in the strength of state governments. Existing transnational functional regions, like the Euregio in border areas of Germany and the Netherlands, are now being formally recognised. Transnational geopolitical regions, like the Barents Region and the Baltic Region, are now also formalised. Cooperation between separate administrative and functional regions in different countries is being strengthened by the formation of systems of regions (Nordgreen 1995), of which the so-called Blue Banana may be an example; or by the creation of alliances of regions, perhaps best illustrated by the so-called Four Motors of Europe. Such cooperation may be bilateral, trilateral, or even multilateral, and need not be characterised by territorial contiguity.

Transnational ties between regions on the sub-state level is a consequence of concurrent moves toward "empowerment" at the regional level. Central governments in unitary states without significant regionalism, peripheral nationalism, or regional nationalism (Paddison 1983) have been decentralising limited and defined state power to regional bodies (e.g. counties), shifting the responsibility for local problem-solving; this is the so-called principle of subsidiarity. Central governments in unitary states having regional nationalism have also devolved powers to regions in an effort to to reduce separatist pressures.

Norwegian regions are increasingly occupied by international cooperation, in particular for industrial development. Initiatives are taken mainly by the county authorities. A survey of Norwegian county initiatives and participation in direct contact and cooperation with regions in other countries (Nordgreen 1994) gives a picture of great variation in the priority that the counties attach to such cooperation, as well as in their choice of channels, degree of organisation, amount of success, etc. Tendencies may be observed in the data, but it is difficult to draw definite conclusions about these processes at this stage.

Transnational regionalisation and sustainability

Environmental sustainability and economic sustainability are inter-dependent, and indeed dependent upon an international, even global context. Not least in an extremely open economy like that of Norway, neither economic development nor environmentally sustainable develop-ment can be fully understood in a national context alone. Norway's influence and control over its economy and environment is limited by the country's strong vulnerability to international forces. Thus Norwegian participation in international forums seeking to influence such forces is decisive for sustainable development.

It is important to interpret international tendencies correctly. This is dependent upon a terminology which is clear and unambiguous. To preserve necessary consistency in the discussion of terms like regions, regionalisation, regionalism, etc., and to prevent the use of trendy labels like "Europe of Regions" becoming just fads, the terminological tools must be employed with precision. The definition of these terms must be improved when existing terms do not altogether enable us to describe the real situation with the necessary clarity. In other words, to gain control over these developments and to draw the best results from from them, even the terminology must be sustainable. As well as presenting Norwe-gian regional policy and current regional activity on the international stage, this paper is intended also to be a contribution to terminological precision. It is important that commentators on these issues, and their readers, have a clear understanding of what is involved in the discussion, and what the terms mean.

Norwegian regional policy in 1995

National regional policy and the Europe of Regions

In the period 1992-1994, Norwegian regional policy has undergone substantial changes, as discussed by Paul Olav Berg (this volume). What have these changes meant for the transnational building of regional alliances as an element of regional development? In 1993, the govern-ment issued a white paper on regional policy---a responsibility of the Ministry of Local Government and Labour (Kommunal- og arbeids-departementet 1993). Regionalisation in Europe was only briefly mentioned; the sense in which the concept was used suggests sub-national territories linked to capitals and other regions without regard to national frontiers. The government saw regionalisation as a response to a political need for a counterweight to supra-national power centralisation, and as being in accordance with the principle of subsidiarity. It saw the end of the Cold War, European integration and the regionalisation of Europe as creating new challenges for Norwegian regional policy, making it obvious that Norwegian regional policy can no longer be independent of general European developments. The Norwegian response to this trend was described in rather general terms. Besides stimulating cooperation between different parts of Norway, the Government intended to emphasise the possibilities for regional contact with Norway's neighbours. Experience gained from the Barents cooperation was thought to hold valuable lessons for other parts of Norway where regional cooperation might cross national borders.

At the same time, the government also issued a white paper on regional planning and area policy (Miljøverndepartementet 1993)---the responsibility of the Ministry of the Environment (Miljøverndepartementet---MD). Here the government approached regional internationalisation in somewhat more concrete terms. It found that most Norwegian counties saw the challenge of increased internationalisation as being mainly in relation to Norway's EU neighbours; but some counties were also looking eastwards, this being particularly important in the northernmost counties, enhanced by incentives developed as a part of the Barents Region cooperation. It found the most important challenge was regional cooperation for developing the potential for the growth of industry and employment within the framework of sustainable development. The government believed this to be an interesting additional perspective for regional planning in Norway. Inspired by a development towards strengthened European regional cooperation, it saw the promise of stronger regional cooperation in Norway on a country section level, recognising that achieving a strengthened position for broader cooperation with regions in other countries is a main goal. The Ministry of Environment declared its approval of counties which had already taken important steps on this path, and of planning in some counties being related to new European challenges.

Nevertheless, these white papers indicate that, in 1993, the government did not regard European regionalisation and building of transnational regional alliances as a major problem or issue of contention in Norwegian regional debate. The government probably did not fear the consequences of such regionalisation for governmental power and for the equitable distribution of welfare and economic growth. The reason for the positive attitude may be parallel to the reasons why the government has for the last twenty years taken an increasingly positive attitude to regional and municipal engagement and responsibility for industrial development. Central government's power to create a desired sustainable economic growth locally and regionally is limited. The government to a certain extent does not feel it is equipped to do this, thus it is decentralising a responsibility it is unable to carry out itself. The prospects of top-down measures for local development succeeding are increased if they are linked with regional and local bottom-up strategies, and if they are administered by a local or regional system for receiving and employing national incentives and other external impulses. The choice is not between national, functional or local, territorial forces. Success is enhanced by harmonising these forces, moreover including external, outside-in forces from juxtaposed national sources or even from other countries (Nordgreen 1993). Success is unlikely to be achieved without a relatively decentralised, regional responsibility for local and regional development in general. Significantly, Norway has a strong, unitary national identity; as a state it is not compromised by competing regional identities. Decentralising is not based upon, has not created, and is unlikely to create separatist regionalism (Selstad 1994).

The Storting (Parliamentary) committee responsible for the follow-up of both white papers, the Committee for Local Government and the Environment, approached the question with greater enthusiasm than the ministries. It sponsored special seminars to publicise development trends on the formation of regions in Europe and Norway, and on internationalisation and the building of networks in business life. It studied examples of network-building and business contacts between Norwegian industry and industry in other countries, regional promotion and international marketing, and found that bodies through which interested foreigners can direct their approaches to Norway have not yet been established.

The majority---consisting of Labour,[1] the Conservatives,[2] the Progressive Party,[3] and the Christian People's Party[4]---found it important that developing regional cooperation structures across state borders in Europe should be exploited in a strategy to strengthen Norwegian regions and Norwegian industry. They asked for a survey of existing regional cooperation and experiences thereof, to advise how government policy can make the single region and the different regional actors (industry, research and educational institutions or local and regional politicians) active, so that they could themselves take part in the process of regionalisation going on in Europe. The majority's conclusion emphasised the importance of stimulating the single region to optimally exploit their own advantages in international engagement. The members from the Socialist Left Party[5] and the Centre Party[6] both reserved themselves from the majority view.[7,8] In the plenary debate of the Storting, regionalisation and regional alliances were scarcely mentioned at all. Only the committee spokesman on regional policy, representing the

Conservative Party, and the spokesman for the governing Labour Party touched upon the question.

Development 1993-94

The counties are increasingly emphasising international cooperation. In a strategy document elaborated by the college of county commune mayors (Kommunanes Sentralforbund 1993) the mayors stated their belief that the counties can be spearheads for industry in the current effort to reach international markets. The conclusion is that the counties must increase their international expertise in order to develop cooperation with regions in other countries.

In 1994, in cooperation with the Nordic Institute for Regional Policy Research, I did a survey of the status in Norwegian counties of direct international activity (Nordgreen 1994). The survey does not allow a comprehensive evaluation of the situation, but rather indicates the situation as seen from different vantage-points---mainly by those responsible for industrial development promotion---in the counties. Initiatives for building transnational regional alliances mainly come from the public sector---the counties themselves. If at all, trade and industry associations at county level only rarely had taken such initiatives. The actors who were expected to be found in the foreground as co-actors or counter-actors for the county commune in promoting transnational alliances were the KAD, the Foreign Ministry, the Ministry of Industry, the Norwegian Export Council, the Central Association of Municipalities and the Industrial and Rural Development Fund (Statens nærings- og distrikts-utviklingsfond---SND).

The respondents who evaluated the role of the Ministry of Local Government were dissatisfied that the ministry did not interest itself in the question of the counties' international engagement and possible participation in the building of transnational alliances. Regions engaging themselves towards eastern Europe, thus getting in touch with the Foreign Ministry's Office for eastern Europe, were much more satisfied with this ministry. No respondents mentioned the Ministry of Industry as offering help. Most respondents who mentioned the Export Council were highly dissatisfied. It is symptomatic that *all* regional Business Advisory Centres which commented on the question also had formalised arrangements with the *Danish* EU Knowledge Centre. Without exception they were all very satisfied with this centre, whose services comprise subscriptions, free telephone service, news bulletins, branch surveys, handbooks, etc. Contact with the Danish centre is more important than with the Norwegian Export Council; their expertise is a result of the long-term accumulation of experience, since Denmark has been an EU member since 1973. Moreover, the Norwegian Export Council gives low priority to small- and medium-sized business. Its organisation and their representatives are patronising towards the regional representatives, behaving as if they where on the international diplomatic stage. Labels like "pompous windbags", "besserwisser", "lip servants" were heard. Their general attitude is strongly coloured by a traditional top-down thinking, with very limited understanding of independent regional engagement or even any knowledge of the topic.

The Central Association of Municipalities seems with very few exceptions to be uninformed and not engaged. The SND is mainly involved in concrete projects connected with single enterprises. The SND wants to engage directly in Russian enterprises if these may be of particular interest for Norwegian industry and trade, and thus may be seen as enterprise development directly serving Norwegian stakeholders.

Beyond 1995

In November 1994, the Norwegian people in a national referendum turned down membership in the European Union, whereas its closest neighbours Sweden and Finland joined. Will this affect Norwegian regional efforts and possibilities as direct international actors? The government indicates that it may be willing to review its regional policy to compensate in some measure for incentives enjoyed by Norway's EU neighbours (Sandal 1995). It emphasises the importance of continued border-regional cooperation and strengthened Nordic cooperation bodies responsible for financing and organising such cooperation. It gives high priority to getting access to the EU's INTERREG II programme. All this is mainly connected with border-regional cooperation that today comprises Norway, Sweden and Finland. All other transnational regional cooperation will be dependent on initiatives from the regions themselves. Government efforts to facilitate this and to take part in enabling regions to engage in such activities may be a precondition for transnational cooperation not leading to increased regional imbalance in Norway.

A sustainable regional terminology

The term "region", and even more specific terms like "functional region", "identity region", etc., are often employed as if they were unambiguous, which they are not necessarily. Regional research requires a precise terminology. Hence in discussing terms like region and regionalisation it is important to understand current phenomena, like the "Europe of Regions". The term Europe of Regions is intended as a description of a tendency in Europe---mainly, but not only, inside the European Union. Without regard to the territorial state governments the regions belong to, and without regard to national borders, regions in this part of the world establish themselves as independent actors nationally and not least internationally. We have what is described as a European "wave" of regionalisation. Regionalisation in this context is defined as the strengthening of a regional level and a parallel weakening of state level. In this context, the regional level is a level below the territorial state that can sometimes transcend national borders.

Some writers consider the establishment of new regions---a number of old regions forming one new region---to be a prerequisite for regionalisation. If the same writers are enthusiastic regionalists, they tend to identify new transnational functional regions, be they bananas or grape clusters, all over the place, since this is the hallmark of a Europe of Regions.

> Considering that theory as well as empirical studies may give several indications, but far from an unambiguous picture, of an emerging Europe of Regions, it is somewhat astonishing to see the great number of thematic maps conveying an impression of one-eyed confidence. There is an obvious discrepancy between regional science analyses with careful conclusions on the one side, and impressive colour slides of development axes, new regional formations, etc. on the other. (Meissner and Nødland 1994)

But is the formation of new, comprehensive functional regions such a prerequisite? Might not contact and common action between several regions be expression of regionalisation even if the regions do not converge into one larger, uniform region unit?

Basic properties of regions

A region is an area with internal similarities distinguishing it from other areas. Fellmann et al. (Fellmann, Getis and Getis 1992) include identification features and hierarchical structures as important properties of regions. If an area can be identified by name, this may in itself induce division into regions. A region is not a point, but an area where certain physical, cultural or other criteria are dominant. A region represents a degree of presence of properties or flows that the region is defined by. The region is surrounded by borders beyond which the properties or flows do not exist to the assumed extent. Borders will often be abstractions made for analytical purposes. A region is defined upon criteria that separate it from surrounding regions. The more the criteria are generalised, the bigger will the region's area be. The more criteria are specified, the smaller the area. Smaller regions are part of bigger regions, in a hierarchy of regions. A hierarchy has a marked order of rank. Hence a hierarchy of regions is a vertical system with subordinate and superior regions. The autonomy of subordinate regions is limited. Superior regions also dominate internal relations in the single subordinate regions.

Besides being part of a hierarchy, the single region may have an internal hierarchical structure. Hence one should distinguish a *region-external hierarchy* and a *region-internal hierarchy*. A region-external hierarchy means that the region is part of a hierarchy of regions, not necessarily having an inner hierarchical structure. A region-internal hierarchy means that the regions have an inner hierarchical structure (Nordgreen 1995). Regions will always be part of a region-external hierarchy. Some regions thereby are superior to other, which thus are subordinate. Several regions may be juxtaposed on the same level in the hierarchy. Not all regions have an internal hierarchy. Whereas a functional region will always have such, homogeneous regions normally will not.

Main types of regions

It is common to classify regions according to four main types---homogeneous, administrative, identity and functional regions. In real life this separation is not always obvious, but it may be useful for analytical purposes.

A *homogeneous region* is the largest possible area where basic homogeneity of one or a combination of physical or cultural properties is found. What is true for one part of the region must be true for the entire region.

An *administrative region* is an area subject to uniform legislation. The same political and administrative governing system prevails inside the region. Terms like political region, planning region are often synonymous.

Identity regions refer to the characteristics that ordinary people---in particular those living or being born there---associate with particular features of the territory, like nature, landscape, dialect, culture heritage, etc. These features may be marked by distinct local particularities, and by the inhabitants' defence of these features from perceived external threat; but also, even at the same time, by the inhabitants' systematic underestimation of the features that give the area status as an identity region, either by their feelings of inferiority, or by lack of knowledge or consciousness of such features. Identity regions may to a lesser or greater extent overlap functional regions. A common feeling of identity may improve preconditions for functionality---loyal customers, loyal employees, etc.

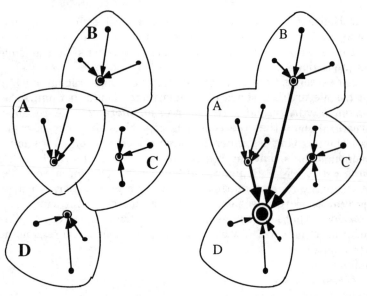

Fig. 1a: Separate functional regions   *Fig. 1b: New region formation*

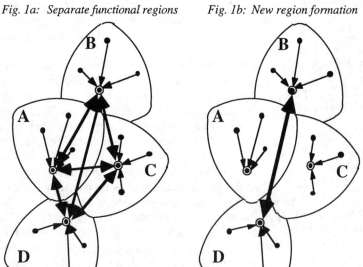

Fig. 1c: Region system   *Fig. 1d: Region alliance*

Figures 1a-1d Types of regional relationships

A *functional region* (nodal region, polarised region) is a spatial system defined by interaction and connection. Functional regions are identified by criteria like a certain function or activity (Jones 1991) or by combinations of these. On the basis of these criteria, functional regions are limited by areas inside the region interplaying more strongly with other areas inside the region than with areas outside. In a functional region, the central place and its surroundings are tied to each other by functional ties. The internal structure is hierarchical. The criteria for a functional region may be set by one variable---as for example a labour-travelling region with a weekly commuting distance as the outer limit; a customer area for daily consumer goods or selected goods outlets; the local newspaper coverage area, etc. The criteria may also be set by a combination of variables. Maps of single variables are then compared to determine transition zones where most variables change.

In analysing regionalisation tendencies in Europe, one should define a combination of single variables tied to interplay within a defined period of time, and then search for transition zones where most of them change synchronically. The hypothesis is that it will be possible to define marked transition zones if all variables of interplay are studied. One will, however, also find that some variables do not change in these zones. Interplay variables like retail trade, labour travel, personal services, road transport services, telephone traffic, and local newspaper subscriptions will probably give quite similar transition patterns. Transition zones for variables as the sale of finished products, the purchase of raw materials, or corporate consulting may not necessarily show convergence with the previously mentioned zones.

Not least, the interplay for some variables will not be present over a territorially contiguous area, fading evenly as distance from the centre increases. Two important conclusions may be drawn. First, the dominating transition zones will define the borders of the functional region, which will be territorially contiguous and cover a limited area. According to economic base theory, production for sale within these borders is to be seen as non-base production (Nordgreen 1995). Second, areas outside these transition zones with which substantial interplay may be identified do not belong to our functional region. Production for sale in these areas is to be seen as base production.

One may not identify functional regions based upon one single interplay feature like export or import of one product or a limited product group, even if the exporting firm is dominating in the export region and the product is important in the import region. The interplay caused by the exporting or importing firm may follow quite different transition zones than all other relevant interplay variables seen together. Exporting firms will often not mark transition zones at all over a territorially contiguous area. A vast area may lie between the export and import areas. There are examples showing that such interplay over a territorially discontinuous area may be identified for many variables, and that a clear hierarchy can even be identified. The relations between colonies and a colonial power may give such a picture. Today one will probably find that such interplay is tied mainly to one good or group of goods, that it even may be possible to identify a hierarchy tied to the routes of this good, but not for the interplay over a broad spectrum.

If interplay between territories does not cover a substantial number of interplay actors and variables, and does not take place inside a hierarchical structure over the entire territory, but rather shows interplay between juxtaposed territories, then the combined territory may not be seen as *one* functional region. Such interplay is horizontal between two or more juxtaposed functional regions. This is important in an evaluation of interplay between regions in Norway and regions in the rest of Europe. *Most of the interplay that may be identified today does not imply that new, consistent functional regions are being formed.* What we are seeing is inter-regional, not intra-regional interplay.

Territorial contiguity

Functional regions are territorially contiguous; they are not separated by interjacent functional regions. If common features appear in two or more areas that are separated by areas without these features, the areas should be defined as two or more functional regions with common features. Functional regions are supposed to have an internal hierarchical structure, which underpins the assumption of territorial contiguity. Attempts to establish a broad-scale public and private sector cooperation between the counties of Hordaland in Norway and Cleveland in England may succeed, but we still have two separate cooperating regions, not a formation of one new functional "Hordaclev" region. One may conclude that only border regions---regions with common border whether this is a nation border or not---may converge into one new functional region.

Unfortunately, it is often said that phenomena like the Blue (London-Milan) and the Green Banana (Barcelona-Milan), are single functional regions. Thus we lose terminological precision. Each of the non-contiguous territories of the banana will have an internal hierarchical structure, whereas this will not be the case for these areas seen together. The prerequisites for the Blue Banana being considered one functional region are significant internal functional interplay stronger than with areas outside the banana, and a uniform hierarchical structure inside the borders of the banana. Such interplay should be present between London and Milan, not only separately between London and Brussels, Brussels and Frankfurt, Frankfurt and Milan. Furthermore, territorial contiguity should not be broken by areas inside the banana belonging to other functional regions than the banana itself. Frankfurt thus should have stronger interplay with London and Milan than with Hamburg, Berlin, Barcelona and Madrid. Region-internal hierarchy as a precondition makes it doubtful whether the Blue Banana can be regarded as *one* functional region. One city should be superior to all others. Cities like London, Brussels, Frankfurt, Munich and Milan all---not one of them--- constitute the highest level in the banana hierarchy. In *one* functional region *one* metropole alone---not several juxtaposed metropoles--- constitute the highest level. Administratively---but by no means functionally---Brussels may be seen as superior to the other cities: "Yes, we have no bananas!"

Regions, regional systems, regional alliances, geopolitical regions

The Blue Banana is contiguous, but composed of several juxtaposed hierarchies with different metropolises on the highest level. The Blue Banana may be seen as a regional cluster or a *regional system.* In a functional region, criterion interplay is stronger between a place and the rest of the region than with places outside. Regional systems have a parallel feature: in a regional system interplay between the single regions in the system is stronger than interplay between any of them and regions outside.

There is a major difference between functional regions and functional region systems: The single region is a pure hierarchy with one single point as its superior level. Functionality in a functional region may more precisely be labelled *vertical functionality.* In the regional system, however, as no region may be considered a point, no single place is the superior level. Interplay between regions in a regional system therefore may be labelled *horizontal functionality* (Selstad 1994)---non-hierarchical functionality between equals. Horizontal functionality may exist on single levels in a functional region---in addition to, but not instead of vertical functionality. If a functional region can be defined by vertical *or* horizontal functionality, then the term functional region would lose its precision. It follows from this that the habit of using "region" when, at best, a regional system is present will have the same consequences. Regions may found cooperation upon horizontal functionality aimed at mutual industrial development. Such cooperation will rarely develop into a hierarchical structure; hence the regions will not converge into one new functional region. In such cases one may speak about *regional alliances.*

The functional flows shown in Figures 1 a-d demonstrate differences between vertically *functional regions, new region formation*---separate regions converging into one functional region, *region systems*---horizontal functionality between mutually equal regions, and *region alliances*---horizontal functionality formalised by agreements between mutually equal functional regions. Top-down region formation like the Barents and Baltic Sea Regions are geopolitical meso-regions. The main reason for such formations are other than just functionality. Thus the primary intentions of the Barents Region obviously are maintaining and developing security and environmental protection in the unstable situation after the breakdown of the Soviet Union. It is not meaningful to describe the geopolitical regions as functional. They may be seen as homogeneous if identified by common problems or challenges. They will never converge into single functional regions, but may eventually show characteristics of functional region systems.

Europe of Regions---?

My survey of international initiatives shows interplay between several regions, even initiatives towards and interplay with regions in other countries. Examples are Hordaland towards Cleveland; Telemark towards Schleswig-Holstein; Oslo towards Gothenburg; Northern Norway towards St. Petersburg, Murmansk, and Arkhangel. Those initiatives may add functional content to geopolitical region formations like the Barents region, the Baltic Sea region and the North Sea region. Primarily the initiatives express priority given by Norwegian regions to create organised functional contact and cooperation between Norwegian and foreign regions without satisfying the conditions for a new functional region to be formed. The initiatives will not change the participating regions' regional status. They join in building a horizontal functional cooperation.

The development of new regions satisfying the criteria for functionality and hierarchical structure as discussed above is not a logical precondition for a Europe of Regions. As increased and strengthened horizontal interplay between mutually equal regions occurs in more countries, independently of national governments, the expression "Europe of Regions" is increasingly heard. The expression may have been invented by the EU to legitimise the reduction of national governments' power; its power to encourage local and regional initiatives through a bandwagon effect should not be under-estimated.

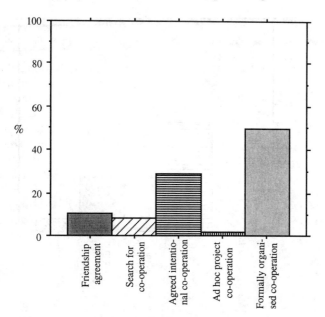

Figure 2   Status of cooperation

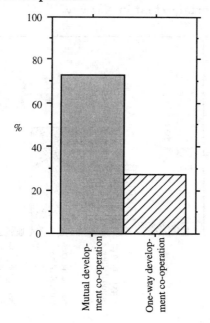

Figure 3   Type of cooperation

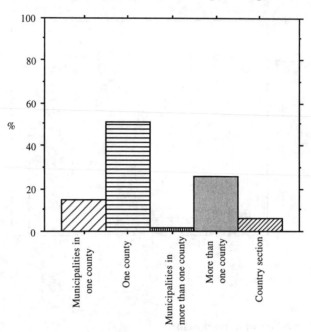

Figure 4   Territorial extent in Norway

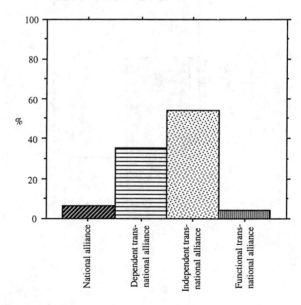

Figure 5   Regional status

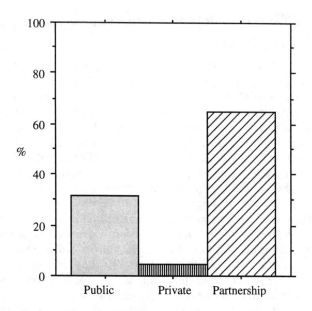

Figure 6   Participating sector

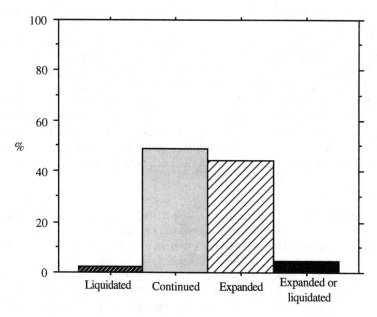

Figure 7   Future aspects

International engagement in Norwegian regions

Background and classification

In my survey (Nordgreen 1994) I have included international initiatives in the fields of industrial development, communications, and exchange of expertise and knowledge, involving the public sector directly or indirectly, and which are reasonably well established. The initiatives were mainly taken at county level. Most initiatives are directed towards European regions, but the capital Oslo also directs some of its initiatives towards places as far away as to Tokyo. A classification of regional international initiatives will not give a perfect picture. Compromise is necessary. The informants were the actors themselves. Investments were not quantified. Minor bilateral initiatives may have been more easily identified than participation in transnational organisations.

The Østfold (Norway)---Bohuslän (Sweden) Cooperation, based upon a contiguous communications infrastructure and an old tradition for close ties (Bohuslän was Norwegian territory till 1658) is classified as one functional region. Nevertheless, increased cooperation inside this territory is not unlike cooperation between regions like Hordaland and Cleveland, which definitely do not constitute one functional region. It would therefore be fair to classify the Østfold-Bohuslän cooperation as horizontal functionality between mutually equal and separate functional regions.

Classification was, however, at times doubtful and uncertain. This is accentuated by respondents being unable to give clear information to found classification upon. No attempt has been made to judge success or a failure: Information sources---the actors themselves---cannot be assumed to have been entirely neutral. The industrial sector is often exceedingly sceptical of public industrial development promotion, and have unrealistic expectations for quick results that may be measured in their own account books. Most initiatives were taken quite recently, whereas such engagements yield their main results in the long term.

Status of cooperation

The status of cooperation indicates how firm, extensive and binding the initiatives are. *Friendship agreement* implies a classical friendship agreement, originally exclusively consisting of cultural and personal exchange programmes, if the agreement is extended also to comprise industrial development. *Search for cooperation* illustrates that the region is presently doing a one-way search for region(s) with which to establish cooperation; or initial contact has been already established, but concrete fields for cooperation are not yet established. *Agreed intentional cooperation* means that cooperation is established with authorities in one or more regions, but that concrete projects or the framework for the cooperation are not yet agreed upon in detail. *Ad hoc project cooperation* indicates that the cooperation is limited to specific types of action, single projects, etc., and thus is not general. Formally organised cooperation is the most complete form of cooperation, meaning that it involves general obligations to cooperate in industrial develop-ment between two or more regions (for example contact mediation, con-crete development projects, etc.).

The distribution of cooperation status appears in Figure 2. Formally organised cooperation is the main tendency, followed by agreed intentional cooperation. The type of cooperation reflects the degree of reciprocity of the initiatives. In *mutual development cooperation*, the Norwegian and the foreign partners assume both will benefit from cooperation. *One-way development* cooperation aims at industrial, possibly also other development in the receiving foreign region. Such cooperation is also called regional development aid. Initially it is a public or partnership solidarity initiative to enhance industry in the receiving foreign region. Through the aid, the receiving region may develop into an interesting business partner, possibly favouring the helping Norwegian partner. In general, national government funding is avail-able for such projects in some foreign countries like Russia, the Baltic countries, etc. Norwegian industry may get development contracts in the initial phase of such projects. This kind of initiative is mainly found in northern Norway under the umbrella of the Barents system. All these are aimed at regions in eastern Europe. The regions may also be engaged in expertise and development cooperation in other sectors than industry, for example environmental protection, health services, developing the public sector, etc. Figure 3 shows the distribution of cooperation types. Mutual development cooperation dominates, while one-quarter of the projects are one-way development cooperation.

Territorial extent of the cooperation

The territorial extent of the Norwegian partner can be classified, whereas the extent of the foreign partner's cannot, mainly because the principles for administrative regions under the national state level differ very much from country to country. *Municipality or municipalities in one county* means that a limited number of municipalities in one Norwegian county take part, with the possible participation of the county itself. Initiatives by single municipalities are not registered, but are probably few in number. *One county* means that one county is responsible for the cooperation, and that possible municipal participation is a result of county initiative. *Municipalities in more than one county* indicates that a limited number of municipalities in more than one county are responsible for the initiative, with the possible participation of the counties themselves. *More than one county* reflects projects where Norwegian counties join forces in international cooperation, and that possible municipal participation is a result of county initiative. *Country section* is an ambiguous term, here used when initiatives comprise more than three neighbouring counties. Figure 4 illustrates the territorial extent of the cooperation. Initiatives by one county dominate, followed by cooperation between more than one county.

Regional status

Will the initiative lead to the formation of a new functional region, or is it an alliance between more than one functional region? The term alliance is usually interpreted as close, firmly organised, binding cooperation that even may include giving up sovereignty to supranational organs. *National alliance* between regions indicates an alliance, permanently or so far only with Norwegian participants, which aims at international initiatives. *Dependent transnational alliance* between regions is cooperation between Norwegian and foreign regions, initiated by the region(s), but as a result of a geopolitical superstructure and/or in its present shape or at the present stage requiring such alliance for funding purposes, etc.; bottom-up actions taken as a result of a top-down initiatives. *Independent transnational alliance* between regions is cooperation without a geopolitical superstructure, and normally a pure bottom-up initiative. A functional transnational region is a coherent functional cross-border region. The distribution of regional status is shown in Figure 5. Independent transnational alliances dominate, followed by dependent transnational alliances. Functional transnational regions are insignificant in number, and all such projects are older than Europe of Regions and less extensive than many of the regional alliances.

Participating sector of society

This classification shows whether the public (municipalities, counties) or private sector alone, or a partnership between the two, participates on the Norwegian side. *Public sector* indicates that only public bodies take part. *Private sector* similarly indicates that only private institutions take part. This category does not satisfy the condition taken above that public participation is a prerequisite. For the initiative to be included, it must be broadly collective and not solely taken by one single firm or a small group of firms, and furthermore is tied directly to a geopolitical superstructure. Possibly the survey has not, even with this allowance, given a full picture. It has been substantially more difficult to get the private than the public sector to respond, partly because responding to surveys like this has a low priority in the private sector, partly because they judge information like this to be sensitive. *Partnership public-private sector* shows cooperation projects where both the public and the private sector take part. Even though private participation in partnerships may be substantial, no cases are registered where a cooperation project is not a result of public sector initiative. The third sector---voluntary organisations---is also from time to time engaged in the initiatives. More or less without exception the sector is engaged by the other actors. The third sector participation is not a result of own exclusive initiatives, and most often third sector organisations do not take part on equal terms. The distribution of participating sectors is illustrated in Figure 6. Partnership projects dominate, followed by purely public projects.

Future aspects

How do the initiators judge the future of the initiative? The label *will be liquidated* indicates that the participants have decided to terminate the project. *Will be continued* similarly means that the project will go on more or less as today. *Will be expanded* indicates that an expansion of the cooperation is agreed upon or is the definite intention by the participants. The category *will be expanded or liquidated* illustrates test projects that in the long run will cost more than they yield if run as today. If they have proven viable they will be expanded, whereas they will be terminated if the outlook is not satisfactory. This category may also represent projects where private sector participants demand relatively quick economic results. If the expectations are believed to have been largely met, the project will be expanded. Are they not, the project will be liquidated. Figure 7 shows how the initiators judge the future. Almost all the projects will be continued or expanded.

The Norwegian government and a Europe of Regions

International activity differs from county to county. One county gives an impression of very high bilateral activity; another of concentrating a lot of resources through multilateral region organisations; several of being in search of the right strategy; some of realising a need for external assistance; most of really needing it. One county rejects the need for any international participation at all.

If Europe of Regions develops into something beyond the fad stage, wide variation in Norwegian regional international activity may lead to regional inequality, so failing to meet the national government's basic objective of just distribution of welfare and economic growth. This may provoke the government's direct intervention in the building of transnational regional alliances. If Europe of Regions becomes the development engine foreseen by many, Norwegian regions and Norway as a nation may then lag behind in economic development. The challenge for the government is thus not to hinder direct regional participation in transnational alliances, but to engage itself in enabling the regions in general, independently of particular and exclusive local and regional preconditions, to take part in the creation and successful management of such alliances.

The uneven degree of regional participation may be explained by several factors, appearing alone or probably in some combination. The phenomenon of a Europe of Regions, being a new concept in Norway, is simply unfamiliar to many. Another reason may be that Norwegian municipalities and counties, in spite of decentralised state power, do not have traditions of direct international activity. Furthermore, independent activity in the building of transnational alliances obviously is strongly tied to the personal characteristics and interests of key figures in the regions. Work in Norwegian local and regional administrations is very dependent upon organisational arrangements and adaptation, whereas the adaptation of the organisations to direct international regional activity is varying, but generally weak. The activity in Norwegian regional and local administration is in general strongly led by top-down instruction. At the same time, instruction from the central authorities in the building of and participation in regional transnational alliances is more or less absent. More research in the field will hopefully encourage the central government to deepen its engagement both in instructing the regions in how to take part in regional alliances aimed at industrial development, and in actively supporting the regions in this endeavour.

Notes

[1] The governing party; initiators of Norwegian application for EU membership.

[2] The mainstream conservative party, strongly favouring Norwegian EU membership.

[3] A liberalist, right-wing and anti-immigration party, split on the EU question, but officially supporting Norwegian membership.

[4] A centrist Christian party with a stronghold in the lay movement,

opposing Norwegian EU membership but supporting Norwegian EEA membership.

[5] A left wing social democratic party established in 1973 in the wake of the EEC referendum of the previous year, composed of the former Socialist People's Party, anti-EEC defectors from the Labour Party and Euro-Communist defectors from the Communist Party. Its main political basis was opposition to Norwegian EEC membership. In 1994, the party officially opposed EU as well as EEA membership, but with a visible minority supporting EU membership.

[6] A centre-right party with strong and traditional ties to the agricultural sector (it is the former Farmer's Party). Strongly opposes Norwegian membership in the EU and the EEA.

[7] The party did not touch upon these questions in their comments, which concentrated upon whether new Norwegian regional policy is a mere adaptation to EEA/EU. The parliamentary process thus gives no hint of this party's attitude and priorities on trans-national, regional alliances.

[8] The party's remarks are concentrated on whether new Norwegian regional policy is a mere adaptation to EEA/EU. The party also says: "This member believes the Barents cooperation to have interesting perspectives, but will underline that this must be shaped according to the premises and needs of northern Norway, and will warn against international big capital being allowed to have a dominating role." Apart from this, the parliamentary proceedings give no hint of this party's attitude and priorities on trans-national, regional alliances.

References

Fellmann, J., A. Getis and J. Getis. 1992. *Human Geography. Landscapes of Human Activities.* Dubuque, Iowa: Wm. C. Brown Publishers.

Jones, M. 1991. *Region som geografisk begrep I.* (Region as a geographical term). Trondheim: Trondheim University.

Kommunal- og arbeidsdepartementet. 1993. *St. meld. nr. 33 (1992-93). By og land hand i hand: om regional utvikling.* (White paper on regional development). Oslo: Kommunal- og arbeidsdepartementet.

Kommunanes Sentralforbund. 1993. *Fylkeskommunen møter framtida: om fylkeskommunenes rolle og oppgaver i Norge.* (The county commune meets the future: On the roles and tasks of Norwegian county municipalities). Oslo: Kommunanes Sentralforbund.

Meissner, R. and S. I. Nødland. 1994. *Transnasjonale regionale allianser i et "Regionenes Europa": motefenomen eller regionalpolitisk paradigmeskifte?.* (Transnational regional alliances in a "Europe of Regions": Fad or regional politic paradigm shift?). Paper no. RF 98/94. Stavanger: Rogaland Research Foundation.

Miljøverndepartementet. 1993. *St. meld. nr. 31 (1992-93). Den regionale planleggingen og arealpolitikken.* (White paper on regional planning and areal policy). Oslo: Miljøverndepartementet.

Nordgreen, R. 1993. The promotive man. In T. Flognfeldt, J. C. Hansen, R. Nordgreen and M. Røhr (eds.), *Conditions for Development in Marginal Regions.* Lillehammer: Oppland College and International Society for the Study of Marginal Regions.

Nordgreen, R. 1994. *Norske regionar og internasjonalt engasjement for næringsutvikling.* (Norwegian regions and international engagement for industrial development). Lillehammer: Lillehammer College.

Nordgreen, R. 1995. *Regionar, regioninndeling og regionalisering.* (Regions, region classification and regionalisation). Lillehammer: Lillehammer College.

Paddison, R. 1983. *The Fragmented State: The Political Geography of Power.* Oxford: Basil Blackwell.

Sandal, J. 1995. *Nordkalotten og regionalpolitikken etter folkeavstemningene: sentrale perspektiver.* (European arctic areas and the regional policy after the EU referenda). Unpublished. Oslo: Kommunal- og arbeidsdepartementet.

Selstad, T. 1994. *Re-regionalisering---periferiens renessanse eller ultraurbanisme?* (Re-regionalising---the rebirth of the periphery or ultra-urbanism?). Unpublished. Lillehammer: Lillehammer College.

9   Sustainable local development in practice: The case of Sykkylven

Roar Amdam

Introduction

Sustainable development can be regarded as a vision, a kind of wished-for situation. Sustainability is a continuous learning process, because we cannot fully know the needs of future generations. If it is held that sustainability is an important issue, then in a democratic and pluralistic state, it can be argued that it is essential that the people support this vision both in their thoughts and practical behaviour. Sustainability can be achieved only through people's actions within a broad learning process. In this paper I discuss some of our experience of the Sykkylven case, where a new kind of planning process was set up to allow people to take part in the creation of a land use plan for the village which pursued the goals of sustainable development. To some extent these goals were achieved.

Learning about sustainability

Compared to the sprawling development patterns that characterise much of today's urban development, considerable advantages can be achieved where the overall goal is to preserve nature and maintain environments by concentrating the urban developments, locating new buildings in areas where encroachments on nature have already taken place, and by utilising each building site more efficiently. The environmental gains can be especially significant if a development strategy that reduces transportation distances and protects new areas from poorly-planned development is combined with better public transportation and measures that limit automobile traffic. These are the main conclusions drawn from analyses of alternatives for land use and development patterns in three Norwegian urban areas (Ness 1992). These environmentally-friendly alternatives are based on the principles mentioned above, with

173

residential construction characterised by low-rise apartment buildings and dwellings of modest size. The analyses show that these environmental alternatives yield considerably lower levels of energy consumption and significantly less degradation of biologically-valuable areas than the established land use policies.

The established land use policies do, however, reflect what most people want and aspire to: a single-family home with a degree of privacy which is a function of the physical (and social) space which separates it from the next house. The more concentrated patterns of housing advocated by the environmentally-friendly alternatives will take some time to become accepted in a sparsely-populated country like Norway, where there is a great deal of land per inhabitant. The ruling values and ideologies, distribution of power and the conditions for governmental planning are obstacles to a radically different approach to urban development. There is, moreover, little support among the population for restrictions on private motorised traffic envisaged by the environmental alternatives.

There is therefore little incentive for municipalities to consider national or global concerns when making decisions about local developments, but it can be argued that they should: "purely local" decisions, when taken in the aggregate, have national and global impacts. Garret Hardin (1968) used the concept of "the tragedy of the commons" to describe the situation that obtains when individual actors compete to maximise their share of resources to which all have free, unrestricted access but which are available only in fixed supply, such as the fish in a lake. Unregulated competition will eventually cause over-fishing; ultimately the fish population is destroyed, and with it the livelihood of the fishers.

Whether this zero-sum principle can really be said to apply to residential development in a country like Norway, which is underpopulated and rich in scenic and natural resources, and where access to house sites is in any case not free but is already restricted by market pricing, is an open question but is one worth asking. The question has both aesthetic and economic dimensions, and the possible answers differ when seen from a societal or an individual viewpoint. For example, at what point is the valued public amenity of the natural landscape irreparably harmed by building a few more private houses in a semi-derelict pasture which is itself not "natural" but was appropriated from nature by an earlier generation? Can ordinary people be persuaded that sustainability directly benefits them in practical ways in the short term, and is not just a set of fashionable, politically-correct ideals which might, in unknown ways, be of benefit to unknown people somewhere else, in places where the relation between people and natural resources is much less advantageous than in Norway; or to as-yet unknown future genera-

174

tions of Norwegians? Will radical policies aimed toward sustainability restrict building land in a way that will simply drive up its cost to the point where only rich Norwegians can afford what many ordinary Norwegians now enjoy: the comfort and privacy of spacious houses set in their own gardens, thus increasing social and economic differences, making Norway a less egalitarian society? At least some Norwegians will have become rich by finding ways to profit from the creation of an artificial scarcity of building land, the direct result of well-intentioned planning controls adopted in the interests of sustainability. How can the market in a resource made dramatically scarcer and more valuable by well-intentioned political manipulation be managed in such a way as to prevent other kinds of less-well intentioned manipulation, including misuses of power and influence, corruption and profiteering?

Bringing the debate about environmental sustainability into the discourse of planning involves learning about sustainability and the limits of nature, matters which are not well understood in development planning in Norway. Learning of this kind can be regarded as a rational process in which the actors are seeking better ways to realise their interests and values (Sabatier 1983). Learning is not only about new means to realise existing goals. Learning can also be a matter of changing old goals and taking up new goals (Offerdal 1992). That is why it is important to discuss learning on different levels, and about learning as an individual process and as a collective process in organisations and communities.

Bateson (1979, 1985), sets out the following typology. *Learning on level O:* learning on this level means no learning at all. New situations that are similar to earlier situations are met with the same solution (derived from laws, manuals, legislation and other stable action models). *Learning on level 1:* learning on this level means choosing among different solutions within an appropriate set of options. *Learning on level 2:* when learning reaches this level, the actor is able to choose among sets of options based on different values. In contrast to the situation at level 1, the actors evaluate the former set of options as poor choices and change to or create another set of alternatives. This is the highest level in the learning process, and that means the actor has learned to learn.

Learning on level O indicates that rules and old practice tell us what is adequate. In given situations, one tries solutions that have been used before. This can be an appropriate, but it is more likely that the action is dominated by routines and must be regarded as an unimaginative response. The actors do not know any other way to act. When we are looking for learning on this level in land use planning in municipalities, we find that the municipality's dominant pattern of action where, for example, a request for new land to build on is routinely met with expansion into the surrounding agricultural land. No other alternatives are regarded as possible solutions. Learning on level 1 is based on the model of the rational, goal-oriented actor. For this actor learning is about relating action to his interests, goals and values. A successful action is an action that is functional for the goals he has, but these goals are unquestioned. Action and learning on this level mean that the dominant action pattern provides opportunities to discuss several possible actions, but the goal is the same. In land use planning this can be illustrated with an example where the municipality's goal is to build a certain number of houses. The procedure will then be to find enough land to build these houses on, and there will be no question about what kind of houses or how much land per house. Thus planning can come simply to legitimate a certain course of action. The planning authority has chosen a course of action that fulfils the goals, but when the criticisms of this course of action arise, the search for other alternatives stops. The planners pervert the planning process into a defence for their chosen course of action. Thus, the planning authority has decided not to learn. In principle, they could discuss other alternatives, but in fact they resist any change to their goals. Learning on level 2 is a kind of paradigm shift including new values, norms and ends. In this situation the actor not only evaluates the different alternatives in order to reach his goal, but he evaluates different goals. Planning in this situation means both a process of making sense and making action; hence many writers describe the process of learning how to learn. Bukve (1991) calls this a cultural revolution, and argues that this process can take place both in organisations and communities. Learning on this level can also become perverted, however: the situation can become one of anarchy if communication between the actors breaks down, the interpretations are in conflict, and engagement disappears.

If we want people in local communities to take part in sustainable development, the process must bring learning up to level 2. If the process does not, nothing will be gained. In this case learning on level 2 means that the vision of sustainability must be the overall goal for land use planning and policy implementation, and it means that if the local actors have really learnt, they will be back in learning on levels 0 and 1, but within a new paradigm. Learning on level 1 is about learning of substance, and learning on level 2 is about process. Both forms of learning come about only through interaction with other people. Therefore individuals learn in a collective interaction process, and collectives learn through individuals. We can find out what collectives as organisations and local communities have learned by studying their processes, rules, routines, positions of people in power, and how they use power. This

learning is maintained through processes of decision and implementation, through socialisation and recruiting. To some extent the
collectives are separate from the individuals, and can autonomously
develop their own understanding of the situation, goals, strategies and so
on (Offerdal 1992). With this brief discussion of learning on different
levels, I will outline the process of planning and the content of the
development plan in Sykkylven.

The case of Sykkylven

Based on our analysis of planning theory and practice, we have divided
planning approaches into the following rough categories (Amdam 1995).
The four approaches do not exclude each other, and local communities
can make use of several approaches simultaneously or combine parts of
them.

Strong control of the means; strong control of the ends. We call
this the *synoptical planning approach.*

Strong control of the means; weak control of the ends. We call
this the *negotiation and advocacy planning approach.*

Weak control of the means; strong control of the ends. We call
this the *disjointed incremental planning approach.*

Weak control of the means; weak control of the ends. We call this
the *transactive planning approach.*

The various approaches correspond to varying degrees of uncertainty and,
normatively, are applied to situations based on their degree of
uncertainty. In general it can be said that most communities today
experience a considerable degrees of uncertainty, but there are great
differences in the way the local organisations are able to tackle and
exploit these uncertainties (Olson 1982). Active local communities are
prerequisites for all the four approaches. Creating and maintaining an
active approach to planning in local communities requires a social process
based on involvement, communication, joint action, personal growth and
learning by participation.

That the interactive forms of policy articulation are important arenas
of mutual learning, developing understanding and ownership of problems
and solutions, have long been understood (Friedmann 1987, Bryson and
Crosby 1992, Forester 1993). Community planning must therefore be
developed to become an overall planning for the community as a whole.
There must be a common arena or "think tank" for all activities in the
community, such as neighbourhood associations, residents' associations,
political parties, state bodies, businesses, organisations, private citizens

and municipal authorities. To this there must be linked a mobilising strategic process that helps to develop a general understanding of challenges and opportunities, visions and strategies. Moreover, there must be concrete plans of action, agreements on their implementation and evaluations that look back at the process and its results, in order to stimulate new understandings based on the activities and results that have or have not been achieved. New understandings can, among other things, contribute to the choice of the field of activity and working methods that are better suited to achieve the desired result.

A voluntary communal method of local planning

The traditional approach to planning and evaluation is to entrust to experts removed from everyday concerns of the municipalities to draw up the plan and undertake the evaluations. The experience of this approach is that it usually reinforces the existing power structure through established actors who take up already-known problems, solve them with traditional solutions and ignore the negative effects. We attempted, therefore, to bring to neighbourhoods, municipalities and regions a collective action approach where all the actors concerned are invited to participate in formulating the problems and the objectives and in implementing the solutions. Such an approach is based on communities or networks of semi-autonomous groups that interact to modify or construct their environment through planning and evaluation processes by means of conflict, negotiation, compromise and mutual learning and adjustment. The method emphasises the importance of mobilisation through establishing arenas such as public meetings, group work, etc., in order to stimulate networks and alliances. We call this method the voluntary communal method (Amdam and Amdam 1990, 1993).

Our efforts are based on the thesis that development work in the local community is a continuous process of thinking and acting. In this process we operate with five functions of the planning system. These functions or variables are (1) the context, (2) mobilisation, (3) organisation, (4) implementation, and (5) evaluation (see figure 1). In order to stimulate those variables we use a planning approach where the development process is organised as a project with strategic, tactical and operative planning and evaluation as elements in the planning system (see figure 2). We link strategic planning to mobilisation, tactical planning to organisation, operative planning to implementation, and reporting to evaluation.

We have developed six work books to support this planning process, to be used in workshops. The key actors or stakeholders are especially invited, but the meetings are open for everyone. The agendas of the workshops are based on plenary discussion and group work, and we use different methods of creative problem-solving to ensure equality between the participants and to make everyone involved in the democratic discourse. The experts take part in the meetings with their diagnoses and scenarios, but they participate in the work groups as "ordinary" members. The work groups brain-storm and make reports to the whole group in plenary sessions.

Project organisation and context

The planning process is usually organised as a project with an administrative committee as the co-ordinating body. We often establish a team for teaching, supervision and evaluation (Amdam, Kleven and Sæterdal 1993). It is important to emphasise that development work can be intensified by way of a project, but that it is nevertheless a continuous process. Organising development work as a project appears to be a form of working of which many municipalities and local communities seem to have little experience, but it can be a useful method of approach when an all-out effort is required for a limited period in a limited area. A well-established project presupposes that the members of the administrative committee have arrived at a reasonable degree of agreement about aims and means, and not least about the limits of, and the mandate for the project. Without the clarification of such questions, internal conflicts within the administrative committee can paralyse the whole project. It is also vital that the participants as far as possible enjoy equal rights when it comes to the terms of participation, and that the formal and informal leaders support the project.

The ideal is that the focus should be on the individual, and that coordination can be achieved through learning by participating in political arenas. Friedmann (1987) claims that transactive planning in society cannot be organised and supported by authority bases in society, but has to grow from within the local communities. The planner who comes from outside can, among other things, help to develop a new self-understanding and improve their skills in self-help, direct action, negotiation and drawing up effective plans of action to achieve changes in policy processes and structures. Transactive planning focuses both on the local power relationships and on national and international government: class structures, sharing of power, resources etc.

Mobilisation and strategic planning

Strategic planning can contribute to a transactive mobilising process by strengthening the local communities' capacity to improve their situation (Friedmann 1987 and 1992). Our means of achieving this is to stimulate the mutual understanding of the characteristics and challenges of development work, and of how one can work to achieve common goals in local communities. This involves focusing attention on structures and processes in the local community, on relationships between the local community and society at large; and it means that the local communities must clarify how to work to influence these elements and relationships. Consequently we stress the importance of strengthening general understanding by establishing new arenas that allow the local inhabitants and other important actors to meet across the traditional boundaries of political administrative levels, administrative systems, and political interests; and also across other boundaries such as age, sex, profession, status, etc. We hope in this way to stimulate the formation of groups, alliances and networks that empowers the people of the local community and gives them new resources to improve their conditions.

These relationships can be illustrated as a learning spiral. After one circuit in the spiral, one is back where one started, but with new knowledge one ends up in a different place. The next question is whether the new knowledge and understanding of the situation are sufficient reasons to provoke reconsiderations of visions, strategies, practices and theories. In the context of mobilisation, this learning spiral must operate at several levels. Levin (1988) refers to this as a process where, as individuals go round the first circuit, they gradually get other individuals, groups and local communities to join them in the spiral of understanding and practice. In the same way, Dryzek (1990) calls this planning for an inclusive democracy, and Sager (1993) speaks of the integration of people and personal growth. Advocacy planning can be used to include weak organised groups in the mobilisation process (Davidoff 1965).

Strategic planning refers to fundamental questions such as what is typical of the situation with its development characteristics and challenges, what sort of future do we want, where should we start and how can we make changes in order to move from the present situation in the direction of the ideal towards which we are working. Questions like this touch on ideological values that can be expected to be fairly stable over a period. It is debatable to what degree planning alone can manage to change such stable values, but over some time changes will certainly be likely, and therefore strategic planning may be used as a tool to stimulate the acquisition of knowledge, to increase awareness and to create a new understandings in the hope that individuals, organisations and communities can change.

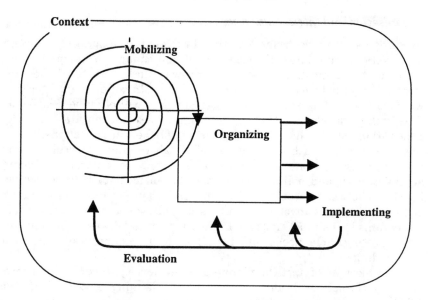

Figure 1 Variables in the process of planning

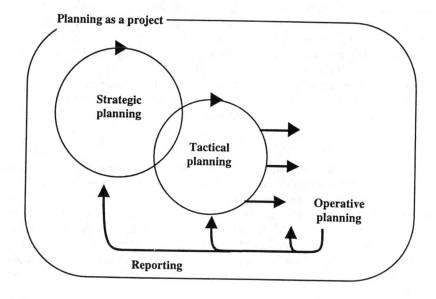

Figure 2 Tools in the process of planning

Organisation and tactical planning

By organisation we refer to the fact that the project, through mobilisation, stimulates the formation of and changes in temporary and permanent organisations that can empower the interests of the local community in both local and national politics. In societies like Norway, which are politically sectored and segmented, it will often be decisive for the further development of local communities to initiate organised cooperation across the boundaries of established organisations. It is therefore vital to achieve a division of labour and cooperation with voluntary associations and organisations, private enterprises, public administration and politicians. It may be an ideal to seek to achieve harmony between local organisations and their surroundings, but in practice situations involving conflicts are unavoidable, simply because the organisations must fight for limited resources between different and often irreconcilable needs and norms in local communities and their surroundings.

The objective of tactical planning is to develop flexible short-term planning through a disjointed incremental planning process (Lindblom 1959). In the first place this involves that we over a period of time give priority to activities in the form of a programme of action. The formulation of the programme is based on programme planning, a form of planning that requires that the people responsible for drawing up the plan of action are in a position of authority (Amdam and Veggeland 1991). Usually, however, these programmes of action can only consider how to use the organisation's resources such as money and labour. Local organisations have scant resources at their disposal and are very dependent on other actors to get things done. Programmes of action can contribute to the production realistic ideas about just what the local organisations can achieve by themselves or in collaboration.

Implementation and operative planning

By implementation we mean the local organisation's capacity to follow up and execute measures and changes, including the evaluation of irregularities, correcting errors, checking quality, etc., to ensure that the implementation as closely as possible matches up to resolutions, activity contracts, programmes of action etc. To make this possible, it is necessary to have project plans that, among other things, state what is to be done, by whom and when. Above all, local organisations have to be empowered with the means to force through democratically-decided measures.

Operative planning refers to the clarification, implementation and evaluation of projects. This type of planning has as its ideal instrumental and synoptical planning (Banfield 1959). A prerequisite is that at the moment of decision there is full awareness of the present situation and clear and unambiguous objectives for the future, so that it possible to decide which alternative offers the best course of action. In practical planning we know that limited projects come closest to this ideal. Strategic and tactical planning can be seen as aids towards establishing the necessary limitations, so that the situation can be made stable and harmonious enough to be amenable to project planning. In every activity that involves other actors, activity contracts should be signed, stating who is to do what, when and how. The drawing up of such contracts can be based on negotiations between actors who depend upon each other (Forester 1987).

Evaluation and reporting

We here refer to the learning process that produces knowledge about events and actions, which can create a new appreciation of the situation, and which in turn can lead to new actions. A policy-making process needs to be subjected to a continual reflexive critique, and this critique must support learning on all the three levels. In instrumental rationality, this is understood as "monitoring" and focuses on changes in context and the implications of the plan, and on whether specified policy objectives are being achieved (Reade 1987). A reflexive critique of a plan needs to attend to these matters but also to keep an eye on whether a plan makes sense. To answer this question, people have to participate in the process and interact in a public discourse. Reporting must be a democratic process with critical questions, but often it becomes a cover-up ritual for undone and unsuccessful activities, and the reports do not produce data that stimulate evaluation and learning on levels 1 and 2.

Learning on level 0 and operative planning. Operative planning is the instrumental mode. Healy (1994) calls this form of planning "management by performance criteria and output targets". The planning organisation has all necessarily knowledge, and actions are secured through command and control. Within the framework of stable action models, the individuals, households, firms and agencies can for themselves work out how to adjust their behaviour simply by following the prescribed procedures.

Learning on level I and tactical planning Learning on this level often means choosing among different solutions within a set of options. In a situation with similar information as in an earlier one, the actors are able to prefer solutions that are appropriate to the situation. To take responsibility is a prerequisite for learning, but often there is a lack of delegated responsibility in the communities. Tactical planning is about how to use the organisation's resources to achieve the goals. In communities there are several organisations with separate fields of working. Usually the actors have to collaborate if they are to succeed in their struggle. The general prerequisite for learning on this level thus becomes the development of partnerships, networks and other forms of collaboration between the actors, and the establishment of action programmes with delegated responsibility for implementation.

Learning on level II and strategic planning. When learning reaches this level the actor can choose among sets of options based on different values and goals. Compared to the situation on level 1, the actors manage to create or change to another set of alternatives. Learning on this level involves a moral dimension (Etzioni 1988), and can be achieved only through interaction and democratic discourses (Forester 1993). This process has to be participation-inclusive, and concerned with consensus-building. This kind of management by arguments (Healy 1994) is important to mutual learning, but agreements on values and strategies are likely to be incomplete and unstable when it comes to practice, especially if they are not rooted in a collective moral spirit.

The place and the project

The genesis of the Sykkylven project was the Ministry of Agriculture's rejection the municipality's land use plan for Sykkylven, and the assignment of the plan to the Ministry of Environment. Instead of simply imposing a new plan, they set up a project with participation from Sykkylven municipality, Møre and Romsdal county, the two ministries, Møre Research and other stakeholders. The main purpose of the project was to create an example of an inclusive democratic plan process and to draw up a development plan for the municipal centre based on a vision of sustainability. The participants saw several problems. One problem was how to make more concentrated use of land in the residential areas and in the office and shopping areas in small villages such as Sykkylven. Another problem was how to resolve conflicts between land use actors when the land to build on is used more intensively. Conflicts in cases like this can be based on conflicts about data, incompatible interests and different values. The main key to this project was to bring new knowledge to the situation, get the different interests on the table and to argue for sustainability. Put simply, to obtain a more sustainable development plan professional academics and local people needed to meet in a broad, inclusive democratic discourse in Sykkylven.

Sykkylven municipality has about 7,000 inhabitants in total, and about 1,500 live within the limits of the plan. Sykkylven is located near Ålesund town in Møre and Romsdal county. The community of Sykkylven was a leader in the industrialisation of Sunnmøre, and is today a leading Nordic centre for the production of furniture. Sykkylven produces about 40% of all furniture produced in Norway, and 80% of the production of soft furniture. The centre of the municipality is also named Sykkylven.   Almost all public and private service production in the municipality is concentrated in the centre. Most of the houses in the office and shopping area were rebuilt after a big fire in 1930, and were built in a grid street pattern. The church, the school buildings, the community house and the sporting fields are located in a green belt along the river. The centre is located on the fjord, but today the main road through the municipality creates a barrier between the centre and the sea. Sykkylven has been continuously settled since prehistoric times, and many ancient artefacts have been unearthed. A recent archaeological excavation found the remains of houses from the Viking age. One of the buildings was about 50 metres long, and housed both people and animals.

Is the new plan more sustainable than the old plan?

Our analysis of the old and the new plan shows that the new plan is different from the old one, especially in the case of residential areas, where the new plan is based on the goal of concentrating the houses. The new plan has stronger emphasis on safeguarding the green areas around the building area, and puts limits on the expansion of building areas. The differences between the old to the new plan illustrate the rationales of the two plans. In the old plan the general goal was to create effective development pattern to meet the needs for building areas. Through the project new values have been added to the process and have gained influence. The new plan gives more priority to the green areas, more intensive use of the developed building areas, stronger safeguarding of the area with the remains of the very old settlement, and the agricultural, natural and outdoor recreational areas. The new plan is more attuned to current norms and goals about land use planning and urban development.   The plan shows that the local community has given priority to a more environmentally-friendly pattern of development. This is a good start for more sustainable development in Sykkylven.

Few empirical investigations on the actual effects of physical planning have been carried out, at least in Norway, but studies support the hypothesis that plans are followed. Ellefsen and Røsnes (1990) show that the municipal master plans have to a large extent been able to regulate different types of protected areas. In a recent study of the municipality of

Elverum, Larsen and Saglie (1995) found that 98% of the amount of area developed between 1970 and 1990 was developed following the zone plan of 1970. Falleth, Kollbotn and Tombre (1995) conclude in their study that in five investigated Norwegian municipalities, development along circumference roads constructed after 1965 has almost been entirely carried out according to the municipal land use plan.

The new Sykkylven plan solves many of the problems in the old plan, but the question about roads still remains. The decision in the municipality council about the road between the office and shopping areas to the school area makes one wonder about to what extent the plan is really accepted. The road will cross the green belt, agricultural land and an area of archaeological value. There was much resistance to this road during the planning process, and the result may be a low degree of acceptance of and legitimacy for the plan, and little support for the implementation of the plan from local actors.

Can the process be recommended?

It is not easy to give an exact answer to this question. Instead, it is better to break down the question into smaller questions. The report from the Ålborg project, a project for planning and developing Ålborg town in Denmark, provides some illumination; the project is thoroughly documented and evaluated by Flyvbjerg (1993). Flyvbjerg analysed the process as one of genesis, design, decision and implementation. He found that the most important parts of the process are before the design phase and after the decision phase. Thus the genesis phase and the imple-mentation phase become the most important, but traditionally the main focus of policy studies is on the design and decision phases. He argues that if we limit our studies to those two phases in the middle of the process, we lose sight of the most important part of the process. In other words, he regards planning as a process that both prepares for the decision and puts the decision through, and that planning must be an integrated part of the whole policy-making process, not only a limited part of it.

Kleven (1990) uses this definition of planning in his thesis about result-oriented planning. He concludes with the statement that formal planning ("Sunday theory") is not the same as real planning ("everyday theory"). For Kleven, and others with the same view on planning, the obvious solution is to separate planning from policy-making. Planning must become more rational and instrumental. Flyvbjerg (1993) thinks that instrumental-rational planning must be viewed in connection with power-rational planning, because these forms of planning interact and have mutual influence on each other. Through power-rational planning it is possible to reach compromises that are beyond what instrumental planning can achieve, although it is an important part of everyday theory and policy.

In the Sykkylven project many central actors were active in the genesis phase when the project was framed and made operational. The central government authorities who rejected the original municipal plan put significant emphasis on the genesis phase. The project was presented as a case of national interest. Sykkylven basked in a certain amount of glory, but the real feeling they was that the community was a client in the hands of the ministries, a client that was unable to handle its own land use planning and land use conflicts. The ministries had rejected the old plan and started a new planning process, and therefore they were obliged to play an important role right through to the end of the project. Altogether the genesis phase did not manage to create sufficient local ownership of the project, and none of the later phases was able to remedy this. This represents a crucial problem with the project, and the main reason why the project so far cannot be characterised as a success. What happened in this phase cannot be described as beneficial. I believe that an equal power situation between the municipality and the central authorities would be a far more preferable starting point. If the ministries had only been looking for a good national example, they ought to have chosen another municipality that was more motivated and had actors with more competence in land use planning and in working with conflicts.

In the design phase of the plan, both the long-term vision part and the short-term action part, the emphasis was on mobilisation, participation and power equality. Apparently this phase went well, but it is important that the project is broadly accepted and that participants are receptive to learning. In the Sykkylven case, powerful actors with strong ownership of the old plan have been more concerned with defending this plan than prepared to consider new values and alternatives. Each proposal that led to changes in the old plan was considered a threat, and attempts were made to defeat it, but not necessarily in the democratic discussion in the open assembly meetings. The project board became the most powerful arena, and in this board the owners of the old plan were well represented.

The weak ownership that many actors had of the project really came to the surface in the decision phase. The mobilising process had created strong support for a more sustainable development plan. When the plan was on the agenda in the municipal council, the lord mayor used his double vote to make the alternative more like the old plan pass. One main conflict was the plan for a road that had been accepted in the old plan. This road was heavily debated in the plan process. The winners in the council got the road to pass close to the farm houses, through the green belt and over a field with many very old archaeological finds. But the last word had not been said, because local representatives of the national government authorities had already said before the decision that they would reject this route if it was decided. Therefore the plan is once again on its way back to the Ministry of Environment.

Our interviews with people in the municipality show that they are tremendously disappointed because the ministries, the county and others who initiated the project, so far not have shown in action that they will support the project in the implementation phase (Amdam, Dimmen and Magerøy 1995). One thing to be learned from this project is that the ministries in an early stage of the project must make clear if they are interested or not interested in taking part in the implementation of the plan. If they are not, I think everyone will be better off if they do not participate at all. Flyvbjerg (1993) has shown that this phase gives many opportunities to exercise power, both to support and to oppose decisions. In the Sykkylven case, the municipality uses the lack of ministerial action and support to promote their own interests. The decision in the municipal council to support an alternative to the old plan can be interpreted as an effort to bring the crisis to a head and thus force the ministries to take part in the implementation of the plan. The logic in this behaviour is that the ministries have invested too much prestige in the project to let it be unsuccessful. So far, this is pure speculation, but time will tell whether this is the case.

The project as a learning process

We presented the learning as a process on three levels, and we linked this to the two-fold purpose of the project, which is learning about process of planning and about the substance of sustainable development in small villages. The question here is what was learned and on what level.

In this project we tried to practice a new kind of planning process based on democratic discourses both in designing and in preparing the implementation of the plan, and many reports from the group sessions were produced. Some actors in the project claimed that the old plan was good enough for the further development of the area, and these were sceptical both to the process and the substance. They argued against participation from the locals in the process because they did not have the professional knowledge about planning, and that the process was too expensive. These arguments particularly came from the actors who had been working with the old plan. They wanted to maintain the traditional approach to planning. They wanted a more rational approach to the process based on the work of the employed professional in the municipal organisation combined with a political planning committee. This had been the process, and ought to be the process.

Most of our informants mentioned the positive aspects of the process. The planning approach with the open democratic process represented a new kind of planning for the local people, and it represented an academic challenge for the professionals. The response after the most intensive process shows that the approach is accepted both by the locals and the professionals. Many external participants in this process saw an opportunity to gain experience about how to put values and visions into practice. An open democratic process was early in the genesis of the process put forward as a prerequisite for the project, and the project has really been implemented with broad participation. The question is, does this represent a new vision for the land use planning and development, and will the planning practice from now on be based on this approach? We found a positive attitude for the broad process among the external professionals, both in practice and in theory. Some of them said that they learned much about the potential of people's participation in land use planning, and that they have continued to use this approach in other similar cases.

In Sykkylven they have used this approach in some smaller cases, but the municipal authorities will not be truly convinced until they see the results. The democratic process was mostly supported by the participants. During this process the municipality was obliged to put the land use conflicts on the agenda, many of the conflicts were solved, and most of the actors were content with the process. The overall evaluation of the process is closely linked to the results and impact of the plan. The plan process and the plan implementation are integrated in their minds. This is understandable, but the risk is that if no results are achieved, the plan process gets the blame. Then the lack of results can undo learning on level 2, and lead back to old habits and a situation with almost no learning.

Those who were sceptical of the plan process were also sceptical of the new plan. One main criticism of the new plan is the lack of potential land to expand on near the office and shopping area. From several sources, there was a strong recommendation to create a relatively stable border between the building area and the agricultural land, so that the farmers can invest in the farm and know that the land will not be taken from them for at least 20 or 30 years. The plan does not go so far, but there are given a sort of assurance for 10 to 15 years. In the old plan a lot more of the agricultural land surrounding the centre was planned to be building area, but the plan had no reflections about when it would be used. The farmers had of course immense difficulties to adapt to this situation.

The same persons who were negative to the process have difficulties with the new and more qualitative and aesthetic aspects in the new plan. They see almost no value in these aspects and claim that the main purpose with the centre is to be a functional frame for the activities within it, and that the centre does not have to be aesthetic. Their guiding value is technical and economical rationality. I think those owners of the old plan are so strongly rooted in their rationale about process and substance that they have rejected almost any new solution, and therefore have learnt almost nothing from this project. However, the new plan represents some new solutions to problems that earlier have been solved in a more traditional way in Sykkylven. If these new solutions are implemented, there has been much learning about substance on level 1.

Indications of learning in this category are expressed in terms like "we see the village with new eyes", and that "threats and challenges for the village have been seen in a different light during the process". The professionals, especially, made analyses of the village and the surroundings as an "architectural room"; this has helped the local people to see new details and the different elements as a part of the whole. These analyses supported the process with knowledge, helped to put new values on the agenda, and had impact on the plan design, but Sykkylven has to prove in their further practice that they have really based the development on a vision of sustainability. There are many opportunities in a plan process to act tactically on behalf of one's own interests, but simultaneously to claim that the action is embedded in democratic and sustainable values.

Conclusions: learning or power?

When we use the term learning as I have in this paper, we can conclude that all three levels of learning are present in this project. The majority of instances places learning on level 1. During the project they learned a new approach to planning. They learned that this approach has been useful in this particular situation, and they claim that they are using the approach, or plan to use the approach, in new situations. I am not sure that they have used this approach only as a tool, or that they have adopted this kind of planning because they accept that a living local democracy has its own and equal value beside the technical and economic values. I am not sure that the environmentally-friendly solutions in the new plan are really rooted in the values of sustainable development. What I am convinced of is that we in this project managed to stimulate a process with opportunities to learn on all three levels, but only the future will show if there have really been learning how to learn.

The weak point in the plan, a prerequisite for real learning, is the lack of an action programme that distributes the responsibility for implementation. We stressed this problem all the way through the process, but the action programme is still missing and this is in our opinion the biggest threat to the success of the plan. When the responsibilities for the implementations are not clearly divided and delegated, everyone can blame each other for the lack of results, and there will be no incentive for further learning. Thus the process can collapse and the community can be forced back to the point at which it started.

References

Amdam, J. and R. Amdam. 1993. *Handbok for kommuneplanlegging etter dugnadsmetoden.* Arbeidsrapport V9314. Volda: Møreforsking.

Amdam, J. and N. Veggeland. 1991. *Teorier om samfunnsplanlegging: en teoretisk introduksjon for planlegging av samfunnsendring.* Oslo: Universitetsforlaget.

Amdam, J. and R. Amdam. 1990. *Strategisk og mobiliserande planlegging: kommuneplanlegging etter dugnadsmetoden.* Oslo: Det Norske Samlaget.

Amdam, J., T. Kleven and A. Sæterdal. 1993. *Gjør det noen forskjell.* Rapport 9312. Volda: Møreforsking.

Amdam, R. 1995. *Development Planning in Local Communities.* Notat 12/95. Volda: Møreforsking.

Amdam, R., S. Dimmen and N. Magerøy. 1996. *Tettstadutvikling med miljøprofil: evaluering av tettstadprosjektet i Sykkylven.* Forskingsrapport nr 10. Volda: Møreforsking og Høgskulen i Volda.

Banfield, E. C. 1973 (1959). Ends and means in planning, in A. Faludi (ed.), *A Reader in Planning Theory.* Oxford: Pergamon Press.

Bateson, G. 1985 (1979). *Mind and Nature.* London: Fontana.

Bryson, J. M. and B. C. Crosby. 1992. *Leadership for the Common Good: Tackling Problems in a Shared-power World.* San Francisco: Jossey-Bass.

Bukve, O. 1991. Råd for uråd? Forsøksverksemd og læring i fire frikommunar, in: L. Rose (ed.), *Det er love å prøve seg.* Oslo: Kommunforlaget.

Davidoff, P. 1973. Advocacy and pluralism in planning behaviour, in A. Faludi (ed.), *A Reader in Planning Theory.* Oxford: Pergamon Press.

Dryzek, J. S. 1990. *Discursive Democracy: Politics, Policy, and Political Science.* Cambridge: Cambridge University Press.

Eztioni, A. 1988. *The Moral Dimension: Towards a New Economics.* New York: The Free Press.

Falleth, E. I., K. Kolbotn and E. Tombre. 1995. *Aktører og arealbruksutvikling langs omkjøringsveger.* Oslo: Norsk institutt for by- og regionforskning.

Flyvbjerg, B. 1993. *Rationalitet og magt.* Odense: Akademisk Forlag.

Forester, J. 1993. *Critical Theory, Public Policy and Planning Practice.* Albany N.Y.: State University of New York Press.

Friedmann, J. 1987. *Planning in the Public Domain: From Knowledge to Action.* Princeton, New Jersey: Princeton University Press.

Friedmann, J. 1992. *Empowerment: The Politics of Alternative Development.* Oxford: Blackwell.

Hardin, G. 1968. The tragedy of the commons. *Science* 162: 1243-1248.

Healey, P. 1994. Development plans: new Approaches to Making Frameworks for Land Use Regulation. *European Planning Studies* 2 (1): 39-57.

Kleven, T. 1990. *"... Det rullerer og det går...": studie av et forsøk med resultatorientert kommunal planlegging.* NIBR-rapport 1990: 23. Oslo: Norsk institutt for by- og regionforskning.

Larsen, S. L. and I.-L. Saglie. 1995. *Elverum utbygging og planlegging 1960-1990.* Oslo: Norsk institutt for by- og regionforskning.

Levin, M. 1988. *Lokal mobilisering.* Institutt for industriell miljøforsking. Trondheim: SINTEF-Gruppen.

Lindblom, C. E. 1959. The science of "muddling through". *Public Administration Review* 19, 2: 79-88.

Ness, P. 1992. *Natur- og miljøvennlig tettstedsutvikling.* Faglig sluttrapport. NIBR-rapport 1992: 2. Oslo: Norsk institutt for by- og regionforskning.

Offerdal, A. 1992. *Den politiske kommunen.* Oslo: Det Norske Samlaget.

Olson, G. 1982. Planleggingens øye, in N. Veggeland (ed.), *Planleggingens muligheter 2.* Oslo: Universitetforlaget.

Reade, E. 1987. *British Town and Country Planning.* New York: Open

University Press.

Sabatier, P. A. 1983. Notes toward a strategic interaction theory of policy ecolution and learning. Paper presented at the conference of the research Group on Guidance, Control and Performance Evaluation in the Public Sector, Center for Interdisiplinary Research. University of Bielefeld.

Sager, T. 1993. *Paradigms for Planning: A Rationality-based Classification.* Trondheim: Norwegian Institute of Technology.

10 The Welsh language, agricultural change and sustainability

Garth Hughes, Peter Midmore
and Anne-Marie Sherwood

In this chapter we explore a number of associations between employment in the countryside, the way in which it is (and will be) affected by pressures on the rural economy, and the effects that these have on linguistic, cultural and intellectual diversity. The context is Wales, which has perhaps the most viable of all the minority Celtic languages: Welsh is spoken by about half a million people, amounting to roughly 19% of the total population (OPCS 1994). At the beginning of this century, virtually half of the population could speak the language whereas at the beginning of the nineteenth century, the language was spoken by the overwhelming majority, including many monoglot speakers. The marked regional variation in the decline of the Welsh language has been intensively investigated, revealing the progressive shrinkage of a once strong heartland area (see, for example, Aitchison and Carter 1994). In large parts of Wales, particularly in the industrial, urban south and along the border with England, Welsh is spoken by a relatively small proportion of residents: in other localities the language continues to be an integral part of everyday life, as the dominant mode of communication. However, even in the communities where Welsh speakers remain predominant in terms of absolute numbers, a reduction in the relative proportion of people able to speak the language has continued.

Both the European Union (EU) and governments of member states now have policies to support and safeguard lesser-used and minority languages. If these policies are defended at all, it is in terms of the welfare and human right of individuals to be able to communicate, and to conduct legal and other business, in their mother tongues. In the United Kingdom, for example, the Welsh Language Act 1993 has sought to enhance the use of Welsh in public and legal affairs and to strengthen the statutory agency, the Welsh Language Board, whose responsibilities include provision of advice on matters related to use of the language.

194

These and other substantial policies have been responses to political activity: there is a clear general connection between language and national or regional identity. Also, in an important if highly contingent way, sustained linguistic diversity may provide a focus countering the tendency of unregulated markets towards the spatial agglomeration of economic activity, identified first by Myrdal (1957), whose analytic tradition has been continued recently, for example, in Massey and Allen (1988). Thus, if more dispersed autonomous control over the local economy may be exercised (following Agenda 21) as a result of linguistic diversity, the latter has an important role to play in reducing unsustainable human activity.

This association between the use of a lesser-used language and sustainability in general may be strengthened by two further arguments, both of which are conditional until coherent supporting evidence has been assembled. The first argument relates to the changing nature of economic activity in the countryside and to the way in which this might be adapted to take advantage of the fragmentation of tourism demand. The second argument suggests that linguistic diversity is similar to biodiversity, and that cultural evolution is comparable in nature to the genetic sort, shifting continuously in response to environmental changes. Some of the consequences of each argument will be considered in turn.

The long-term decline of natural resource prices (and incomes based upon their exploitation, though not necessarily the rate of their production) has reduced employment in industries such as agriculture, forestry, fishing and mining which, it goes without saying, are proportionately over-represented in marginal, peripheral regions. This redistribution and technological transformation has had other consequences though, especially on the mobility of the urban population and on the type of activities sought for relaxation and leisure. One of the effects of the demise of conventional mass tourism is a new, hungry search for authenticity: experiences close to nature and a pace and style of life different from the everyday (Urry 1990: ch. 5). Linguistic diversity may thus become an asset which, since it is embedded in a different cultural tradition, is an attractive symbol which can generate new incomes and employment. In this contemporary context, "cultural tourism" may assist in sustaining marginal regions and their cultural integrity: though the proposition is a fragile one. Today's tourist may become tomorrow's resident, thus weakening irreversibly the essence of the initial cultural appeal (see, for example, Day 1989; Bramwell 1994; Lane 1994).

Cultural fragility is also the basis for the second set of arguments. These are that linguistic diversity, like biodiversity, is both scientifically valuable and an important part of the complex of systems that comprise and mutually support the biosphere. The first aspect has been proposed with some vigour by linguistic scientists in defence of threatened languages, exploring the idea that:

> . . . linguistic diversity is important to human intellectual life---not only in the context of scientific linguistic inquiry, but also in relation to the class of human activities belonging to the realms of culture and art . . . (Hale et al. 1992: 35).

These arguments are assembled on the basis of the need to examine diversity of grammatical structures in order to gain insight into the development of language, the fundamental building block of human societies, in much the same way that, for example, soil structure in semi-natural woodland can be used as a control to determine the extent of erosion and degradation in adjacent cultivated land (Peterken 1993: 195-6). The morphological and phonological structures of language are also important in cultural expression, since they underlie the historical development of verse and music, crucial to the culture of Wales. Unlike genetic diversity, of course, techniques have been developed to record linguistic structures: consequently, languages without native speakers can be classified as moribund and may, to an extent, be artificially reconstructed (as with Hebrew and, possibly, Cornish). However, there may be more to the process of cultural evolution which is not yet understood, that may have yet be assimilated from future study of living, spoken languages. Krauss compares endangered languages to the situation with regard to the most threatened biological species: perhaps 10% of the 4,400 mammal species and 5% of the 8,600 bird species are seriously at risk or extinct. Of the world's 6,000 languages, "the coming century will see the either the death or doom of 90% of the world's languages . . ." (Krauss 1992: 7), which will make the scientific task of investigating human evolution and identity considerably more difficult.

A development of arguments in this evolutionary vein draws on Norgaard's (1992, 1994) ideas about the convolution of culture and society within the context of their natural environments. He suggests that these have adapted social systems and practices which are suitable from the conditions in which they are located, and that geographical patches of linguistic and cultural diversity formerly existed between natural barriers of mountains, seas, deserts and rivers. The decline of this diversity has been due to increased mobility of information, goods, people and. latterly, services. Norgaard argues that failure to appreciate the co-evolutionary nature of social, economic and environmental changes has resulted in development failure. One of the implications of this proposition is that the co-evolutionary view is supportive of cultural pluralism: conventional thinking (described as modernism by Norgaard) is antagonistic.

Table 1
Estimated number and proportion of Welsh-speakers in the workforce by county, Wales, 1981-1991

County	1981		1991	
	%	nos.[2]	%	nos.[2]
Clwyd	17.6	24,960	15.5	26,400
Dyfed	46.4	56,420	42.6	56,490
Gwent	2.4	4,030	2.1	3,660
Gwynedd	62.4	48,870	60.2	55,220
Mid Glamorgan	5.6	11,210	5.8	11,360
Powys	20.7	9,190	15.7	8,050
South Glamorgan	5.2	7,850	6.0	9,510
West Glamorgan	14.7	20,320	12.6	16,900
Wales	17.5	182,850	16.9	187,590

[1] Sample results have been grossed up by a factor of 10: the standard error is approximated by the square root of the number of sample observations in each particular class.

[2] Usually resident persons in employment (including those on a government training scheme).

Source: OPCS

Table 2
Estimated numbers of Welsh-speakers employed in the top twelve industrial classes, Wales, 1991

Ranking of Industrial Sub-Classes (SIC) [1]	Welsh Speakers	Total Persons	Non-Welsh Speakers [2]
All Employed Persons	187,590	1,110,180	922,590
Industry Code			
93 Education	21,460	77,950	5th
01 Agriculture and horticulture	17,290	35,560	16th
64/65 Retail distribution	16,190	116,510	1st
95 Medical and other health services; veterinary services	15,700	81,270	4th
91 Public administration; national defence	15,190	85,400	3rd
50 Construction	15,100	88,470	2nd
96 Other services provided to the general public	8,240	43,810	8th
66 Hotels and catering	8,170	58,650	6th
83 Business services	6,470	47,210	7th
61 Wholesale distribution (except dealing in scrap & waste)	4,900	30,710	10th
97 Recreational services and other cultural services	4,840	24,860	14th
81 Banking and finance	3,790	18,940	18th

[1] According to the number of Welsh speakers employed in each industry sub-class: sample results have been grossed up by a factor of 10.

[2] Comparable ranking.

Source: OPCS

Table 3
Welsh- and non-Welsh-speakers in employment
by age structure, Wales, 1991

Persons in Employment [1]	All ages	16-29 yrs.	30-44 yrs.	45 to pension	Pension & over
	%	%	%	%	%
Non-Welsh Speakers					
Total in employment	100.0	29.2	38.5	29.6	2.7
Managers/proprietors in agriculture & services	100.0	19.5	37.3	37.7	5.5
All other occupations	100.0	30.0	38.6	28.9	2.4
Welsh Speakers					
Total in employment	100.0	26.8	36.6	32.6	4.0
Managers/proprietors in agriculture & services	100.0	16.2	33.6	39.3	10.9
All other occupations	100.0	28.2	37.0	31.7	3.0
All Employed Persons					
Total in employment	100.0	28.8	38.2	30.1	2.9
Managers/proprietors in agriculture & services	100.0	18.7	36.4	38.1	6.8
All other occupations	100.0	29.7	38.4	29.4	2.5
Proportion of Welsh Speakers:	%	%	%	%	%
a. In total employment	17	16	16	18	23
b. In agricultural occupations	25	22	23	26	40
c. In all other occupations	16	15	16	17	19
Ratio of b to a	1.50	1.40	1.44	1.42	1.72

[1] Excluding those on a government training scheme

Source: OPCS

Table 4
Forecast agricultural employment requirements, Wales, 1994-2005

County [1]	1994		2000		2005	
	FTE [2]	FT	FTE	FT	FTE	FT
Clwyd	2,799	2,091	2,635	2,029	2,481	1,969
Dyfed	13,284	9,504	12,055	9,056	10,944	8,629
Gwynedd	5,520	4,038	5,140	3,896	4,789	3,760
Powys	7,727	5,654	7,275	5,486	6,849	5,324
Objective 5b Area	29,330	21,287	27,106	20,467	25,063	19,628

Source: Hughes, et al. 1995

Even though these arguments are, as yet, unsubstantiated, the scale of government resources and action devoted to Welsh language policy suggests that they may be taken seriously. It is therefore surprising that until comparatively recently, even a basic knowledge of the economic activities of the Welsh-speaking labour force and the extent to which these might differ from the rest of the British population has been lacking, particularly since the decennial Census of Population gathers information not only on the occupational structure of the working population in Wales but also its linguistic composition. In this context, data commissioned from the Office of Population Censuses and Surveys (OPCS) has provided the basis for an exploratory study (Jones 1989, Chapman et al. 1990). This work drew on basic cross-tabulations of linguistic status and industry employment defined by the Standard Industrial Classification or SIC (CSO 1979; OPCS 1991), for each of the county districts in Wales at the 1981 Census. The data was unique, in the sense that it was not part of the statistical output published by OPCS, nor had it been previously requested by any other researcher.

Standing alone, however, the 1981 data was of limited value, being almost ten years out of date and representing a view of prevailing economic circumstances at a single point in time. Once the results of the 1991 Census of Population were made available, a fuller and more up-to-date investigation became possible and in 1992, a further set of cross-tabulations was commissioned from the OPCS. This data was subsequently obtained in November 1994 and represents a new source of information on the Welsh-speaking population of Wales. Our purpose in this paper is to report on the initial findings of an examination of this database (Hughes and Sherwood 1995) and to discuss the implications for the survival of the Welsh language under changing economic conditions. The questions raised in this introductory section form a wide-ranging and interesting backcloth to the preliminary investigation of census results, and may assist in identifying fruitful avenues for further research.

Economic activity and linguistic diversity in Wales

According to estimates derived from the results of the OPCS 10% sample, the total number of usually-resident persons in employment in Wales amounted to 1.1 million in 1991. Of these, just under 17% (representing some 187,600 persons) were Welsh-speaking. Although the absolute number of employed Welsh speakers increased marginally between 1981 and 1991, the increment was more than matched by a rise in the number of non-Welsh speakers employed over the same period. Consequently, the relative proportion of Welsh speakers in the total workforce continued to fall, reflecting the trend of previous years. The proportion of Welsh-speakers in the resident population (age three years and over) taken as a whole, is comparable at 18.5% (OPCS 1994).

Table 1 indicates that the regional balance of the Welsh language remained virtually unchanged during the intercensal period, with the predominantly rural counties of Dyfed and Gwynedd accounting for 60% of all Welsh speakers employed in Wales in 1991. This pattern reflects the linguistic composition of the resident population, in which the latter two counties are seen to be the main strongholds of the Welsh language, in both absolute and proportionate terms (Aitchison and Carter 1994). At the other extreme, considerably smaller Welsh-speaking communities are evident in the more industrialised areas of south Wales, particularly in Mid and South Glamorgan and in Gwent where less than one in ten of the workforce are able to speak Welsh, again reflecting the linguistic structure of the resident population overall. A map illustrating the counties and districts of Wales is included in the appendix.

Linguistic characteristics and industry of employment: The all-Wales perspective

When examined according to Standard Industrial Classification, there is an element of conformity as well as diversity in the patterns of economic activity shown by the Welsh- and non-Welsh-speaking populations in employment. However in a broad comparison of the two linguistic groups, the most immediately observable differences in industrial employment relate to manufacturing and to the agriculture, forestry and fishing sectors. These differences were evident at the 1981 Census and were maintained during the intercensal period. Whereas the agricultural category accounted for 10% of all Welsh speakers employed in 1991, the corresponding figure for the employed monoglot English-speaking population was considerably lower at 2%. The latter group have fuller representation in the manufacturing industries, where approximately 23% of the non-Welsh-speaking workforce were employed, compared to only 13% of the Welsh-speaking group.

A clearer picture of differences between the two linguistic groupings is provided by an examination of the 1991 Census data at a more dis-aggregated level. Table 2 lists the individual industry sub-classes occupying the top twelve positions with regard to the absolute numbers of the Welsh-speaking workforce. It is shown that education employs the highest numbers of Welsh speakers and, in fact, accounted for over 30% of all Welsh speakers working in the combined "other services" industry division in 1991. In terms of ranking, this category is followed by employment in the agriculture and horticulture sub-class (SIC, code 01 activities), retail distribution and medical and other health services.

Sub-classes which contribute to the manufacturing sector are absent from the register of foremost employers.

For comparative purposes, the final column of Table 2 indicates the corresponding position of each particular industrial sub-class with respect to employed non-Welsh speakers. In this case, nine of the classes listed are re-ordered since three-quarters of the top twelve are common to both linguistic groups. Unsurprisingly, the retail sector emerges as the principal single employer for the non-Welsh-speaking group, with the construction trades and public administration occupying second and third places. For non-Welsh speakers, the 9th, 11th and 12th positions are accounted for by employment in manufacturing, reflecting the greater numbers working in these industries. Employment in agricultural and horticultural activity ranks only 16th.

An assessment of the relative strength of the Welsh language within each broad industry division supports the absolute positions of each linguistic group, described in Table 2. Bearing in mind that virtually 17% of the employed population fall into the Welsh-speaking group on an all-Wales basis, Welsh speakers figure most highly within agriculture, forestry and fishing, and accounted for 47% (agriculture: 49%; forestry: 28%; fishing: 23%) of all those employed in this sector in Wales in 1991. Approximately one-fifth of persons working in other services are Welsh-speaking (although this proportion rises significantly, to 28% in education) and 19% are engaged in the energy and water supply division. However, the manufacturing industries taken as a whole exhibit a disproportionately low number of Welsh speakers. Only 1 in 10 of the manufacturing workforce were able to speak Welsh in 1991.

Linguistic characteristics and industry of employment: Welsh county and district analysis

The geography of the Welsh language, including proximity to the English border, has implications for the linguistic features of national employment activities, reflected at a regional level. Agriculture is a major employer in the predominantly rural counties of Wales where, broadly speaking, the Welsh language remains more highly represented in local communities. Conversely, employment in manufacturing and the service sectors is of greater overall significance in the relatively urban and industrialised areas of the more anglicised districts to the south. Consequently, in 1991, agricultural (code 01) activities represented the largest numbers of Welsh speakers employed in Dyfed and Powys and ranked a close second in Clwyd. In Gwynedd the situation is not so clear cut, due to the relatively large size of the Welsh-speaking community overall: approximately 10% of employed Welsh speakers were working in

201

each of the retail distribution, education and construction sub-classes, only exceeding the numbers engaged in agriculture and horticulture by a marginal 2%. In the counties of Mid, South and West Glamorgan and in Gwent in south Wales education rather than agriculture was the principal employer of the Welsh-speaking labour force in 1991.

However, two striking features emerge from a district-level examination of the linguistic composition of industry of employment: the relatively lower proportions of non-Welsh speakers who are agriculturally employed in the most rural counties of Wales and the comparatively higher proportions amongst the manufacturing workforce in the more industrialised areas of the south. Subsequent discussion is mainly confined to the rural counties case, since this is the main focus of our interest in the census returns. The proportion of Welsh speakers working in the agricultural sector is compared with that of the total workforce, for individual Welsh districts, in Appendix II(b).

With the exceptions of all the county districts in Gwent and South Glamorgan, the most anglicised districts of Brecknock and Radnor in Powys, Wrexham Maelor in Clwyd and the Rhymney Valley in Mid Gla-morgan, the agricultural sector across Wales employs a conspicuously higher proportion of Welsh speakers than might be expected from the linguistic structure of each district. This is a position which is not matched by any other industrial grouping and applies both within and outside rural Wales although, in the latter case, the overall numbers engaged in farming are relatively small. With regard to the pre-dominantly rural counties---that is Clwyd, Dyfed, Gwynedd and Powys--- the association between agriculture and the Welsh language is particularly strong in the districts of Colwyn and Glyndwr (Clwyd) where 75% and 70% of those working in the sector are Welsh-speaking; in Carmarthen, Ceredigion and Dinefwr (Dyfed); and in Gwynedd, where over 75% of the agricultural workforce of all districts, are able to speak Welsh. Additionally, it is perhaps more significant that in those districts where the Welsh language is relatively under-represented, for example, in Preseli and Aberconwy, the ability to speak Welsh remains a characteristic of those engaged in farming.

Even in Mid and West Glamorgan in south Wales, where less than 1% of the employed population is engaged in farming activity, the sector continues to figure significantly in the employment of Welsh speakers, despite the relatively anglicised nature of local communities. This is particularly the case in the districts of Merthyr Tydfil, Ogwr, Rhondda and Neath. It is also notable that in the most agricultural district of the Lliw Valley in West Glamorgan, half of those engaged in farming are able to speak Welsh, compared with 32% of those employed in the district as a whole.

Statistical significance of observed sample results

The association between the ability to speak Welsh and industry of employment was tested using a simple chi-square procedure. The test was applied to all 37 county districts of Wales and the results are summarised in Appendix II(a). In most cases, the calculated chi-square values were much higher than the critical values at both the 1 and 5% levels of probability, suggesting a statistically-significant association between the ability to speak Welsh and industry of employment. Furthermore, a more detailed examination of the data identified agriculture as a major contributor to the chi-square value at a district level, indicating a strong association between agricultural employment and the use of the Welsh language.

Agriculture and the Welsh language

A principal conclusion arising from the examination of OPCS data is that a clear relationship exists between the ability to speak Welsh and industry of employment and that agriculture is a major source of this association. The agricultural sector in Wales has remained a significant employer of Welsh speakers and, as such, represents a major source of income within Welsh- speaking communities as well as in the wider rural economy. In this section, we investigate some of the possible reasons for the existence of this important link between agriculture and the Welsh language: clearly, the effect of age structure may be an influential factor. The comparison of employed Welsh and non-Welsh speakers presented in Table 3 shows that a relatively higher proportion of the Welsh-speaking workforce are to be found in the older age groups. Additionally, in comparison with the labour force overall, a higher proportion of the agriculturally-employed fall into the older age categories of both linguistic groups.

A measure of the strength of this age effect is provided by comparing the percentage of Welsh speakers working in agriculture with that of the labour force in general, for each age group: the results are given at the foot of Table 3. The ability to speak Welsh is shown to be a characteristic feature of those employed in agricultural occupations across all age groups, with a notably stronger tendency amongst those over pensionable age, although the absolute numbers in this category are relatively small. This would suggest that whilst age is a contributory factor in the association between agricultural employment and the Welsh language, it is not the only factor, and consideration must also be given to other potential causes.

The predominance of family farms in Wales and the stability and social cohesion that this has given to the rural Welsh-speaking community may be of considerable interest in this context. The significance of family farming in Welsh agriculture is illustrated by an examination of the agricultural labour force statistics compiled from the June Agricultural Census. These show that only a small proportion of the labour used on Welsh farms is provided by hired workers and that labour input is dominated by farmers, their wives or husbands and other members of the family. Furthermore, the census indicates that owner-occupation, rather than farm tenancy, is the prevalent form of land tenure: there are just under 30,000 farm holdings in Wales, of which some 21,000 are owner-occupied, a further 3,000 or so being partially farmed by their owners.

In support of the relative stability of the existing farm structure, farm sales data indicates that few holdings change hands within a locality and those that do are usually comparatively small units which become amalgamated with neighbouring farms. Only about 1% of the million and a half hectares of agricultural land in Wales is sold annually, representing about 600 transactions or 2% of holdings, and most of these sales involve farms of under 100 hectares (Welsh Office, various years). There are considerable obstacles to entering the industry other than through marriage: these factors, combined with the substantial capital requirements of farm purchase (land, buildings and stock) and with competition from neighbouring local farmers wishing to expand, all help to restrict access to Welsh agriculture. Consequently, relatively few farms in Wales are sold to outsiders. These structural characteristics have promoted a high degree of stability in the farming population. Farms are inherited within the family and successive generations of Welsh speakers become socially and economically tied to particular localities, reinforcing the continuity of the traditional farm structure.

Moreover, the mobility of farming families outside agriculture is often restricted by a lack of transferable skills, as well as a strong attachment to farming as a way of life. Only small numbers of farmers leave agriculture through choice and departures from the industry are often only precipitated by financial and other external pressures. Other sectors of the economy have exhibited a far greater freedom of movement between industries, thus increasing the contact between Welsh and non-Welsh-speaking communities.

Some additional evidence on the relationship between social factors and the survival of the Welsh language in agricultural communities is drawn from a survey, undertaken in the early 1990s, of some 300 farmers in two of the most rural and Welsh-speaking areas of Wales, namely, the Cambrian Mountains and the Lleyn Peninsula (Hughes and Sherwood 1992). The survey indicated that the vast majority of farmers questioned felt that job satisfaction was central to their way of life, as well as their livelihood, and there was a general reluctance to give up farming, even under circumstances where financial rewards might prove to be greater. A large proportion of the farmers interviewed had been brought up on the family farm, had remained in farming all their lives, had acquired their farm through inheritance, and had lived on their existing farms for a considerable number of years within their present localities. Finally, many expressed the hope that they would be succeeded by a family member.

In summary, the geographical isolation of farms, the traditional structure of the industry and the nature of farming itself---young farmers' clubs, traditional market days, the pattern of the farming year, shearing, harvesting---all help to promote a sense of identity within the agricultural community and have maintained a traditional way of life which is embedded in the use of the Welsh language. Religion has also played an important part in preserving the cultural identity of Welsh farming communities, with their support for the chapel and the conduct of religious services in Welsh.

Future agricultural prospects in rural Wales

Public policies for agriculture have been one of the major factors determining the size and structure of the agricultural sector and its contribution to the rural economy. Considerable funds have been channelled to rural areas as a result of the EU's CAP and structural policies, as well as significant financial resources drawn directly from the national budgets of member states. Furthermore, farmers in the EU have benefited from both the protection of internal markets by the CAP and from subsidised exports to world markets. All of this is now changing, and in this section we consider firstly, the future policy environment for Welsh agriculture and secondly, the likely implications for farm incomes and employment in Wales.

The agricultural policy environment

In 1992, the EU agreed the most significant changes in its agricultural policies since its inception and, for the UK, since British entry into the EU in 1973. The 1992 CAP reform firmly established a new direction for policy, encompassing major changes in the method of support: from one which sustained the market prices of the various agricultural commodities at relatively high levels, by protecting the European market from foreign competition, to one in which support is provided by direct payments to farmers. The pressures which led to the 1992 reform are well-known and do not require elaboration. It should be emphasised, however, that these changes will continue to have substantial effects on the agricultural sectors of individual member states and that further "reforms" are inevitable. In particular, further changes may be necessary to facilitate the enlargement of the EU to include the six countries of eastern Europe, with whom it has signed Association Agreements, and to enable it to meet its existing and potential future obligations for freer international trade.

Given the political problems that were encountered in gaining acceptance of the 1992 CAP reform, it is unlikely that further radical changes are imminent. What is more probable is that the use of existing policy instruments will intensify in the medium term as international, budgetary and other pressures on the CAP increase. Consequently, a potential scenario for the future is envisaged as a period of two to three years in which the 1992 CAP reforms are consolidated and extended is followed by a tightening of restrictions on agricultural output and a downward pressure on prices towards the end of the century. It is likely that growing dissatisfaction with the distortions produced by these policies, and their costs, will encourage their eventual withdrawal; consequently, the development of a freer market policy is envisaged in the long term, in which market considerations are clearly separated in policy from socioeconomic objectives. Support for this view has been expressed by Buckwell et al. (1994: 17) and Davenport (1995: 80).

This is the policy environment that EU farmers and, specifically, farmers in Wales are likely to face sooner or later despite the fact that, in the short term, the potential impact of the 1992 CAP reform has been postponed (softened) by compensation payments. Indeed, in Wales, these payments together with the added cushion of successive devaluations of the green pound, lower interest rates and reduced inflation have provided some respite to the declining farm incomes of the late 1980s and early 1990s. In the longer term, however, there is likely to be renewed pressure on farm incomes and employment in rural Wales and hence on the continued survival of Welsh-speaking communities and their way of life.

Agricultural incomes and employment in rural Wales

Rural Wales is identified as the counties of Gwynedd and Powys; the districts of Colwyn and Glyndwr in Clwyd; and the districts of Carmarthen, Ceredigion, Dinefwr, Preseli and South Pembrokeshire, in Dyfed. These administrative districts broadly identify the extent of the Objective 5(b) region in Wales, in which areas having low incomes and a high dependence on agricultural employment are eligible for assistance through the EU's structural funds. All of the districts where Welsh-speaking communities are overwhelmingly reliant on agriculture now fall within the (recently extended) Objective 5b area in Wales.

The economic prospects for agriculture in rural Wales are complex, particularly in terms of jobs that might be lost from agriculture, and require remedial intervention. Whilst it is almost certain that the loss of jobs will continue, the rate and distribution of this loss will be influenced by trends in agricultural policy, the local job-creation efforts of development agencies, and the degree to which linkages, adding value to farm output, can be established. Nevertheless, a forecast of the potential impact throughout the districts of rural Wales can be made on the assumption of the most likely outcomes. These are summarised in Table 4 and indicate the extent to which full-time and full-time-equivalent labour requirements are likely to change from current levels to the years 2000 and 2005 (Hughes et al. 1995). These forecasts make clear that there is a high probability of severe loss of agricultural employment in Welsh rural communities over the coming years.

Since the decline in the number of agricultural workers appears to have reached a nadir, the loss of agricultural employment is likely to focus on full-time farmers, rather than workers. This, together with the limited availability of off-farm work, amounts to a weakening of the family farming structure, with related social as well as economic repercussions. Given the strong link between the farming community in Wales and the use of the Welsh language, it is clear that there may be important cultural implications arising from such developments.

Prognosis and future research directions

Policies to promote the Welsh language have been primarily concerned with legal status and education and, as far as policy recommendations for economic development are concerned (and there have been a great many in Wales), these have apparently lacked any explicit consideration of their potential influence on the survival of the Welsh language. Clearly, however, such policies can and will continue to have wide-ranging effects on Welsh-speaking communities, not all of which can be assumed to be beneficial.

It would appear that there is considerable scope for further research into the links between agricultural change and the Welsh language, or indeed, between economic development more generally and the maintenance of cultural and linguistic diversity. What, for example, is the experience of Welsh speakers who have been unable to remain in the agricultural sector? What jobs are available and are they able to continue to live in Welsh-speaking communities? In addition, the agricultural changes now taking place are likely to have much wider implications for the long-term future of the Welsh language. Such changes will not only act directly, through their impact on the social fabric of family farming but also indirectly, because the existence of a Welsh-speaking agricultural community helps to sustain a wider infrastructural framework in rural Wales: a framework which reflects and supports the linguistic diversity of the area which it serves.

In this respect, it is appropriate for agricultural suppliers and other industries providing farm services in Wales to employ Welsh speakers. In rural primary schools where the majority of local pupils are Welsh-speaking, the ability to speak Welsh is also a requirement for teachers. Similarly, banking services employ large numbers of Welsh speakers in rural Wales in order to offer a bilingual service to their clients, many of whom are engaged in the farm sector. The interactions between economic change and their cultural effects are important: if declining agricultural prosperity and employment has negative knock-on effects for the "Welsh-ness" of rural communities, it follows that the overall demand for services provided in Welsh may also decline. In rural areas, these processes of change might also promote a contraction in the quality and quantity of the services themselves, further eroding the relative stability of Welsh-speaking communities. The old maxim from the Irish Gael-tacht, cited by Williams (1989: 46) is equally applicable in Wales: "No jobs, no people; no people, no Gaeltacht". He argues that the key to the survival of the Welsh language is the degree to which its speakers are settled in economically-viable communities.

It is our contention, therefore, that in Wales---and this situation is reflected in other parts of the EU---there is a crucial, but mainly neglected, cultural dimension to economic development. This is an aspect which needs to be explored in relation to the potential conflict between policies for development and stated social objectives. In the case of employment creation schemes, for example, these need to take account of more than just the number of jobs created in rural Wales. Locational factors, skill requirements and availability, linkages with the rest of the economy and potential multiplier effects are also important (see, for example, Midmore et al. 1993): their social and cultural impacts may in turn affect the ability to attract tourist income to substitute for the loss of agricultural incomes. Equally, population loss can lead to abandonment of traditional land management practices, which affect the cultural attractiveness of the countryside as well as having potentially detrimental impacts on the natural environment. Conflicts will exist between objectives and the inter-relationship between economic develop-ment and cultural issues is a legitimate policy consideration.

There is also a need for comparative study within the EU, since many of the questions raised are likely to be relevant to the position of other European lesser-used and minority languages, and cultural identities. A further issue is that of the extent to which development policies can be adapted in order to take the cultural dimension into account. Since complex and often sensitive regional considerations concerning equal opportunities and human rights necessarily become involved, it is likely that in practice, there will be substantial obstacles to policy formulation. Increasingly, however, there is some indication that such issues are being addressed. Within the EU, with respect to agriculture and rural development, there is growing evidence of a more holistic approach (European Commission 1988). Whilst the assertion by Von Meyer (cited in Ockenden and Franklin 1995), that:

> . . . agriculture's most important contribution to rural development is no longer the production of feed and food, but the protection and promotion of rural amenity, ecological integrity and cultural identity . . .

is perhaps an overstatement, there can be no doubt that agricultural policy must be more fully integrated with wider policies for rural development in the future. We suggest that policies for sustainable rural development need to be broadened in order to give more explicit consideration to their social and cultural consequences.

Appendix 1
Counties and districts of Wales

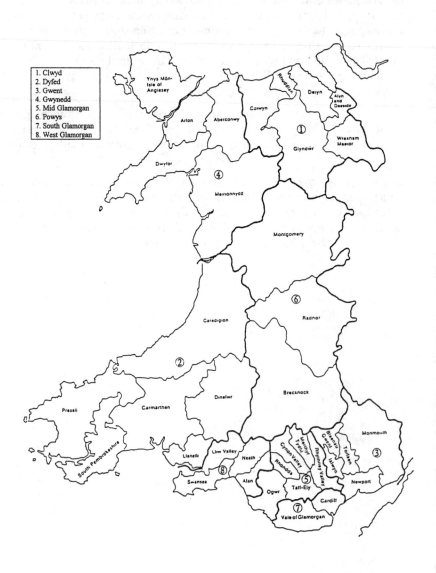

1. Clwyd
2. Dyfed
3. Gwent
4. Gwynedd
5. Mid Glamorgan
6. Powys
7. South Glamorgan
8. West Glamorgan

Source: OPCS

Appendix 2
(a) Chi-square values for observed sample results, and
(b) Welsh-speakers as a proportion of total employed in agriculture,
Wales, 1991

County	District	Values for Chi-square 1981	1991	1991 : Welsh Speakers % in agriculture	% of total [2]
Clwyd	Alyn and Deeside	38.53	50.42	23.6	5.7
	Colwyn	179.87	192.85	75.2	26.4
	Delyn	93.74	64.53	30.4	14.5
	Glyndwr	79.94	142.22	69.9	39.2
	Rhuddlan	57.00	58.56	54.5	13.9
	Wrexham Maelor	94.86	90.15	4.8	10.5
Dyfed	Carmarthen	55.61	69.17	73.3	56.1
	Ceredigion	30.84	66.66	73.6	59.3
	Dinefwr	22.73	29.79	76.4	66.5
	Llanelli	66.84	40.06	64.3	42.8
	Preseli	142.38	166.62	53.4	25.2
	South Pembrokeshire	9.94	18.81	9.3	7.0
Gwent	Blaenau Gwent	9.69	17.09	0.0	1.2
	Islwyn	3.84	17.26	0.0	2.7
	Monmouth	43.94	24.86	1.0	1.9
	Newport	27.36	37.63	2.3	2.3
	Torfaen	6.68	14.69	0.0	2.2
Gwynedd	Aberconwy	120.24	91.45	76.0	35.0
	Arfon	35.01	29.58	80.6	72.8
	Dwyfor	59.28	67.18	84.0	75.1
	Meirionnydd	61.67	100.63	88.7	65.4
	Ynys Mon	44.50	86.98	90.8	62.8
M. Glam.	Cynon Valley	67.08	33.48	9.1	6.7
	Merthyr Tyfdil	25.82	25.06	18.2	4.0
	Ogwr	78.52	65.82	15.9	5.6
	Rhondda	27.11	52.79	20.0	4.1
	Rhymney Valley	26.95	36.66	0.0	5.8
	Taff-Ely	75.72	75.90	12.5	7.5
Powys	Brecknock	95.95	49.13	13.2	18.5
	Montgomeryshire	72.66	105.16	35.2	18.7
	Radnorshire	13.50	25.62	1.3	3.5
S. Glam.	Cardiff	219.45	245.95	5.9	6.1
	Vale of Glamorgan	58.03	37.63	4.7	5.7
W. Glam.	Lliw Valley	48.51	43.11	50.0	32.0
	Neath	24.27	51.90	22.2	10.1
	Port Talbot (Afan)	19.89	24.10	14.3	6.5
	Swansea	47.78	47.58	9.5	8.2

1% level : χ^2 critical value:	21.7	23.2	
5% level : χ^2 critical value:	16.9	18.3	

[1] Welsh speakers as a proportion of total employed in the combined agriculture, forestry and fishing division (SIC, code 0).
[2] Welsh speakers as a proportion of total employed in each district.

References

Aitchison, J. and H. Carter. 1994. *A Geography of the Welsh Language 1961-1991.* Cardiff: University of Wales Press.

Bramwell, B. 1994. Rural tourism and sustainable rural tourism. *Journal of Sustainable Tourism* 2: 1-6.

Buckwell, A., J. Haynes, S. Danidova, V Courboin, and A. Kwiecinski. 1994. *Feasibility of an Agricultural Strategy to Prepare the Countries of Central and Eastern Europe for EU Accession.* Final report to Directorate-General of the European Commission, 16 Dec. 1994.

Central Statistical Office. 1979. *Standard Industrial Classification* (revised 1980). London: HMSO.

Chapman, N. D. C., G. O. Hughes and M. E. Jones. 1990. *Dadansoddiad o Gyfrifiad 1981 ar weithgaredd economaidd a'r iaith Gymraeg / Analysis of the 1981 Census for Economic Activity and the Welsh Language.* Aberystwyth: Department of Economics and Agricultural Economics, University of Wales.

Davenport, M. S. 1995. Changes in the pattern of world trade in agricultural products. In B. J. Marshall, and F. A. Miller (eds.), *Priorities for a New Century: Agriculture, Food and Rural Policies in the European Union.* Centre for Agricultural Strategy, CAS Paper 31, Reading.

Day, G. 1989. "A million on the move?": Population change and rural Wales. *Contemporary Wales* 3: 137-159.

European Commission. 1988. *The Future of Rural Society.* Commission communication transmitted to the Council and to the European Parliament on 29 July 1988. COM(88) 371 final, Bulletin of the European Communities, (4/88).

Hale, K., M. Krauss, L. J. Watahomigie, A. Y. Yamamoto, C. Craig, La V. N. Jeanne and N. C. England. 1992. Endangered languages. *Language* 68: 1-42.

Hughes, G. O., A.-M. Sherwood and P. Midmore. 1995. *The Implications of CAP Reform for Rural Wales.* Report to the Development Board for Rural Wales and Welsh Development Agency (unpublished). Aberystwyth: Welsh Institute of Rural Studies, University of Wales.

Hughes, G. O. and A.-M. Sherwood. 1995. *Economic Activity and Linguistic Characteristics in Wales: Analysis of Census of Population Results, 1981-1991.* Unpublished report, *To Mentor a Business.*

Aberystwyth: Welsh Institute of Rural Studies, University of Wales.

Hughes, G. O. and A.-M. Sherwood. 1992. *Socio-economic Aspects of Designating the Cambrian Mountains and the Llyn Peninsula as Environmentally-sensitive Areas.* Final report to the Welsh Office, Aberystwyth: Department of Economics and Agricultural Economics, University of Wales.

Jones, M. E. 1989. *The Linguistic Implications of Agricultural Change.* M.Sc. dissertation. Aberystwyth: Department of Economics and Agricultural Economics, University of Wales.

Krauss, M. 1992. The world's languages in crisis. *Language* 68: 4-10.

Lane, B. 1994. What is rural tourism? *Journal of Sustainable Tourism* 2: 7-21.

Massey, D. and J. Allen. 1988. *Uneven Re-development: Cities and Regions in Transition: A Reader.* London: Hodder and Stoughton.

Midmore, P. 1988. *An Analysis of Agricultural Statistics for the Mid-Wales Development Area.* Unpublished report to the Development Board for Rural Wales. Aberystwyth: Department of Agricultural Economics and Marketing, University of Wales.

Midmore, P., G. O. Hughes, D. I. Bateman, N. D. H. Chapman, C. Ray, M. Haines and N. H. Lampkin. 1993. *An Integrated Agricultural Strategy for Rural Wales.* Unpublished report to Development Board for Rural Wales. Aberystwyth: Department of Agricultural Sciences, University of Wales.

Myrdal, G. 1957. *Economic Theory and Under-developed Regions.* London: Duckworth.

Norgaard, R. B. 1992. Coevolution of economy, society and environment. In P. Ekins and M. Max-Neef (eds.), *Real-life Economics: Understanding Wealth Creation.* London: Routledge. Pp. 76-86.

Norgaard, R. B. 1994. *Development Betrayed.* London: Routledge.

Ockenden, J. and M. Franklin. 1995. *European Agriculture: Making the CAP Fit the Future.* Chatham House Papers. London: The Royal Institute of International Affairs.

Office of Population Censuses & Surveys (OPCS). 1991. *Census 1991: Definitions, Great Britain.* London: HMSO.

_____. 1994. *1991 Census: Cyfrifriad 1991, Welsh Language/Cymraeg, Wales/Cymru.* London: HMSO.

Peterken, G. 1993. *Woodland Conservation and Management.* 2nd ed. London: Chapman and Hall.

Urry, J. 1990. *The Tourism Gaze.* London: Sage.

Welsh Office. (various years). *Welsh Agricultural Statistics.* Cardiff: Welsh Office.

Williams, C. H. 1989. New domains of the Welsh language: Education, planning and the law. *Contemporary Wales* 3: 41-76.

Part Three
SUSTAINABLE APPROACHES TO TOURISM DEVELOPMENT

11 Environmental interpretation as a disciplinary interface in sustainable development

Richard Prentice

Interpretation defined in the context of sustainable development

Environmental policy now ranks with economic and social policies as a component of an integrated political agenda in marginal regions (cf. Prentice 1993a): not just as an ideology of "green" awareness but more tangibly both as a quality of life issue for residents and as an "export" product for tourists to enjoy. For its inherent and immediate qualities, but also frequently for its earnings potential, environmental sustainability enters political debate. For such debate to be informed, scientific and interpretative attention needs to supplement sensory awareness and ideological passion. Sustainable development is here defined in the practical sense as being development which does not have unacceptable opportunity costs in terms of physical and social environments, policy objectives and tourists' demands. Intentionally, this definition encompasses both weak sustainability and strong sustainability as criteria (Glasson et al. 1994). Weak sustainability is the criterion that the physical environment may be irrevocably exploited if there is substitutability between the environment in question and others. Strong sustainability is the criterion that any irrevocable exploitation is unacceptable. In practice, however, issues of sustainability often focus on remote, "rural" landscapes and communities in need of export industries competitive in the modern economy. Increasingly, some forms of tourism have been regarded as one form of development potentially acceptable in these areas (Murphy 1985, Prentice 1993a and 1993b, Commonwealth Department of Tourism 1994, STB 1994, WTB 1994, Wight 1994). Tourism development of this kind requires not just accommodation provision, but also attraction development; in other words, it requires the design, development and promotion of tourism products where they did not exist before. The interpretation of place, or environment, is seen as potentially one such form of sustainable tourism development. For example,

> Ecotourism is nature-based tourism that involves education and interpretation of the natural environment and is managed to be ecologically sustainable. This definition recognises that "natural environment" includes cultural components and that "ecologically-sustainable" involves an appropriate return to the local community and long-term conservation of the resource (Commonwealth Department of Tourism 1994: 17).

From the perspective quoted above, the resource is not just the environment visited by tourists, but also its interpretation to them, thereby enhancing the core resources of landscape, fauna, flora and the like. Even the most unlikely industrial relicts are being developed in this way as unique selling points of marginal areas: most notably the coal mining pasts of Cape Breton and Wales (Prentice et al. 1993, Prentice 1994a).

Interpretation is defined as the identification and explanation of what may be seen or imagined at a place. Interpretation may be achieved through a wide range of media, including verbal communication, music, smells, displays, notices and labels, diagrams, information panels, models, "touch-tables", boardwalks, guidebooks, puzzles, guided walks, period rooms, audio-visual techniques, virtual reality, other computer interactive techniques, and theatre. The ubiquitous heritage or visitor centre is a further form of the product, with a range of museum variants such as open-air museums, museum villages and living history museums (Shafernich 1993). Heritage and visitor centres often represent a recently-developed but substantial tourism resource in marginal regions. For example, in Great Britain, Forest Enterprise advertises thirty-six of these centres as introductions to its forests, representing a significant tourism resource for Wales, the Scottish Highlands and the borderlands of Cumbria, Northumbria, and Galloway in England and Scotland. While heritage and visitor centres may be thought of as gateway media, orientating the tourist (and meeting all the interpretative demands of many), the advantage of many low-technology media to sustainable tourism development is that they are comparatively cheap to install and maintain, and can be non-intrusive when used outdoors.

Interpretation may be of real artefacts, activities or settings, or equally of their staged or contrived equivalents. Interpretation can take place at different levels of objective. Most simply, it is the pointing out of what may be significant in that which is being viewed. More elaborately, interpretation may enhance the experience of a place, thereby yielding insight into what is being seen. More elaborately still, interpretation can facilitate the understanding of the social, economic and physical environmental systems inherent in a place, through the enhancement of learning. As such, interpretation as a minimum may have an informational, experiential or educational function. It can range from window-shopping on (or gazing at) the environment,[1] to fieldwork ("getting one's boots dirty"); ranging from passive to active learning. So defined, interpretation is different from entertainment in objective; not that interpretation should not be entertaining, but rather that it should be more, providing as a minimum a metaphorical window on the world present, past or imagined futures, through which the visitor may at least gaze.

However, other objectives are also common beyond this minimalist stance. Environmental interpretation is frequently a process of communicating to people the significance of a place so that they can enjoy it more, understand its importance, and develop a positive attitude towards conservation. As such, interpretation is used to enhance the enjoyment of place, to convey symbolic meanings, and to facilitate attitudinal or behavioural change. The latter is frequently an objective of interpretative provision in treasured environments, such as national parks (and, indeed, as education of the tourist may be found in the Australian quotation given above). However, interpretation can have a wider role, and one beyond the scope of this paper: the pertinence of interpretation in promoting national identities and as a means of propaganda are examples of the application of these objectives to goals set on a wide ideological canvas, and demands a questioning of the motivations inherent implicitly or explicitly in interpretative provisions. Nationalisms are generally made; they do not simply happen (Shafer 1972, Taylor 1985, Prentice 1990 and 1991a). Interpretation can be used to facilitate a sense of belonging; it can be used to include or to exclude, and as such is a tempting political tool. Equally, implicit in the recognition that all interpretation is value-laden is the questioning of whose values are being interpreted to whom. In a multicultural Europe, issues such as these are increasingly the subject of academic attention. How does one seek to interpret the contribution of German and Russian influences in the Polish landscape, for example; or of the English and Scottish in Ireland? The interpretation of slavery presents similar issues, but also that of the morality of making people confront a past, and why this should be attempted:

> Teachers I have worked with, doing Black case studies on access courses etc., have testified to the value of having objects in hand and how the physical impact of handling shackles has successfully brought out the enforced and constraining elements in the process of keeping

African people enslaved. Clearly there is a strong case for bringing this emotional subjectivity to bear on the study of history . . . . When exhibiting some shackles at an open day in a Black studies centre, adults acknowledged the value of physical learning but were loathe to take up the opportunity. In some instances there was an objection to being offered the opportunity of handling. Those against it argued that it is too emotionally frightening to make that contact. (Morris 1995: 15)

As implicitly value-laden, interpreters may need to be as careful that their product is equally sustainable socially as it is sustainable in terms of impacts on the physical environment. More generally, principles of interpretation for sustainable development need to be derived, possibly at least in part mirroring the Australian principles of ecotourism development listed in Appendix 1.

Interpretation may be supplied to the visitors to a place, but equally to its distant viewers in space or time. Modern electronics increasingly offer the potential of separating the need to visit a place from its interpretation, through virtual reality systems and the Internet (Williams and Hobson 1994). Art gallery collections may increasingly be accessed remotely, and selectively, for example by artist, picture types or period and place. The Museum of Scotland Advanced Information Computer Systems (MOSAICS) is intended to give remote access to images of artefacts in the collection, and also to facilitate their examination in "three dimensions" on the user's computer screen in perspectives and detail unavailable to most visitors in reality. Equally, classroom education or library research can be thought of as a more traditional form of interpretation removed from the actual place to which it may refer. What we are as yet unsure about is whether developments in electronic technology, by removing interpretation from the place interpreted, will become an encouragement to tourism, to see in reality what has been experienced in remote form; or whether such developments will act as substitutes for tourism. If such developments are in fact jointly consumed with tourism, increased passive awareness of environmental issues (Prentice 1993a) coupled with increasing computer access, may well lead to an expansion in tourism trips to attractive environments, so as to see in reality that already seen remotely. On-site interpretative provision needs be able to respond to this demand, and planned as part of an overall strategy including remote and local interpretative needs. In this scenario, on-site and remote provision are inherently tied together as a tourism product, and one of particular relevance to the marginal regions of the Atlantic Rim.

As to date much interpretative development has been based upon hunch rather than science, the objective of this paper is to review issues pertinent to the development of interpretative provisions as a form of sustainable tourism development. In doing so, more issues will be raised than answered, and elements of an agenda for research thereby identified.

Interpretation as enhancing experience

Tourist consumption can be either instrumental to a higher goal (such as understanding) through gaining experiences of place, or simply experience-seeking with no higher goal. The latter is known as hedonic consumption, as it is generally orientated to pleasurable consumption. However, for physical and cultural environmental "products", experiences are rarely so hedonic that no insight is gained (Prentice et al. 1993), in contrast to pleasure park or fair ground thrills, for example. As such, the tourism market is clearly differentiated by attraction providers: those seeking to provide purely hedonic experiences and those seeking to provide instrumental but also pleasurable experiences. As such, successful tourist attractions increasingly focus explicitly on the facilitation of experiences for their visitors. The focus of this paper is with those seeking to provide more than just hedonic experiences.

For example, the Oban Sea Life Centre is promoted as "breathtaking . . . endearing . . . amazing . . . thrilling . . . enchanting . . . relaxing . . . involving . . . entertaining" (Oban Sea Life Centre promotional leaflet 1995), and its St Andrew's equivalent as "endearing . . . involving . . . exciting . . . endearing . . . relaxing . . . touching" (St Andrew's Sea Life Centre promotional leaflet 1995). Deep Sea World at North Queensferry provides the experience of shoals of fish swimming around the visitor, through the illusion of a sea bed tunnel. In this manner the product is not the fish but the experience of close encounters with fish. Likewise, Discovery Point at Dundee seeks to provide an "adventure" involving the visitor:

> As you attend the launch in 1901 and listen to the speeches, imagine the thoughts of the crew as they prepare for the voyage into dangerous uncharted waters. (Discovery Point promotional leaflet 1995)

In their imagination visitors are taken back in time, as in a historical drama, novel or film, or placed in a different physical environment.

Attractions of this kind are seeking to provide simulated means of psychologically immersing visitors in their exhibits, thereby involving, absorbing, or engrossing their visitors' thoughts and imagination and providing a partial illusion of being in a different time or place (Bitgood 1990, Shafernich 1993). Interpretative media may in this sense be seen as a "technology of imagination" (MacDonald 1992). Attempts at immersion are a response to criticism of more conventional display techniques which have been shown not to engross all visitors (McManus 1989). Immersion as a goal of interpreters may seem superficially similar to the concept of flow (Csikszentmihalyi and Csikszentmihalyi 1988) found in psychology, which partially describes a similar state of engagement; principally a loss of the sense of time passing, a lack of self-consciousness, and the dominance of intrinsic rewards. However, flow is also characterised by intense participant involvement, deep concentration and a transcendence of the sense of self. It also predicts optimal experience in situations where challenges given and skills offered exceed personal averages. As immersion may not involve challenge, nor unusual demands on skills, deep concentration, intense involvement or transcendence, flow is more appropriately equated with extreme immersion. As a principal objective for interpreters, the facilitation of flow is unrealistic, as the extents of involvement, challenges and skills demanded are unrealistic expectations of many tourists seeking to gaze on history or place. Immersion, with its focus on settings, is a more realisable objective in product design.

Not all immersion is stimulated by simulated settings. Hill and forest walks may likewise be thought of as a mix of experiences immersing participants, but using non-simulated, but often managed environments as settings. Mixes of experiences include, for example:

challenge	fun	exhilaration	exhaustion
excitement	fear	peace	concern
relaxation	stimulation	boredom	refreshment
amazement	achievement	tiredness	upset
adventure	inspiration	communion	uplift
escape	beauty	fulfilment	invigoration
recreation	information	enlightenment	awe
thought	immersion	entertainment	relief

Forest and mountain experiences are potential products of many marginal regions of the Atlantic Rim; potential in the sense that for many tourists such resources need to be managed, particularly in terms of perceived risk. The image of the backpacker becoming the frontiersman and not wanting any human contact is a minority product, at least in Britain. Remoteness, the extent to which an individual perceives him or herself as removed from the sights and sounds of human activity, may not be the appropriate product to seek to provide, unless a minority demand is being met. As such, so-called primitive or semi-primitive experiences, out of sight or sound, or distant, from human activities (US Dept. of Agriculture 1990), should not be thought to be a dominant demand in the design of attractions, even in many national parks. In contrast, the interpreted experience may be part of the managed product demanded. For people in Britain, at least, land management and naturalness may not conflicting sentiments (Prentice 1992) however contradictory they may seem otherwise: interpretation is part of "managed naturalness". This is perhaps unsurprising in view of the importance of gardening as a leisure activity in Britain, and the management of flora which gardening involves, both in design and maintenance.

Not only may tourist experiences be particular to a place, they may be particular to individual visitors and may, or may not, be dependent upon the enhancement of the core product (for example, a walk) by interpretation. For walkers seeking to reach the summit of Ben Lomond, for example, the relevance of interpretation may be slight, except to identify the views from the summit. But in less dramatic landscapes, where the physical challenge may be less, interpretation may convert an otherwise unnoteworthy landscape into something appreciated. Likewise, for some of the visitors at Loch Lomond for whom the walk to the summit of Ben Lomond is unwanted or too demanding physically, interpretation of the oak woodlands around the lakeside is a potential enhancement of their visit to the loch. In other words, attention to market segments (sub-groups) is required in interpretative design, and the realisation that different types and extents of interpretative provision are needed, rather than single products. In practice, however, the single interpretative product strategy is frequently found; its designers implicitly assuming that every visitor either wants the same interpretative messages or ought to. These segments need to be defined in terms of the experiences gained, and possibly the longer-term benefits gained.

To remark that visitors bring with them a range of memories and values is self-evident, but pertinent to whether or not interpretation is likely to be effective. If interpretative provision is to stimulate cultural imagining we need to understand the visions and particular predispositions for particular imaginings which are brought by tourists to attractions (MacDonald 1992); in particular, we need to understand their misconceptions. Nor at present do we know how the experiences we seek to facilitate through interpretative products are influenced by, and in turn influence, the general values held by market segments. Nor have visitor segments at attractions been defined even in terms of generalised value systems (Pottick 1983), such as the desire for respect from others, security, self-respect, belonging, relationships, accomplishment, enjoyment and self-fulfilment. Nor has the issue of complex choice (Stewart and Stynes 1994) been addressed generally as a basis of tourism demand.

Complex choice is where decisions have long-term implications, where the decision process is extended over time, and where the framing of the problem may change as decision-makers learn more about themselves. In other words, learning, adaptation and feedback processes are essential to understanding complex choices. Of potential relevance to environmental sustainability, a complex choice system relating macro-issues of "green" consumerism, to consumers' cognitive frameworks, to their decision processes and to their behaviour as tourists can at present only be sketched rather than fully defined or calibrated. Yet the definition of the elements in such a model and their use in identifying market segments is essential if environmentalism is to be promoted as both an ideology and tourism product. In contrast, at present our understanding derives from segmentations of tourist demand generally.

Reference to segmentations of tourist demand generally shows that the demand for interpreted products seems increasingly world-wide among the affluent and educated middle classes. For example, when reviewing tourism markets around the Pacific Rim, Helber (1995) has commented,

> The ageing of the baby boomers is creating a new demand for health and wellness centres, gourmet food and beverage experiences, soft adventure travel and boutique/retreat resorts which emphasize personal attention and a strong sense of place.

> The growth and increasing affluence of minority populations and the expanding middle class of rapidly developing countries in regions such as Southeast Asia will bring renewed interest in luxury facilities and amenities which equate to self-fulfilment, status, image-building and quality of life. Elderly populations are broadening their interests through travel to destinations that combine learning experiences with leisure and recreational activities. (Helber 1995: 4, emphases added)

Evidence from Europe, North America and Asia confirms the generality of these trends (Prentice 1994b, Richards 1994). Such demands are part of the wider post-modernist conceptualisation of consumption as a mix of internalised meanings and external symbolism (Doherty et al. 1992). Increasingly, demand is for non-standardised tourism products by the groups identified above (Poon 1989). Indeed, *in*authentic interpretations of environment may suffice as meanings and symbols if educative needs are subordinate to experiential needs. Degrees of contrivedness in attractions may be found from the uncontrived but ruined industrial structure, through the museum with artefacts removed to it from their original location, to the heritage park with authentic buildings in an inauthentic townscape, to the park with inauthentic buildings to the fantasy or dream park which is totally contrived. As such, interpretation can range from the authentic to the inauthentic, and still provide a product acceptable to some tourists (if not to educators and academics).

Agenda-setting for interpretative provision

As an emergent science, environmental interpretation has to date largely relied upon other disciplines to define its subject matter and audience. In other words, use has been made of literatures derived already, which have usually been produced for purposes other than interpretation beyond their immediate discipline. As such, much interpretation has been supply-led in terms of its informational base. However, if the objective of interpretation is to meet the diverse needs of consumers, and in doing so thereby to popularise academic disciplines, environmental interpretation needs increasingly to determine these other agendas as much as responding to them. In particular, relevant disciplines need to be identified, and their inter-linkages, potential and present, defined. Such linkages span the traditional arts, science and management disciplines.

Such linkages may be defined in two ways. Either through professional assertion, or through consumer preference. In the long run the latter is the appropriate basis for product development, as it places a central focus on the needs of the consumers of interpretation. This is the service industry model of product development whereby the transiency of services as memories and promises is implicitly recognised, as is their essentially one-off production run quality of personal tailoring and consumer involvement in their delivery (Irons 1994). However, our present lack of knowledge as to these preferences impels reliance upon professional judgement. The latter should, however, be viewed as an intermediate strategy for product design; while in the meantime greater attention is paid to consumer evaluation of environment. This intermediate strategy encompasses both what we seek to provide and what objectives we evaluate provision by.

Basing interpretation on what tourists value in the environment

Much of the existing literature on consumer valuation of the environment has been economic, and often summary in style. As such it addresses a price to be placed on environment, rather than the aspects of the environment which are culturally valued. These studies derive from the welfare economist's concern to measure intangibles in a manner by which they may be reduced to a comparable basis of assessment to other more tangible costs and benefits. However, if opportunity costs are accepted as the fundamental basis of valuation, attempts to measure the monetary value placed on environments by the consumer are only one means of expressing valuation, since some opportunities which may have to be forgone to allow a particular use may have no unambiguous monetary value.

The economic methodologies may be divided into those which require some form of customer survey to elicit expressed values (for example, contingent valuation) and those which measure observed behaviour as a proxy for values (for example, travel-cost method and hedonic pricing). Contingent valuation directly asks the respondent for his or her willingness to pay towards the preservation of an asset (Hanley 1989, Benson 1993, Farber et al. 1993, Turner 1993, Bateman et al. 1994, Grosclaude and Soguel 1994, Willis 1994). The travel-cost method assumes that environmental value is related to the travel cost incurred in reaching that environment (Balkan and Kahn 1988, Willis and Garrod 1991, Randall 1994). Hedonic pricing attempts to evaluate environmental attributes from among other attributes determining prices actually achieved in the marketplace (Garrod and Willis 1992, Kask and Maani 1992). For example, all other things being equal, in a given destination area hotels with panoramic views of lakes and mountains should be able to charge higher prices than those located next to the area's rubbish tip, and this premium should be able to be estimated statistically through multiple regression. A note on terminology is opportune, emphasising the diverse disciplinary inputs into tourism analysis. In this case, the term "hedonic" refers to the pleasurable elements incorporated into the function defining price, rather than to pleasurable consumption as the sole objective of experience as defined earlier. In this case an economist or geographer is likely to imply a different model in their use of the term "hedonic" than is implied by consumer behaviouralists!

The travel-cost method and hedonic pricing are essentially techniques of inferred valuation, but the latter may give some insight into the elements affecting the valuation. Irrespective of their summary nature, by definition, hypothetical valuations are unreal and may, or may not, apply to real circumstances. Likewise, inferred valuations rely on the adequacy of the inference made. For example, it is assumed that travel cost incurred implies a valuation of the environment visited, rather than a valuation of a broader tourist experience or a response to imperfect information. Nor does it allow for the effect of consumer surplus, where some tourists might have paid more to reach a destination had they have needed to. Whereas such a method may be valid for long journeys (intracontinental or intercontinental perhaps), the logic of interpreting travel costs as a valuation of the destination is less clear for more local travel which may be multi-faceted.

Leisure science has also addressed the issue of valuation, in terms of the attributes gained from leisure. As such, this literature has a pertinence to the valuation of environment. This literature sees leisure as multi-faceted and identifies dimensions of experience from which environment may be valued. This literature also suggests hierarchies of demand. One such hierarchy may be termed the Manning-Haas-Driver-Brown Sequential Hierarchy of Recreational Demands (Manning 1986, Prentice 1993c, Prentice and Light 1994). This hierarchy identifies four levels of demand: activities, settings, experiences and benefits. Level 1 represents demand for activities themselves. Level 2 concerns settings, including environmental, social, and management settings, and the experience of these settings for particular activities being pursued. Finally, Level 4 demands refer to ultimate benefits which come from satisfying experiences derived from participation and can either be psychological or societal. The Manning-Haas hierarchy implies that all experiences are instrumental to benefits, and therefore have particular relevance to non-hedonic consumption. However, the identification of such benefits can be problematic as tourists' identification of them may be dependent on their personality, articulateness and thoughtfulness. For this reason, an alternative hierarchical approach can be used to inform this hierarchy.

This alternative hierarchical framework is termed the Means-End Chain (Gutman 1982 and 1988, Perkins and Reynolds 1988, Klenosky et al. 1993). Like the Manning-Haas hierarchy, the usefulness of the scheme is the ability to link the concrete and the abstract entities into a single framework. It specifically focuses on the linkages between the attributes that exist in products (the means), the consequences for the consumer provided by the attributes and the personal values (the ends) which the consequences reinforce (Reynolds and Gutman 1988). Simply expressed, the means-end chain works on three levels of abstraction: product attributes, consequences and personal values. For the understanding of tourist experiences and benefits, a focus on the consequences of attributes (which may be attributes of activities or settings) is important. Of critical importance to operationalising this methodology is the why question, for example, "Why, or in what ways, did you find that beautiful?" or "Why is that important to you?" This methodology is known as laddering.

Demand hierarchies of these kinds offer the potential by which we can identify the dimensions by which tourists value environment, thereby providing the basis for interpretative design based on consumer needs. They also offer the opportunity of the substitutability of activities or settings to achieve the same ends. Such substitutability may include substituting environments as different settings, by encouraging tourists to substitute holiday destinations through promotion and interpretative product development. This possibility offers both an opportunity and a challenge to marginal regions seeking to develop tourism products through interpretative developments. The opportunity is to divert tourists from more established destinations, usually for additional rather than main holidays. The challenge is to ensure that the interpretative product is sufficiently distinctive not be to readily substitutable by one elsewhere.

Developing interpretative provisions in the absence of consumer information

A basis for interpretative developments in a scientific understanding of how tourists value environments, and importantly, how valued experiences can be facilitated through interpretative products, remains at best an objective. It does not presently exist to inform developments. As such, interpretative science is at most emergent, a proto-science so to speak. With optimism, the term "science" will be used. However, currently the definition of both what to interpret and whether or not that interpretation is effective is largely a matter of practice, reliant on professional judgement, and is frequently technology-led, and therefore cost-led. Exceptions are principally to be found in the museum profession, where traditional museum objectives are being questioned in an increasingly competitive world, and different museologies are being advocated.

Most environmental interpretative design is undertaken in the absence of regional interpretative strategies, although exceptions in this regard can be identified, notably in Ireland (Browne 1992). A distinctive Irish product is being built around five key themes, namely:

Live Landscapes (for example, mountain and moorland, bogs and wetland)

Making a Living (for example, emigration and famine, working with the sea)

Saints and Religion (for example, pagan Ireland, early Christianity)

Building a Nation (for example, invasion and conquest, the Anglo-Irish)

Spirit of Ireland (for example, literary Ireland, language, folklore, legend)

More usually designation strategies identify reserves or conservation areas without an overall strategy to integrate their interpretation nationally or regionally, or indeed to justify their selection as regional examples of landscape or other environment (Prentice 1993a). Regionally important geological or geomorphological sites in Britain (NCC 1990) are one exception to the latter failing. Without strategic guidance, the interpretation of local environments can lead both to duplication and to omission. It can also hinder the development of tourist trails seeking to integrate attractions into packages facilitating themed experiences.

At present practice largely defines what we consider important to interpret. Much of this information is abstracted from established academic disciplines which determine their research agendas with little, if any, reference to the interests of a wider public in their subject, other than in terms of funding. The principal disciplines included as feeders of interpretation are environmental management, the physical environmental sciences, archaeology, historical geography and history; secondary disciplines are the leisure sciences and consumer behaviour. The inclusion of environmental management is a reminder of its recurrence in the ideology of interpretation as environmentalism, and serves further as a reminder of the value-laden nature of interpretative science.

This present situation is deficient in that interpretative science is in effect tagged onto more established academic disciplines, traditionally having influenced some archaeologists in their site investigations, but little else. A more optimistic picture is where interpretative science is more integrated into the other disciplines directly, and indirectly via environmental management. This view points to the pertinence of environmental management as an associated focal point of disciplines, and therefore implicitly emphasises our need to more fully understand environmentalist motivations among tourists. In this more optimistic view, interpretative science affects the content of other disciplines, giving it a pro-active role. In effect, interpretative proto-science has become interpretative science. Not only should interpretative science be linked directly to agenda determination in those disciplines through which messages are likely to be gained, it should also be linked directly in agenda formulation to consumer behaviour, and through this, to leisure sciences. In other words it should be linked to the understanding of consumers' demands for interpretation, and implicitly to their valuation of environmental elements as worthy of interpretation as tourism products.

Just as our current judgements as to what is pertinent to interpret rely on practice, so does what we choose to evaluate. Evaluation has so far not been a prominent part of interpretation; professional best practice has usually been assumed, rather than demonstrated through rigorous evaluation. This is particularly problematic as the experiences and benefits derived by visitors to attractions can not be reliably understood from casual observation. Of the formal evaluation which has been undertaken, most has focused on what visitors notice at attractions (Herbert 1989, Light 1995a), their experiences while visiting (Prentice et al. 1993, Beeho and Prentice, 1995), what they learn or fail to learn during their visit (Prentice 1991b, 1993d and 1995; Light 1995b), or on their memories of an attraction subsequent to their visit (McManus 1993). As yet too few studies have been undertaken to enable the making of other than very hesitant recommendations about the effectiveness of individual media, or of media mixes. The general point, however, is that until we know what tourists value in the environment, and incorporate this preference structure in our interpretative planning, we cannot make this the focus of our evaluations. In other words, not only have we little scientific proof that the media commonly used in interpretation are effective to different types of tourists, but we may be choosing inappropriate criteria by which to judge effectiveness.

Conclusions

Tourism is about experiences of place, and environmental interpretation in its minimalist form can potentially meet demands for information, experiential insight and education. As such interpretative provisions are products which can meet the demands of some market segments, principally those tourists for whom hedonic experiences are not the primary objective of their visit. Surprisingly, we know little about tourists' experiences, and if interpretative provisions are to have their greatest effect, research attention needs to be directed to the experiential elements of tourism, and the benefits tourists derive from being tourists (cf. Prentice 1993d). As so little is presently known, inductive methodologies are implied as a basis for beginning to remedy these deficiencies (cf. Beeho and Prentice 1995).

In its minimalist form, interpretation can provide a metaphorical window on the world. However, such a function is usually enhanced with other objectives: principally, that of conveying the significance of places or artefacts, and that of inducing a positive attitude towards conservation. Potentially, interpretation relates to much wider tourism strategies to develop ecotourism or heritage tourism and to environmentalist ideologies. Generally, the potential of interpretation at the strategic level has been ignored, although this paper has drawn attention to notable exceptions to this in Irish and Australian policy. Much greater strategic planning of interpretative provision is desirable if themed experiences of place are to be promoted as distinctive selling points of marginal destinations. Nor do we adequately understand the potential of interpretation as a means of encouraging environmentalist ideologies. As a basis for such developments we need first to understand the tourist as a "green" consumer. The marginal regions of the Atlantic Rim are the potential beneficiaries of such developments, and as such need to seize the initiative in research of this kind.

As interpretation is now commonplace at attractions it might be thought to be non-problematic. This view implicitly assumes that professionals know best. Such an assumption is untested, and likely in part at least to be wrong as professionals have not systematically researched consumer valuations of the environment as the basis for their designs. At most we understand consumer demands from summary likes and dislikes recorded in national tourist board surveys. But in any systematic way we do not know how consumers value elements of the environment; and particularly how tourists value environmental elements. At best interpretative products have generally been test-marketed, rather than based upon in-depth market research. Central to a research agenda for interpretation must be the way in which tourists value environmental elements, and how such valuations can inform how we interpret the environment to tourists. Such analyses need to be related to those of tourist experiences, so that comparable market segments can be defined.

At present we also lack a systematic understanding of the effectiveness of interpretative media. Because of this, interpretative provisions may be less effective than they could be, and in consequence the tourist experience may be unnecessarily sub-optimal. This situation has serious implications for the relative competitiveness of destination areas, particularly those more marginal to traditional tourism flows. As yet interpretation is a proto-science, and needs to become a science. A research agenda for interpretation needs to focus on the effectiveness of media and of mixes of media. Once again, marginal regions could usefully seize the initiative in such research.

The discussion has shown that interpretative science has the potential to become a disciplinary focus, along with environmental management. Both environmental interpretation and management are inherently multidisciplinary, and need to partake in research agenda setting. Australian policy provides an example of interpretation and management being developed together at a national level. Regional strategies to operationalise this focus may be desirable, and once again marginal regions could usefully take the initiative here. By realising that environmental interpretation is inherently multi-disciplinary, the role of the professional interpreters ceases to be one of specialist designers working in media, and becomes extended to include strategic design, consumer behaviour, environmental appraisal and performance review.

The recognition of the potential of interpretative science in the development of tourism products relevant to the post-modernist consumer implicitly offers challenges to the current practice of interpreting the environment; challenges which are all the more pertinent to marginal economies seeking to develop tourism products. It also implies that contemporary tourism products will need to be increasingly thought through before they are developed, thereby increasing the entry costs to tourism provision. For marginal regions the investment needed to successfully compete for tourists is likely therefore to increase.

Note

[1] Sarah Clarke of Queen Margaret College, Edinburgh, is operationalising such a perspective at Deep Sea World.

Acknowledgement

The comments of Ms Sarah Clarke and Ms Sinead Guerin, both of Queen Margaret College, Edinburgh, on aspects of this paper during its drafting are gratefully acknowledged.

Appendix 1
Australian Principles of Ecotourism Development

1   To facilitate the application of ecologically-sustainable principles and practices across the tourism industry.
2   To develop a strategic approach to integrated regional planning based on ecologically sustainable principles and practices and incorporating ecotourism.
3   To encourage a complementary and compatible approach between ecotourism activities and conservation in natural resource management.
4   To encourage industry self-regulation of ecotourism through the development and implementation of appropriate industry standards and accreditation.
5   Where appropriate, to support the design and use of carefully sited and constructed infrastructure to minimise visitor impacts on natural resources and to provide for environmental education consistent with bioregional objectives.
6   To undertake further study of the impacts of ecotourism to improve the information base for planning and decision-making.
7   To encourage and promote the ethical delivery of ecotourism products to meet visitor expectations and match levels of supply and demand.
8   To facilitate the establishment of high quality industry standards and a national accreditation system for ecotourism.
9   To improve the level and delivery of ecotourism education for all target groups.
10 To enhance opportunities for self-determination, self-management and economic self-sufficiency in ecotourism for native peoples.
11 To examine the business needs of operators and develop ways in which viability can be improved, either individually or through collective ventures.
12 To seek to ensure that opportunities for access to ecotourism experiences are equitable and that ecotourism activities benefit host communities and contribute to natural resource management and conservation.

Source: Commonwealth Department of Tourism 1994

References

Balkan, E. and J. Kahn. 1988. The value of changes in deer hunting: A travel cost approach. *Applied Economics* 20, 533-539.

Bateman, I., K. Willis and G. Garrod. 1994. Consistency between contingent valuation estimates. *Regional Studies* 28, 457-474.

Beeho, A. J., and R. C. Prentice. 1995. Evaluating the experiences and benefits gained by tourists visiting a socio-industrial heritage museum. *Museum Management and Curatorship* 14, 229-251.

Benson, J. F. 1991. Value of non-priced recreation on the Forestry Commission estate in Great Britain. *Journal of World Forest Resource Management* 6, 49-73.

Benson, J. F. 1993. A technique for valuing non-priced recreational features of commercial forests. *Leisure Sciences* 15, 149-158.

Bitgood, S. 1990. *The Role of Simulated Immersion in Exhibition.* Center for Social Design Technical Report No. 90-20. Jacksonville, Alabama: Jacksonville State University.

Browne, S. 1992. A strategy to interpret Ireland's history and culture for tourism. In Bord Failte, *Heritage and Tourism: The Second Conference on the Development of Heritage Attractions in Ireland.* Dublin: Bord Failte.

Cameron, T. A. 1992. Combining contingent valuation and travel cost data for the valuation of non-market goods. *Land Economics* 68, 302-317.

Commonwealth Department of Tourism. 1994. *National Ecotourism Strategy.* Canberra: Commonwealth of Australia.

Csikszentmihalyi, M., and I. S. Csikszentmihalyi (eds.). 1988. *Optimal Experience: Psychological Studies of Flow in Consciousness.* Cambridge: Cambridge University Press.

Dittmar, H. 1992. *The Social Psychology of Material Possessions.* Hemel Hempstead: Harvester Wheatsheaf.

Doherty, J., E. Graham and M. Malek (eds.). 1992. *Postmodernism and the Social Sciences.* Basingstoke: Macmillan. .

Farber, S., and A. Rambaldi. 1993. Willingness to pay for air quality: The case of outdoor exercise. *Contemporary Policy Issues* 11, 19-30.

Garrod, G., and K. Willis. 1992. The environmental economic impact of woodland: A two-stage hedonic price model of the amenity value of forestry in Britain. *Applied Economics* 24, 715-728.

Glasson, J., R. Therivel and A. Chadwick. 1994. *Introduction to Environmental Impact Assessment.* London: UCL Press.

Grosclaude, P., and N. C. Soguel. 1994. Valuing damage to historic buildings using a contingent market. *Journal of Environmental Planning and Management* 37, 279-288.

Gutman, J. 1982. A means-end chain model based on consumer categorisation processes. *Journal of Marketing* 46, 60-72.

Hanley, N. D. 1989. Valuing rural recreation benefits: An empirical comparison of two approaches. *Journal of Agricultural Economics* 40, 361-374.

Helber, L. E. 1995. *Redeveloping Mature Resorts for New Markets.* Pacific Asia Travel Association Occasional Paper no. 12. San Francisco, Calif.: PATA.

Herbert, D. T. 1989. Does interpretation help?, in D. T. Herbert, R. C. Prentice and C. J. Thomas (eds.), *Heritage Sites: Strategies for Marketing and Development.* Aldershot: Avebury. Pp. 191-230.

Irons, K. 1994. *Managing Service Companies.* Wokingham: Addison-Wesley.

Kask, S., and S. A. Maani. 1992. Uncertainty, information, and hedonic pricing. *Land Economics* 68, 170-184.

Klenosky, D. B., C. E. Gengler and M. S. Mulvey. 1993. Understanding the factors influencing ski destination choice: A means-end analytical approach. *Journal of Leisure Research* 25, 363-379.

Light, D. F. 1995a. Visitors' use of interpretive media at heritage sites. *Leisure Studies* 14, 132-149.

_____. 1995b. Heritage as informal education. In D. T. Herbert (ed.), *Heritage, Tourism and Society.* London: Mansell.

MacDonald, S. 1992. Cultural imagining among museum visitors. *Museum Management and Curatorship* 11, 401-409.

Manning, R. E. 1986. *Studies in Outdoor Recreation.* Corvallis: Oregon State University Press.

McManus, P. M. 1989. What people say and how they think in a science museum. In D. Uzzell (ed.), *Heritage Interpretation 2.* London: Belhaven.

_____. 1993. Memories as indicators of the impact of museum visits. *Museum Management and Curatorship* 12, 367-380.

Morris, G. 1995. Issues, ethics and morality when working on the Transatlantic Slavery Gallery. *Interpretation* 1 (1), 14-16.

Murphy, P. E. 1985. *Tourism: A Community Approach.* New York: Methuen.

Nature Conservancy Council. 1990. *Earth Science Conservation in Great Britain: A Strategy.* Peterborough: Nature Conservancy Council.

Perkins, S. W., and T. J. Reynolds. 1988. The explanatory power of values in preference judgements: Validation of the means-end perspective. *Advances in Consumer Research* 15, 122-126.

Poon, A. 1989. Competitive strategies for a "new tourism". In C. Cooper (ed.), *Progress in Tourism, Recreation and Hospitality Management 1.* London: Belhaven.

Pottick, K. J. 1983. Work and leisure. In L. R. Kahle (ed.), *Social Values and Social Change.* Praeger: New York.

Prentice, R. C . 1990. "The Manxness of Mann": Renewed immigration to the Isle of Man and the nationalist response. *Scottish Geographical Magazine* 106, 75-88.

_____. 1991a. The impact of economic restructuring on the cultural identity of the Isle of Man. In M. Leroy (ed.), *Regional Development around the North Atlantic Rim.* Swansea: The International Society for the Study of Marginal Regions.

_____. 1991b. Measuring the educational effectiveness of on-site interpretation designed for tourists. *Area* 23, 297-308.

_____. 1992. The Manx National Glens as treasured landscape. *Scottish Geographical Magazine* 108, 119-127.

_____. 1993a. *Change and policy in Wales: Wales in the Era of Privatism.* Llandysul: Gomer.

_____. 1993b. Community-driven tourism planning and residents' preferences. *Tourism Management* 14, 218-227.

_____. 1993c. Motivations of the heritage consumer in the leisure market: An application of the Manning-Haas demand hierarchy. *Leisure Sciences* 15, 273-290.

_____. 1993d. *Tourism and Heritage Attractions.* London:

Routledge.

_____. 1994a. Promotional mix. In S. F. Witt and L. Moutinho (eds.), *Tourism Marketing and Management Handbook.* Second edition. Hemel Hempstead: Prentice Hall.

_____. 1994b. Heritage: A key sector of the "new" tourism. In C. P. Cooper and A. Lockwood (eds.), *Progress in Tourism, Recreation and Hospitality Management 5.* Chichester: Wiley.

_____. 1995. Heritage as formal education. In D. T. Herbert (ed.), *Heritage, Tourism and Society.* London: Mansell.

Prentice, R. C., and D. F. Light. 1994. Current issues in interpretative provision at heritage sites. In A. V. Seaton (ed.), *Tourism: The State of the Art.* Chichester: Wiley.

Prentice, R. C., S. F. Witt and C. Hamer. 1993. The experience of industrial heritage: The case of Black Gold. *Built Environment* 19, 137-146.

Randall, A. 1994. A difficulty with the travel cost method. *Land Economics* 70, 88-96.

Reynolds, T. J., and J. Gutman. 1988. Laddering theory, method, analysis and interpretation. *Journal of Advertising Research* February-March, 11-31.

Richards, G. 1994. Cultural tourism in Europe. In C. P. Cooper and A. Lockwood (eds.), *Progress in Tourism, Recreation and Hospitality Management 5.* Chichester: Wiley.

Scottish Tourist Board. 1994. *Scottish Tourism Strategic Plan.* Edinburgh: STB.

Shafer, B. C. 1972. *Faces of Nationalism.* New York: Harcourt Brace Jovanovich.

Shafernich, S. M. 1993. On-site museums, open-air museums, museum villages and living history museums. *Museum Management and Curatorship* 12, 43-61.

Stewart, S. I., and D. J. Stynes. 1994. Toward a dynamic model of complex tourism choices. In J. C. Crotts and W. F. van Raaij (eds.), *Economic Psychology of Travel and Tourism.* New York: Haworth Press.

Taylor, P. J. 1985. *Political Geography.* London: Longman.

Turner, R. K. (ed.) 1993. *Sustainable Environmental Economics and*

Management. London: Belhaven.

U. S. Department of Agriculture, Forest Service. 1990. *Recreation Opportunities Spectrum: Primer and Field Guide.* Washington, D.C.: U.S. Government Printing Office.

Wales Tourist Board. 1994. *Tourism 2000: A Strategy for Wales.* Cardiff: WTB.

Wight, P. 1994. Environmentally-responsible marketing of tourism. In E. Cater and G. Lowman (eds.), *Ecotourism.* Chichester: Wiley.

Williams, A. P., and J. S. P. Hobson. 1994. Tourism---the next generation: Virtual reality and surrogate travel, is it the future of the tourism industry? In A. V. Seaton (ed.), *Tourism: The State of the Art.* Chichester, Wiley.

Willis, K. 1994. Paying for heritage: What price for Durham Cathedral? *Journal of Environmental Planning and Management* 37, 267-278.

Willis, K., and G. Garrod. 1991. Valuing open access recreation on inland waterways: On-site recreation surveys and selection effects. *Regional Studies* 25, 511-524.

12 Eco-tourism in remote areas of Norway: Just green veneer?

Thor Flognfeldt, Jr.

Introduction

Studying tourism development is a very complex field. Examining tourism and sustainability are even more complex, even though most studies ignore the most complex issues, including transport to and from the destination areas. Most studies limit their scope to a small community or a marginal region. They often regard tourism as an event taking place at a small site during a short period of time. The aim of this paper, in contrast, is to look at the whole trip and present some reflections on the sustainability of tourism in a broad sense.

The northern parts of Scandinavia have a large market potential when marketing focuses on green tourism destinations or as a part of an eco-tourism product. The aim of this paper is to focus on how eco-tourism as a destination product might have other than "green effects" for the rest of the total trip. If the majority of tourists entering the areas still are coming by their own car or camper van, the success of green tourism in the north will produce environmental problems in some of the corridors they are passing through coming from the south.

Most studies of eco-tourism are site-oriented in a narrow sense. They emphasize what is happening only at the final destination of the complex tour and do not look at the other parts of the journey. This means that describing a site as an eco-tourism product might be regarded as adding a green veneer to a highly polluting activity. From a marketing point of view this way of giving flavour to the product will be a very important one, but we should also consider other ways of examining those products described as "green".

I will not argue that how to arrange the tourists' behaviour at the destinations is of little importance. There is still much to gain both for the local ecosystems and for the future respect of tourism as a trade, if we adjust the products offered in marginal areas to the existing environment and to the needs of the people living there. For example, better management of sewerage and waste are important parts of tourism development, everywhere.

Sletvold (1994) has described the sustainability of the coastal tourism development in northern Norway mostly from the view of local communities including natural and cultural elements. It is very important that this discussion continues. If, however, we really want to make tourism greener, in a broader sense, we must pay closer attention to how we plan and organise the whole trip. In this regard looking at the means of transportation, from the point the tourists leave their homes until they return home, will be an important research field in the years to come. This could mean putting more emphasis on the revitalisation of existing railway systems---especially those using electricity generated by hydro-electric power stations---as the prime transporter of tourists to remote destinations. This could also mean trying to slow down the speed of car-ferries and cruise ships. This might also mean trying to fill up empty spaces in scheduled buses and even in private cars.

Høyer (1995) has attempted to produce energy accounts of different modes of travelling. His research describes both the energy consumption by a local inhabitant living at different locations in Norway and that for frequent travellers to a cottage in the mountains. Research like that of Høyer will create a new and more serious discussion about different types of tourists and the sustainable environment, including bringing much wider areas into the discussion of pollution. The aim of the paper is primarily to show how a more route-oriented analysis could be used to describe different products, and to throw some light on possible sources of positive effects, and to identify problem areas in eco-tourism.

Green tourism, eco-tourism and sustainable tourism

This paper will not include a full discussion on the meaning of different concepts describing tourism and sustainability. Other papers (e.g. Flognfeldt 1992, 1993, 1995) have previously dealt with this subject. Defining sustainable tourism as "the acceptable pace of change" might be the only way of fitting tourism and sustainability together. For my purpose, however, a clarification of the area and route dimensions is necessary. In general the term "green tourism" is more useful as a marketing slogan for separating nature-based destination products from "plastic theme parks", than it is as a research subject. The term "eco-tourism" might be divided into at least two parts, based on different ways of describing tourism. First, "destination ecosystems" take into account only the effects shown at the site of the specific product elements examined even if they sometimes include the nearest region to that site. The eco-tourism concept is analysed only from the site in question. Second, "eco-route systems" look at the whole trip a tourist makes, including the departure from and return to the tourists' homes. For research purposes we then have to aggregate individual trips to route patterns. Of course, to get deeper into the ecosystems of different routes is a very complicated matter, in which both destination and route studies must play a role. The term "sustainable" will be used only to facilitate an examination of the effects on the complete ecosystem. I intend to show what kinds of challenges expanding the ecology view of tourism into studies of eco-route systems will present to the fields of geographical research on tourism.

Basic movement patterns in Scandinavian tourism

There is, as yet, no complete study of the different movement patterns of tourists in Scandinavia, even though many guest studies the last seven years have given some consideration to the route dimension. By "guest studies" I mean interviews of tourists when they are travelling and when enquiring for information about their route. Before describing some actual movement patterns, I want to show five different ways of travel as a leisure-time tourist in Scandinavia. This segmentation is based on the Campbell 1966 model and describes movement patterns as well as suggesting possibilities for producing more environmentally-friendly trips.

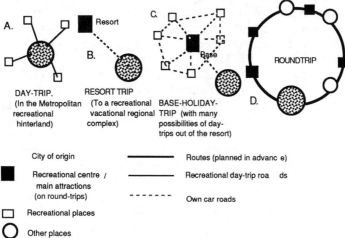

Figure 1 Modes of recreational or vacational travel

Source: Flognfeldt 1995 based on Campbell 1966

Day trips: trips which start and finish at home during the same day. The need is to offer better possibilities closer to the bigger towns, i.e. the Nordmarka forests by Oslo.

Resort trips: trips to a place where the major part of the stay is at the accommodation location. The need is to offer transportation that is more ecological than private cars.

Base holiday trips: the prime trip is going from home to a single place with a long stay. The visitors then take day trips out of the accommodation area, i.e. to visit attractions. The need is to offer a system of public transport to these attractions.

Tour-operated round trips: mainly by coaches, where the travellers visit new places every day and night. The need is to fill the coaches as much as possible and

Round trips by private cars or camper vans: in principle organised as the tour-operated ones, but those driving in private cars have more freedom of individual choice during the trips.

The last two modes are very similar in structure, but the tour-operated ones cannot be changed much during the trips. People travelling on coach routes have decisively chosen their routes before they left home. Summing up the patterns of tourists travelling by car or camper van coming from the southern and middle parts Europe to Scandinavia, the pattern is represented in figure 2. The possibilities of further developing green products in the sparsely-populated areas of northern Scandinavia are great. The very important question of sustainability is how and where the eco-tourists choose to go on their way to the final destination and back home. Today most of them either go by private car or by camper van, driving thousands of kilometres to find a really remote place to stay for a short time. For many research workers this final destination is the only one included in their research on the sustainability of tourism.

As shown in figure 2, there are some communities located at the narrow entrances to Scandinavia that may suffer if more "green" car tourists enter our part of the world. The Øresund between Denmark and southern Sweden is one of those areas, Kristiansand and Larvik in southern Norway are two others. In the spring of 1994 the Swedish government decided to build a bridge across the Øresund many years after the Danes accepted this proposal. The new bridge might substantially lower the threshold to get to northern Scandinavia by car or camper van even more. More than twice as many cars will be passing through Denmark and the southernmost parts of Sweden in ten years' time.

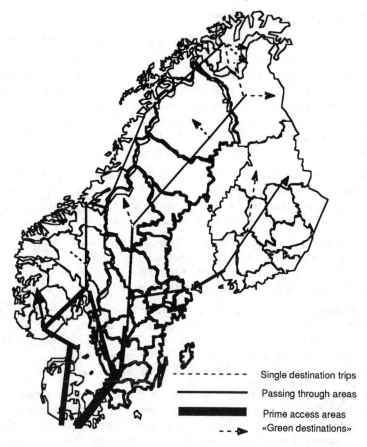

Figure 2   Patterns of car-based traffic to the "green" parts of Scandinavia

Other areas on the route northwards are characterised by traffic passing through. In Norway the city of Trondheim is one such area, Nordland county another. The challenges of planning for being a nice place to pass through are not over-focused, and often plans are presented as if the areas had other functions, i.e. acting as resorts. Along with these patterns are the networks of local and regional public transport. Most of those transport opportunities have an excess supply with many free seats during the whole year, including the peak summer season. These questions need to be discussed much more, and the discussion should be based on real figures on traffic rather than on vague hypotheses.

Describing the whole trip

From my point of view too much of the focus on eco-tourism is only upon organising the tourists' behaviour at their destinations. Of course the way a destination is organised is of great importance: Hawkes and Williams (1993) give fine examples of how much there is to gain by looking seriously to both destinations and other product elements. Nevertheless, much discussion and research are lacking, for instance a discussion on how to use the existing railway system more and reducing the use of private cars. Some questions are:

Could the primary travelling pattern be organised so that more tourists are sharing the same vehicles? This is a challenge both to tour operators and to the promoters of "green" destinations who aim their advertising at people travelling by private car.

Is it possible to expand the use of trains, coaches and boats instead of developing varieties of green tourism based exclusively on the private car? This is a challenge both to the scheduled transportation industry and to politicians who decide the structure of subsidised transport.

Is it possible to stop promoting further development in areas if this leads to too many disadvantages for the areas on the routes to the destination? Who will decide in which areas development will be stopped? If this is not possible, the focus must be on reducing the effects on on-route places by bypassing or compensating them.

It is important to emphasize that there is no conflict between a route focus on eco-travel and the important work of bettering the ecological standards at a site or in a limited rural area. The problems are that the understanding of the route dimension in all tourism activities has a much lower priority than destination studies in a decentralised planning structure like that of Norway.

Interviews carried out in the Jotunheimen area of Southern Norway during the summer of 1995 show at least two contrasting types of tourists, which are illustrated by the following examples. In the first, a coach was filled with 45 Japanese tourists travelling 500 km from Oslo to Geiranger. They stopped for 25 minutes in Lom to visit the Stave Church and spent on average 20 NOK in the destination area. The second example is that of German or Dutch couples and family units travelling five persons together in a camper van spending three weeks in the same area with the purpose of "doing everything". They do really adjust to local rules and visit state-subsidised local attractions, but are officially regarded as "unwanted tourists" by the Norwegian Minister of Environment (Berntsen 1995).[2]

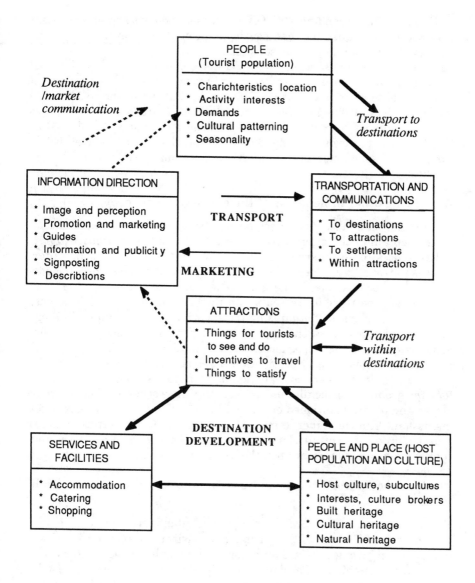

Figure 3 The Tourism Environment

Source: Travis 1989

Coach visitors spending 20 NOK locally on their way to an overnight stay will not even pay for road development or the use of the area. The camper van people do pay for some of the investments in tourism infrastructure and do buy some of their food in local stores. They often travel around in low speed and take short daily trips. Still the stereotype of that type of tourism is that it is polluting, in contrast to the coach round trippers, who are thought to be more valuable. A study which compares these stereotypes to reality has been be done by Flognfeldt and Onshus (1996). The patterns of expenditures show that people travelling in camper vans spend more money in the region than those in tour-operated coaches.

Describing other dimensions of the eco-tourism concept

If we really want to examine eco-tourism systems, we will have to look more deeply into the alternatives offered to the tourist concerning alternative places to go, alternative ways of travelling or even to the alternatives to travelling. There are a number of research questions still to be answered. For example, is there any alternative to travelling itself: can conditions be bettered for recreation in the areas near to people's homes? Are there other ways of organising trips, perhaps by combining different modes of transport at a cheap price to compensate for the many inconveniences during the trips, mostly at terminals? Can internal transportation systems at most destination areas be developed for the benefit of tourists? (In Norway most public bus transport systems are designed for two groups: schoolchildren and commuting workers). The work of Høyer and others mentioned earlier will help us to set a new agenda for discussion. The consequence may be to reformulate the nature of rural tourism; ironically, of all Norwegian tourism structures this is the one that is most heavily reliant upon the use of private cars.

Eco-tourism in northern Scandinavia: who is gaining and who is losing?

The northern parts of Scandinavia and Finland are among the last wildernesses of Europe. If the greening of tourism markets continues, we might expect strong pressure on areas in the north because they have a satisfying accessibility. Parallel to this development there might also be a pressure on more remote and unprepared areas. By "unprepared" I mean areas without any plans for recruiting tourists or managing them. Today there is a tendency to call all types of nature-based tourism products either green tourism and eco-tourism. The discussion of these forms of tourism focuses only on some aspects of the tourism product. I call this a green veneer because the green parts are the surface ones, and when we go more deeply into the matter, problems come to light. The polluting passing-through traffic all the way up to northern Norway is much more difficult to examine and to work with than organising a small destination area. In this paper, I have aimed to show that so-called green tourism products might not be the ecologically right ones.

Notes

[1] An earlier version of this paper was presented at the Arctic and Eco Tourism Symposium, Troms, Norway, September 28-30, 1993.

[2] Twice during the spring of 1995, Thorbjorn Berntsen, Minister of the Environment, said that these tourist only empty their toilets in streets of built-up areas. Berntsen is well-known for such remarks, but this shows the status of knowledge about important tourism questions at that Ministry.

References

Berntsen, Torbjorn. 1995. Interviews and statements by the Norwegian Minister of Environment, Torbjorn Berntsen.

Campbell, C.-K. 1966. *An Approach to Research in Recreational Geography.* University of British Columbia, Department of Geography. Occasional Paperts no 7. Vancouver.

Flognfeldt, Thor. 1992. Area, site or route: The different movement patterns of travel in Norway. *Tourism Management* 13 (1).

_____. 1993. Area, site or route: How types of travel and accommodation are leading to differences in the use of activities and attractions. *Tourism Recreation Research* 2.

_____. 1995. *Area, Site or Route.* (Areal, sted og reiserute). Bergen: Fagbokforlaget.

Flognfeldt, Thor and Terje Onshus. 1996. *The Expenditure Patterns of Tourists in Ottadal Valley During the Summer of 1995.* Working paper no. 25. Lillehammer: Lillehammer College

Hawkes, S. and P. Williams. 1993. *The Greening of Tourism---from Principles to Practice: A Casebook of the Best Environmental Practice of Tourism.* Burnaby, B.C.: Center of Tourism Policy and Research, Simon Fraser University.

Høyer, Karl Georg. 1995. Unpublished lecture on energy accounts of different modes of travelling to the Hemsedal resort in Norway. Presented at Tiltakskonferansen 1995, Lillehammer.

Kosters, M. 1992. Tourism by train: Its role in alternative tourism. In Valene L. Smith and W. R. Eadington (eds.), *Tourism Alternatives: Potentials and Problems in the Development of Tourism.* Philadelphia: University of Pennsylvania Press.

Mathieson, Alastair and Geoff Wall. 1982. *Tourism: Economic, Physical and Social Impacts.* New York: Longman.

Seaton, A. V. (ed.). 1994. *Tourism: The State of the Art.* Chichester: John Wiley and Sons.

Sletvold, Ola. 1994. Northern coastal tourism: Concepts, resource basis and sustainability strategy. In A. V. Seaton (ed.),*Tourism: The State of the Art.* Chichester: John Wiley and Sons.

Smith, Valene L. and W. R. Eadington. 1992. *Tourism Alternatives: Potentials and Problems in the Development of Tourism.* Philadelphia: University of Pennsylvania Press.

Travis, Anthony S. 1989. Tourism destination areal development (from theory into practice). In Steven Witt and Lois Moutinho, *Tourism Marketing and Management Handbook.* New York: Prentice Hall.

Witt, Steven and Lois Moutinho. 1989. *Tourism Marketing and Management Handbook.* New York: Prentice Hall.

13   Eco-tourism: Rhetoric or a new prospect for the periphery?

Peter Sjøholt

Part I: Some general problems

Introduction

The concept of eco-tourism scarcely existed in the literature only fifteen years ago. In the recent past it has gained a popularity which is staggering. It is estimated today that 10% of world tourism is nature-based travel, and the volume is increasing. Far from all of it can be characterised as eco-tourism, however. As is the case with other popular terms, the concept seems to convey a multiplicity of connotations and has different meanings to different people. Definitions abound and the phenomenon is not clearly perceived by researchers, public authorities or politicians. If we were to try to find a common denominator that could cover the meaning of the term in some breadth and with some precision, we could adopt the following definition, which was proposed as a guideline for a prospective Eco-Tourism Society (Epler Wood 1991):

> Purposeful travel to natural areas to understand the culture and the natural history of the environment, taking care not to alter the integrity of the ecosystem, while producing economic opportunities that make the conservation of natural resources beneficial to local people.

This definition was originally conceived in connection with tourist development in the Third World. It is, however, sufficiently general to define eco-tourism anywhere. This statement points to a series of qualities that appear to be inherent in eco-tourism, and which serves as a point of departure for discussion.

The nature of eco-tourism

In the above citation, attention is focused on the requirement that the type of travel in question should be particularly motivated and purposeful. Culture as well as nature is its object. The integrity (or quality) of the ecosystem, both natural and cultural, should be left undisturbed. It is this conservation or preservation imperative which is inherent in the Norwegian saying of nature reserves: "Here you are always welcome if nobody can see that you have been here". This type of tourism should at the same time be organised so that local people can reap the benefits. Economic gains should fall to the local community. No hint is directly made in the statement of the idea of sustainability, but this is a logical corollary of the quest for the integrity of the system.

If due weight is given to the properties mentioned above, and they all are taken seriously, many features must at the same time fit together in order to label the phenomenon as eco-tourism. We are furthermore struck by the many restrictions on the practise of eco-tourism, if viewed on a world basis. A delicate balance evidently exists between the different demand and supply factors which characterise the system.

If we turn to the *demand* factors, a true eco-tourism immediately stands in contrast to many of the characteristics found in the motives of today's mainstream tourist clientele. Very many of these tourists are, as we all know, motivated by a search for relaxation, a relief from daily chores; they are driven by "sunlust" rather than "wanderlust". They are in search, for a short period, for a social life which is not too demanding of personal adjustment, in reality not too different in values from what they are accustomed to, simultaneously combined with as low costs as possible. In order to cater to these demands, the provision of services to the mainstream tourist is dependent on some scale of development of the service institutions. International standards are incessantly being upgraded to meet standard requirements, which also add to the necessity of developing economies of scale. The consequences will easily be adverse to the qualities required by eco-tourism. Meeting the requirements of standard mainstream tourism may thus easily lead to the violation of the integrity of the ecosystem, and more often than not it will mean leakage of production out of the local community rather than multiplier effects within it.

The typical eco-tourist, in contrast, is a more active person making demands on himself as well as on the surroundings. He is a more individualistic consumer, and differs very often from others in the same situation. Eco-tourists encompass all types of people, varying from elitist holiday-seekers to ordinary people. This makes the development and management of supply rather problematic. If developers and organisers are to keep strictly to the nature of the activity, great care has to be exercised as far as the dimensions of development are concerned, so that the carrying capacity, whatever this may mean, is not surpassed either in the physical or in the local cultural environment. Economy of scope rather than of scale characterises this type of tourist activity.

Eco-tourism need not necessarily be associated with nature reserves, national parks or other restrictions on development and land use, which were the settings from which the concept was originally derived. It is also highly compatible with patronising the cultural landscape, a point strongly stressed by Messerli (1994). According to him, conservation and utilisation, production and reproduction must be seen as interdependent elements and reciprocal principles of development. An agricultural landscape and certain farming systems are therefore as important elements in nature-based or "green" tourism as is untouched nature. However, the combined natural-cultural idiosyncrasies of attractions call for an interference on a rather small scale by man-made systems, particularly as regards heavy infrastructure. On the whole, eco-tourism, as we conceive it, implies activities which are adverse to crowding, thus being most easily implemented in non-central areas and mainly in the periphery.

Organising and practising eco-tourism

Considering the development of nature-based tourism from the *supply* side, we are confronted with many conflicts and dilemmas. Developing a tourist product implies a neat interplay of several functions and actors. The industry consists of a very intricate production system, which relies on many linkages both backward and forward in the production chain. According to Britton (1991), the production system includes activities which are part of producing and selling both travel itself and a host of different tour products associated with it. It also encompasses the social groups and cultural and physical elements which make up the attractions. Finally it also consists of organising, regulating and controlling agencies both in the private and public sphere. For a tourism that aims at a praxis, which takes care not to exceed important thresholds, all these determining factors and the intricate network of actors and agents easily create pressures which threaten to exceed these thresholds.

The first and foremost concern in any production system is to make the different activities *economically* sustainable. In a capitalistic system this means highest possible or at least a satisfactory return to capital, which under the reigning system also means some return to scale. This requirement permeates nearly all the elements which unite to make up the tourist product: accommodation enterprises, man-made attractions and transport companies. Much as we might wish the other aspects of sustainability (the cultural milieu and artefacts, important social relations and surplus generation---accumulation) to be taken care of on behalf of the local community, when it comes to economic viability, this factor tends to reign supreme. Herein lies the main dilemma for a viable eco-tourism. Considering the demand side, just relying on a particular and unique demand and on a particularly motivated group of customers who patronise a supply developed beyond the organised capitalistic-oriented tourism may turn out to be an illusion. If eco-tourism is going to be viable and sustainable in the long term, it must be organised in a way that takes into account important economic parameters. If left to haphazard development, mainly built on ideological foundations, the danger is great that supply will not match demand and the tourists' expectations. I will argue that the perception by many proponents of eco-tourism of infrastructure, production systems and coordinating organisation aiming at combining tourism with well-functioning local communities and sustainable environments and habitats is still wishful thinking, particularly in the periphery. As an industry, it is very patchily developed and rudimentarily integrated into organised tourism, particularly in developed countries.

Provided that the above diagnosis is correct, the problem before us will be to combine relevant elements making up the production system and tailor it to the needs of eco-based tourism. This calls for great flexibility in development with due regard for costs and benefits. Particularly important in this context are the economic parameters. The failure to incorporate these is perhaps the reason why this type of tourism, notwithstanding all the backing from politicians and other official authorities and emerging NGOs, who are trying to reap benefits from it, so easily collapses into more conventional forms of tourism organised by big business. Certainly, there are examples of nature tourism as a renumerative business. Thus Boo (1990) found that spending by elitist eco-tourists in Latin America was far higher than that of conventional tourists. However this only happens occasionally, and it is an established fact that more than 80% of this income is exported back to the industrialised countries. This trend has been observed in many developing countries, of which Costa Rica is a good case in point. This country is hailed as a practitioner of an eco-tourism prototype, which could serve as a model for other countries as well. However, on closer inspection, much of what is marketed as "green" tourism in that country turns out to be mere rhetoric. After a decade of development in this field the results are rather modest, even if positive examples can be found. On the whole, the practices of the activities do not differ significantly from conventional tourism and the local spin-offs are frustratingly low. Most of the activities are induced and organised from the outside and generally on a large scale with a substantial leakage both of input factors and surplus back to the developed world (Acuña Ortega 1995).

Comparatively little research is done on preconditions for and results of this and other alternative forms of tourism, especially on a global scale. This is particularly the case when considering the activities as part of a wider production system, in a social context and from the point of view of its spatial requirements and impacts. In Norway, for example, research has up to now mainly consisted of studying bits of the problem sectorally, this being the case whether we consider research from the angle of problem orientation or research targets. From an economic view-point product quality has loomed large, as have studies of the profitability of individual enterprises and the effects of marketing; all legitimate and important elements, but there have been no attempts to give a holistic view. Many surveys have also been made of tourists as consumers and of the use of different attractions by different types of tourists. These studies are interesting in themselves, but often cut off from a wider context. Few, if any studies cover the present theme. Against this background it is high time to advance further in bridging the sectorial aspects and making connections between the components. As we have seen, this is particularly important for the study of alternative tourism. There are many issues before us in that context, and, fortunately, concrete projects are now being launched in that direction. This will be the theme of Part II of this paper.

Part II: Some pertinent issues and research projects

The case for more in-depth research

As we might conclude from Part I, there is only a rudimentary emerging knowledge and only fragmented theorising on the issue of "green" tourism or eco-tourism. Still we are confronted with many more questions than answers. Certainly, some of the issues linked to this field are pertinent also in other types of tourism. If we want to approach the matter from a more general and critical point of view, it cannot be detached from what Britton (1991) called the wider structures of tourism and what Shaw and Williams (1994) made more precise as a production system or part of a production system within a wider leisure context, a phenomenon which "cannot be separated off from the social relations within which it is embedded". This certainly puts restrictions on the way of and scope for organising and developing eco-tourism as an industry, as we have also pointed out above. Particularly, however, it presupposes clearer concepts and images of this branch of the industry than we up to now have been able to provide. In other words, it presupposes more fundamental research.

Among the many issues that should be looked at more thoroughly, we find the problem of sustainability, or the meaning of sustainability, transferred to this particular field. This is very intimately associated with the host communities of this type of tourism, their reactions and their need for adjustment. This type of tourism is generally small scale and based on nature as the main attraction. The different qualities inherent in nature will therefore have important impacts for location of the activities and for the ways they are organised. Increasingly the industry is also being linked to cultural qualities, the cultural landscape per se is one of them, and an increasingly important element in eco-tourism. It is, however, part and parcel also of a wider cultural environment and heritage, including a host of artefacts. As it is simultaneously an industrial activity, the tourists' willingness to pay for keeping up the ecological balance, and thus counterbalance opportunity costs, will always remain crucial; so will the organisation and regulation of tourist flows, particularly in fragile areas.

There is a great need for light to be shed on these and many more issues, and for more analysis to be done. This challenge has now been taken up in Norway. When the Norwegian Research Council through a special programme for tourist research invited scholars to apply their special research interests in the field in the autumn of 1994, the problem of tourism and concern for nature and culture was one of the main themes of the invitation. Particular emphasis was put on the interaction between cultural, social and ecological qualities and attractions, as the Council found these aspects very little illuminated by recent and current research. Simultaneously, more knowledge would be crucial, not only for their academic interest, but as a contribution to help develop long term sustainability in the widest meaning of the term. The response to the invitation was encouraging. In the remainder of the paper I am going to dwell on three of the issues which are taken up and discuss them briefly as a means of broadening our understanding. Looming large among the topics is sustainable tourism and consumption in the light of the concept of sustainability. Intimately linked to it are the qualities of nature as a factor in location of tourism and nature-based tourism and its relations with the host communities, as well as the importance of the cultural heritage.

Sustainable tourism and the concept of sustainability

This project takes its point of departure in the fact that there has been a lot of discussion about, but little precise knowledge of tourism and its impact on the ecosystem. The goal of research is therefore to explore whether it is possible by relying on existing theory and the empirical knowledge-base to make the concept of sustainable tourism more precise. A second question following upon a possible clarification is to what extent that which today is labelled "green" tourism can be considered sustainable. And as a third issue, it is of interest to know how sustainable tourism is marketed by tourist agencies, organisations and enterprises.

The first part of the research theme is the most difficult both as far as contents and methodology are concerned. Answers are sought by reviewing the existing literature systematically in order to determine the criteria for the use and management of "nature" and the "cherished cultural traditions" which are reflected in the cultural landscape and the built environment as well as in handicrafts, folk music, etc. In addition to this clarification there is the question of the value basis for sustainability. Where are the limits to exploitation, who is going to define them and on what criteria? It is hypothesised that in order to keep up sustainability it is necessary to maintain the capital source intact or nearly intact, as this is a precondition for reproduction both of natural and sociocultural resources. Into this perspective must be inserted the importance of local knowledge about the use and management of nature and about the nurturing of local traditions in the built environment, in food culture, dance and costume and in the patterns of interaction. This is a clear extension of the concept of sustainability beyond what was defined by the Brundtland Commission, and is considered necessary in this particular field.

The second and third main themes, how sustainability is materialised, could be illuminated by having revealed how far the different tourist operators and producers are willing to go in this direction; it can be approached by studying both attitudes to and practice of "green" tourism through their concrete products in a sample of enterprises. In addition, the national and regional plans and other conditions laid down by the authorities and their following up should be inquired into and evaluated in the light of these authorities' attempts to exert control.

This research proposal is very ambitious, and will, if properly managed, enable us to widen our understanding substantially. The basic clarifications it sets out to attain are crucial in many fields of work and could serve as a very important frame of reference both for future research and for viable management of the industry. It could, if properly carried out, provide a useful framework for discussing eco-tourism in its different aspects. We should, however, be aware of its limitations. It does not pretend to give answers about the scope and organisation of the activities, as linked to the economy, which must always loom large for market-based activities. Neither will the results from the project give us the means for coming to grips with conflict issues between the particular type of tourists concerned and the local host communities. To the latter problem we now turn.

Nature-based tourism and its adjustment to the host communities

The background for the interest in this theme is manifold. First, it reflects the fact that nature is a growing attraction, and, second, as a corollary, that it is increasingly being taken advantage of commercially. Third, this may lead to conflicts. The third problem may be contingent on a number of socioeconomic and cultural idiosyncrasies and the way the local community is organised; to this sphere belong property rights and other rights to resources. The conflicts provoked may be with local recreational interests and may even originate in identity problems like the symbolic content of the scenery as local people perceive it. A negative attitude towards tourists may also be reinforced by the insignificant income accruing to the local community from this type of tourism. Whatever the reactions from the local community, this is a topic little researched both in a global and a Norwegian context. Conflict issues are touched on by Mathieson and Wall (1982) and explained as a result of lack of planning and management. Causes probably penetrate far deeper than this, so this should be a rewarding research theme. The project focused on in this context will among other problems seek to highlight which forms of nature-based tourism are most conflict-prone: the one attracted by an organised supply or the type instigated by individual tourists, who (in Norway) use their legal right to roam about freely outside cultivated areas. Important both for a deeper understanding of the problem and as a means of future adjustment, it will study how problems are handled by different actors, both private and public. The latter actors are particularly interesting to study as they have the right to impose regulations and restrictions.

Results from this study will give valuable input, both for broadening our knowledge base and for practical measures in conflict-prone areas. It may seem a flaw that the question of the magnitude of tourist penetration as an explanatory variable is not explicitly signalled in the proposal. This is also part of the sustainability issue, and might link the present project to the former one. Simultaneously, conflict studies like this one could be extended into the cultural realm by asking what are the limits of absorption of green tourists under different conditions for not violating cultural values and idiosyncrasies.

Quality of nature as a factor of location of tourist activities

This project is motivated by our present lack of knowledge of how tourists perceive crucial environmental qualities and how these qualities are managed by landowners and public authorities. This may have a bearing on future planning and the location of tourist activities. It can, moreover, contribute increased knowledge of environmental tourist products, which have to be sustained if they are going to have a long-term value. Of importance to uncover in this investigation are the qualities which are particularly emphasised by tourists, and whether there are differences in their assessments, contingent on types of tourists. Do mass tourists differ from eco-tourists, and are there differences according to nationality ? Does cultural background foster particular demand for natural qualities? Looming large in such a study is the problem of the management of resources. Tourists can give valuable feedback on the strengths and weaknesses of the Norwegian management praxis in a comparative perspective, and the owners of land, whether private or public, can reveal their perceptions on their particular role in management. This is particularly important, since the Norwegian ownership structure, with small, scattered units and the right of free movement outside cultivated land, may impact upon the way resources are managed. This may be pertinent to the ability of the system to maintain future resources.

Culturally-based resources

Inherent in the problem of nature and the ecologically-sound management of tourism is a balanced use of cultural heritage and associated cultural artefacts. All types of transition exist between nature and culture in this respect. Physical preconditions may be important for the enjoyment of particular cultural experiences, and there is wear and tear as a result of too-heavy tourist loads. It is important to find how the enjoyment of cultural artefacts and values is affected by different types of organisation and traffic volumes. When will formal arrangements of the supply of attractions turn negative for different groups and lead to diminishing returns? A project asking these questions will also be incorporated into the Research Council package together with a study giving a broad analysis of the use of the cultural product by the tourists. As frequency of visits by tourists will be one of the variables in the model areas, we hope in this way to throw some light on the rather imprecise concept of carrying capacity, which may be different for different people. One crucial comparison will be how local people and tourists experience tourism's use of cultural heritage and how this use impacts upon the relations of people to the cultural milieu and its artefacts. This is in a general sense intimately linked to sustainability: a long-term pre-condition also for further economic gain.

Conclusion

It was argued, by way of introduction, that our knowledge of eco-tourism is limited. Evidence of this was given in the subsequent discussion. What we have presented in this paper is, accordingly, more questions than answers to some pertinent issues, which are intimately linked to each other. Certainly, the programme of which the above mentioned projects are a part covers far more issues, among which is a broad analysis of the tourist production system, and which may have as a by-product some evaluations of the preconditions for and impacts of eco-tourism. On the other hand, many gaps still exist in the programme. Thus we need a more far-reaching analysis of the economic relations of small scale nature- and culture-based tourism and a broad assessment of its economic organisation. How are we to channel demand in better ways and how are we to match supply and demand? What role ought planning to play in this respect and what could be taken care of directly by the market? It is only when such questions are answered that we will be able to answer the question in the title: whether eco-tourism is rhetoric or a genuine prospect for the periphery. It is a pity that the research world is generally divided, either being exclusively geared towards ecological and environmental matters per se and ignoring economic prerequisites and consequences, or primarily engaged in purely economic analyses. To be sure, in the portfolio of projects linked to eco-tourism, there is one catering to national economic matters, exploring how much people are willing to pay in order to conserve nature. Unfortunately, answers to this question do not illuminate the problem of economic viability and sustainability when it comes to organising both ecologically- and economically-sustainable forms of tourist activity. This issue will have to be incorporated in a follow-up of the projects. However, as matters stand, even without this more exact knowledge of a vital problem, we are in a position to conclude that eco-tourism, important as it may be in transferring resources from the outside, will never be a panacea for solving the more profound structural problems of economically marginal areas.

References

Acuña, Ortega M. 1995. *Ecotourism in Costa Rica.* Paper presented at Department of Geography, NHH,UiB, Bergen.

Boo, E. 1990. *Ecotourism: The Potential and Pitfalls.* Washington, D.C.: World Wildlife Fund.

Britton, S. 1991. Tourism, capital and place: Towards a critical geography. *Environment and Planning, Society and Space.* Vol. 9.

Epler Wood, M. 1991. Global solutions: An ecotourism society. In Tensie Whelan (ed.), *Nature Tourism: Managing for the Environment.* Washington, D.C.: Island Press.

Mathieson, A. and G. Wall. 1982. *Tourism: Economic, Physical and Social Impacts.* London: Longman Scientific and Technical.

Messerli, P. 1994. The dilemma of the Alps: Balancing regional development and environmental protection in particularly attractive regions. In *Regional Policies and the Environment.* NordREFO 1994: 2.

Shaw, G. and A. Williams. 1994. *Critical Issues in Tourism: A Geographical Perspective.* Oxford: Blackwell.

14   A sustainable strategy for scenic landscapes

Jeanne Meldon

Introduction

The Fifth Environmental Action Programme, *Towards Sustainability,* requires environmental concerns to be integrated into all European Union policies including tourism. There is nothing particularly new about the concept of sustainability. More recent, however, is the general acceptance that more sustainable behaviour is the key to current and future well-being. Sustainability is a process, not a state, hence it is more meaningful to talk in terms of how rather than what.

As part of the process of operationalising the Fifth Environmental Action Programme, the European Commission established the LIFE financial instrument for the environment. Its aims and objectives are to link policy with practice by funding demonstration projects according to different priorities. Thus, in 1993, priority actions included examining means of integrating tourism and environment in a rural context. It was under this priority that Bord Failte---the Irish Tourist Board---and An Taisce---the National Trust for Ireland---obtained funding for the scenic landscapes[1] project.

Background

Tourism is one of Ireland's most significant socioeconomic activities. One of the principal resources upon which the tourism industry depends is the environment: the unspoilt landscapes and habitats, the areas of natural uplands and undeveloped coastlines. Bord Failte, in its *Tourism Development Plan 1994-1999,* proposes a network of national scenic landscapes as a key initiative to protect significant natural and scenic areas. It is proposed that protection will be achieved not by acquisition but by appropriate management strategies involving national and local authorities, as well as the voluntary and private sectors. The intention is that the special recognition of these areas will result in a comprehensive conservation programme for the areas in the country of high scenic quality.

But the landscape is not just a scenic backdrop for the touring visitor. It is a dynamic, living environment in a constant state of change. In an Irish context much of the landscapes which we so much admire is the product of centuries---indeed millennia---of human activity. The small fields and rolling pasture lands, the fishing boats at the pier, the forestry plantations, the mussel rafts in the bay, the timber processing factory, not to mention the new holiday cottages and hotels, all represent the asset value of the landscape from the perspective of those who live and work in that environment. How can the growth and development of these activities be reconciled with holding onto the picture postcard image of stone walls and whitewashed cottages?

Some form of management strategy is called for to ensure that the essential character-giving elements of the landscape resource are conserved and at the same time the resource is developed to the full to provide a sustainable future for local communities. The challenge is to identify a strategy which will facilitate development and conservation and will reconcile often-conflicting interests in the landscape, thus allowing growth in employment and incomes at the local level and at the same time maintaining the quality of the landscape and the environment which has given rise to that economic activity in the first place.

Project proposal

Bord Failte was concerned with maintaining and improving the quality of the landscape so that the marketing of the landscape as a tourism product would be enhanced. But the tourism resource can be destroyed by tourism itself. An Taisce, the National Trust for Ireland, through its work on the EU's structural funds and their environmental effects, had looked at some of the impacts of increased tourism spending in vulnerable areas and found an absence of a coherent policy for sustainable development. Following a round table on the Fifth Environmental Action Programme early in 1993, Bord Failte invited An Taisce to join with them in applying for funding to the European Commission's LIFE 93 programme for a pilot project to test the question of how the areas of outstanding scenic landscape could be protected and yet developed for tourism.

Scenic landscapes: definition and objective

Scenic landscape areas are defined as areas where significant scenic qualities are protected by the integrated development and management of key resources without recourse to acquisition of land by public authorities. Each scenic landscape comprises area of outstanding landscape quality but also contains the range of socioeconomic activities and infrastructure as well as the human and physical resources necessary to sustain rural communities. Initially the objective was to create a new tourism product in the form of some kind of designation or park status which would readily identify these areas as special and at the same time put in place a management strategy which would protect and conserve their essential character-giving elements.

Through this project, Bord Failte, in partnership with An Taisce, the National Trust for Ireland, hoped to demonstrate how a management strategy might be used to sustain areas of high scenic quality so as to maintain the resource for a range of socioeconomic activities including tourism. The most vulnerable and most diverse areas in terms of natural resources often coincide with the areas of greatest tourism potential. The project examined how existing socioeconomic activity, land use planning and rural management could be integrated to achieve the objective of creating environmentally sustainable scenic landscapes, with the involvement of local authorities, regional tourism organisations, farming organisations and other relevant agencies as local partners.

Methodology

Pilot areas

An inventory of areas of outstanding scenic quality was carried out in 1977. From this basis an indicative map of some 25 areas was included in Bord Failte's Development Plan. For the purposes of the pilot project, three of these areas were chosen for detailed analysis. These were south-west Cork/Kerry, Sligo-Leitrim and the south-east river valleys. The impacts of tourism are not spread uniformly throughout even the scenic areas, so a deliberate decision was made to include areas with different levels of tourism pressure. The areas selected also crossed over county (administrative) boundaries, contained cohesive landscape units, and were not already under the protection of a national park designation (which involves protection through land acquisition by the state).

South-west Cork/Kerry and Beara

This area, which includes a small part of Kerry, extends from Bantry to Kenmare and includes the Sheep's Head peninsula. It is characterised by spectacular coastal scenery as well as magnificent mountain landscapes. The area is rich in archaeological sites, historical monuments and places of scientific interest, and already has a well-defined tourism image.

Sligo-Leitrim

This area extends from Strandhill to Lough Melvin and includes the Glenade valley, Glencar and Lough Gill. The landscape is characterised by dramatic mountain cliffs, waterfalls, lakes and sandy bays. It is an area rich in archaeological and historical sites ranging from Carrowmore cemetery to Parkes Castle and the decaying splendour of Lissadell House. The area includes well known tourist resorts such as Strandhill and Rosses Point as well as places of tourism interest such as Glencar, Ben Bulben and Lough Gill. The mountains to the north of Glencar are an area of largely untapped potential. This area shares a boundary with Northern Ireland. The permanent cessation of violence in the north would bring dramatic changes to the tourism industry in this part of Ireland with a huge increase in the number of visitors from Northern Ireland and farther afield anticipated.

The Barrow/Nore/Suir river valleys

This area includes the valleys of the Barrow, the Nore and the Suir, as well as the Blackstairs Mountains to the east, extending from Kells village in the west to Bunclody in the east. It is characterised by wooded hill slopes dissected by major river valleys, attractive villages at river crossing points and typical pastoral scenery. The Blackstairs mountains are an area of particular scenic beauty. It is an area rich in castles and abbeys, great houses and parklands, dolmens and churches, with the medieval city of Kilkenny to the north and the Viking settlement of Waterford to the south.

The tourism potential of much of this area has hitherto been under-exploited. Apart from Kilkenny City which has long been a significant tourism destination of national significance, and the attraction of specialist interests for angling and equestrian activities and more recently golf with the opening of Mount Juliet, much of the area has not been regarded as a tourism destination. Objectives for the development of rural tourism and touring areas are particularly applicable to this area.

Inventory and analysis

The designation or recognition of scenic landscapes requires first and foremost an inventory of resources and activities in order to identify the character-giving elements. The project has identified the key elements of the pilot areas under the following headings: ecology, flora, fauna, geology, landscapes; archaeology, folklore/folklife, language and place names. Existing designated areas such as areas of scientific interest, proposed natural heritage areas, nature reserves and special protection areas have been identified and mapped and the relative significance of each recorded. Of equal importance are the socioeconomic activities which ensure the survival of a living community. The principal activities which dominate the rural environment have been analysed with particular reference to agriculture, forestry, fisheries including aquaculture, and of course tourism.

Consultation

The inventory gave a clear picture of the present state of the landscape and current strategies for its protection and management. The next step was to identify the processes of change. This was undertaken through data analysis and through consultation at national, regional, and local level with a wide range of interests and agencies to clarify priorities for protection and management of the landscape.

It is increasingly recognised that top down strategies alone are an inadequate response to the needs of local communities, and that imposed strategies will not be effective. Any proposal to designate or recognise certain landscapes had to involve from the outset extensive consultation, particularly at local level. An extensive process of community consultation was undertaken using local media, semi-structured interviews and public meetings. The essence of this phase of the work was to ask people in local communities how they felt about their own areas; what they saw as the key elements and how they wanted these sustained into the future and whether they wanted to see tourism become the anchor of the local economy. Consultation is not a single-step process: to be meaningful and useful it has to be an on-going process which both informs and is informed by the development of a management strategy.

Designation or recognition?

Initially it was assumed that the outcome of this phase of the work would result in the designation of the core areas as scenic landscape areas which would aspire to some form of statutory protection and control. However it became apparent as the work progressed that designation in that sense was not the appropriate response. Analysis of best practice elsewhere and a review of existing designations within Ireland undertaken as part of the research indicated that strict designation can result in more problems than it can resolve. This is particularly the case in regions such as those concerned here, where one is dealing with large heterogeneous zones dominated by a landscape resource which is the product of centuries of human activity.

It also became clear as the process of consultation with both official agencies and local communities widened and deepened that there was considerable antipathy to the notion of designation. Traditional activities may be declining, but that does not mean that scenic landscapes should become some sort of tourist reserve where the local population takes second place. Tourism is not a panacea for solving the problems of declining agriculture and marginal incomes in peripheral rural areas. It is only one of a number of activities which can facilitate sustainable rural communities.

Management strategy

The key issue in protecting yet developing the resources of scenic areas is the control of externalities, or to put it more positively, the integration of different sectoral activities. Peeling back the layers to examine the real issues on the ground has exposed the complexity of the underlying structures. It is not easy to unravel all the strands to create a new present. It is not easy or possible or indeed even desirable to satisfy all demands. Each sector, each local group, each agency is working to its own agenda. The outcomes often produce conflict such as that between the development of aquaculture and the preservation of coastal scenic views; or the expansion of forestry and the maintenance of the traditional farming landscape, facilitating economic survival for farmers on marginal incomes at the expense of hillside erosion; or improving infrastructure and changing the inherent character of the local landscape, as through building one-off housing in the countryside to maintain the local population but affecting what others may perceive as an unspoilt landscape.

The resolution of such conflicts provides the key challenge for sustainable management of the rural landscape. What is needed is a strategy which takes account of the totality of the environment, which supersedes the individual concerns of sectoral interests. The mechanism proposed for conflict resolution in such areas is a scenic landscapes forum. This would provide the basis for a conciliation or mediation service between conflicting interests to resolve planning issues. It was proposed that the forum would establish a scenic landscapes bureau would act as an advisory centre providing design guidelines on issues as diverse as the development of depuration plants for the mussel growing industry; the design of road improvements and guidelines for new housing in sensitive environments; and the creation of a new interpretative strategy for the local cultural and physical heritage.

Conclusions

The approach of the scenic landscapes project is widely applicable to peripheral areas throughout Europe. Detailed implementation will vary depending on local circumstances but the following key concepts will remain valid: a mutual recognition of the special qualities of scenic landscapes; an acknowledgement of the community stake in the landscape and its resources; community involvement in the formulation, implementation and monitoring phases of landscape protection; a partnership of development and environmental interests working through consensus; conflict resolution as the basis for management; and the integration of sectoral activities through an area based management strategy.

At the commencement of the project it was assumed that the designation of scenic areas would be the most sustainable basis on which to establish a strategy for protection of the landscape. However, a key finding of the project has been the realisation that designation is not the appropriate response for living landscapes which have been largely shaped by the imprint of human activity. Retaining the special qualities of such areas while at the same time facilitating development depends on acknowledging the dynamic of change while maintaining the essence of cultural continuity. The development and promotion of sustainable tourism in special landscapes is possible and desirable only in the context of a strategy for sustainable communities. Recognition as the basis for protection involves continuing community ownership of the resources. Sustainable activity is best promoted through awareness, understanding and consensus.

Note

[1] A summary report on the project has been published: see J. Meldon and C. Skehan, 1996. Copies are available from An Taisce, Tailors' Hall, Dublin 8, Ireland.

Acknowledgement

This paper owes much to my colleague, Conor Skehan, an environmental consultant who has been involved in the scenic landscapes project since its inception.

Reference

Meldon, J. and C. Skehan. 1996. Tourism and the landscape: Management by consensus. Dublin: An Taisce and Bord Failte.

15 Tourism and alternative employment among farm families in less-favoured agricultural regions of Wales

John Hutson and David Keddie

A recent study of some 400 family farm households across seven regions of Wales focused on pluriactivity, that is *non-agricultural* work done by members of farm households in a situation where declining farm returns require new ways to generate income.[1]   On-farm non-agricultural pluriactivity rates on Welsh farms were double that of Europe in general and were particularly associated with tourism and work done by spouses. This paper looks at the kinds of tourist enterprises found, gives the views of those who provide these services and considers the part such enterprises might play in sustainable development.   If the future of the countryside is really in leisure and tourism, then down on the farm this is not viewed as being without its problems.

Pluriactivity

The research sample reflected Welsh farm structure, where the dominant type is livestock farming, with dairying and arable in lowland areas. Four-fifths of farms were between 25 and 250 acres. Most families (79%) owned their farms but farm household incomes were generally low with 56% earning less than £15,000 and 13% less than £5,000 per annum. Sixty per cent of farm households in the study were pluriactive and the most important source of extra income was from off-farm activity by household members other than principal farmers (Davies et al. 1993). Only 20% of principal farmers were pluriactive---emphasising the view that part-time farming was not "real" farming. However, the availability of off-farm paid work was vital for successors to support themselves as they gradually succeeded to management of the family farm as well as enabling them to invest income in the future of the family business.

Opportunities for waged work locally are also important for spouses, since the declining economic and social status of farming has imposed pressures on farmers' wives to stay in jobs or to return to work. Pressure to do paid work is not only financial, for maintaining household income, but cultural, in that most married women today are engaged in paid work. Going out to work is seen by many women as a source of social independence, giving women their own life beyond farm and family. Thus, as we have suggested elsewhere, policies and funding should encourage local labour markets which can provide the off-farm work which is able to make the greatest contribution to household survival (Hutson and Keddie 1995).

On-farm, non-agricultural pluriactivity rates in Wales at 41% were twice that of Europe in general at 19.6% (Brun and Fuller 1991). In Wales, these higher levels are most noticeable among spouses and much of this kind of activity is based in the tourist sector, especially in the north and west of the country. The study showed that 20% of farms used buildings and fields to generate income. The use pattern was for caravans (34%), rented accommodation (32%), general farm tourism (17.%), activities such as fishing, other sports or workshops (11%) and tents (6%) (Davies et al. 1993).

Sustainable development

In terms of providing a sustainable livelihood, tourism must be a *supplementary* source of income for the small scale, self-financed enterprise. Even in a country where some 75% of the population now see the countryside in terms of a recreational area, there are few tourist enterprises of a scale, and with sufficient year-round demand, to provide a full-time livelihood. However, it is important not to dismiss supplementary income sources as being unimportant. Firstly, they are vital to sustaining farming which, as the main creator and maintainer of the landscape, is itself a primary tourist resource. Secondly, they are important for providing income-earning opportunities as well as a chance to meet current cultural expectations and personal independence for spouses or partners---especially women. Thirdly, they provide a future for the farm business in that alternative income sources locally mean that children who will eventually be successors and inheritors can stay in the area while still working and investing in the farm. Thus, supplementary income sources provide ways of both sustaining and aiding the continuity of rural businesses, households and livelihoods.

Forms of small-scale tourist provision

The main forms of small-scale sustainable tourist provision are in offering accommodation or leisure activities. Farms can provide sites for camping or touring caravans, bed and breakfast or self-catering accommodation. Visitors can go horse riding, mountain biking or canoeing. Ventures such as farm tours for schools, working horse centres or gardens may attract visitors. Farm shops selling farm-produced cheese, vegetables or even chocolate products may encourage tourists to visit and buy direct. Tourism can also develop in new directions with impetus from guests. For example, camping and bed and breakfast projects have developed into leisure enterprises with the development of horse riding or mountain biking enterprises, as the following comments show:

> **Mrs:** People were starting to come in with caravans and they were asking, "Is there somewhere we can get a ride?"---as this is riding country---and it sort of took off from there. It wasn't planned, it just evolved on its own and was built up steadily.

or

> **Mr:** Last year, people who used to stay bed and breakfast a couple of years ago, were camping in our fields and suggested the idea of mountain bikes. Also I saw an article in The *Independent* (newspaper) about how popular mountain biking was and the nearest other place was miles away. We might revive bed and breakfast, but mountain bikes are more lucrative than bed and breakfast by a long shot---over double.

> **Mrs:** Bed and breakfast disrupts your life, so do the mountain bikes---but at least they're not in the house with the bikes!

For the small-scale enterprise, however, tourism is an uncertain market. Even for basic bed and breakfast or camping, a farm needs to be in an attractive setting near to a through route to readily attract custom. Too many farms are unable to meet either of these requirements. Tourism tends to be seasonal and few places have a year-round appeal. In any one local area saturation can quickly be reached. Everyone cannot do bed and breakfast and it is unlikely that there can be more than one "theme park" in a region. In Britain, there is always the problem of the weather!

Combining two businesses

All those involved in pluriactivity reported the strain of combining two jobs and spoke of the effects which one job can have on the other. On-farm tourism has its own problem of strangers coming on to the farm which is often seen as intrusive and may mean that the farm has to be tidied up for public presentation (just as the house and even personal living arrangements must be for bed and breakfast). There is an on-going tension between the (necessary) mess of farming and what the tourist expects---a clash of rural idyll and the actual processes of agricultural production. This is expressed in the following comments:

> **Son:** Our next door neighbour does bed and breakfast and makes more money out of the bed and breakfast than what he does farming! But we've never done it, father wouldn't cope with that! People walking around---it isn't that tidy a place---can't have them walking around!

or

> **Mr:** Oh, Jiw, Jiw! (Lord, Lord!) Oh no way! On a stock farm like us now, cattle on the yard all messy and you can't take the mess and the visitors, and we've got milking in the morning, that takes the time!

In some instances, disused or traditional farm buildings can be developed as tourist accommodation. However, the capital investment needed for this may be beyond the means or wishes of many farm businesses, as these informants say:

> **Mr:** We have a caravan to let which we bought specifically for tourism in 1974-5. And there's an old building outside we would like to convert into chalets to let. Capital is a problem, although there is a good grant on that at the moment---about 90%. Half the roof has been re-tiled and we've put in Velux windows thinking we would use it as a holiday cottage but we've not progressed from that!

or

> **Mrs:** We've got redundant buildings and he'd like to convert them but er . . .
>
> **Mr:** Well, the expense is too much. I couldn't see me getting my money back. You're talking about £25-30,000.
>
> **Q:** You'd then have two properties to sell?
>
> **Mr:** Well it would be, but looking at it the other way, we've got privacy now. I'd prefer to have privacy!

270

So, quality of life may be affected, as this farmer also observed:

> If you're gonna sort of have people living in a terrace of holiday cottages, you might as well be living in a terraced house in Fishguard!

On-farm tourism retains family labour on the farm---wives, especially, are still available to carry out regular farm jobs as well as being there to help out whenever an extra person is needed. Thus, much tourist activity reinforces a traditional feminine supportive role on the farm. Several farmers mentioned that if their wives had had to go *out* to work it would alter the farming system which at present relied heavily on their work. However, the following woman farmer, recently separated, saw tourist provision as a way she might get the farm going again since it was source of income which allowed her to be on the farm at all times.

> **Mrs:** I'd like to do bed and breakfast again and caravanning and camping which my husband stopped, I'd like to go back into that.
>
> **Q:** Isn't that a lot of work?
>
> **Mrs:** Yes, but if I could do bed and breakfast I'd give up going out to work, I get more satisfaction from being at home than going out to work. I'd rather be at home! I can see things that need doing, but I can't afford to stay at home!

Effects on family and household organisation

There is a great deal of hard work involved in servicing tourist accommodation with all the cleaning, washing and cooking involved---especially with guests who only stay one night. As these women say:

> **Q:** And have you ever thought about bed and breakfast?
>
> **Mrs:** Oh no, I couldn't cope with that because I don't like housework (laughs). I'd enjoy the cooking side, because I like cooking! But er, no, I couldn't cope with bed and breakfast because I couldn't stand the housework!

or

> **Mrs:** But I still---whether I have one person or two---I've still got to do the washing! And there's another thing, I've got a double bed and a single bed in one room. Well you can bet if I have a single person in, they'll always sleep in the double bed! I've never had anybody yet that has gone into the single bed! (laughs)

Children, especially daughters, can be an important source of help. As another woman said when asked why she didn't do bed and breakfast:

> Well, if I had a daughter---but I'm on my own, I haven't got time!

The actual house and its layout can be as important as the family type, size and point in the developmental cycle. In large farm houses which can be divided easily into family and guest areas, or in households where children have left home already, there may be accommodation which can be readily used for bed and breakfast. However, more often, bed and breakfast leads to a great deal of domestic disruption with family members having to restrict their use of living rooms, bathrooms and children even having to give up bedrooms. As this man says:

> My wife did bed and breakfast and evening meal at the time. We split the farmhouse into two. Kept doing it for a few years after having children---which helped pay for electric fences! Stopped because the children needed an extra bedroom and had to go without a bathroom and toilet and had to use the outside toilet and shower. It's more difficult with children!

A common account was that it was possible to do bed and breakfast when the children were young and after they had left home, but when they were adolescents you could not get them out of their rooms. Also, elderly parents may move in as the children leave:

> **Mrs:** . . . the summer just gone I did bed and breakfast here for a few weeks. I stopped because my father was unwell and he moved in. My last bed and breakfasts went out in the morning and my father moved in in the afternoon so that was the end of it! And it was going quite well too! I would have done well probably for another month you know, 'till the end of the season anyway and that was quite fun, people from all over the place!

Guests in a house create a need for special behaviour on the part of family household members. There is a loss of privacy which many resent and which puts others off going into it. Thus, many prefer to let caravans or cottages as visitors may be distanced from the farm as well as from the domestic life of the household, but opportunities for sociability and contact remain. The costs are more in terms of capital outlay and maintenance. Caravans can give the chance to try out letting with very little capital outlay---but they are not so attractive in wet weather!

Tourist provision can lead to tension between spouses especially where the husband resents the intrusion of outsiders into both his domestic routine and into the farm environment. Wives, on the other hand, often say that meeting visitors is something they enjoy and that it gives them a chance of sociability which they could not otherwise get on the farm. Many establish regular customers who return each year and some say that they make "real friends" whom they can visit in return. In addition, it includes them in the local network of bed and breakfast providers which gives both status and contacts in the neighbourhood.

> **Mrs**: I like meeting people and er we have a card from them sometimes. You know, it's mostly a Christmas card. And one family, they've come here for three years. And they're, you know, they're like friends now, not like er visitors. And we called to see them then when we were in Stratford in October, and they were so pleased to see us! You know, I enjoy that part of it! George doesn't enjoy it very much because the children always want to see the milking you know. He doesn't like that!

Farming is perceived as a masculine occupational culture while tourism, at least in its *service* aspects, is seen as a feminine one. Those enterprises which are an extension of the domestic arena---bed and breakfast, self-catering cottages or caravans, even camping---tend to be seen as women's work and to run somewhat uneasily beside the farm enterprise. Often, because of their seasonal nature, they seem to be tolerated as disagreeable features of the summer season. The more active enterprises such as mountain biking may have more men working in them and, as the scale of investment and income rises, men's involvement tends to increase.

Contribution to household income

The social costs of tourism related work are such that some say they would only do bed and breakfast as a necessity---if they were desperate for the money. For many others it is a source of that little bit extra, of pocket money, something to spend on the house which does not have to come from the farm account.

> **Q**: And now you've done up the house have you any plans to do bed and breakfast?
>
> **Mr**: Not at the moment.
>
> **Mrs**: No.
>
> **Mr**: Unless it gets that we have to! It would have to be for financial need. You know, it would have to be for the money and for nothing else!

or

> **Mrs**: Well, I'd always wanted a caravan. Perhaps I do miss people, you know, and er, I suppose at the time I thought that it would be a nice bit of pocket money for me, because I don't like taking money out of the bank, you know. Because I know we've got an overdraft and I thought if that money would be there, I could spend on the house and buy things for the house. I put it away and, you know, if we need a new carpet or I'm after two new chairs and they'll come from that. But er, you know, I think things for the house are things that we could do without. It seems wrong taking it out of the bank when that's got to be really used for paying off the overdraft!

Some, in the main those who did *not* do bed and breakfast, stressed that the right attitude was important---with so much competition you had to provide a good service. Others saw it as a possible future strategy.

> **Mr**: Yes. Oh, yes! Bed and breakfast would be good. But it depends on your house doesn't it? And it depends on whether you're cut out for that kind of thing, you know! Yes, that would suit a lot of people but it wouldn't suit us!

or

> **Mrs**: You know, we'd love to make money but would it be worth it and all the implications and it would be far too much hassle! I think also it's going to reach some sort of saturation point that there's only a certain percentage who want a farm cottage holiday or whatever and unless you do something really very, very well then, you know, you're not going to succeed!

or

> **Mr**: As far as the tourism is concerned you've got to specialise in it and the competition is quite keen, and um, I don't feel that tourism is the thing for us really. But, at a later stage, there'll be younger members of the family that will be left without, can't get a job and it's a last resort, it will probably be worth thinking about it then. But you've got to get in and really do a good job of it, and there's a possibility then that you can get something out of it---doing it sort of half-hearted, it's not on!

Increasing bureaucratic controls and changing fashions

Legislative controls covering hygiene, fire, health and safety are now becoming widespread and restrictive. Regulations may even affect visitors' access to parts of the farm which might otherwise be made available as part of a farm tourism package. Competition locally may be fierce and visitors expect increasingly high standards. They are no longer happy to just join in another family's routine as a house guest, but expect a separate and special place as a client. As these couples explain:

> **Mrs:** I mean with all the rules and regulations that they're going to bring in. I mean in some ways I don't know whether I'll be bothered next year if I'm truthful and abide by the rules they'll bring in and what they think people will want! I mean I don't think it's worth it!

> **Mr:** It's getting now that people don't want bed and breakfast anyway. They want a hotel room and facilities at a cheap rate. That's what they want. You know, they want sort of er separate toilet facilities and showers and all this sort of thing!

> **Mrs:** Toilet facilities and en suite, you know, all like this that and the other---a "Teasmade" in the room!

> **Mr:** Well, you know if they want that they can go down to Fishguard and pay £40 a night instead of £12, but this is how it's getting now, I think. The older generation are all right, you know. You have an elderly couple come and they say, "Oh that's lovely!" you know, all this sort of thing and "Is that too much trouble?" and this sort of thing! But the younger generation, "Oh, no bath, no separate bathroom!" and this sort of thing!

or

> **Mr:** And you're supposed to get your Health and Safety certificate!

> **Mrs:** I know a friend of mine that she could put up sort of a couple of families, then it makes ten by the children and you're supposed to have a separate kitchen. Well how ridiculous!

> **Mr:** You know, it's just gonna kill it, because people just won't bother like. Unless you're doing it on a large scale which is getting into the guest house, sort of hotel business---it's not sort of farmhouse bed and breakfast! That's one of those things that make you think, well, is it worth it? You know, sort of having people coming and going. I mean we get on tremendously well with the majority of people who come and stay here like. I mean it's nice to have a chat with them and you know, but sometimes you think, well you know, why should I allow them to invade my privacy just for that little amount of money when you've got to live up to all these other rules and regulations?

Getting clients

Most people advertise locally, and being on a local network means visitors are sent on when others are full. For some, who come from other parts of the country, parents or relatives may place advertisements in *their* local papers. Others use commercial agencies.

> **Mrs:** We've had it (a caravan) three summers. I advertise it and this year we let it for about 11 weeks. My Mum put it in one of her local papers the first year we had a caravan. And we didn't have it until June, so we didn't advertise until then and my Mum put it in one of the local papers, and a couple and their two small children came from Leamington Spa, which is only about 6 miles from Mum. And they've been coming here for three years!

or

> **Mrs:** I've had a reasonable year with my cottage, best year so far any way! Not quite as good as I'd hoped. I went with a new agency to advertise it this last winter and they sort of suggested that I might get 30 weeks' bookings. But with the Gulf War in the spring and the recession bookings all round were down and they got me 24 weeks---which was very good, I mean I'd never managed to get, I think 16 weeks was my own best that I'd managed to do with my own advertising and everything, so . . .! I just have to pay a fee, an annual sort of fee, subscription really, and then they take care of everything after that. They do all the advertising, they do all the bookings, they just send me details of all the families that they've booked in and with telephone numbers so I can contact families if there's any queries. You know, if I want to know do they need a cot or you know, are they bringing a dog with them, will they require any extra things and you know, what do they want putting in the cottage before they arrive and that sort of thing? So I can get that contact, I can get to know the customers but I don't have any of the hassle of the possibility of double booking or people paying a deposit and then not sending the balance and things like that. They do all that. So it means I can spend my labour time more effectively on actually looking after them and looking after the people that come, you know. Taking care of their needs and then if they want to know things and, you know, book things for them and send them off to places of interest and, you know, find out about buses and everything else that they need to know, you know so it's erm, it's good!

Larger enterprises

Our qualitative sample included two larger tourist enterprises. The first was a farm with a four acre garden, run with family labour, which last year attracted 8,000 visitors. Two sons were away doing agricultural courses, one on a horticultural course as a result of interest in the garden which he might take over in time. The farmer, who had been brought up on the neighbouring farm, bought this farm in a very run down condition as a hobby farm. Ill health, however, had forced him to retire from a salaried job and he had had to work the farm full time. It had been a struggle to build the place up because it had been so run down: "That's been my downfall! I've had to buy everything!". His neighbours are all farmers who inherited going concerns. His wife goes out to work from 6.30 am to 2.00 pm then she works on the garden. Keen gardeners, they opened their garden for charity for a few years; then, encouraged by the response, they opened it commercially in 1989 and had 400 visitors. Four years later they expanded the garden, planted thousands of bulbs to give a good show at Easter and have 8,000 visitors. He now spends £700-£800 a year on advertising. He was very bitter that while there were all sorts of grants available for farming, there was nothing for his garden enterprise. He had also run into opposition from the local authorities about putting up sign boards for the garden.

The other enterprise was based around a complex of caves and underground caverns which were discovered on the farm in 1912 and parts of which were opened to the public by the present farmer's father in 1939. The business has expanded considerably with extra attractions such as a café, nature trails, riding and a dry ski slope. His current ambition is to build up the enterprise into a full day out for the family, but he has been involved in a constant struggle with the National Park authorities for approval for his latest schemes for achieving this---a shire horse centre and a museum of farming since Neolithic times.

> (The caves) are unalterable. The problem is we have got to find a way of getting people to come back, and the only thing we can do is to give them something new every so many years. It is a problem because, as I say, I think anybody looking at the business would say, well what you want here is a great chunk of fun! We do heavy geology---Carboniferous and Silurian---all heavy stuff, you've really got to sit and concentrate! And now we would have liked a softer, more fun approach!

Business peaked in the 1970s and 80s when it was averaging 180,000 visitors a year. By 1992 visitors were down to 90,000. This he put down firstly to fewer people coming on holiday to Wales, as it is cheaper to go abroad for a holiday (40-45% of his visitors come from the south east of England). He was particularly concerned about competition from Disneyland. Secondly, he blamed falling numbers on his failure to provide a full day's entertainment. He had had to reduce his permanent staff of six down to four and might have to reduce his temporary summer staff of 42. He stressed that he tried to employ local people. He had spent around £15,000 researching and planning the museum idea and he was very frustrated at the National Park's response to his plans---especially as they took over a year to consider his applications.

> I am now at my wits' end with the National Park because I do not have any more ideas! I mean if I can't get museums through, if I can't get Shire horses through, I mean what can I do? I mean if I were suggesting putting in a dodgem track with a sixty foot high loop the loop, fair enough, I don't expect anybody to have any sympathy. But I'd have thought things like shire horses and farm museums . . .! Not necessarily the best things for the company, but obviously we have to think of things that stand some hope of going through the Park. We are standing still and, as a company, going backwards!

Although the two enterprises were very different in scale and capital involvement, both saw their main problem as a lack of support from, even conflict with, local agencies--especially from those most concerned with environmental sustainability.

Tourism and sustainable development

A third of farm households in the Welsh study reported that they needed extra income from other sources to provide a sustainable livelihood, and 21% of such farms were involved in on-farm non-agricultural work, most of which was associated with tourism. In this context, small-scale tourist ventures such as those providing accommodation, campsites and on-farm leisure activities do seem to meet a need to develop local social, cultural and material resources while avoiding dependency and indebtedness.

The countryside and a farming way of life can be used to attract visitors with relatively little capital outlay. Farm tourism can increase household income and contribute to farm projects. It is a source of sociability both with tourists and among neighbours who are engaged in similar activities. Those involved in tourism may be more likely to engage in "environmentally-friendly" practices and to keep farms and yards tidy for visitor appeal. Farmers are thus made directly aware of the views of non-farmers towards both the countryside and to farming itself. In several cases, ideas for further developments such as riding stables, or mountain bike trails have come from the demands of tourists themselves. Moreover, where a region is involved with tourism there may be a knock-on effect on the rural economy as a whole, thus providing more off-farm work for farm household members---including potential successors.

However, farm tourism is not without its problems. Seasonality is a constraint in many areas which only really attract tourists in the summer. Also local landscapes are not equally attractive, and there are limits to the amount and range of provision which can be put on in any one area without reaching saturation. Tourism tends to fit better with some types and sizes of farm, household forms and stages in family development. Visitors on the farm and in the household can lead to disruption and loss of privacy. A further difficulty mentioned is the increasing number and restrictive nature of bureaucratic controls.

Thus, some form of regional policy and organisation could be very helpful to promote the attractions of a region, to advise providers on what is needed by tourists and to co-ordinate local provision and bookings as well as acting as a pressure group for providers. For example, there is some indication that visitor demand is moving in the direction of rented accommodation rather than bed and breakfast. This is cheaper for the tourist, but more expensive in terms of capital outlay for the farmer. Expert knowledge and advice is needed to encourage and co-ordinate such developments. Once the investment risk can be calculated more accurately, this sort of provision actually fits rather well with some cultural expectations as it minimises the domestic disruption and loss of privacy which many complain about or say puts them off going in for this sort of tourist venture.

However, there were other aspects of cultural resistance to tourist enterprises. "Proper" farming was seen as full-time farming. Those who engaged in other activities were "playing at it", were "incomers" or even "failed" farmers. Overall, our survey showed that there was a great reluctance to borrow coupled with a low incidence of indebtedness---even for mortgages (18%) and bank overdrafts (33%). Pluriactivity in general was mostly found in the £5,000-£15,000 income category---where farms were being improved or where investment was needed---and levels of borrowing were higher on these pluriactive farms. There was a perceived difference in outlook and motivation between those who inherit a farm and those who buy and build one up. Local or incomer and Welsh or English distinctions were also associated with such differences. However, such ethnic contrasts seem to be based on differences of a practical kind--- established farmers have less *need* to borrow---rather than any simple cultural avoidance of risk-taking and entrepreneurial endeavour (Keddie 1992). Moreover, reluctance to borrow seems sensible in view of most farmers' lack of market knowledge concerning tourist development.

Another cultural aspect is the feminisation of small-scale tourist accommodation. Much of the on-farm pluriactivity which is associated with tourism is done by spouses---rather than by principal farmers or other members such as children. Thus it tends to be "women's work", done mostly by wives to increase household income rather than providing a means of maintaining children as successors to the farm. In most cases the money gained goes on household expenses and maintaining the home. But it may also go to the farm to pay for particular projects or needs such as electric fencing.

Thus, small scale tourism seems to reproduce established cultural patterns in terms of gender divisions and occupational culture. Servicing the needs of tourists is seen as an extension of women's traditional and existing roles---feeding the men (farm workers) and feeding the family. It combines with the notion of "real" farming above so that providing tourist accommodation is acceptable in so far as the husband remains a full-time farmer and it is the wife who manages the tourist enterprise. And, insofar as women say that income from tourist provision tends to go on the house (rather than on the farm), the combination is again culturally acceptable. From one point of view this may be seen positively as facilitating such developments into this occupational culture---they may be more acceptable because they will not change things too much. However, seen negatively it does tend to reproduce differences and divisions.

Conclusion

It is clear that there is still a considerable gap between the public's perception of the countryside as a recreational area and farmers' and their families' willingness and ability to engage in tourist provision. However, small-scale tourism is an effective and sustainable supplementary source of income---for the middle range of farms, if they are in an attractive locale, at the early or late stages of the family cycle, if the spouse is prepared to do the work and if the farmer is prepared to tolerate the effects on the farm and the loss of privacy. Self-catering tourist accommodation or leisure activities which involve financial borrowing and men's labour require a more fundamental commitment by both spouses. This is where some sort of regional organisation of expert advice, publicity and booking services could become an important facilitator. Even at the most local level, involvement in bed and breakfast can provide a source of contact and co-operation between neighbours---a source of sociability as well as a marketing base in a rural neighbourhood. A longer-term feedback is that the more farmers and their families are involved in tourist provision, the more they will become aware of alternative views about the countryside and its future as well as being encouraged to farm in more environmentally-sensitive ways which help to maintain the landscape.

Note

[1] The research was funded by the Economic and Social Research Council as part of the Joint Agriculture and Environment Programme and was carried out by the Rural Surveys Research Unit and the Department of Economics and Agricultural Economics at the University of Wales, Aberystwyth and the Department of Sociology and Anthropology at the University of Wales, Swansea.

References

Bateman, D, G. Hughes, P. Midmore, N. Lampkin and C. Ray. 1993. *Pluriactivity and the Rural Economy in the Less-favoured Areas of Wales.* Aberystwyth: Department of Economics and Agricultural Economics, University of Wales.

Brun, H. and A. M. Fuller. 1992. *Farm Family Pluriactivity in Western Europe.* Oxford: Arkleton Trust.

Davies, L., W. J. Edwards and J. W. Aitchison. 1993. *A Comparative Study of Pluriactivity in the Less-favoured Farming Areas of Wales.* Aberystwyth: Rural Surveys Research Unit, University of Wales.

Hutson, J. and D. Keddie. 1993. *Household Work Strategies in the Brecon-Merthyr and Fishguard Regions of Wales.* Swansea: Department of Sociology and Anthropology, University of Wales.

Hutson, J. and D. Keddie. 1995. Pluriactivity as a strategy for the future of family farming in Wales. In R. Byron (ed.), *Economic Futures on the North Atlantic Margin.* Aldershot: Avebury.

Keddie, D. 1992. Welsh farming and the entrepreneurial spirit. *Planet* 95: 30-35.

Part Four
SUSTAINABLE DEVELOPMENT
OF AGRICULTURAL COMMUNITIES

16 Farm diversification and sustainability: The perceptions of farmers and institutions in the west of Ireland

Mary Cawley, Desmond Gillmor and
Perpetua McDonagh

Introduction

The economies of most marginal regions traditionally have been heavily dependent upon agriculture. The role of agriculture has diminished as their economies have diversified but this process has lagged behind and occurred to a lesser extent than in the more developed regions. Thus the proportion of the workforce reliant on farming and the proportion of the land devoted to agriculture remain comparatively high (Fenton and Gillmor 1994). In the west of Ireland, for instance, direct employment in agriculture is 25% of all employment and 78% of the land is used for agricultural purposes, with much of the remainder being mountain, peat bog or forest. The population is predominantly rural, with 74% of the people living in the open countryside or in settlements of less than 1500 population.

The agriculture upon which marginal regions are so dependent has come under considerable pressures in recent times (Goodman and Redclift 1989, Bowler 1992, NESC 1992). This has resulted from the need to curtail the escalating costs of farm support and disposal of surplus production, together with growing concern about the detrimental impacts which modern farming is having on the environment. Under the reform of the Common Agricultural Policy (CAP) of the European Union (EU) and the measures of national governments, efforts have been made to curtail production through reduced price incentives and quantitative controls on output of the main products. This has exerted income pressures on farmers and greatly restricted the possibility of responding in the traditional way of increasing production in the conventional enterprises. The pressures are felt in common with agriculture elsewhere but farming in marginal regions tends to be more vulnerable because of less favourable land resources and farm structure, adverse social conditions and poor market accessibility. The predominantly small farm businesses of marginal regions have much less scope for following the option most commonly adopted, that of increasing farm efficiency. Because of limited employment opportunities in marginal regions, there is also less scope for obtaining off-farm jobs though this is a significant adjustment strategy (Fuller 1990, MacKinnon et al. 1991, Shucksmith 1993).

In these circumstances, it may be expected that some farmers would turn to another course of action, that of farm diversification through the adoption of alternative farm enterprises (AFEs). These are farm-based activities outside the mainstream of modern conventional agriculture and include enterprises such as agri-tourism, farm forestry, new types of livestock, organic agriculture and on-farm processing. It would seem logical also from the perspective of marginal regions seeking sustainable development, that the potential should be explored for putting three of their most abundant and important resources---agricultural land, the rural environment and farm families---to these alternative uses. Such development would be based on the indigenous resources of the areas and would mobilise the skills and expertise of their resident people. The scope for AFE development has expanded greatly with the changing demands of modern economies and societies, opening up new market opportunities to be exploited. This is reinforced by state policies and incentives to promote rural diversification and farm practices which are less damaging to the environment than modern intensive agricultural production. Thus farm diversification offers the scope for being a significant element in the sustainable development of marginal regions: economically, socially and environmentally.

The potential opportunities and constraints of farm diversification were reviewed in general terms by Gillmor (1995). This chapter has developed out of and is an extension of that discussion by investigating the perceptions of farmers and institutions concerning the adoption of AFEs in a marginal region, the west of Ireland. Farm diversification does not occur in isolation but through the interaction between the internal environment of the farm and the external institutional environment. The farmer-institution interface is a critical element in this process. Thus it was decided to explore both the opinions of farmers, on whom adoption is ultimately dependent and who have the experience of the real world of farming, and also the perceptions of institutions associated with AFEs, which deal with numbers of farmers and so may be expected to take broader perspectives in certain respects. Some other aspects of the study are reported in Cawley et al. (1995).

While the west of Ireland was the study area in general, attention in the farm survey in particular was focused on the counties of Galway and Kerry as representing the varied conditions occurring in the region. Within each county a sample of 100 farms was selected for a questionnaire survey, with a distinction being made between AFE adopters and non-adopters. The non-adopter subsample was obtained by taking randomly 60 farms from the list of Farm Accounts Data Network (FADN) farms in each county and then, for the 11% of these farms which were found to have AFEs, substituting non-adopters from a random fall-back sample list. A list of diversified farms was compiled from all the varied relevant sources, involving a thorough search to ensure that the list was as comprehensive as possible. An adopter subsample of 40 farms was selected in proportion to the total number of farms known to be involved with the different types of AFE in each county.

From a total of 71 institutions identified as being associated in some way with farm diversification, a sample of 36 was chosen to represent the diversity of organisations and the spatial scales at which they operate. Identified key personnel in 45 institutional divisions were interviewed, multiple interviews being conducted in the three most important organisations. Institutional involvement with farm diversification included AFE promotion and development, the provision of information and advice, lobbying government departments and contributing to policy formulation, the provision and administration of grant schemes and of other finance, marketing, research, education and training, and representation of farmers.

The context of farm diversification

In relation to farm diversification in the context of sustainable development, it was decided first to seek the views of the different groups of respondents on some general agricultural issues. This was done using the methodology devised by Beus and Dunlap (1991) to measure adherence to conventional and alternative agricultural paradigms. Four pairs of contrasting statements were chosen from the items used by Beus and Dunlap as being relevant to farm diversification in sustainable development (Table 1). A five-point scale was placed between each of the two contrasting positions, with the mid-point (three) representing a neutral view. Respondents were asked to circle one number for each item. In interpreting Table 1, it should be borne in mind that the conventional farmers in the west of Ireland are not representative of modern highly industrialised agriculture for, while there are progressive commercial farmers, the majority are of a more traditional type.

The first two pairs of statements were related in questioning attitudes associated with short-term profitability versus the long-term sustain-ability of the land and farm. The mean scores indicate that all three groups of respondents tended towards favouring sustainability rather than profitability in both pairs of statements and the percentage dis-tributions show the range of scores (Table 1). In both instances, the diversified farmers were more committed to sustainability than were the conventional farmers and it is interesting that the institutions were even more so, more markedly in respect of the first pair of statements. These perceptions of those associated with diversification augur well for its role in the maintenance if rural land and communities.

The three groups diverged in their attitudes towards the third pair of statements, with the conventional farmers tending to see farming more as a way of life and the other groups seeing it, more strongly, as primarily a business. There was a dichotomy amongst the non-diversified farmers, however, as one-quarter of them strongly agreed with farming being primarily a business, though the majority held more traditional views. It is important that there should be a business attitude in AFE development and this was reflected in the diversifiers and associated institutions.

The fourth pair of statements addressed attitudes towards the relative merits of specialisation in general agriculture, not referring to AFEs. While conventional farmers were more disposed towards specialisation in either crops or livestock, the other groups were more disposed towards more mixed farming systems. In the latter instance, however, the tendency was quite marginal and substantial proportions of respondents were undecided. Nonetheless this indicates a shift away from seeing specialisation as a mark of agricultural progress by those who are adapting most quickly to the changing circumstances in farming.

It is interesting that in relation to each of the four pairs of statements there was the same sequence of mean scores, with the opinions of the diversified farmers being intermediate between the those of the conventional farmers and the institutions. This suggests that the institutions and diversified farmers have common elements in their thinking and that the opinions of the institutions are further removed from those of conventional farmers than are those of diversified farmers.

That farm diversification is perceived to be a significant development in the rural economy was demonstrated by three-quarters of both groups of farmers having thought AFEs to be a sign of a real change in Irish agriculture, with less than one-tenth considering that they were not. By a ratio of four to one, they felt that AFEs would increase rather than decrease over the next five years. Diversification is being entered predominantly as a long-term commitment, as indicated by 90% of those who had adopted it, with only one respondent considering it to be specifically short-term. This favourable perspective of diversification as a sustainable venture was reinforced by three-fifths of adopters feeling that the introduction of an AFE had a positive impact on their quality of life, whereas only two respondents felt that the effect had been negative.

Reasons for AFE adoption

The experiences and perceptions of farmers

When adoptive farmers were asked to give up to three reason why they had established an AFE, the financial consideration of increasing or maintaining farm income was the leading single factor, having been mentioned by more than half of respondents (Table 2). Yet, while income generation was the major stimulus, 55% of the adopters estimated that the AFEs provided less than 10% of gross farm income. While it must be borne in mind that most of the enterprises were at an early stage of development and that the farmers had difficulty in calculating contributions to total income, it is possible that the realities of AFE income generation may not match the expectations. The other financial factor of government grant aid was mentioned by just one-fifth of respondents. Yet it was found that only 31% of the AFEs had been established without state financial assistance and these were mainly bed and breakfast enterprises for which grant aid was generally unavailable. Also the adoption of particular AFEs often coincided with the introduction of corresponding grant aid schemes. Thus the role of state grants as a stimulus to farm diversification may be greater than acknowledged by the farmers.

The socio-personal dimension has been demonstrated to be of importance in agricultural decision making in general (Ilbery 1985) and so this is likely to apply also to farm diversification. Almost two-fifths of farmers gave personal interest as a reason for establishment and over one-fifth related adoption to a change in personal circumstances (Table 2). The chance element in establishment was of some significance and the opportunity to meet people was a minor factor. While only six farmers mentioned previous experience as a reason, eighteen adopters had such experience. Thus it was evident that the combined personal influences had been important in the adoption process.

Availing of an under-utilised resource was ranked joint second as a reason for AFE establishment, principally by those using poor quality land for forestry and empty rooms for tourist accommodation. The resource of farm location was of lesser significance as a factor, being relevant mainly in relation to tourism areas. The human resource element figured less prominently than might have been expected in a region of limited employment opportunities. The provision of employment, principally for family members, was mentioned by only one-eighth of farmers. Although marketing opportunity was ranked fourth in importance, its mention as a reason for AFE establishment by only a quarter of respondents suggests a lower level of market-led development in farm diversification than would be desired.

Institutional perceptions

The institutional responses as to what their organisations consider to be the main reasons why farm families and businesses are adopting AFEs, with allowance for mentioning of up to five factors, are shown and compared with the reasons given by farmers in Table 2. The need to supplement farm income was the predominantly perceived reason for adoption, being mentioned by four-fifths of the institutional divisions, so that it was emphasised even more strongly than by the farmers them-selves. Associated with this and ranked second was the response to CAP reform. This may be combined with the more lowly-placed availability of government grants, together indicating a stronger emphasis on the role of the state in farm diversification than that attributed by the farmers. Conversely, although one-third of institutional respondents acknowledged the influence of changing attitudes, the role of personal reasons was rated more lowly than the experiences of farmers would indicate. Another difference related to the generation of family employment, which was ranked fourth by the institutional respondents but placed only ninth in the farmers' own experience. This divergence was attributable mainly to overemphasis on labour provision by those institutions involved primarily with conventional agriculture, so that they placed it even above the influence of CAP reform.

In order to explore a different dimension of the adoption process as perceived by the institutional respondents, they were asked to indicate the types of farm, with regard to certain specified characteristics, that have shown the strongest tendency to adopt particular AFEs. The respondents did not specify the types of farm with regard to approxi-mately one-half of the AFEs. For those which were identified, the respondents felt that the strongest tendencies to adopt had been shown by: small to medium farms; farms on mixed to marginal land; farms with drystock but not arable farms; farms in the west; farmers of middle to young age; farmers with young families. The other characteristics specified by the respondents as identifying farms which had been more likely to adopt AFEs were mainly those on which there were initiative, contacts, high levels of education and available capital. Support for some of these institutional perceptions was provided by a comparison of the samples of adopters and non-adopters, which showed that those farmers who had diversified tended to be younger, better educated, have more contact with the advisory service, and be more likely to be married and have children than were conventional farmers.

Barriers to the development of farm diversification

Despite the number and strength of the reasons for farm diversification, the low level of adoption suggests that there are also substantial barriers to AFE development. These were explored with both farmers and institutions. The non-adoptive farmers were asked to give up to three main reasons why they had not established an AFE. The institutional respondents were asked what they considered to be the main barriers or constraints to the participation in AFEs by farm families and farm businesses. The institutional perception of constraints is compared with the reasons given for non-adoption by farmers in Table 3.

It is evident that deficiencies in the availability of capital and expertise must be major hindrances to farm diversification, as there was agreement between the reasons given by farmers for non-adoption of AFEs and the perceptions of constraints by the institutions in highlighting these as two barriers to development, with the institutions focusing more strongly on them (Table 3). Every institutional respondent identified the lack of private capital as a constraint and ten of them added the related financial consideration of an insufficient level of grant aid. Inadequate capital was cited as one of their main reasons for non-adoption by over one-third of farmers, including two who specifically mentioned difficulties in obtaining loans. To the 37 institutional respondents who identified lack of knowledge or education concerning AFEs as a constraint, may be added the specific references to marketing education and technical advice or information, emphasising the great importance attached by the institutions to deficiencies in expertise as a barrier to farm diversification. Lack of knowledge about AFEs was ranked third by the non-adoptive farmers as a reason for not diversifying.

The major differences between the farmer and institutional perceptions of barriers related to the role of socio-personal factors. Their preference for traditional methods of farming was identified quite clearly as the main reason for not establishing an AFE, having been mentioned by almost one-half of farmers (Table 3). Conversely, the persistence of traditional methods was ranked only fifth by the institutional respondents, having been mentioned by less than half of them. Furthermore, they identified no other influences of a specifically socio-personal nature. Yet age was one of the four dominant reasons for non-adoption by farmers, a lack of interest was significant and poor health was a minor factor. The personal attitudes of farmers would also have been important in their identification of risk aversion, avoidance of extra pressure of work, satisfaction with existing income and lack of time as reasons why they did not diversify.

While the institutional respondents greatly underestimated the role of socio-personal influences, they placed much importance on the more objective constraints of inadequate on-farm facilities and market restrictions. The market potential should be a prime consideration in any AFE development, so it must be of concern that the lack of market opportunity was considered a negligible reason for non-adoption by the farmers. It suggests that farmers may not give sufficient attention to marketing in the decision-making process. Yet market considerations are likely to have been major components in the assessment of unsuitable farm location and uncertainty of returns as significant constraints by both farmers and institutions.

A later barrier to the development of farm diversification arises if some farmers, having adopted one or more AFEs, subsequently cease these activities. This in itself reduces the level of development but also acts as a disincentive to other farmers to adopt farm diversification. The number of farmers in the sample surveys who had abandoned an AFE was too small to provide any basis for analysis or consideration of reasons. The institutions were asked to provide reasons for lack of success for those farms for which diversification had proved unsuccessful. The response to this question was low, however, because the institutional respondents had little experience of such failures and perhaps in part because they did not wish to acknowledge association with them.

The main reason for lack of success given by the institutional respondents, mentioned by nine of them, was changing market conditions. This was followed by four reasons, each with six to five mentions. They were: lack of investment capital, lack of professionalism, bad management and lack of marketing skills, thus relating to deficiencies in the financial and human resources. Other reasons for lack of success were mentioned only three to one times and comprised: insufficient financial returns, lack of technical information, location and lack of communication skills.

The regional context

While the need for farm diversification as a component in sustainable development is considerable in marginal regions, it is important that there should be a realistic appreciation of the comparative competitive position of such regions. It might be found, for instance, that the attributes which have retarded other forms of development also restrict farm diversification. Then it would be desirable that there should be national policy decisions concerning the appropriate balance between promoting AFEs in areas to which they are most suited and promoting them in areas where the need for them is greatest.

It is evident that there must be substantial and complex spatial variation in the potential for farm diversification. Most of the factors which were identified as encouraging and hindering its general development have spatial expressions. With regard to the individual AFEs, their locational influences vary considerably, for instance those for agri-tourism, farm forestry and vegetable production being quite different. While recognising that much of the complexity would be concealed, the perceptions of institutions were explored with regard to the comparative advantages and disadvantages of the study areas for the development of AFEs in general. Their assessments would be useful because of the perspectives which they would have through operating at a range of spatial scales from local to national and through the variety of functions which they perform.

Most of the areas' advantages and disadvantages which the institutional respondents identified relate to farm diversification in general, though the inclusion of some specific AFEs indicates the importance attached to these (Table 4). This was most notable with regard to agri-tourism, to the extent that it was mentioned by three-quarters of the institutional divisions and its potential was regarded as by far the most important advantage of the study areas. This significance reflects in part the role which tourism plays in west Galway and in south and west Kerry, which have major coastal, upland and human attractions for tourists. Also specifically mentioned were the advantages for organic agriculture, relating to the low intensity of agriculture and the clean environment, and for farm forestry, relating to the extent of marginal land and the favourable conditions for tree growth. Individual enterprises were not identified amongst the disadvantages of the areas, apart from two references to the lack of a tradition in processing.

It may be regarded as a considerable potential strength of the areas that the two advantages most mentioned with regard to farm diversification in general were their unrealised resource potential and the good image of the areas. The favourable green environmental image of the west of Ireland is in itself a huge resource which could be a great asset in the marketing of farm products and services. The ranking next of a tradition of changing enterprises and willingness to adopt AFEs may be attributed in part to institutional contact being mainly with the more progressive element amongst the farm population. Specification of the diversity of soil and land types as an advantage suggests that the institutions consider diversified development to be more sustainable and desirable, rather than undue reliance on a single AFE.

Table 1
Percentage distributions and mean scores for attitudes towards farming by non-diversified farmers, diversified farmers and institutions

N. Non-diversified farmers
  (n = 117)
D. Diversified farmers
  (n = 73)
I. Institutions
  (n = 29)

1. Strongly agree with the view in the left-hand column
2. Mildly agree with the view in the left-hand column
3. Undecided
4. Mildly agree with the view in the right-hand column
5. Strongly agree with the view in the right-hand column

		1	2	3	4	5	Mean score	
Farming should protect long-term productive capacity of land	N.	30	26	10	18	13	2.58	Farming should seek profit maximisation from land
	D.	42	27	19	10	1	2.00	
	I.	72	21	7	0	0	1.34	
Goal should be productivity and profitability of farm	N.	12	3	26	26	32	3.65	Goal should be quality and long-term farm condition
	D.	7	8	9	25	53	4.10	
	I.	0	7	7	34	52	4.31	
Farming is a business	N.	26	9	5	26	35	3.36	Farming is more a way of life
	D.	55	8	7	18	12	2.25	
	I.	62	10	10	7	10	1.93	
Farms should specialise in either crops or livestock	N.	46	11	9	12	22	2.53	Farms should have both crops and livestock
	D.	22	8	32	18	21	3.07	
	I.	3	21	38	17	21	3.31	

Table 2
The main reasons for adoption of farm diversification, as given by diversified farmers and perceived by institutions

Reasons	Reasons for adoption given by farmers (n = 80)		Reasons for farmer adoption perceived by institutions (n = 45)	
	No. of mentions	% of mentions	No. of mentions	% of mentions
Increase of income	45	21.6	35	26.3
Utilise farm resources	31	14.9	16	12.0
Personal interest	31	14.9		
Market opportunity	20	9.6	12	9.0
Change in personal circumstances	19	9.1		
Grant availability	17	8.2	6	4.5
By chance	14	6.7		
Use farm location	13	6.2		
Employment	10	4.8	16	12.0
Previous experience	6	2.9		
Opportunity to meet people	2	1.0		
Response to CAP reform			23	17.3
Change in attitudes			12	9.0
Example farms			4	3.0
Farm type			3	2.6
Rural development			3	2.6
Farm wives			3	2.6
Total	208	100.0	133	100.0

Table 3
The main barriers to farm diversification, as given by non-diversified farmers and perceived by institutions

Reasons or constraints	Reasons for non-adoption given by farmers (n = 107)		Constraints on farmer adoption perceived by institutions (n = 45)	
	No. of mentions	% of mentions	No. of mentions	% of mentions
Traditional preference	52	18.2	20	8.0
Insufficient capital	38	13.3	45	18.0
Lack of knowledge	36	12.6	37	14.8
Age of farmers	35	12.6		
High risk	26	9.1		
Not wanting extra work	18	6.3		
Disinterest	14	4.9		
Unsuitable location	14	4.9	14	5.6
Insufficient labour	10	3.5	1	0.4
Have adequate income	10	3.5		
Uncertain or low returns	8	2.8	20	8.0
No time	7	2.5		
Developing existing enterprise	5	1.8		
Poor health	5	1.8		
Inadequate market	4	1.4	35	14.0
Inadequate on-farm facilities			32	12.8
Restrictive regulations			11	4.4
Insufficient grant aid			10	4.0
Lack marketing education			10	4.0
Inadequate technical information			8	3.2
Land area or quality			5	2.0
Total	282	98.9	248	99.2

Table 4
Institutional perceptions of the main advantages and
disadvantages of the study areas for farm diversification

Advantages	No. of mentions	Disadvantages	No. of mentions
Tourism potential	34	Remoteness	25
Unrealised resource potential	20	Poor land quality	11
Good image of area	16	Lack of capital	10
Willingness to change	15	Age profile	9
Land diversity	10	High production costs	8
Organic potential	9	Traditional attitudes	7
Size of farms	7	Low skills	6
Forestry potential	6		

The areas' disadvantages for farm diversification identified by the institutions are essentially a listing of what are perceived in general to be attributes of many marginal regions. This is epitomised by the dominance of remoteness, mentioned by over one-half of respondents, and presumably it relates in particular to inaccessibility to markets. Other disadvantages were quite evenly spaced in the ranking, comprising unfavourable conditions with respect to land quality, investment capital, age structure, climatic conditions, production costs, traditional attitudes and skill levels. Little can be done to alter some of these perceived attributes but the listing contributes to identification of some of the features to which remedial attention should be given in marginal regions.

Farmers held a generally positive view of the future role of farm diversification in the development of marginal regions. Those who felt that particular AFEs have a contribution to make to the future of their region exceeded those who felt that they had not by more than three times, though one-fifth were uncertain. When they were asked to specify these contributions, the potential to increase employment and help to stabilise the population was that most strongly identified, followed by the development of the region's resource potential, both highly relevant to sustainable development. The main strategies other than farm diversification which might aid the survival of farm families in these regions, as perceived by the institutional respondents, were the provision of off-farm employment and small businesses, the development of community infrastructures and initiatives, and the improvement of efficiency in conventional agricultural enterprises.

Issues which need to be addressed

Having explored perceptions of the influences affecting farm diversification in marginal regions, it was felt desirable to identify more specifically those where change should be promoted in order to effect sustainable development. Thus the institutional respondents were asked to indicate the main general issues that need to be addressed in order to ensure the future successful development of AFEs. Institutions should be able to take a broad perspective of these issues but their responses were supplemented by farmer assessment of the importance of some individual influences.

The single issue identified by most of the institutions as needing to be addressed was marketing and its importance was emphasised by them during the interviews. Just over one-half of the farmers considered the existence of a marketing organisation to be a very important factor when establishing an AFE, a lower rating than those given to the availability of capital and of government grants. Earlier consideration of incentives and constraints had shown that marketing was assessed as being one of the significant factors but, as here, institutions stressed marketing somewhat more than did farmers. Thus it seems desirable to emphasise to farmers, especially, the importance of assessing market potential in decisions about farm diversification, as it is essential that the process should be market-led if it is to be economically sustainable. It is vital that marketing structures and the development of markets for alternative farm products and services should be given a high priority. The institutions were optimistic concerning market prospects; two-thirds of respondents assessed them as being good or very good and only one-sixth considered prospects to be less than that.

Assessed by the institutions as being the next most important issue to be addressed was the area of education, training and information. Again just over one-half of farmers considered the availability of advice and information and of training courses to be very important. Training courses were assessed as being of lesser importance by diversified farmers than by non-diversifiers, suggesting that familiarity with some enterprises may lead to a realisation that there is less mystique relating to them than other people assume, or perhaps in some instances to justify their own non-attendance at courses. Lack of knowledge or education had been ranked as the third most important constraint by both farmers and institutions. Participation in AFEs requires new knowledge and skills, so it is vital that adequate training and advice should be provided in order to ensure the development of the appropriate technical and management expertise.

The need for structures to facilitate AFE development was ranked third as an issue to be addressed, and the concept of integrated rural development and the structure of grant aid were placed joint fifth. These three issues combined suggest a very strong desire for a new and thorough administrative approach to farm diversification. If combined as one issue, they would have constituted the leading concern, accounting for 30% of all the nominations, compared with 18% for marketing. They suggest a strong feeling that farm diversification should be seen as a rightful and important part of integrated rural development, that it should be supported by adequate state grant incentives and that proper structures should be established to facilitate the whole process. The implication is that in each of these respects the current situation was seen as being far from satisfactory. When asked to assess the significance of government financial assistance alone, 83% of farmers rated its availability as being very important. Thus the level and the targeting of support need consideration.

The other issues which were stated as needing to be addressed indicated concerns with the quantity and quality of production, the economic viability of AFEs, back-up services, restrictive regulations, the need for research, the professional approach of farmers and capital availability. It is surprising perhaps that capital availability, which was rated so highly as a barrier to AFE adoption by both farmers and institutions, was mentioned by only three institutional representatives as needing to be addressed. In apparent contrast, having capital available for investment was rated as being very important by over four-fifths of farmers. Eligibility to borrow from a bank was considered to be very important by three-fifths of non-diversified farmers and one-third of diversified farmers. Although capital was not nominated by the institutions as a major issue needing attention and many farmers who diversified regarded credit eligibility as less of a problem than others would have anticipated, the overall impression gained from the research was that development could be greatly facilitated by easier access to capital. This relates especially to the considerable caution shown by lending agencies towards most alternative enterprises, so that freer access to credit should be a component in any effort to promote development. There is also a reluctance to borrow on the part of some farmers, especially the older conventional farmers.

The importance of the socio-personal dimension in the diversification process was demonstrated but this received little reference in the institutions' perception of issues to be addressed. This may result, not only from the apparently lesser institutional awareness of the significance of these influences than that of the farmers, but also an appreciation that these constraints are amongst the most intractable and a feeling that there may be little that can be done in relation to some of them. This may be relevant in relation to personal interest in the AFE, which was considered to be very important by 88% of diversified farmers, though only by 60% of those who had not diversified and so would have had a lesser understanding of its significance. Interest can be promoted to some extent but critical is the need for a reorientation from some traditional attitudes held by many farmers and an acceptance of the necessity for change and for an entrepreneurial approach.

Conclusion

There is an increasing acceptance that farm diversification has a part to play in planning for the sustainable development of rural communities in marginal regions such as the west of Ireland and that this role should be actively promoted while not overstated. Diversification was seen by those associated with it as contributing to the long-term maintenance of farm land, farm businesses and farm families, rather than as merely a palliative for short-term income problems in agriculture. It was evident from the perceptions of the reasons for the adoption and non-adoption of farm diversification and of regional advantage and disadvantage that there are certain major incentives and constraints affecting development in marginal areas. The fact that these are the influences perceived by those most intimately associated with the farm diversification process gives this identification considerable validity and significance. This led on to the specification of issues which were considered to be important and needing to be addressed. AFE adoption could be made more effective through amelioration of some of these influences but others would be less amenable to manipulation. It is important that this promotion should be done in the context of proactive and coherent policy and planning for the expansion of farm diversification if it is to realise its potential to contribute to the sustainable development of marginal regions.

Acknowledgement

This study was done when the authors were participating in a programme of collaborative research by the Departments of Geography at the Universities of Leicester (UK), Caen (France) and Dublin (Ireland), the Scottish Agricultural College (UK), CEMAGREF (France), Teagasc (Ireland) and the Department of Agricultural Economics at the University of Patras (Greece). Part of the farm questionnaire used was developed at Leicester and Caen and the institutional questionnaire at Trinity College Dublin. The research project was funded under the European Union CAMAR Programme.

References

Beus, Curtis E. and Riley E. Dunlap. 1991. Measuring adherence to alternative vs. conventional agricultural paradigms: A proposed scale. *Rural Sociology* 56, 3: 432-460.

Bowler, Ian R. (ed.). 1992. *The Geography of Agriculture in Developed Market Economies.* Harlow (Essex): Longman.

Cawley, Mary, Desmond A. Gillmor, Anthony Leavy and Perpetua McDonagh. 1995. *Farm Diversification: Studies Relating to the West of Ireland.* Dublin: Teagasc.

Fenton, Alexander and Desmond A. Gillmor (eds.). 1994. *Rural Land Use on the Atlantic Periphery of Europe: Scotland and Ireland.* Dublin: Royal Irish Academy.

Fuller, Anthony M. 1990. From part-time farming to pluriactivity: A decade of change in rural Europe. *Journal of Rural Studies* 6, 4: 361-373.

Gillmor, Desmond A. 1995. Diversification on farms in the development of marginal regions: Potential opportunities and constraints. In Reginald Byron (ed.), *Economic Futures on the North Atlantic Margin.* Aldershot: Avebury. Pp. 163-181.

Goodman, David and Michael Redclift. 1989. *The International Farm Crisis.* London: Macmillan.

Ilbery, Brian W. 1985. *Agricultural Geography: A Social and Economic Analysis.* Oxford: Oxford University Press.

MacKinnon, N., J. M. Bryden, C. Bell, A. M. Fuller and M. Spearman. 1991. Pluriactivity, structural change and farm household vulnerability in Western Europe. *Sociologia Ruralis* 31, 1: 58-71.

NESC. 1992. *The Impact of Reform of the Common Agricultural Policy.* Dublin: The National Economic and Social Council, Report No. 92.

Shucksmith, M. 1993. Farm household behaviour and the transition to post-productivism. *Journal of Agricultural Economics* 44, 3: 466-478.

17   Will Wales stay green in the absence of rural policy?

Siân Pierce, Gareth Rennie and Eifiona Thomas

Introduction

In shaping a strategy for rural Wales for the remainder of this decade and into the next century, it is vital that policies take account of the life experiences of the inhabitants of the areas that are designated rural. Current concepts of rural land use are restricted by traditional views of rural agriculturally-based development and of established settlement patterns. As rural societies become more diverse and problems such as rural poverty and lack of small-scale economic development becomes more significant for the rural communities of Wales, there needs to be a greater flexibility in the land use control systems and the types of development deemed suitable in rural areas. The absence of a specific policy document from the British government relating to rural issues within Wales is addressed in this chapter.

The "rural problem"

The concept "rural" is one that engenders endless terminological debate and confusion (Shucksmith et al., 1994). Within an academic discourse (Halfacree 1993), particularly in the disciplines of sociology, agricultural economics and geography, a re-theorisation of "rural studies" has begun. Recent debate has focused upon the definitions that characterise rural areas as "problematic" or "contentious" (Cloke 1987, Hoggart 1988) which are diametrically opposed to a lay discourse in which

> each generation of country dwellers and observers sees what it wants to see in the land: romantic beauty, nostalgic traces of the rustic past, peace, tranquillity; despoiled landscapes, brutal intrusions of modernisation. (Mingay 1989: 6)

Rural life is often the subject of sentimental commentary from academics and non-academics alike (Hoggart and Buller 1987) evoking a "familiar, changeless place [which is] part of the idea that we have of ourselves as a nation" (*Sunday Express* 25.9.94). The countryside thus is "viewed as the repository of all that we cherish and hold dear" (Newby 1991). In this paper we contend that rural Wales dances to another tune, linguistically, socially and culturally, and that central and local government policy for the territorial area designated rural Wales should not be driven by an engine which is facing the wrong direction. Defining rural areas is, however, problematic and runs the risk of amalgamating areas which are fundamentally different. In defining "rural" we have used the Organisation for Economic Development's 1993 strategy document *What Future for our Countryside?* in which rural areas are defined as

> . . . comprising the people, the land and other resources, in the open country and small settlements outside the immediate economic influence of major urban centres. RURAL is a territorial or spatial concept. It is not restricted to any particular use of land, degree of economic health, or economic sector. (OECD 1993: 11)

Such a definition is coterminous with the definition provided by the Commission of the European Union in *The Future of Rural Society*, in which rural areas are generally understood to

> extend over regions and areas presenting a variety of activities and landscapes comprising natural countryside, farmland, villages, small towns, regional centres and industrialised rural areas. (Comm [88] 371: 15)

The area covered by rural Wales, as defined by the British government and its agencies, embraces almost three-quarters of the land mass of Wales, yet has only 22% of the population (Welsh Office 1994b). Launched in 1977, the Development Board for Rural Wales (DBRW) was created to promote economic and social development in mid Wales and has ". . . responsibilities for 40% of the land area of Wales". The Welsh Development Agency (WDA), formed two years prior to that, has a brief to "secure and improve the economic, environmental and social development of those areas of rural Wales for which WDA has a remit" (WDA 1992).

It is clearly inappropriate to treat Wales as homogenous in terms of experience and circumstances. In 1988, the Welsh Affairs Committee of the House of Commons regretted the fact that Wales "presented a series of distinct, and at times contrasting, images to the outside world and argued that prospects for inward investment would be aided by the presentation of a unified 'single' face of Wales which would then be promoted by the various governmental and non-governmental agencies" (Humphreys in Herbert and Jones 1995: 133). However, it is possible to identify some general features similar to those which characterise many other rural areas in the United Kingdom and Europe, such as low population density per hectare, the decline of agriculture and other primary industries as employment and income sources with knock-on effects throughout the local economy, high levels of part-time and casual employment, and low wages and income levels (Thomas and Day 1992: 37).

> Rural Wales continues to suffer problems associated with peripheral-ity, agricultural decline and inadequate economic structure together with related social and cultural issues. . . it is a rural area in need of economic development and structural adjustments. (Welsh Office 1994a)

In the first tranche of awards of funding under the Objective 5b status of the European Union's Regional Development Fund, much of Wales was designated as meeting the specific criteria relating to the "development of rural areas" (EU 1988: 60). However we choose to define it, rural society in Wales is changing fast in its social and demographic structures, the languages its people speak and the attitudes they express are being changed before our eyes (Lle Neis i Blant?: 1993). Yet the future of the economy of rural Wales, and its people and culture, are intertwined. The nature of Welshness and "yr hen ffordd Gymreig o fyw" (the old Welsh way of living) has always been heavily dependent on and influenced by the natural environment. The bards who have sung about Wales wrote about the habitat, its tradition of patronage and landscape. Many continue to sing about farming experiences, of working the land and about the merits of "Y Fro Gymreig" (the Welsh heartland).

CAP in hand?

By the start of the 1980s, the regional dimension of the "farm problem" had become obvious and had been described as "farming in crisis" (Commins 1990). Marginal farming areas had been left behind in the race for increased farming profits and were suffering socioeconomic depression. One issue of increasing concern was the debate centred on the contribution these areas should make to overall production as these areas are also valued for alternative purposes. Despite valuable stocks of "care goods" these areas continue to have an endemic problem of low farm income. There is a long-established recognition of the contribution of agricultural populations in the maintenance of a vital rural economy in such areas. These factors of low income and problems of depopulation have led to a series of European measures. The first of these included the designation of these zones in 1975 as "Less-favoured Areas" (Directives 75/268/EEC Mountain and Hill Farming in LFA 75/269/EEC and 75/276/EEC).

Traditionally, the more elite landowning group has always been well represented within British political circles. There are strong farming lobbies, notably the National Farmers' Union and the Country Land-owners' Association, by definition interest or "insider" groups (Schwarzmantel 1993) which are accepted by government as the legitimate representatives of particular interests in society (Finer 1966) and are regularly consulted on issues deemed relevant to them. These tend to be representative of the more commercial sectors of farming in the wealthier, productive regions of Britain and of organisations based on agriculture (Beer 1971, Howarth 1985). Members of the same groups, however, were among the first to protest and to express concern at the impact of agricultural intensification on rural landscape: this was seen as a national asset and its conservation of great consequence. Conservation of scenic beauty (and associated habitats) was considered to be a public concern which could best be addressed by policy developments and the extension of current legislation.

Heightened public awareness towards both environmental and food goods during the Thatcher period (1979-1990) ensured that the British government promised a move towards establishing reformed policy for agriculture for the nineties. This new policy framework was outlined in the government white paper *This Common Inheritance* (Department of the Environment 1990).

In the mid 1980s, government was lobbied for stricter legislation to curb "damaging" agricultural activities; this was particularly timely in the context of growing surpluses leading to grain and butter mountains. Steps taken were to re-focus farming effort to redress the situation. Rather than to intensify under government guidance as had been encouraged through the intervening fifteen years, farmers were advised to extensify---to diversify or to adopt environmentally-friendly alternatives. Under Article 19 of the European Community's Directive 797/85 and the revision of the 1986 Agricultural Act, the Ministry of Agriculture Fisheries and Food (MAFF) and the Welsh Office Agricultural Department (WOAD) were able to identify areas where the intrinsic environmental characteristics of the area were being threatened by farming activities and to designate these areas to receive monies from European Agricultural Guidance and Guarantee Funds for farming activities other than those leading to traditional production. The first round of Environmentally-sensitive Areas (ESA) were designated in 1986/7 and included Mynyddoedd y Cambria in Wales. In January 1988, a further seven areas were identified in the second round including the Pen Llyn area and an extension to the Mynyddoedd y Cambria scheme. During 1992-93, further new areas were designated, namely Bryniau Clwyd, Ynys Mon, Preseli, and the Radnor area. The Cambrian Mountains designations were also extended; see Figure 1. These schemes attempt to conserve agricultural landscapes created through the regionally-differentiated evolution of the industry and to maintain these diverse, visually-rich areas in the changing face of agricultural intensification. On the basis of the Countryside Commission's[1] recommendations (Countryside Commission 1986), the sites were designated as those considered to have a high conservation value with visual appeal or historic interest where such designations could also constrain output (Gaskell and Tanner 1991, Gilg 1991, MAFF 1989). The value of these schemes in terms of the potential they offer to wildlife conservation has been described by Woods (1989) and Mather and Woods (1989). Regionally typical landscapes are conserved such as the earth banks and small scale landscape of Pen Llyn with its diversity of alkaline wetland, semi-natural grassland and coastal heaths. This contrasts significantly with the wilder upland scenery of Mynyddoedd y Cambria. The designation of each ESA is required to be attuned to the specific requirement of rarity of habitats and landscapes it is established to protect. It is widely applicable to areas with differing conservation objectives and as such allows easy application and administration with fine adjustment to conserve the features of interest in each ESA.

Farmers and landowners are voluntary participants in these schemes and as such they are able to opt in or out, to adopt the responsibility for maintaining biodiversity or not. From the outset, therefore, agri-environmental schemes in Wales have been administered based on the principle of subsidiarity.[2] Although this concept was not identifiable in the policy documents of the schemes their voluntary nature meant that the first steps towards local sustainability was being taken by the farming community itself.

These schemes may therefore be viewed from different perspectives. Ecologically they should be seen as an opportunity for areas such as Ynys Mon, Pen Llyn and the Preseli to move towards rural sustainability, as the most recently developed schemes indicate that lessons have been learnt in that farmers' expectations are better understood and that scheme detail allows for positive conservation work such as rebuilding earth banks and other types of habitat restoration. Work of this nature has been going on already in the national parks in Wales (see Figure 2) to some extent through individually-negotiated agreements. As such, the Tir Cymen[3] scheme available in the Eryri, Dinefwr and Bro Gwyr areas since July 1992 is in fact a formalisation of these types of agreements to the wider farming community with financial input from the Countryside Council for Wales,[4] up to a maximum £3000 per year per farm. Through the process of reducing production, the concept of extensification of farming also contributes to general agricultural decline. The role of the farmer becomes landscape custodian again. European agricultural policy as it is currently being applied by central government seems to be encouraging economic decline through increased competition and specialisation within the agricultural sector. At the same time as handouts are available to farmers in more marginal areas for conservation farming or to do nothing, in the more prosperous lowlands they are still encouraged to produce if they so wish.

It may be concluded that the numerous agri-environmental grants available in Wales for extensification and farm woodland activity indicated a shift in emphasis by central government and European policy back towards a mixed agricultural industry with lowered inputs: a neo-traditional way of life for the farmers of the more marginal agricultural areas, at least. Politically there seems to be a hidden socioeconomic agenda based on the dependence of increasingly marginalised rural areas both on the governing urban core but also on the high input productive regions with which they compete. This situation does not seem encouraging to sustainability at the local level in rural Wales.

Agricultural ecosystems typify an area of concern where the sensitive integration of economic policy with environmental policy is vital. It is also an area where policy guidance is weak. The post-modern agricultural society (Murdoch and Pratt 1993) is characterised by polarisation of farm units in terms of size, income and enterprise specialisation (Bowler 1985, Newby 1991, EU 1988). The implementation of the European Union's Common Agricultural Policy throughout Britain has led to regional differentiation and widely differing farm incomes. A consideration which the agricultural industry must take on board as a result of the sustainability debate is the need, not only to de-intensify production but also to accept the weakening of its role as the engine of rural communities, whilst recognising its responsibility for the maintenance of environmental quality and landscape amenity. The burden of bringing British agriculture into sustainability is mainly being borne by farming communities of the more marginal areas; set-aside has received a lukewarm welcome in the productive lowlands but would not, in most cases, be accepted as a whole farm strategy. It seems therefore that post-Rio pressure on agriculture is applied in contradiction to the ideal of sustainability of natural resources, specifically that highly productive land is exploited through the utilisation of energy-costly inputs of capital accumulation on very large farms. This seems to contradict the overall concept of global sustainability.

Planning in Wales during the 1990s

The last two years have seen a gradual dismantling of the structures that enable strategic land use planning in rural Wales. The influence of the former Secretary of State John Redwood has been an important part of this process and the relative autonomy granted him has allowed the pursuit of agendas which were not entirely that of the government. Not only was the Secretary of State an enthusiastic supporter of local government reorganisation (bequeathed to him by his predecessor) but he presided over the systematic dismantling of the strategic structures and systems that bridge the divide between central and local government.

Before entering upon an examination of strategic planning in Wales, and the growing gap between England and Wales in this respect, it is necessary to examine the theoretical or ideological background that has led to this situation. Local government reorganisation in Wales has been promoted as a means to give local communities back some control over their local area:

> People naturally seek to belong to a community they can understand, and they then expect to be able to exert some control over it. (Redwood 1993: 54)

The reorganisation of the two-tier system starts

> . . . from the two propositions that good borders must define natural communities, and that where possible local government should be conducted through a single council rather than a multiplicity. (Redwood 1993: 58)

Local government should be relevant to the community that it represents, both geographically and in scale, and rather than being a service provider each authority should be an enabling authority, with services being contracted out to the private sector. Strategic planning should be the role of central government and then only for issues such as transport. It is evident that strategic planning is equated with regional planning, regional planning with regional government, and regional government with a federal Europe.

> The idea that there should be regional government in the United Kingdom could be damaging to county, city or rural district authorities, taking power away from them and imposing new burdens upon them. Yet it is regional government that the European Community is looking for. . . . (Redwood 1993: 58)

Attitudes to planning in general also seem ambivalent; as a source of intervention in the marketplace it is obviously an anathema, but planning is recognised as central to the local government function, and particular attention is drawn to rural planning. What emerges is a wholly suburban viewpoint towards rural areas and rural planning:

> Urban dwellers are coming to see farmers as rural gardeners on a grand scale, manicuring the field, hedgerows and trees so that we can all enjoy the feeling of extended parkland and garden beyond the city edges. (Redwood 1993: 56)

Wales is thus split between industrial south and north-east where the people do not spend effort on portraying England as the "old enemy" and rural Wales where "a different spirit is alive" (Redwood 1993: 60).

Local government reorganisation in Wales in April 1996 will replace the existing two-tier system of eight county councils and thirty-seven district councils[5] with a single tier of twenty-two unitary authorities. At present the planning function is split between county and district with the counties being responsible for strategic planning through their structure plans[6] and bearing responsibility for strategic issues such as minerals planning. Upon reorganisation, the statutory functions of the counties will be absorbed by the new unitary authorities. However the strategic planning function presently implemented through structure plans will disappear and although structure plans will remain in force, they are likely to grow out of date very quickly and there will be no mechanisms for monitoring of policies or their modification. Until there is complete coverage of Unitary Development Plans, the development plan in Wales will very quickly come to consist only of the Local Plan.

The need for a strategic direction to planning in Wales was recognised by the then-Secretary of State for Wales in September 1990 when the Assembly of Welsh Counties, in collaboration with the Council of Welsh Districts, the National Parks and other bodies, were invited to take the lead in reviewing the strategic planning guidance relevant to structure planning and local planning in Wales. A further impetus for this work was provided by the publication in March 1993 of the government white paper on local government reorganisation. The Assembly produced a series of reports (1992, 1993a, 1993b) which were published in May 1993 and identified the main strategic issues that would affect Wales in the subsequent ten to fifteen years. In the foreword to the overview report, John Pembridge, chair of the strategic planning advisory committee, stated that

> There is a need for a strategic vision if Wales is to prosper in the twenty-first century and local authorities in the Principality are willing to work with the Welsh Office to develop the strategic land use policies which will achieve that objective. (Assembly of Welsh

Counties 1993a: iii)

The Assembly carried out a wide-ranging consultation exercise which produced a consensus of opinion which clearly highlighted the need for the development of a comprehensive planning policy strategy for Wales, the development of new policy guidance (for waste management, energy and the Welsh language in particular), the revision of existing policy guidance, and the need for a sub-regional dimension to strategic planning in Wales.

It is the call for a sub-regional dimension which is perhaps the most important. Section three of the overview report, "The Character of Wales Today" illustrates the fact that the problems facing rural north, west and mid Wales are not the same problems that face urban south and north-east Wales. The Assembly, though unable to make any recommendations, suggested that sub-regional guidance should be concerned with a number of strategic planning issues, but more importantly should provide "the forum for translating the concept of sustainable development into meaningful land use policies" (1993a: 21). This is one of the roles of strategic planning that is growing in importance and has hitherto only really been uppermost in the minds of county-based strategic planners; as the newly elected president of the District Planning Officers Society admits: "while I understand the concept of sustainability, I admit that I am much less clear on what it means in practical terms when it comes to putting forward specific proposals in a local plan" (Wright 1995).

Despite having received the Strategic Planning Guidance in Wales documents in May 1993, there seems to have been little indication to date that their content has been either implemented or even considered by the Welsh Office. Certainly there has been no attempt to encourage or impose any system of issue-based sub-regional strategic planning within the reorganisation of local government. It is assumed within local government that in time informal strategic structures between the new authorities will develop. There is little evidence that such a spirit of co-operation exists even within the new shadow authorities themselves.

The Assembly of Welsh counties stated that apart from the need for a sub-regional dimension to strategic planning in Wales, the way forward should include the development of new planning guidance and the revision of existing policy guidance. Not only has this not been pursued, but new guidance and revised guidance published by the Department of the Environment in England have not been published, as is the norm, in Wales but have been subject to the veto of the Secretary of State for Wales. The director of the Country Landowners' Association commented recently on the lack of guidance and of rural initiatives in Wales:

One day the Welsh Office might surprise us by launching a countryside initiative ahead of government departments in England, but until that happens we are forced to view the belated launch of the Moorland Scheme as yet another example of Wales being left behind in the field of public rural policy. (*Western Mail* 1995).

Planning legislation has long been supplemented by government advice in the shape of circulars and latterly Planning Policy Guidance notes (PPGs) and Mineral Planning Guidance notes (MPGs). This guidance has provided vital interpretation of the statutes, advice on their implementation, and has provided the framework for strategic planning in the form of the development plan. The situation that Wales and its new Secretary of State face is that a number of significant PPGs and MPGs are either missing altogether or have not been reviewed in line with revisions carried out by the Department of the Environment in England. The main loss is the expected PPG on strategic guidance for Wales expected following the publication of PPG12 (Development Plans and Strategic Planning guidance in Wales) and the report of the Assembly of Welsh Counties. At present, however, other losses include PPG13 (Highway Considerations in Development Control), PPG23 (Planning and Pollution Control) and PPG7 (Nature Conservation). Importantly, also, revised versions of MPG6 (Guidelines for Aggregates) and MPG13 (Opencast Coal) despite having been issued as national guidance in England lack the Welsh input contained in the pre-publication drafts.

It is perhaps useful at this point to examine in more detail what this lack of guidance and loss of strategic planning through local government reorganisation means for sustainability in rural Wales. The planning of aggregate minerals development provides an illustration of the effects of changes in guidance and in the systems of control and implementation. At present all control over mineral exploitation is carried out by specialist officers within the county councils. These councils have a statutory duty to process planning applications for minerals development, produce a Minerals Local Plan,[7] and carry out periodic reviews of all mineral sites. They are also responsible for the monitoring and enforcement of planing conditions placed on those sites. This is carried out within the context of specific minerals legislation and guidance.

It has been necessary over the years for mineral planning officers not only to develop as specialist planners, as the legislation and guidance have become more and more specific, but many are also specialists in the minerals industry, geology or land reclamation. Minerals planning has developed as a specialist highly technical profession in its own right and what could be termed a specialist corps of officers within the County structure has developed to administer the system. There has also been a reciprocal development in the administrative structures designed to implement the control and strategic planning of minerals development.

In 1975 a Government Select Committee reported on Planning control over minerals working. The report of the Stevens Committee, named after its chairman Sir Roger Stevens, recognised the strategic nature of minerals planning and the need for a consideration of long-term mineral planning on three levels, that of government, local government and the minerals industry (Anon 1976). Minerals planning had already been recognised as a strategic function of local government, and after the 1974 reorganisation of local government became a county function. The strategic nature of minerals development was further confirmed by the establishment of sand and gravel working parties in 1969 in the south east of England and the establishment of Regional Aggregate Working Parties (RAWPs)[8] in the 1970s which were standardised and formalised following the publication of the Advisory Committee on Aggregates (the Verney Committee).

Regional Aggregate Working Parties carry out surveys of supply and demand in their areas and feed information into national guidance through annual reports and a national coordinating group; they also have important roles in liaison between the industry and local government and in initiating research. A national forecast of regional demand is produced by the Department of the Environment and this pattern of future requirements for aggregates, and the inter- and intra-regional flows of aggregates, are then used to produce local figures and in the formulation of local minerals policy. MPG6 is the mechanism that is used to separate the national forecast of demand into regional guidance.

Although it has been strongly suggested that RAWPs will continue in some form or another, local government reorganisation in Wales is likely to see an end to the relationship that has developed between local, regional and national planning in aggregate minerals. The first step in this process has been the refusal of the Secretary of State to publish a revised MPG6 in line with the Department of the Environment in England. This has left a policy vacuum and has forced both the North and South Wales RAWPs to consider issuing their own forecasts of aggregate demand for the next ten years. These will, however, be unlikely to be adequate in terms of the revised national forecast in particular where export demand is concerned. The revised English MPG6 is also important in that for the first time it makes consideration of sustainability in aggregates planning and sets targets for the recycling of demolition wastes and the use of secondary aggregates such as china clay waste, slate waste and colliery shale, an emphasis which has been lost to Wales (Anon 1994).

Not only is the structure and mechanisms of strategic aggregate mineral planning under threat but the officers administering that system are also threatened by reorganisation. A recent survey of county councils in Wales carried in connection with this paper showed that at present there are no specific arrangements in place for the transfer of minerals planning to the unitary authorities. Of the options that are available for the future administration of mineral planning, a lead authority approach, a joint minerals team, or individual officers in each authority it is apparent that it is the latter, simplest option that is the preferred one. Not only will that mean the dissolution of the so-called "mineral teams" that have developed but because of the size of the new authorities each officer will be unlikely to be dedicated to minerals planning exclusively. This body of professional experience and knowledge is a vital resource in itself and one which is generally undervalued in local government and it has to be recognised that "mechanisms need to be found to ensure that the quality of professional advice can be maintained" (Goode and Tyldesley 1995).

The implications for the rural communities of Wales are significant. Such a system for the planning of minerals and specifically aggregates and opencast coal could result in a free-for-all where decisions on minerals applications are made purely on local issues. On one hand this could bring decision-making closer to the community and increase the influence of the public. However, on the other hand---and this is more likely---it will leave the system open to abuse, to hijacking by interest groups from both sides of the development equation and ultimately lead to an uneven spread of development. Areas of high unemployment or of limited employment opportunities such as rural Wales may find themselves unable to resist the pressures for minerals development whilst the urbanised areas of Wales become more successful in preventing such development taking place, so increasing the demand for suitable mineral sites. This is a pattern which is already evident on a national basis and which is only kept in check by strategic planning structures. It is not only true of aggregates, open cast coal and general minerals development but of other development types and presents a real threat to the communities of rural Wales, to the designated areas[9] of rural Wales and to the implementation of the principles of sustainability within the planning process.

Local Agenda 21

Local Agenda 21 was derived from Principle 10 of the Rio Declaration following the third World Conference on Environment and Development in July 1992. This principle requires local people to be included in all aspects and in each step of the decision-making process involved in managing natural resources and economic development within their own communities. Local authorities in England have been supported in initiating this process by the Local Government Management Board (LGMB 1994). In certain areas of Wales this process has been set in motion by the formation of environmental fora. These are based on workshop sessions where interested individuals and representatives of environmental and development groups are drawn into round table discussions on aspects of "the rural" such as the economy, quality of life, transport and energy. Local authority input into these fora adopts a facilitating role in the period leading up to the creation of a recommendation document. One of the objectives of the forum is to feed local opinion and expertise into the formation of local government policy through a participatory process. The objective therefore in Wales was to submit documentation to the newly-formed unitary authority for consideration for inclusion as part of the local development strategies following the formation of the new authorities (the authority is not legally required to implement the proposals).

The Prince of Wales, in a speech to the chief executives of the new shadow councils, has recently shown concern that local environmental issues would be low on their list of priorities for the new unitary authorities. He emphasised the importance of the Local Agenda 21 programme in Wales and even more vitally that it should be distinctly identifiable as a Welsh agenda: "I would expect Local Agenda 21 projects in Wales to have a distinctive flavour, reflecting the country's special culture, geography, social conditions and needs."

Environmental groups, in conjunction with local authorities, now have the responsibility of plugging the gap in strategic planning identified within Local Agenda 21. In Wales, both these sectors are under pressure, through reorganisation, lack of funding and, in the case of the Welsh environmental groups, a lack of membership (Hughes 1995). What membership they have is probably not representative of many sections of the communities they purport to represent and their degree of influence on the "decision-making process" is minimal---they are outside the "ruling power elite" (Mills 1956).

The rural white paper

Government response to ensuring sustainable development has widely differing emphases and rates of activity in Wales and England. In November 1994, the Department of Environment and Ministry of Agriculture Fisheries and Food (MAFF) jointly announced that a rural white paper would be published in mid-September 1995. This paper will be relevant only to England. In the press release, the then-Minister of

Agriculture, William Waldegrave, commented:

> We are drawing up a positive strategy to take us into the next century. Rural life is not set in aspic and, quite rightly, there is a lively debate about how change is affecting those who live and work in the countryside. The white paper will act as a focus for discussion and ideas. (MAFF press release 22.11.94.)

The importance of local participation in this initiative was outlined by the Right Hon. John Gummer, Minister of the Environment, who said:

> We want to hear from everyone with a stake in the future of our countryside. The rural white paper will not be about government policy alone. Everyone who values our countryside has a part to play in its future. (MAFF Press release 22.11.94).

The consultation period was two months, during which time a comprehensive range of agencies was invited to comment and contribute ideas and models. The formation of this policy document for England will therefore be a partnership endeavour by government and non-statutory groups: a positive approach towards a more integrated, pro-active policy framework for rural areas.

> It is intended that the white paper should present a long-term strategic vision of the future of our countryside into the next century. The white paper will be prepared within the context of the government's sustainable development strategy. It will set out the practical implications of sustainable development in rural areas, economically, socially and environmentally. . . . (MAFF letter to interested organisations, 1994).

In England, the Country Landowners' Association (CLA) responded to the call for ideas with a submission document entitled *Towards a Rural Policy: a Vision for the 21st Century.* This response typifies the ideology of predominantly lowland "winners" (Haines 1994) or market successes and presents a comprehensive and detailed analysis. Twenty-five objectives are set out for this policy and "lead departments" (their emphasis) in central government are identified. These objectives range from countryside sport through transport, environment to institutional government and central government, including a recommendation for "a new department of state, adequately structured to reflect the need for integrated policies for rural areas" (p. 41). Their vision for the white paper is based on "the need for a move towards a broader-based rural policy, with clear objectives for agriculture, the rural environment and rural socioeconomics" (p. 2).

English Nature's response is a comprehensive strategy of actions under four key objectives: enriching bio-diversity, a new focus for farming and forestry, conserving England's character, and planning for rural sustainability. Their view of the white paper is that it should "present a strategy for rural areas based on the principle of sustainability, with the goal of integrating economic, social and environmental aspects in the formation of rural policy, to ensure that people's essential needs are met while maintaining and enhancing the natural heritage" (*Towards a Rural Policy: a Vision for the 21st Century:* 2).

It is because of the rapid rate of change in rural Wales that calls are increasing for a white paper on the subject, a paper that would help us define the kind of rural lifestyle we want in the next century, help us preserve aspects we don't want to lose while allowing the country areas to evolve as places where people can live complete lives. Such a white paper for England is being prepared by the Department of the Environment but the Welsh Office believes that it already has a suitable framework for rural development in place. Among the numerous planning subjects which ought to conform to a strategy for rural Wales are housing, energy and transport (*Western Mail* 23.12.94). Similar clarion calls for the investigation into the needs of rural areas have come from Cynog Dafis M.P. and Merfyn Williams, Director of the Campaign for the Protection of Rural Wales (CPRW). In preparing this paper we sought the opinions of the body in Wales corresponding to English Nature and the Countryside Commission, namely the Countryside Council for Wales, and were advised: "This rural white paper would not be relevant for Wales, only England" (pers. comm. 26.5.95.).

Conclusion

Because of the lower than average income in rural Wales, the high unemployment rates and the projected further contraction of the agricultural work force there is an obvious need to re-assess rural policy; merely reforming the CAP is insufficient in such areas. A region acclimatised to a production-oriented system will experience shock on the removal of subsidies on production. This may lead to acute depression and deprivation. Within a "developed" member state of the EU, this decline must be confronted and resolved by new and comprehensive rural policies which de-sectoralise rural space. Within Wales numerous fora have been established to address several spheres of rural concern. Local Agenda 21 offers an enormous opportunity for incorporating public participation into decision-making in Wales. In a pluralist society there is seemingly a place for all opinions. There is abundant hearsay evidence that some of the opinions being articulated are not necessarily those which reflect the interests of rural Wales.[10]

316

Local government reorganisation in Wales has resulted in the loss of structures enabling strategic planning. Furthermore there has been a reduction in the guidance to planning legislation offered by government through the Welsh Office. It is vital for efficient land-use planning that it is conducted within a strategic framework, particularly so in the case of minerals and waste disposal. It is argued here that formal systems are required within local government to produce regional or sub regional strategic guidance, and that full government guidance in the form of PPGs and MPGs is a necessary first step to achieve this.

What we have advocated in this chapter is the adoption of a "greenprint" strategy, specifically assembled for the needs of Wales towards the twenty-first century. This would allow for local dynamism, whilst safeguarding amenity and wildlife conservation and which would derive its priorities from the sociocultural characteristics of the communities it serves.

Notes

This is a revised version of a paper presented at the XIII International Seminar on Marginal Regions in July 1995. It is acknowledged that subsequent to this presentation a rural white paper has been published for Wales and that certain planning policy guidance notes have also been issued and that these will be the subject of further papers by this research group.

[1] The government agency responsible up to 1991 for countryside conservation other than purely nature conservation which was the responsibility of the Nature Conservancy Council. From 1991, in Wales these two agencies merged to form the Countryside Council for Wales.

[2] Voluntary participation by local actors.

[3] A voluntary agri-environmental scheme piloted in these three areas where project officers negotiated individual farm agreements with landowners to carry out activities which benefit the environment and leisure uses of land for fixed payments, e.g. stone walling and access agreements.

[4] The government agency for formulating and applying environmental policy and countryside management.

[5] The pattern of local government in England and Wales, prior to April 1996, consisted of sub-regional county councils and their constituent district or borough councils. Functions of the councils were divided on

317

the basis of strategic services such as highways, education, libraries, and social services at county level and local services at district or borough level.

[6] Forward planning has been achieved at local level by use of a two-tier system, operating in tandem with the two-tier local government system. Structure plans represented county level strategic planning containing broadly-based policies and proposals. Local plans represented the means for making specific land use provision and policies at district or borough level, in conformity with the strategic requirements of the structure plan for that area. In unitary authorities both these forward plans have been replaced by the requirement to produce a two-part unitary development plan.

[7] County councils have also been required to produce specific local plans on minerals. While entitled a local plan, the strategic nature of minerals issues has meant that it has been produced at the higher county level.

[8] Regional aggregate working parties consist of representatives of county planning authorities and of the minerals industry constituted to provide regional guidance on patterns of consumption and demand. Wales comprises two such working parties, on each for north and south Wales. The future of these working parties is unclear as is their future membership.

[9] Areas designated as protected areas for nature conservation or landscape conservation.

[10] Since 1979, central government in Britain has devolved a fair measure of its powers to autonomous bodies, the so-called quasi-autonomous non-governmental organisations ("quangos"). In Wales, public debate has turned upon the manner in which nominees are proposed for roles in such bodies.

References

Assembly of Welsh Counties. 1992. *Strategic Planning Guidance in Wales: Report for Consultation.* Cardiff.

_____ . 1993a. *Strategic Planning Guidance in Wales: Overview Report.* Cardiff.

_____ . 1993b. *Strategic Planning Guidance in Wales: Reports.* Cardiff.

Bowers, J. and P. Cheshire. 1983. *Agriculture, the Countryside and*

Land Use: An Economic Critique. London: Methuen.

Bowler, I. R. 1985. *Agriculture under the Common Agricultural Policy: A Geography.* Manchester: Manchester University Press.

Campaign for the Protection of Rural Wales. 1991. *Agriculture and Rural Wales.* Welshpool.

Cloke, P. and G. Edwards. 1986. Rurality in England and Wales 1981: A replication of the 1971 index. *Regional Studies* 20: 289-306.

Commins, P. 1990. Restructuring in advanced societies: Transformation, crisis and responses. In T. Marsden, P. Lowe and S. Whatmore (eds.), *Rural Restructuring: Global Processes and their Responses.* London: David Foulton.

Countryside Commission. 1983. *What Future for the Uplands?* Cheltenham: Countryside Commission.

Countryside Commission. 1986. *Outline Proposals for Environmentally-sensitive Areas in Britain.* Cheltenham: Countryside Commission.

Countryside Council for Wales. 1993. *The National Park Authority.* Bangor: Countryside Council for Wales.

Development Board for Rural Wales. n.d. Rural Wales Action. Newtown.

Department of the Environment. 1990. *Our Common Inheritance.* London: Her Majesty's Stationery Office.

Department of the Environment. 1994. *Minerals Planning Guidance Note 6: Guidelines for Aggregate Provision.* London: Her Majesty's Stationery Office.

European Economic Community. Directives 268/75, 269/75, 276/75.

English Nature. 1995. *Rural White Paper: English Nature's Response to the Government Consultation.* Peterborough: English Nature.

European Union. Directive 797/85.

Finer, S. E. 1966. *Anonymous Empire: A Study of the Lobby in Great Britain.* London: Pall Mall Press.

Gaskell, P. T. and M. F. Tanner. 1991. Agricultural change and ESAs. *Geoforum* 22, 1: 81-90.

Gilg, A. 1991. Planning for agriculture: The growing case for a conservation component. *Geoforum* 22, 1: 75-81.

Goode, D. and D. Tyldesley. 1995. Recommendations for future working. *ECOS Conservation Comment.* April.

Haines, M. 1994. Innovation and diversification. Paper presented at the conference, *Rural Europe: Enterprise, Innovation and Opportunity,* Llangollen, Wales, 21-22 April 1995.

Halfacree, K. H. 1993. Locality and social representation: Space, discourse and alternative definitions of rural. *Journal of Rural Studies* 9: 23-27.

Herbert, T. and G. E. Jones. 1995. *Postwar Wales.* Cardiff: University of Wales Press.

Hoggart, K. 1990. Let's do away with rural. *Journal of Rural Studies* 6: 245-257.

Hoggart, K. and H. Buller. 1987. *Rural Development: A Geographical Perspective.* London: Croom Helm.

Howarth, R. W. 1985. *Farming for Farmers: A Critique of Agricultural Support Policy.* London: The Institute of Economic Affairs.

Humphreys, R. 1995. Images of Wales. In T. Herbert and G. E. Jones (eds.), *Postwar Wales.* Cardiff: University of Wales Press.

Local Government Management Board. 1994. Community participation in Local Agenda 21. Local Agenda 21 roundtable guidance document.

Lowe, P. et al. 1986. *Countryside Conflicts: The Politics of Farming, Forestry and Conservation.* Aldershot: Gower.

Lle Neis i Blant? 1993. Aberystwyth: Creu Côf.

Mather, M. and A. Woods. 1989. Making the most of environmentally-sensitive areas. *Conservation Review* 3.

McEwan, M. and G. Sinclair. 1983. *New Life for the Hills: Policies for Farming and Conservation in the Uplands.* London: Council for National Parks.

Mills, C. W. 1956. *The Power Elite.* New York: Oxford University Press.

Mingay, G. E. (ed). 1989. *The Rural Idyll.* London: Routledge.

Ministry of Agriculture Fisheries and Food. 1989. *Environmentally-sensitive Areas.* London: Her Majesty's Stationery Office.

Ministry of Agriculture Fisheries and Food. 1994. Press Release, 22

November 1994.

Ministry of Agriculture, Forestry and Fishing. 1994. Letter to interested organisations.

Murdoch, J. and A. Pratt. 1993. Rural studies: Modernism, post-modernism and the post-rural. *Journal of Rural Studies* 9 (4): 411-427.

Newby, H. 1991. The future of rural society: Strategic planning or muddling through? In *Strategies for the Rural Economy.* CAS Paper 26, Centre for Agricultural Studies: University of Reading.

Pearlman, D. and J. Pearlman. 1994. Is the right to roam attainable? An aspiration or a pragmatic way forward? Paper presented at the Rural Study Group, Institute of British Geographers' conference, *Accessing the Countryside,* September 21-22, 1994.

Redwood, J. 1993. *The Global Marketplace: Capitalism and its Future.* Glasgow: Harper Collins.

Report of the Committee on Planning Control over Mineral Working. 1976. London: Her Majesty's Stationery Office.

Royal Society for the Protection of Birds. 1984. *Hill Farming and Birds: A Survival Plan.* Sandy: Royal Society for the Protection of Birds.

Schwarzmantel, J. (ed). 1993. *Structures of Power.* Hemel Hempstead: Harvester Wheatsheaf.

Shucksmith, M. et al. 1994. *Disadvantage in Rural Scotland.* Summary Report. Perth: Rural Forum.

Shoard, M. 1980. *The Theft of the Countryside.* London: Temple Smith.

Shoard, M. 1987. *This Land is Our Land.* London: Paladin.

Sunday Express. 25 September 1994.

Thomas, D. and G. Day. 1992. Rural Wales: Problems, policies and prospects. *Contemporary Wales* 7: 37-49.

Thomas, E. E. 1993. The socioeconomic context of agricultural and ecological change in the Llyn peninsula. Unpublished Ph.D. thesis, University of Liverpool.

Welsh Development Agency. 1992. *Overview of Activities.* Cardiff: Welsh Development Agency.

Welsh Office
1994a. *Rural Wales Objective 5b plan 1994-1999.*
1994b. *European Opportunities for Rural Wales: The Member State*

Dimension.

Westmacott, R. and T. Worthington. 1974. New agricultural landscapes. Cheltenham: Countryside Commission.

Western Mail. 23 December 1994.

Western Mail. 9 May 1995.

Welsh Office Agricultural Department. 1986. *Agricultural Improvement Scheme: Grant Information.* Cardiff: Welsh Office Agricultural Department.

Welsh Office Agricultural Department. 1992. *Socioeconomic Monitoring Reports for the Welsh ESAs.* Cardiff: Welsh Office Agricultural Department.

Woods, A. 1989. Reforming the CAP. *Conservation Review* 3: 41-44.

Wright, A. 1995. Planners left to pick up the pieces. *Planning* 1118: 10.

18 The impact of Irish dairy industry rationalisation on the sustainability of small farming communities

Proinnsias Breathnach and Michael Kenny

Introduction

In the second half of the 20th century, the Irish dairy industry---in common with the experience of agriculture throughout developed market economies---has been subject to restructuring processes arising from what some writers have termed the second agricultural revolution (Healy and Ilbery 1985) but which Bowler (1992) more correctly refers to as the third such revolution. This involves "the progressive extension of techno-logical, organisational and economic rationality into the arena of farm operations, linking them even more closely to the other sectors of the economy, both materially and in ethos" (Wallace 1984, quoted in Healy and Ilbery 1985: 2). The specific outcomes of this rationalisation process have been summarised by Bowler (1992) under the three headings: inten-sification, concentration, and specialisation.

This paper traces the process of rationalisation in the Irish dairy industry in the 20th century and discusses some of its economic and social outcomes, with particular reference to its impact on communities of small dairy farmers. Initially, however, the paper provides some back-ground information on Irish agriculture in general, and on the early growth of the Irish dairy cooperative sector in the late 19th and early 20th centuries.

The nature of Irish agriculture

Irish agriculture is dominated by pastoralism, with less than ten per cent of improved farm land devoted to tillage. Over two thirds of gross agri-cultural output is generated by cattle rearing and milk production, which each account for about one third of the total. Irish farming is almost entirely owner-operated, and farm size is generally quite small in relation to the ability to generate incomes comparable to those in the non-farm sector. Today the average farm size is about 26 hectares (64 acres), with about two thirds of all farms below that size. Only 11% of farms are in excess of 50 hectares.

The origins of the dairy cooperative sector

Small farmers, with their limited resources, have always been vulnerable to exploitation by those who purchase their output or supply them with inputs, typically in the form of high input and/or low output prices, frequently exacerbated by problems of indebtedness. The obvious response to this situation has been for small farmers to organise themselves into cooperative groups for joint purchases of inputs or downstream processing of outputs, thereby outflanking private operators in these sectors (Hart 1992).

In the case of Ireland, cooperative organisation gained what eventually became virtually a monopoly foothold in the late 19th and early 20th centuries in the dairy sector. Irish dairy farming is largely concentrated in two particular regions: the Mid-Munster Intensive Dairying Region (with an adjoining Southern Dairying Region) in the south of the island, on the one hand, and the Northern Dairying Region, on the other (Figure 1). Beef rearing predominates in most other areas.

Ireland's first cooperative creamery was established (in the heartland of the Mid-Munster Intensive Dairy Region) in 1889, and the cooperative system subsequently spread rapidly, firstly in the surrounding Munster region, from where it then leapfrogged to the Northern Dairy Region. However, privately-owned creameries (the first of which was established in 1884) proliferated even more rapidly, so that these accounted for two thirds of the almost 800 creameries which were in operation by 1905, when creamery numbers in Ireland reached their apex (Daly 1991). There was strong rivalry between the two systems in many areas, sometimes amounting to cut-throat competition for the milk supplies of local farmers (Bolger 1983).

Rationalisation of the dairy industry

This competition was mainly responsible for setting off a process of profound reorganisation and rationalisation in the Irish dairy industry stretching over the 20th century. This process has mainly occurred in a series of five distinct (albeit overlapping) episodes: the elimination of the private creamery sector, amalgamation of cooperatives into larger units, centralisation of milk processing, closure of auxiliary or branch creameries, and concentration of on-farm milk production.

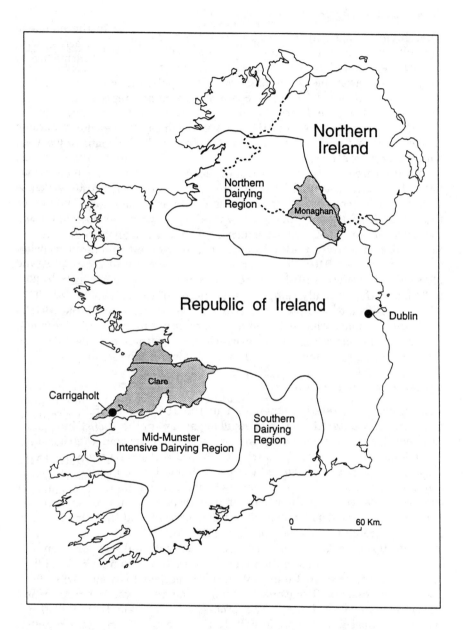

Figure 1   Ireland: Dairying regions and case-study areas
Source: Haughton and Gillmor 1979, Gillmor 1984

Elimination of the private creamery sector

The slump in agricultural prices after First World War created very difficult circumstances for the creamery sector, a position which was further aggravated by on-going milk wars between rival private and cooperative operations competing for milk supplies in many areas. The newly independent Irish Free State government stepped in via the establishment of the Dairy Disposal Company (DDC) in 1927 with a remit, in effect, to take over the private creamery sector and insolvent cooperatives and to either close these down altogether or transfer them to surviving cooperatives.

Within three years, the DDC had acquired 170 private creameries (80% of the total), about half of which were closed down, with a quarter transferred to cooperative ownership and a quarter operated directly by the DDC itself (mainly in areas where there were no suitable local cooperatives to which the creameries could be transferred). Some insolvent cooperatives were also acquired, as were all remaining private operations in the 1940s. The overall effect of this initial rationalisation phase was a reduction in the number of cooperative creameries from 336 to 215, and the virtually complete elimination of the private sector. The DDC continued to operate its portfolio of creameries until the 1970s, when the company was abolished and its constituent creameries sold off, mainly to the large cooperatives which had by then emerged via the process of amalgamation discussed in the following sub-section.

Cooperative amalgamation

After a period of relative stagnation in the 1940s and 1950s, the Irish dairy industry entered a phase of rapid expansion in the 1960s, due partly to general economic buoyancy in both the domestic and international economies, and partly to the introduction of direct government supports. New economic policies involved the abandonment of protectionism and a consequent need for the restructuring of indigenous industry in order to prepare it for growing conditions of free trade. A number of sectoral studies were carried out in pursuit of this objective, and that for the dairy industry recommended the amalgamation of dairy cooperatives into larger groups in order to achieve economies of scale and specialisation.

The first major amalgamation took place in 1964 when four of the five cooperative societies in County Waterford merged to create Waterford Cooperative Society (Breathnach 1992). The fifth was eventually absorbed eleven years later. The process of amalgamation set off in Waterford subsequently spread rapidly throughout the industry rapidly. The 188 cooperatives in existence in 1960 were reduced to just 35 in 1990. There is a high level of differentiation among those remaining, with the top four accounting for one half of total turnover. The process of amalgamation between cooperatives has generally been accompanied by considerable rationalisation within cooperatives. From a spatial point of view, the two most important forms of rationalisation have been the centralisation of milk processing and the closure of the branch creamery structure.

Centralisation of milk processing

Prior to amalgamation, all individual cooperatives would have had their own milk processing operations (usually butter manufacture). Following amalgamation, processing was usually discontinued in the smaller locations and centralised in the major plants which in most cases diversified into other processing activities such as cheese, casein, yoghurt and milk powder production. The former processing locations have either continued to provide existing store and retail functions, been sold off or been closed down altogether.

The closure of branch creameries

The spatial structure of the early creamery system in Ireland was based on a system of central processing plants and a network of auxiliary or branch creameries where milk was separated, with the cream being sent on to the central processing plants and the skim milk being returned to the farmers for feeding to calves and pigs. However, the development of modern forms of transportation and the increasing tendency to use all the milk in dairy processing meant that the branch system was rendered redundant.

Initially, the separating function was discontinued, but the branches continued to act as assembly points, to which milk was brought by farmers for transfer to trucks for onward delivery to central processing plants. However, growing levels of milk output per farm meant that economies of scale in long-distance deliveries of milk from individual farms were increasingly attainable. As a result, the assembly function of the former branch creameries has also largely disappeared, although it still survives in some areas where dairy herds are too small to warrant direct collection from farms. The general disappearance of the branch creamery had a major impact on economic and social interaction patterns in dairying districts where the trip to the creamery had been a central feature of everyday life.

Concentration of milk production

The final process of rationalisation which has occurred in the Irish dairy industry in the last thirty years, and which is the main focus of the remainder of this paper, has been the growing concentration of milk production among a declining number of increasingly large producers. This is linked to the inability of smaller producers to meet the increasing demands of the industry in terms of equipment, material inputs, skills and hygiene standards. It is also linked to a growing preoccupation among dairy cooperatives with economic profitability at the expense of the broader social concerns which played a key role in the earlier days of the cooperative movement.

Nationally, 110,000 farmers were supplying creamery milk in 1966. Of these, 98% were supplying less than 15,000 gallons (one gallon being equal to 4.55 litres) each per annum (O'Dwyer 1968). By 1988, the number of suppliers had been reduced by more than one half (to 49,500). Of these, only 54% were now supplying less than 15,000 gallons, and between them, these accounted for just 19% of total supplies. At the same time, the 5% of suppliers who each were producing over 60,000 gallons accounted jointly for 21% of all supplies (Agriculture and Food Policy Review Group 1990).

This process of concentration is, of course, a general feature of recent agricultural change in advanced market economies and has

> . . . served progressively to polarise the farming community into a minority of highly capitalised, large-scale enterprises, which account for a growing proportion of total agricultural production, and a vulnerable majority of inadequately capitalised farms whose ability to provide their proprietors with a livelihood is being increasingly undermined. (Wallace 1985: 499)

Those farmers who have been squeezed out of dairying have generally been pushed into less intensive enterprises (particularly beef production) which give a lower return. As the great majority of the farms in question are small in area, this means that already low incomes have been reduced even further in most cases. Many of these farmers have been able to obtain off-farm employment to supplement their incomes, while some are in semi-retirement. However, a large proportion now depend on the state social welfare system for a large proportion of their income, while many who are entitled to this assistance do not avail of it for one reason or another. For these latter in particular, who depend on meagre land resources for almost all of their income, extreme poverty is an everyday reality (Kelleher and O'Mahony 1984).

The impact of concentration on small-farm dairy regions

While many of the small farmers who have been squeezed out of milk production are spatially interspersed with larger producers in the main dairy regions, the impact of concentration has been especially great in districts where dairy farms are generally small in scale. This is typically the case in the Northern Dairying Region, and also in peripheral and upland areas in and around the main Mid-Munster dairy region. The following subsections give an account of the impact of concentration in two such districts.

Case study: County Clare

Clare is a predominantly small farming county located at the western edge of the Southern Dairying Region (Figure 1). While the average farm size in 1991 (26.2 hectares) was almost identical to the national average, the county's agricultural land is mainly marginal in quality---most of the county is categorised as "severely handicapped" under the EU Less Favoured Areas scheme. While specialist dairy farms accounted for only 31% of all farms of over five hectares in 1991, within the county, dairying is disproportionately concentrated towards the southwest where average farm size is lower (Horner et al. 1984). Mannion et al. (1993) analysed trends in the dairy industry in the county following the introduction of the milk quota system by the European Union in 1984. This system placed an overall cap on national milk production and allocated each dairy farm a milk quota based on existing production levels; thereafter, individual farmers could only increase output by acquiring quotas given up by other farmers. The following subsection is based largely on the findings of Mannion et al.

In County Clare, the number of dairy farmers declined by 29% to 2,332 between 1984-92. Over 90% of those leaving dairying had been producing less than 9,000 gallons per annum. Despite this, in 1992 almost one-half of remaining suppliers were still in this category, compared with just 14% supplying in excess of 20,000 gallons---considered to be the threshold of viability for full-time dairy farms. From a sample survey it was calcu-lated that, for remaining farmers in the less-than-9,000 gallon category, farm income represented just over half of household income, the rest coming from welfare payments (26%) and off-farm income (19%). These farmers had an average household income from all sources of IR£6,628, compared with IR£14,986 for those supplying in excess of 20,000 gallons and the average earnings of industrial workers for 1992 of IR£12,700.

Small-scale suppliers generally possess land, most of which is classed as not being very suitable for dairying; partly as a result, stocking rates are low (1 hectare per livestock unit), while farm sizes are small and average output per cow is also low (582 gallons compared with 800-1,000 in the core dairy areas). These all combine to give low overall incomes from dairying. Given that this category of dairy farmer also tends to have inadequate on-farm dairy facilities, that only 10% of their milk is of top quality, that very few of them have any agricultural education, that only about a half have any contact with the agricultural advisory service, and that almost one half have no child dependants, it is clear that a large proportion of them have no long-term prospects of remaining in dairying.

This is particularly the case given new EU regulations regarding standards of on-farm dairy equipment and buildings. The great majority of dairy farmers in County Clare currently fail to meet these standards, including not only 91% of those in the less-than-9,000 gallon category, but also 57% of those supplying more than 20,000 gallons. Clearly, very considerable investment will be required to meet these standards, and many farmers will be unable to make this investment. All told, it is estimated that up to three quarters of the 2,332 remaining dairy farmers in the county are at short- or medium-term risk of leaving dairying. Of these, almost one half are considered to be definitely non-viable on the basis of inadequate resources and facilities, and poor household structure. Were all of these to drop out of dairying, it would mean that only just over a half of the dairy farmers in operation in 1984 would be still in business.

Further insight into the impact of concentration at local level is provided in a case study of the parish of Carrigaholt, located at the southwest extremity of County Clare (Figure 1). In 1965 the parish had a population of 1,240, divided into 293 households, including 264 farm households, of which 220 were supplying creamery milk. Including employment generated by dairying (farm labourers, creamery workers, etc.) and services supported by dairying, over 90% of the parish's families were dependent on income arising from the industry. However, the average milk output per farm was low, at 3,100 gallons, reflecting the small farm size structure of the parish.

By 1992, the number of farms supplying creamery milk had dropped by 45% to 120. However, the average volume of milk supplied by those remaining has almost quadrupled since 1965 to 14,280 gallons. In fact, the total volume of milk produced in the parish doubled between 1965 and 1984, when the milk quota system was introduced. Thereafter, milk output from the parish has declined by an average of three per cent per annum, due mainly to sales out of the district of milk quotas by farmers abandoning dairying. The income loss from dairying is the equivalent of ten full-time jobs being lost every year to the district.

While dairying remains central to the economy of the parish of Carrigaholt (accounting for 70% of earned income in 1992), concentration of production has had a severe demographic impact on the locality. The number of farm households declined by 40% between 1965-92, leading to an overall population loss of 35%. The number of dairy farmers has declined at an even faster rate i.e., 45%. The drop-out rate from dairying accelerated markedly following the introduction of the quota system. Between 1984-92 the number of drop-outs was 66 (7.3 per annum) compared with 54 (2.8 per annum) over the previous 19 years. Drop-outs were mainly concentrated among the smallest suppliers: three quarters were supplying less than 9,000 gallons annually.

Despite outmigration and a certain degree of diversification of the local employment base, there has been a significant growth in unemployment in the parish. The proportion of the labour force claiming unemployment assistance grew from zero in 1965 to one-fifth in 1992. There has been a considerable contraction in the parish's service base, with the number of shops down from nine to three, the number of post offices down from three to one and the number of public houses down from seven to five. All of the parish's four branch creameries have had their processing activities terminated. While contraction of the service base is attributable to broader processes than depopulation, and while not all outmigration may be attributed to concentration in dairy production, it is clear that there is a strong link between all three phenomena.

Nor is the decline in the number of milk suppliers likely to cease. In fact, no less than two-thirds of the remaining 120 dairy farmers in the parish are thought to be at immediate or medium-term risk of getting out of milk production, due mainly to small quotas, poor farm facilities and financial difficulties . In addition, the continuing trend for milk quotas to leave the parish means that the income associated with these quotas no longer circulates locally. Given its peripheral location, the prospects of significant employment diversification in the parish (despite some recent tourism-related developments) are limited. Further contraction in dairy production and its related income will therefore add very considerably to the cycle of outmigration, population decline and service contraction, given a continuation of current policies regarding milk production.

Case study: County Monaghan

County Monaghan, along with adjoining County Cavan, is the main focus of milk production in that part of the Northern Dairying Region located in the Republic of Ireland (Figure 1). It is a county of mainly small farms: the 1991 average size of 16.7 hectares was two thirds of the national average and half the average size in the main dairy counties in the south. All of the county is included in the EU Less Favoured Areas scheme, most in the "disadvantaged" category, but with some in the "severely handicapped" category. An analysis of trends in the dairy industry in the county following the introduction of the quota system was carried out in 1993 by Macra na Feirme (a young farmers' organisation). The following subsection is based largely on the findings of this report (Monaghan Macra na Feirme 1994).

In the mid-1970s, approximately 4,500 farmers in the county were milk suppliers---90% of the entire farm population (Irish Times, May 5, 1977). By the time the milk quota system was introduced in 1984, the number of milk suppliers had already fallen to 3,223, and this figure declined by a further 36%, to 2,047, in the following eight years. Almost 90% of those who got out of milk production between 1984-92 had been supplying less than 10,000 gallons per annum. Even then, the average output of the remaining suppliers, at 18,209 gallons, remained below the 20,000 gallons considered necessary to achieve economic viability. In fact, only 30% of producers exceeded that figure, with 43% continuing to supply less than 10,000 gallons. Only 63 farmers reached the 20,000 gallons viability threshold between 1984-92, compared with the 1,182 who got out of dairying entirely in the same period.

In addition to small scale of production, the dominant characteristics of those ceasing milk production are that they tend to be elderly and have no successors: almost one half of sub-10,000 gallon suppliers who abandoned milk production after 1984 were unmarried. However, the demographic structure of those remaining in dairying in 1992 continued to show cause for concern, with almost 40% (including a quarter of those supplying over 20,000 gallons) having no apparent successor. All in all, it is estimated that up to two-thirds of dairy farmers in Monaghan are at risk of leaving milk production, and that 40% will actually do so by the early part of the next decade. Added to those who have already left since 1984, this would amount to an overall decline of 60% in the number of milk suppliers in the county in less than 20 years.

A local case study contained in the Macra na Feirme report covered an area with a population (in 1993) of just 138, representing 51 households, and located some 12 km from the nearest town. In 1970, 40 (three-quarters) of the area's households were engaged in farming, almost all (37) in dairying. The overall supply of milk from the area more than doubled between 1970-93, due partly to an increase in the number of cows but mainly to a major increase in average output per cow (from 480 to 800 gallons). However, in the same period the number of dairy farms dropped by just over one half to 18. Overall, average output per farm rose from 4,700 gallons in 1970 to over 21,000 gallons in 1993---a more than four-fold increase. Thus, the proportion of community income arising from dairying has grown from 21.5% to 34.4%, but this is now shared by a much smaller group of continuing dairy farmers.

The Monaghan local case study shows indications of greater employment diversification than in Carrigaholt, with six farmers having moved into mushroom growing, although most of those who left commercial milk production opted for suckler cows and, more typically, drystock rearing, both of which give much lower returns per acre than dairying. The availability of off-farm industrial jobs has increased significantly, although this has been almost exactly counterbalanced by the decline in local service workers. Overall, however, there has been a noticeable weakening in the demographic structure of the community, with the total population having dropped by 22% (from 172 to 134) between 1970-93. The main contribution to this decline came from the young dependent population, which declined by one-third in the same period. Thus, while the total number of households fell by just two to 51, there was a noticeable ageing in the remaining population.

Policy responses

Dairying is the only form of farm enterprise which offers the prospect of a reasonable living standard for small farmers in Ireland today. However, such a living standard remains beyond the reach of the majority of small dairy farmers. This will inevitably mean a continued haemorrhage from dairy production, leading to even lower farm incomes and an ongoing exodus from agriculture. While much of the current emphasis in Irish rural development is on farm diversification (including new agricultural product lines, agri-tourism and agri-forestry), the evidence thus far is that such diversification tends to be largely restricted to young, relatively well-educated farmers with access to capital (Commins 1996), characteristics which (particularly in combination) are relatively rare among those who are most at risk of ceasing dairy production. Similarly, while the LEADER programme has been having a significant impact in generating alternative non-farming income and employment opportunities in rural Ireland (Kearney et al. 1994), the evidence here is that these are falling far short of compensating for employment and population losses arising from agricultural contraction. This in turn leads to further erosion of the service base and of social and community life in rural Ireland---ingredients which, along with adequate living standards, have been identified by the National Economic and Social Council (1994) as the essential components of an effective policy for sustainable rural development.

The retention of the maximum number of milk suppliers in the farming sector is therefore of crucial significance in maintaining the socio-economic viability and sustainability of small-farm dairy communities in Ireland today. This requires measures to assist potentially viable dairy farmers to acquire the additional resources they need to encourage them to remain on in dairying. These include extra land, expanded milk quotas and dairy herds, improved equipment and facilities, and enhanced technical abilities to exploit these resources to their maximum potential. A first step in this direction would be the provision of special aid (grants and low-interest loans) to allow remaining small dairy farmers to upgrade their facilities, to purchase, or lease (on a medium- to long-term basis) available quotas, and to expand their dairy herds. A potentially important step in these directions has been the recent introduction of a subsidy scheme to help small milk producers to purchase additional quotas, in conjunction with parallel measures to give dairy farmers in disadvantaged areas priority access to quotas made available when other farmers in their localities cease production (Commins 1996).

There is also a need for a pro-active input from the state agricultural advisory service in order to upgrade the skills and technical abilities of small dairy farmers, among whom education and training levels have traditionally been low. This would reverse the trend of recent years, where the state advisory service has become increasingly commercial in its orientation, responding to the needs of larger farmers who are prepared to pay for the service, and more or less abandoning the small farm sector as having little long-term future. A gesture in this direction was made in the Operational Programme for Agriculture, Rural Development and Forestry 1994-99 (part of the Community Support Framework for the disbursement of EU Structural Funds to Ireland), where provision was made for a farm viability service focusing on small farms. However, the resources devoted to this scheme are quite meagre relative to the overall funding envisaged by the Operational Programme (Commins 1996).

Many small dairy farmers will nevertheless still not be in a position to expand their operations unless they are able to expand the area of their farms via purchase or long-term leasing of additional land. Such farmers are generally unable to compete with larger farmers on the open market for land. This points to the need for an effective land policy which will give favoured treatment (via appropriate forms of financial assistance) in the acquisition of available land to younger (and suitably trained) farm operators in particular (including new entrants to farming). The type of land policy which had been operated by the Land Commission (abolished in the 1980s) had become discredited by bureaucratic inefficiency and political interference, while the Farm Modernisation Scheme introduced by the then EC in 1975 proved largely ineffectual in small farming areas, due mainly to the absence of adequate numbers of Development Farmers (the main focus of the scheme) in these areas and insufficient incentives to attract a significant uptake of the parallel Farm Retirement Scheme. While the report of the Interdepartmental Committee on Land Structure Reform (1978) advocated intervention in the land market in order to channel available land in the interest of land reform (a proposal which was accepted in principle by the government of the time), in fact no government since then has had the stomach to tackle the land structure question and, with the subsequent political shift towards deregulation and market orientation, this question has been taken off the policy agenda (Commins 1996). Thus, in the recent National Economic and Social Council (1994) report on rural development, the question of land structure reform is hardly broached at all, the main emphasis being on farm diversification and the expansion of non-farm employment opportunities in rural areas.

Even with the kinds of policies advocated here, it is inevitable that there will be a continued substantial contraction in the number of dairy farmers for reasons mainly related to inadequate resources and age structure. Older farmers without successors should be encouraged to retire, and a policy is required to give younger qualified local farmers favoured access to this land, either through purchase or leasing. Younger farmers with little prospect of making a go of dairying should be encouraged to switch to alternative enterprises while undergoing training for appropriate forms of off-farm employment likely to keep them in the area. In this respect, the LEADER and similar programmes need to focus part of their attention to the specific needs of small farmers.

In the case of Clare, even with the policy measures being recommended here, it is estimated that 35% of the current population of dairy farmers in the county will eventually leave dairying; however, this will still leave almost twice the number which is likely to survive based on a continuation of current policies. The total cost of a package of subsidies and grants required to allow the maximum number of potentially viable dairy farmers in Clare to remain in dairying was estimated by Mannion et al. (1993) at IR£15 million. Given the alternative cost of supporting the more than 700 farmers who would otherwise have to leave dairying, and the social and economic benefits to the communities concerned of maintaining the farm population at a higher level than would otherwise be the case, this is considered to be a worthwhile investment.

Conclusion

As observed at the outset, one of the conventional arguments in favour of agricultural cooperatives has been that they provide the small producer in particular with a degree of protection and countervailing power in their transactions with input suppliers and with the downstream processing and marketing sectors. However, the image of the cooperative as the protector of the small producer has long been obliterated---as have the small producers themselves, to a considerable extent. This may be attributed in part to the increasing control of cooperatives exercised by professional managers whose primary concerns are growth and profitability rather than the welfare of their weaker members (Tovey 1982; Curtin and Varley 1992).

However, undoubtedly of greater importance is the power of market forces in a situation of growing competitiveness in European and world markets. In this situation, the very survival of cooperatives is seen as being dependent on increased efficiency which in turn is seen as requiring the elimination of those suppliers who are regarded as being incapable of reaching the desired levels of efficiency. In this respect, once again, the Irish experience simply reflects international trends. As Wallace (1985: 501) has observed:

> The formation of agricultural cooperatives has long been a favoured response to the difficulties encountered by small- to medium-sized farmers in their dealings with the rest of the economy. However, their theoretical benefits as non-capitalist institutions are realised only infrequently and the more successful they are as businesses, the more they tend to reinforce the prevailing market forces favouring large operators.

A major problem for the Irish dairy cooperatives is that, notwithstanding the advanced stage which the process of amalgamation has reached, even the largest of them remain small relative to their major European competitors. In 1990, the largest Irish cooperative had a turnover only one-third and one-half that of its Dutch and Danish counterparts, respectively (*Irish Times,* September 20, 1991). While the big Irish cooperatives have undergone considerable expansion in recent years, this has mainly been achieved through a process of overseas acquisitions (Breathnach 1996). More significantly, in order to fund this expansion, most of these cooperatives have sold off substantial portions of their share capital to private investors. This inevitably entails that their decision-making will be less concerned with the needs of their member-suppliers, and increasingly concerned with the needs of these private investors (i.e. profit level and share price).

It is clear, therefore, that little assistance for the plight of small dairy farmers will be forthcoming from the large cooperatives which dominate the processing of milk supplies in Ireland. It suits the interests of these cooperatives to concentrate milk production in the hands of the largest and most efficient suppliers. This in turn has serious implications for the small-scale dairy farming sector and the regions in which this sector is concentrated. This is not simply a question of agricultural change since, as we have seen, the rapid contraction in the numbers of small dairy farmers in areas where they previously predominated has far-reaching social and economic ramifications beyond the immediate farming community. It is essential, therefore, that the structural problems of small dairy farmers should be regarded not just as an agricultural problem, but as a crucial consideration for rural development policy in general. Accordingly, it seems appropriate that these problems should occupy a central position in the Area-Based Integrated Development Strategy advocated by the National Economic and Social Council (1994) as the basis for future rural development policy formulation and implementation in Ireland.

References

Agriculture and Food Policy Review Group. 1990. *Report*. Dublin: The Stationery Office.

Bolger, P. 1983. The dreadful years. In C. Keating (ed.), *Plunkett and Cooperatives*. Cork: Bank of Ireland Centre for Cooperative Studies, University College, Cork. Pp. 111-118.

Bowler, I. R. 1992. The industrialisation of agriculture. In I. R. Bowler (ed.), *The Geography of Agriculture in Developed Market Economies*. Harlow: Longman. Pp. 7-31.

Bowler, I. R. and B. W. Ilbery. 1987. Redefining agricultural geography. *Area* 19, 4: 327-332.

Breathnach, P. 1992. The development of the dairy industry in County Waterford. In W. Nolan and T. P. Power (eds.), *Waterford: History and Society*. Dublin: Geography Publications. Pp. 707-732.

_____. 1996. The internationalisation of the Irish dairy processing industry. Paper given to the Conference of Irish Geographers, Galway.

Commins, P. 1996. Agricultural production and the future of small-scale farming. In C. Curtin, T. Haase and H. Tovey (eds.), *Poverty in Rural Ireland*. Dublin: Oaktree Press. Pp. 87-125.

Curtin, C. and T. Varley. 1992. Cooperation in rural Ireland: An approach in terminal crisis? In M. Ó Cinnéide and M. Cuddy (eds.), *Perspectives on Rural Development in Advanced Economies*. Social Sciences Research Centre, University College, Galway. Pp. 111-122.

Daly, P. 1991. The early development of the creamery system in Ireland 1880-1914. Unpublished M. A. thesis, Department of Geography, St. Patrick's College, Maynooth.

Gillmor, D. A. 1984. Regional patterns in farming. *Bulletin of the*

Department of Foreign Affairs 1010: 11-14.

Hart, P. 1992. Marketing agricultural produce. In I. R. Bowler (ed.), *The Geography of Agriculture in Developed Market Economies.* Harlow: Longman. Pp. 162-206.

Haughton, J. P. and D. A. Gillmor. 1979. *The Geography of Ireland.* Dublin: Department of Foreign Affairs.

Healey, M. and B. W. Ilbery. 1985. The industrialisation of the countryside: An overview. In M. J. Healey and B. W. Ilbery (eds.), *The Industrialisation of the Countryside.* Norwich: Geo Books. Pp.1-26.

Horner, A. A., J. A. Walsh and J. A. Williams. 1994. *Agriculture in Ireland: A Census Atlas.* Department of Geography, University College Dublin.

Interdepartmental Committee on Land Structure Reform. 1978. *Report.* Dublin: The Stationery Office.

Kearney, B., G. E. Boyle and J. A. Walsh. 1994. *EU LEADER 1 Initiative in Ireland: Evaluation and Recommendations.* Dublin: Department of Agriculture, Food and Forestry.

Kelleher, C. and A. O'Mahony. 1984. *Marginalisation in Irish Agriculture.* Dublin: The Agricultural Institute.

Mannion, J., J. Phelan, J. Kinsella and M. Kenny. 1993. *A Strategy for Retaining the Maximum Number of Milk Suppliers in County Clare.* Shannon: Rural Resource Development/LEADER County Clare.

Monaghan Macra na Feirme. 1994. *Milk Quota and Its Effects.*

National Economic and Social Council. 1994. *New Approaches to Rural Development.* Report No. 97. Dublin.

O'Dwyer, T. 1968. Structural changes in milk supply in a cooperative creamery area. *Irish Journal of Agricultural Economics and Rural Sociology* 1, 2: 207-219.

Tovey, H. 1982. Milking the farmer? Modernisation and marginalisation in Irish dairy farming. In M. Kelly, L. O'Dowd and J. Wickham (eds.), *Power, Conflict and Inequality.* Dublin: Turoe Press. Pp. 68-89.

Wallace, I. 1984. Towards a geography of agribusiness. Unpublished paper quoted in Healey and Ilbery (1985).

Wallace, I. 1985. Towards a geography of agribusiness. *Progress in Human Geography* 9, 4: 491-514.

19 Addressing the sustainability of rural populations: Migration trends in the Republic of Ireland, 1971-1991

Mary Cawley

Introduction

Recent discussion relating to the sustainability of rural systems has devoted considerable attention to the potentially deleterious effects on human health and on physical environmental quality of high-intensity methods of agricultural production (Commission of the European Communities 1992). The sustainability of rural economies during the transition from labour-intensive Fordist to capital-intensive, knowledge-based, post-Fordist methods of production, which seek proximity to scientific expertise and major markets, also receives attention in European Union (EU) and national government-funded initiatives such as LEADER (Champetier 1992). Relatively less attention is devoted in current debates to the demographic aspects of sustainability, although population retention is undoubtedly an underlying objective of many rural development initiatives. The maintenance of viable economies in rural areas requires that critical population masses which include the economically-active age groups, who play a special role in generating enterprise, maintaining birth rates and providing a basis for social action, are retained (Whitby and Powe 1995). In any particular national context, it is important for effective economic and social planning that population trends are monitored and that inter-area variations are identified. It is known that demographic structures are becoming increasingly differentiated between rural areas with implications for the capacity of different populations and areas to benefit adequately from any development measures that may be introduced. There is evidence forthcoming from several Western European countries of a close association between rural regeneration and proximity to large centres of population (Hoggart et al. 1995). At the same time, a gradual abandonment of peripheral geographical areas is taking place. Social and economic peripheralisation is becoming more common among rural subgroups, resulting in major societal inequalities and high welfare costs in both Europe and the United States (Cloke 1992, Furuseth 1992).

Migration assumes a particularly important role in the context of rural demographic sustainability. Migration trends reflect underlying economic conditions and in turn have impacts for social and economic structures. Outmigration from rural areas is known to be biased towards the younger, more economically-active age groups whose loss contributes to the well-recognised cycle of cumulative decline (Lowe et al. 1986). Yet, few studies address the composition of the net migration loss in any detail at a scale that permits its significance within broader national migration trends to be appreciated more fully. This paper adopts such an approach to the analysis of migration in the Republic of Ireland where the scale of continuous loss among the younger working-age groups in selected small town and rural localities had, by the late 1980s, raised serious concern relating to the demise of communities and of service structures (Euradvice 1994). Attention is directed to the ability of some 160 sub-county census districts to retain their school-leaving and working-age groups, as revealed in net migration trends during the 1970s and the 1980s. These two decades witnessed marked changes in economic conditions and in the distribution of employment opportunities within the state, as well as a gradual withdrawal by government from regional economic planning. Smaller-scale agricultural producers and their families, in particular, experienced reductions in their incomes from farming arising from price controls, the introduction of quotas on output and curtailed off-farm employment options. The research focuses on the relationship between net migration and size of place, as a method of identifying the role of a critical population mass in retaining the economically-active age groups. The paper reports results for both highly urbanised districts and those where a majority of the population resides in the open countryside or in small towns. Whilst the focus of the International Seminar on Marginal Regions is on the latter areas, it is appropriate that rural migration trends should be viewed within the broader national context.

Data sources and study method

Information relating to migration for the Republic of Ireland is available from census place of birth data and from a question included at each census since 1971 which elicits place of residence precisely one year before the census date. The place of birth data provide insights into broad patterns of movement between areas of the state and from over-seas, but are of very limited value as a measure of recent migration. The one-year data are compiled for counties and for towns of 1,500 population or over but not for other sub-county census districts. Sample-based information relating to inter-county migration is available from Annual Labour Force Surveys but these document broad trends only. Because of the limited coverage of migration available from census sources, an exercise was undertaken to estimate net migration for five-year age groups using the forward survival method (Shryock et al. 1976). Survival ratios derived from appropriate Irish Life Tables were applied for this purpose.

The analysis is based on the census periods 1971-1981, 1981-1986 and 19861991. A census was not conducted in 1976, as a cost-cutting measure during a period of economic recession, hence the use of one census period only for the 1970s (a partial census was conducted in 1979 but the partitioning of the decade into an eight-year and a two-year period is not particularly useful for present purposes). There were 157 Rural Districts (RDs) in 1971, together with five County Boroughs (CBs) which contain major cities, giving a total of 162 areal units. Fifty-two of the 157 RDs contain Urban Districts (UDs) within their boundaries, which include all but two of the larger towns in the state (Figure 1). The town areas do not, however, coincide with the UD areas: many towns overbound the urban district boundaries. In addition, town boundaries are subject to change at the time of a census to incorporate recent housing development adjoining the existing built-up areas. Age data for the revised town areas are not available for the preceding census year and net migration for most towns cannot be calculated separately from that for the RD in which they are located. To provide constant areas over time the populations of the UDs have been combined with those of the RDs in which they are located in estimating migration.

The CBs numbered five in 1971 and 1981 (Dublin and the neighbouring city of Dun Laoghaire, Cork, Limerick and Waterford) and six in 1986 and 1991 when Galway was classified as a CB for the first time. Changes in the boundaries of some of the CBs took place over the three census periods: Waterford CB was extended in 1979 as were Dublin CB and Galway CB in 1985. Age data are not available for the revised areas at the preceding census in these cases. In calculating intercensal migration, the pertinent CB was combined with the adjoining RD (RDs in the case of Dublin for 1986-1991) from which it received population.

Migration was estimated for males and females separately in the principal youth, school-leaving and working-age groups: those aged 0-4 to

45-49 in 1971 (aged 10-14 and 55-59 in 1981) and those aged 0-4 to 50-54 in 1981 and in 1986 (aged 5-9 and 55-59 in 1986 and 1991). Net migration is expressed as a rate per 1,000 of the average of the pertinent age groups in the initial and the terminal census years and is correlated with the total population in the initial year of each intercensal period. Pearson Product Moment correlation values are used to measure the relationship between net migration and size of place. As a guide to the strength of the relationship, significance levels are cited which would apply if the data were randomly distributed.

Population change and distribution in context: 1971-1991

During the 1970s, the Republic of Ireland registered one of the highest rates of population growth in western Europe. This equalled 1.56% per annum, and has been attributed to the relatively high birth rates then current, and to net inmigration to improved employment opportunities during the first half of the decade (Kennedy et al. 1988). The effects of international recessionary conditions on the national economy were apparent by the end of the decade in rising unemployment rates and renewed net outmigration, and the first half of the 1980s was marked by lower rates of population growth (0.54% per annum). The second half of the 1980s witnessed the re-emergence of population decline, of 0.1% per annum, for the first time since 1961. Broad patterns of population change by RD indicate that all areas, except the most remote, made gains during the 1970s (Horner and Daultrey 1980). These gains tended to be modest outside the zone of influence of urban centres. The number of districts registering decline and the rates of decline increased throughout the 1980s (Cawley 1990, 1991; Walsh 1991a).

At an aggregate level, town growth and rural decline have been features of Irish population change since the early twentieth century (Cawley 1991). In particular the capital city Dublin, as the admin-istrative centre of a highly centralised state, has absorbed large numbers of internal migrants (Walsh 1991b). In 1991, the Greater Dublin area, which includes Dublin CB, Dun Laoghaire CB and the adjoining suburbs, contained 26% of the total state population. Offsetting the dispro-portionate growth of Greater Dublin by reducing inmigration to that area became an aim of regional industrial policy in the late 1960s (O'Malley 1992). Both large regional growth centres and some 200 smaller towns, distributed throughout the countryside, were selected for infrastructural investment. Overseas industry, attracted by tax concessions and cash grant incentives, was allocated a central role in employment creation (Industrial Development Authority 1972). This programme of regional employment creation undoubtedly contributed to the expansion of the employment base in both large towns and cities and in smaller urban places and to population retention, during the 1970s in particular (O'Farrell and Crouchley 1983). The disproportionate growth of the Dublin region continued, however, because of continued inmigration and because of the relatively high rates of natural increase associated with the young population structure of the region.

The role played by manufacturing employment creation in regional population retention during the 1970s was complemented by a number of other state-led developments. These included the establishment of Regional Technical Colleges, with the aim of meeting the skill demands of new industry, in nine centres, most of which had already been designated for industrial development. The introduction of regional structures in a wide range of state agencies also contributed to expand service sector employment in key cities and towns. Even within the agricultural sector, where demands for labour in general decreased in the wake of capitalisation following accession to membership of the European Community (EC) in 1973, new off-farm opportunities were provided in the processing of agricultural produce (Brunt 1988). A range of factors was therefore at work during the early 1970s which facilitated population retention on a widespread scale throughout the state. By mid-decade, however, escalating production costs associated with increased oil prices and competition from EC imports contributed to the closure of some older-established manufacturing enterprises, notably in the east, north-east and south-east (National Economic and Social Council 1983). By the end of the decade, reduced amounts of mobile international investment were available for the continued expansion which was necessary to absorb the increasing numbers of school-leavers who were entering the workforce. Increases in levels of unemployment and in net outmigration followed.

Net migration and size of district

Small population size districts dominate in the Republic of Ireland. With the exception of the CBs (five in 1971 and 1981, and six in 1986 and 1991), few districts contained a population in excess of 50,000 in any census year under consideration (Table 1). A majority of the districts with populations of 30,000-50,000 and 20,000-30,000 contain UDs as do approximately one-half of the districts with 10,000-20,000 population. It is only in the case of RDs with fewer than 10,000 inhabitants that UDs are for the most part absent. In many of these cases small towns are present. The distribution of RDs by size illustrates that the presence of sizable cities and towns and proximity to CBs have an important influence on population mass (Cawley 1994).

The number of districts used in the analysis of migration varies slightly between census periods because of CB boundary revisions. The initial analysis for 1971-1981 was based on 161 districts (rather than 162, because a boundary change in Waterford CB was accommodated by combining it with Waterford RD), that for 1981-1986 on 159 districts and that for 1986-1991 on 163 districts. County Dublin consisted of four districts in the 1971-1981 period (Dublin CB, Dun Laoghaire CB, Dublin North County and Dublin South County), of one unit in 1981-1986 (County Dublin) and of four districts in 1986-1991 (Dublin CB, Dun Laoghaire-Rathdown, Dublin Fingal and Dublin Belgard). A two-stage analysis was pursued in examining the relationship between net migration and population size of district. All districts were included initially. Because of the large populations of the CBs, and notably of Dublin CB, these extreme values were likely to have a marked influence on the magnitude of the correlation coefficient. For this reason, the analysis was re-run omitting the CBs (plus Galway RD and Municipal Borough for 1971-1981, County Dublin for 1981-1986, and, because of its large size, Cork RD and Cobh UD for 1986-1991). The results of the various sets of analyses are presented in Tables 2 and 3.

Net migration by size of district, 1971-1981

When net migration was correlated with size of place for all 161 census districts for the years 1971-1981, gains to three age groups emerged as being significantly correlated with population size of place (although the relationship is not a linear one, as squaring their values illustrates). These were were the 1981 female 15-19 age cohort and the 1981 male and female 20-24 age cohorts (Table 2). Scattergrams of the values point to net gains in these school-leaving and young working-age groups having taken place in a limited number of large size places and particularly in Dublin CB. Net migration losses to these age groups were registered by many other districts, of varying size. There is a significant negative relationship between net migration and population size, in the case of the 1981 female 30-34 and 35-39 age cohorts, reflecting losses in the larger districts and gains in relatively smaller districts. The corresponding male age cohorts also display negative migration trends with size of district but the relationship is relatively less significant than among females. Movement of females from CBs to the smaller towns and rural localities of origin undoubtedly takes place on marriage as do career-related moves by single females. The explanation for the variation lies in large part in another phenomenon; namely, the imbalanced structure of the population of smaller districts in 1971. Because of higher outmigration among females than among males from less urbanised parts of the state in the past, the number of males exceeded the number of females in such areas in 1971. Similar net numerical migration gains among both sexes over the years 1971-1981 yielded considerably higher rates for females than for males in small population-size districts. A net loss was recorded to Dublin CB's male and female 40-44 age cohort through outmigration during the previous decade. In the remaining age cohorts, gains and losses were registered by districts of varying size, with Dublin CB being a net loser in all cases, so contributing to the weak negative correlation values recorded.

The second stage of the analysis omitted the CBs of Dublin, Dun Laoghaire, Cork, Limerick, Waterford CB and RD combined, and Galway MB and RD. Positive relationships between migration and size of place emerged across a wide range of age groups. Higher net gains by larger size places, of children moving with their parents, are reflected in a positive relationship between net migration to the 1981 10-14 male and female age cohort and size of place in 1971. Limited numbers of small size places registered net migration losses to this age cohort over the decade. Examination of the pertinent scattergrams reveals that the relationships between size of place and net migration depicted by other values are not as clear-cut as might appear at first sight. A majority of districts experienced net losses to their 1981 male and female 15-19, 20-24 and 25-29 age cohorts through migration over the previous decade and particularly in the case of the latter two groups. The areas where gains occurred in the 15-19 cohort appear to relate, in part, to increased education-related movement to regional centres in the wake of improved opportunities being made available from the early 1970s on. The significant positive correlation values registered overall reflect lower losses in large than in small places among these school-leaving and young working-age groups. Even some of the larger size districts registered losses pointing to movement from them to the CBs, and to a lesser extent overseas, among the working-age cohorts.

A positive relationship is present between net migration and size of place in the case of the 1981 male 30-34, 35-39, 40-44 and 45-49 year age groups, but not in the case of the 30-34 and 35-39 year female age groups. The explanation for this contrast lies in the depleted female age cohorts in smaller districts in 1971 which produced relatively high net migration rates for such districts, thereby contributing to weak negative correlation values. Evidence of both gains and losses through migration across a range of district sizes is apparent from the scattergrams for the 1981 male and female 50-54 and 55-59 age cohorts.

During the 1970s, therefore, net migration gains were made by the CBs at the expense of smaller districts, through education and employ-

345

ment-related movement among the late teen and early twenty-year age groups. The CBs, and particularly Dublin CB, experienced net losses of people in their later twenties, thirties and early forties to smaller places through residential-related overspill as well as through some employ-ment-related movement. Net migration gains and losses to the 1981 40-45 and fifty-year age groups were distributed across a range of size categories but Dublin CB was a net loser in all cases. When the CBs are omitted from the analysis, large size districts emerge as experiencing net migration gains or relatively lower net losses among the school-leaving and young working-age groups than their less-populated counterparts. Net gains through migration to the 30 and 40 year male age cohorts were associated with increasing size of district.

Net migration by size of district 1981-1986

Strong positive relationships between the net migration rate per 1,000 for the five years 1981-1986 and the total population in 1981 were present in the case of only two age groups, when all 159 districts were included in the analysis. These were females aged 15-19 and 20-24 in 1986 (Table 2). Examination of the pertinent scattergrams indicates that much of this education and employment related movement took place to County Dublin. A majority of districts experienced net losses to these age groups. In the case of the 1986 20-24 male age cohort, net migration gain was also related positively, but less strongly, with size of place, reflecting lower employment opportunities for males than for females in Dublin CB during the first half of the 1980s. Net migration was negatively related with size of place in the case of all other age groups, most notably in the case of females aged 30-34 in 1986. The scattergrams of the values reveal net outmovement from larger places and particularly from County Dublin, although to a lesser extent than during the 1970s.

The second stage of the analysis excluded County Dublin and the four county boroughs, leaving 154 districts. The scattergrams reveal a dominance of net losses through migration to the 1986 15-19, 20-24 male and female and the 25-29 male age cohorts during the preceding five years. Losses among these school-leaving and early working-age groups were greatest in the smallest districts, particularly in those with less than 10,000 population. Some movement took place to the CBs but migration overseas was undoubtedly involved also (National Economic and Social Council 1991). Net migration gains to the 1986 female 25-29 and male 30-34 cohorts increased as size of place increased but many districts with less than 10,000 population and some with 10,000-20,000 population experienced a depletion of these cohorts. The female 45-49 cohort was the only other 1986 cohort where a marked relationship was registered between net migration and size of district. The generally weak relationship between net migration between 1981 and 1986 and size of place, in the case of the 40 and 50 age cohorts, reflects the absence of any clear-cut relationship with size: gains and losses were registered in districts of varying size. The main trends emerging during the first half of the 1980s are, therefore, continued outmovement from small size districts to larger places for education and employment and widespread losses of both males and females across a range of age groups in districts of varying size.

Net migration by size of district 1986-1991

The initial analysis of net migration by size of district for the second half of the 1980s was based on 163 districts (Table 3). The correlation values point to movement of young children with their parents from Dublin CB. Dublin CB continued to attract school-leavers and persons in the early working-age groups, as reflected in the significant positive correlation values recorded for migration gains to the 15-19 and 20-24 year 1991 age groups. Net losses through migration from these age cohorts were almost universal outside Dublin CB and a limited number of other CBs. Net migration losses were, however, greatest in census districts with less than 10,000 population. A negative relationship between net migration in 1986-1991, and size of place in 1986, was registered in the case of the 30-34 and 35-39 female age cohorts. This reflects relatively high net inmigration being recorded by small districts with depleted female age cohorts.

Significant positive relationships between net migration and size of place emerged in the case of the 15-19, 20-24, 25-29 year male and female and the 30-34 year old male age groups when the CBs were excluded from the analysis. Examination of the pertinent scattergrams reveals that, as in the previous five years, the pattern being represented is one of some gains and lower losses in large than in small size places. The underlying pattern is one of widespread loss of the school-leaving and young working-age groups across districts of varying sizes. Increasing numbers of places with a population of 20,000-30,000 and 30,000-50,000 were involved, pointing to a deterioration of employment opportunities for younger workers during the second half of the 1980s. In the case of the older working-age groups, the low correlation values reflect gains and losses in places of varying size associated with varying local employment conditions. Exclusion of the remaining districts in County Dublin (155 areas) and indeed of Cork RD and Cobh UD (154 areas, the values for which correspond closely with those for 155 areas) from the analysis does not modify the correlation values to any appreciable extent.

Table 1
Combined urban and rural districts, classified by size grouping

Population	Number of RDs+CBs				Number of RDs containing UDs (excl. CBs)			
	'71	'81	'86	'91	'71	'81	'86	'91
<10000	78	73	72	71	4	4	4	4
10000-20000	52	47	45	49	26	21	20	22
>20000-30000	20	20	21	18	17	14	15	13
>30000-50000	6	13	15	15	5	11	11	11
>50000	6	9	9	9	-	2	2	2
Total	162	162	162	162	52	52	52	52

Source: Census of Population, Ireland, 1971, 1981. 1986, 1991

Summary and conclusion

This paper started from the premise that demographic sustainability per se merits attention as a research focus and that migration trends are indicative of the ability of social and economic systems to operate in a sustainable way. A better understanding of the composition of migration flows and of the relationship between net migration and population mass are, it is argued, necessary inputs to the design of effective policies for rural economic and social development. The Republic of Ireland is an appropriate context for such a study because of the central role which migration plays in population change at both national and sub-national levels. By the end of the 1980s, very serious concern was emerging among communities in western areas, in particular, relating to the erosive effects for society and economy of continued outmigration among the economically-active age groups. Decline was limited to a small number of smaller-sized districts during the 1970s but the number and the size of districts experiencing decline increased as the 1980s progressed. In order to identify the structure of demographic change in some detail, net migration was estimated for sub-county districts for the youth, school-leaving and working-age groups.

348

Table 2
Relationship between (a) net migration 1971-1981 and size of place
in 1971, and (b) net migration 1981-1986 and size of place in 1981

Age group in 1981		Correlation coefficients			
		(a) 1971-1981		(b) 1981-1986	
		161 districts	153 districts	159 districts	154 districts
5-9	M			-0.159*	-0.084
	F			-0.147	-0.047
10-14	M	-0.090	+0.227**	-0.024	-0.154
	F	-0.090	+0.264**	-0.046	0.052
15-19	M	+0.094	+0.267**	+0.148	+0.256**
	F	+0.247**	+0.402**	+0.237**	+0.348**
20-24	M	+0.274**	+0.394**	+0.171*	+0.184*
	F	+0.317**	+0.471**	+0.219**	+0.485**
25-29	M	+0.089	+0.342**	-0.043	+0.296**
	F	+0.097	+0.344**	-0.152	+0.171*
30-34	M	-0.160*	+0.279**	-0.120	+0.185*
	F	-0.298**	-0.028	-0.183*	+0.021
35-39	M	-0.167*	+0.279**	-0.127	-0.001
	F	-0.287**	-0.059	-0.150	-0.098
40-44	M	-0.170*	+0.198*	-0.085	-0.018
	F	-0.153	+0.153	-0.074	+0.043
45-49	M	-0.055	+0.278**	-0.024	+0.081
	F	-0.070	+0.172*	-0.007	+0.170*
50-54	M	-0.070	+0.143	-0.049	-0.049
	F	-0.049	+0.059	-0.037	-0.028
55-59	M	-0.049	+0.050	-0.055	-0.037
	F	-0.023	+0.152	-0.009	+0.162

* Significant at 0.05 level   ** Significant at 0.01 level

Table 3
Relationship between net migration 1986-1991
and size of place in 1986

Age group in 1991		163 districts	158 districts	155 districts
			Correlation coefficients	
5-9	M	-0.195*	+0.002	-0.046
	F	-0.174*	-0.010	-0.106
10-14	M	-0.025	+0.030	+0.040
	F	-0.023	+0.066	+0.101
15-19	M	+0.290**	+0.267**	+0.269**
	F	+0.425**	+0.409**	+0.421**
20-24	M	+0.309**	+0.232**	+0.177*
	F	+0.455**	+0.460**	+0.496**
25-29	M	+0.029	+0.334**	+0.390**
	F	-0.092	+0.267**	+0.279**
30-34	M	-0.067	+0.219**	+0.217**
	F	-0.227**	+0.047	-0.063
35-39	M	-0.110	+0.025	+0.007
	F	-0.190*	-0.047	-0.082
40-44	M	-0.030	+0.009	+0.063
	F	-0.092	-0.020	-0.018
45-49	M	-0.087	-0.071	-0.072
	F	-0.059	-0.045	-0.099
50-54	M	-0.089	-0.093	-0.177*
	F	-0.051	-0.029	-0.049
55-59	M	-0.111	-0.061	-0.078
	F	-0.046	+0.002	+0.040

* Significant at 0.05 level** Significant at 0.01 level

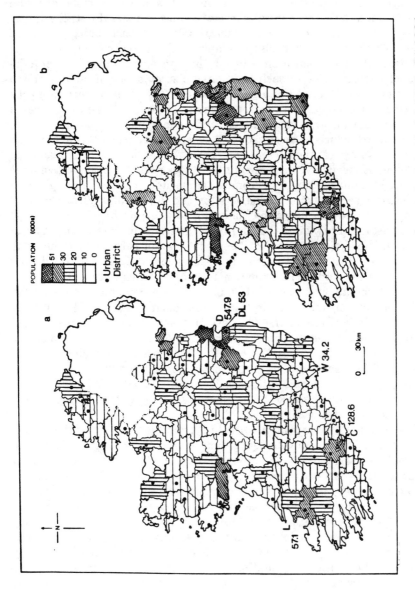

Figure 1   Population of Rural Districts (including Urban Districts): (a) 1971, (b) 1981

A number of broad trends were identified, which corroborate the findings of research at regional and county levels, whilst elaborating on the more detailed geographical aspects of those trends. First, the larger centres of population, and Dublin CB in particular, attracted school-leavers from other districts during the three census periods, a finding that is not surprising given the concentration of higher educational opportunities in such locations. The evidence of labour-related migration to such centres is highest for the 1970s. This pattern might be expected since embargoes on recruitment to the civil service were in operation during the early 1980s and employment opportunities in general were reduced, associated with economic recession throughout the decade. Many of those who left their home locality in search of employment moved overseas during the latter period (National Economic and Social Council 1991). Secondly, gains and losses were registered across the size spectrum of districts for the 30, 40 and 50 age cohorts during all three census periods pointing to the role of particular local conditions in influencing the ability of districts to retain and attract people in these age groups. Evidence of gains of persons in their early forties by smaller population size places is apparent, particularly during the 1970s, when industrial employment opportunities were being created on a widespread basis across the urban hierarchy, but renewed out-movement of persons in their late forties emerged also. The greatest losses were registered in the smallest places. Thirdly, the rates of net migration loss tended to increase over time as did the number and size of districts registering net losses. Fourthly, net losses of females exceeded those of males, most notably in the school-leaving and 20-24 age cohorts. Fifthly, districts with populations of less than 10,000 and 10,000-20,000, which are outside the zone of influence of large centres of population, registered the highest net losses.

The results of the research point to growing losses among the school-leaving and young working-age groups on an increasingly widespread geographical scale in the Republic of Ireland during the two decades under review. Districts with less than 10,000 population which are characterised by weak urban employment structures and lie beyond the zone of influence of larger centres of population were particularly vulnerable to population loss throughout the two decades. This phenomenon has not been highlighted at a national scale in research to date and raises major questions about the capacity of such districts to maintain the critical population thresholds that are necessary for sustainable social and economic activity. During the first half of the 1980s, increasingly larger size districts also experienced losses to their working-age groups, a pattern that became even more marked during the second half of the decade. The scale of the net migration loss and the details of its composition, identified by this research, underline the value of monitoring migration trends in geographical detail for broad areas of territory. These findings also suggest strongly that increased attention needs to be given to the location of new investment in the Republic of Ireland so that the disparities between more-urbanised and less-urbanised areas do not become exacerbated. The Irish government sought to offset inter-regional economic disparities from the late 1980s on by decentralising selected state services to regional centres and by promoting urban renewal programmes, through tax incentives, in the larger cities and towns. Investment associated with LEADER initiatives may also have helped to retain working-age people in smaller places. An assessment of the full demographic impacts of recent initiatives awaits the detailed results of the 1996 census of population. The findings of this study suggest, however, that a co-ordinated approach to the location of investment for employment provision is necessary if disparities in the sustainability of populations and of social and economic systems between small town and rural areas, and urban hinterlands, are not to become more marked in the Republic of Ireland.

References

Brunt, Barry. 1988. *The Republic of Ireland.* London: Chapman.

Cawley, Mary. 1990. Population change in the Republic of Ireland 1981-1986. *Area* 22, 1: 67-74.

_____. 1991. Town population change 1971-1986: patterns and distributional effects. *Irish Geography* 24, 2: 106-16.

_____. 1994. Desertification: Measuring population decline in rural Ireland. *Journal of Rural Studies* 14, 4: 395-407.

Champetier, Yves. 1992. In a word. *Leader Magazine* 1 (1): 12.

Cloke, Paul. 1992. Rural poverty: Some initial thoughts on culture and the underclass. In Ian R. Bowler, Christopher R. Bryant and M. Duane Nellis (eds.), *Contemporary Rural Systems in Transition, Volume 2: Economy and Society.* London: CAB International. Pp. 29-45.

Commission of the European Communities. 1992. *Towards Sustainability: European Community Programme of Policy and Action in Relation to the Environment and Sustainable Development.* Brussels: CEC.

Euradvice Ltd. 1994. *A Crusade for Survival: Final Report of Study of the West of Ireland.* Galway: Developing the West Together.

Furuseth, Owen. 1992. Uneven social and economic development. In Ian R. Bowler, Christopher R. Bryant, and M. Duane Nellis (eds.), *Contemporary Rural Systems in Transition, Volume 2: Economy and Society.* London: CAB International. Pp. 17-28.

Hoggart, Keith, Henry Buller and Richard Black. 1995. *Rural Europe: Identity and Change.* London: Arnold.

Horner, Arnold A. and Stuart Daultrey. 1980. Recent population changes in the Republic of Ireland. *Area* 12: 129-35.

Industrial Development Authority. 1972. *Regional Industrial Plans 1973-1978.* Dublin: Industrial Development Authority.

Kennedy, Kieran A., Thomas Giblin and Deirdre McHugh. 1988. Population and labour force. In Kieran A. Kennedy, Thomas Giblin and Deirdre McHugh (eds), *The Economic Development of Ireland in the Twentieth Century.* London: Routledge. Pp. 139-58.

Lowe, Philip, Tony Bradley and Susan Wright (eds.). 1986. *Deprivation and Welfare in Rural Areas.* Norwich: Geo Books.

National Economic and Social Council. 1983. *Report No. 67: An Analysis of Job Losses in Irish Manufacturing Industry.* Dublin: Government Publications.

_____. 1991. *Report No. 90: The Economic and Social Implications of Emigration.* Dublin: Government Publications.

_____. 1994. *Report No. 97: New Approaches to Rural Development.* Dublin: Government Publications.

O'Farrell, Patrick. N. and Roger Crouchley. 1983. Industrial closures in Ireland 1971-1981. *Regional Studies* 17: 411-29.

O'Malley, Eoin. 1992. Problems of industrialisation in Ireland. In John H. Goldthorpe and Christopher T. Whelan (eds.), *The Development of Industrial Society in Ireland.* Proceedings of the British Academy 79. Oxford: Oxford University Press. Pp. 31-52.

Shryock, Henry S., Jacob S. Siegel and Edward G. Stockwell. 1976. *The Methods and Materials of Demography.* New York: Academic Press.

Walsh, James A. 1991a. The turn-around of the turnaround in the population of the Republic of Ireland. *Irish Geography* 24, 2: 117-25.

_____. 1991b. Inter-county migration in the Republic of Ireland: patterns and processes. In Russell King (ed.), *Contemporary Irish Migration.* Geographical Society of Ireland, Special Publication No. 6.

Dublin: Geographical Society of Ireland. Pp. 96-110.

Whitby, Martin C. and Neil Powe. 1995. Recent British experience of promoting rural development. In Andrew K. Copus and Pamela J. Marr (eds.), *Rural Realities: Trends and Choices.* Proceedings of the 35th EAAE Seminar, Aberdeen, Scotland, June 1994. Aberdeen: Aberdeen School of Agriculture. Pp. 297-312.